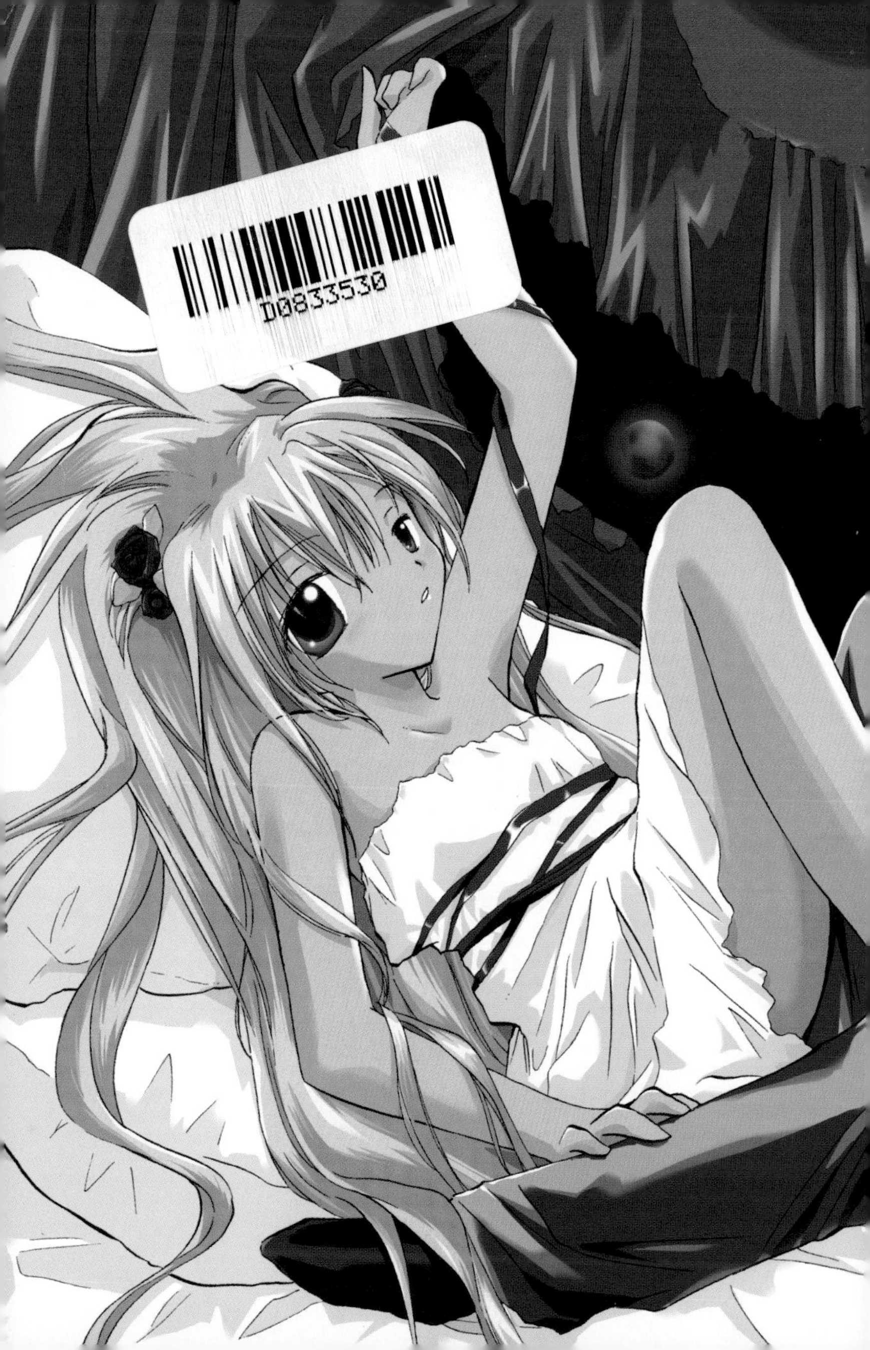

CONTENTS

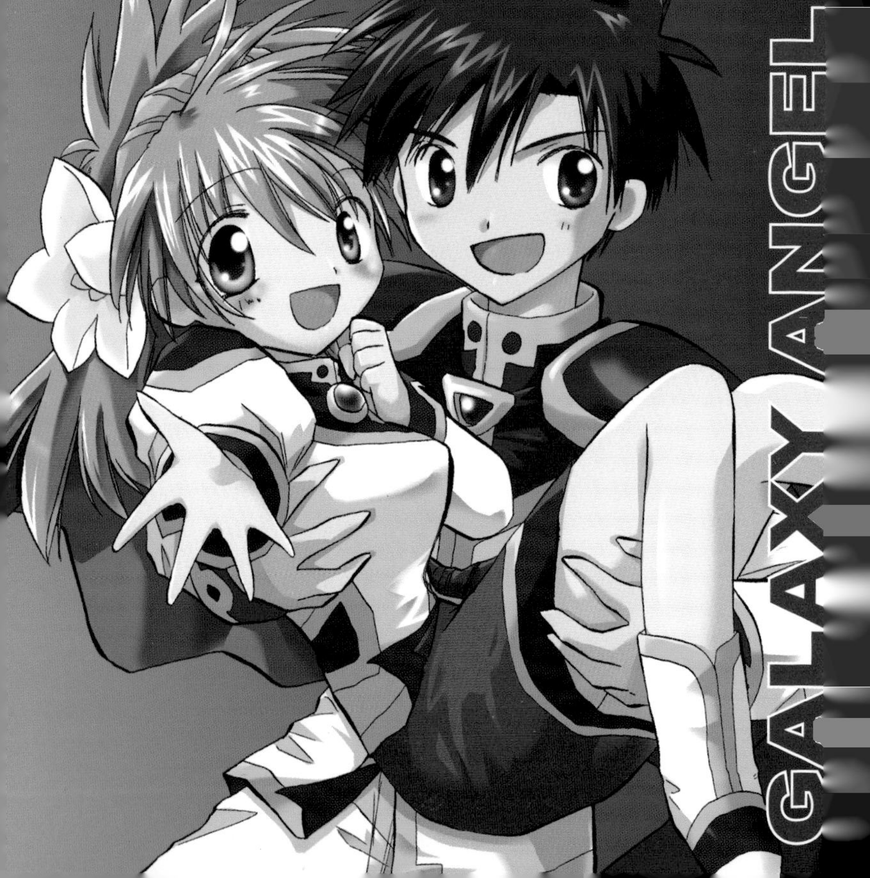

GALAXY ANGEL

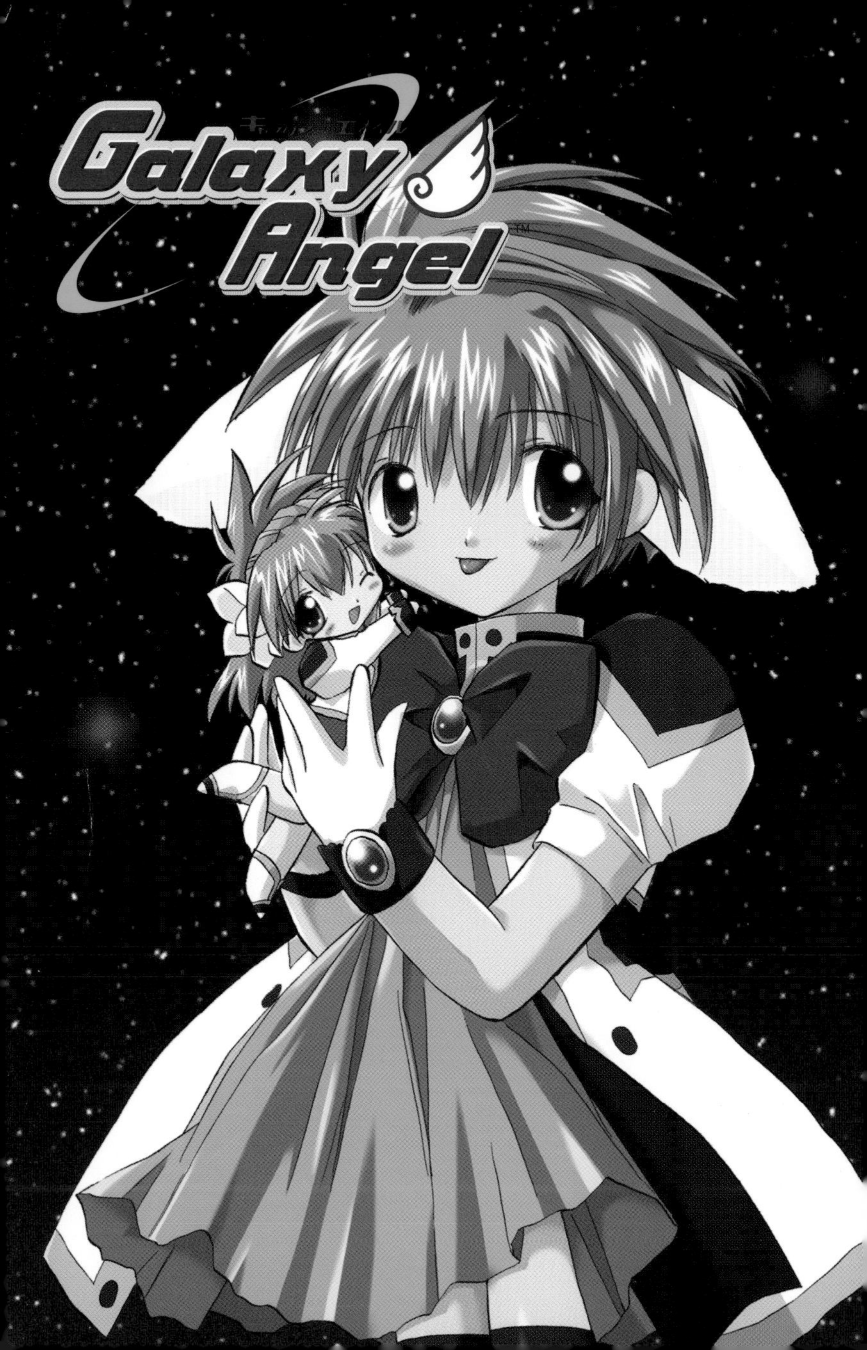
Galaxy Angel™

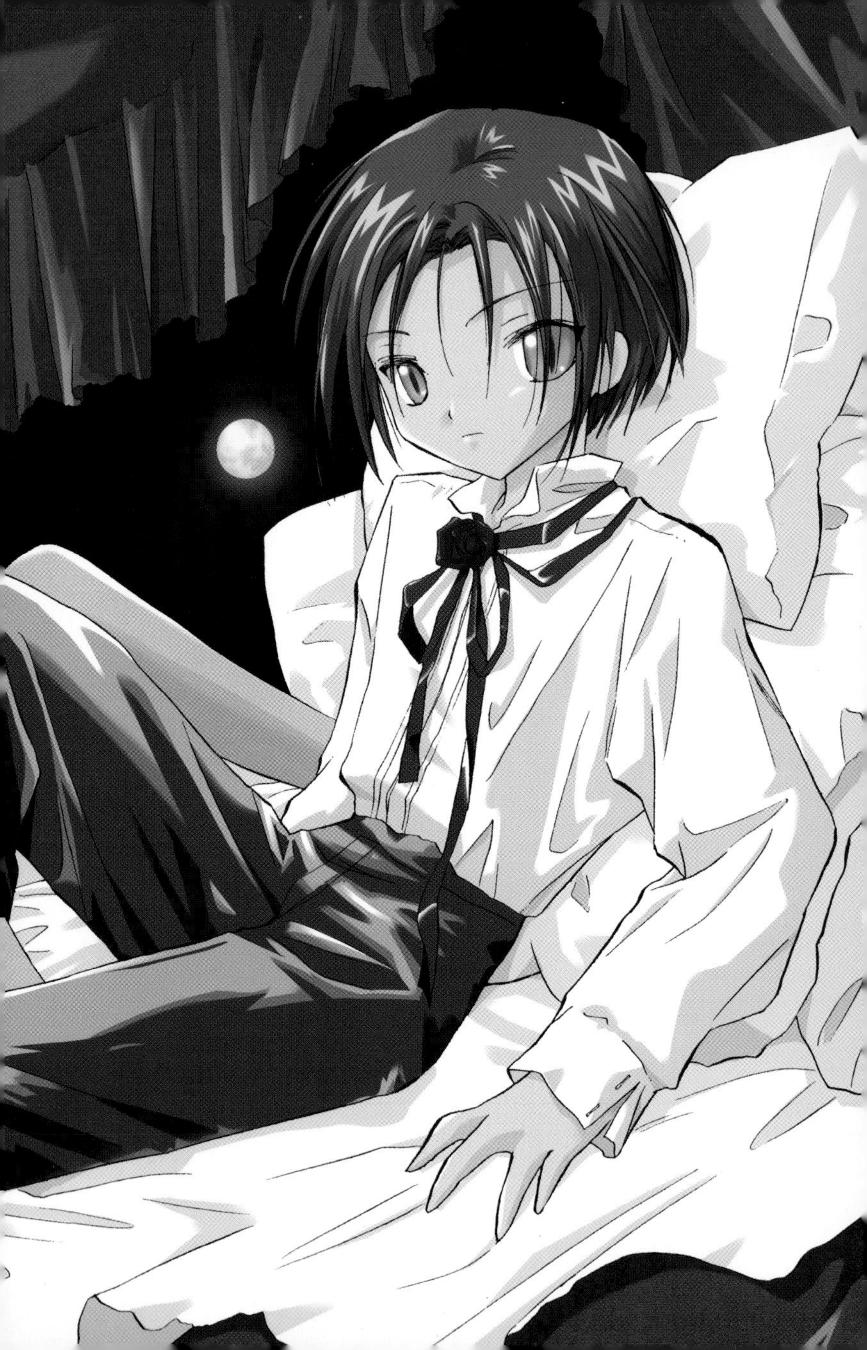

ギャラクシー エンジェル

Galaxy Angel 3

by Kanan
Supervised by Ryo Mizuno
Original Concept by BROCCOLI

brought to you by
BROCCOLI BOOKS
A DIVISION OF BROCCOLI INTERNATIONAL USA

Other titles available from Broccoli Books

Galaxy Angel™ Volume 3

English Adaptation Staff
Translation: Ken "KJ1980" Wakita
English Adaptation: Jason R. Grissom
Clean-Up, Touch-Up, & Lettering: Chris McDougall
Cover Design & Layout: Chris McDougall

Editor: Satsuki Yamashita
Sales Manager: Ardith D. Santiago
Managing Editor: Shizuki Yamashita
Publisher: Hideki Uchino

Email: editor@broccolibooks.com
Website: www.bro-usa.com

A BROCCOLI BOOKS Manga
Broccoli Books is a division of Broccoli International USA, Inc.
12211 W. Washington Blvd, Suite 110, Los Angeles CA 90066

ISBN: 1-932480-22-6

Published by Broccoli International USA, Inc.
First printing, June 2004

All illustrations by Kanan with the exception of pg. 185, Harvester by IKUSABUNE.

ANIME GAMERS

BROCCOLI INTERNATIONAL USA
www.bro-usa.com

10 9 8 7 6 5 4 3 2 1
Printed in the United States

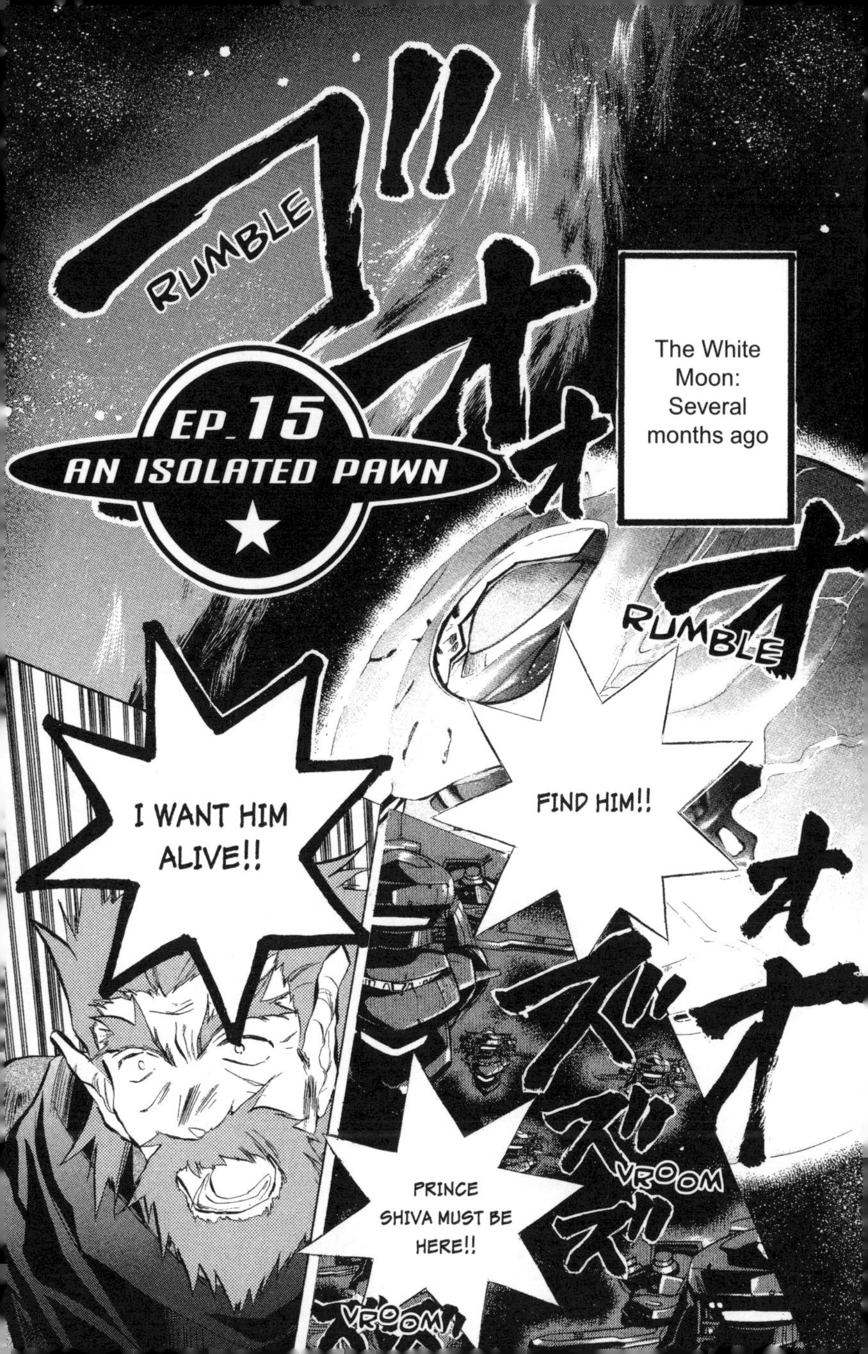
The White Moon: Several months ago
EP_15
AN ISOLATED PAWN
RUMBLE
RUMBLE
FIND HIM!!
PRINCE SHIVA MUST BE HERE!!
VROOM
I WANT HIM ALIVE!!
VROOM

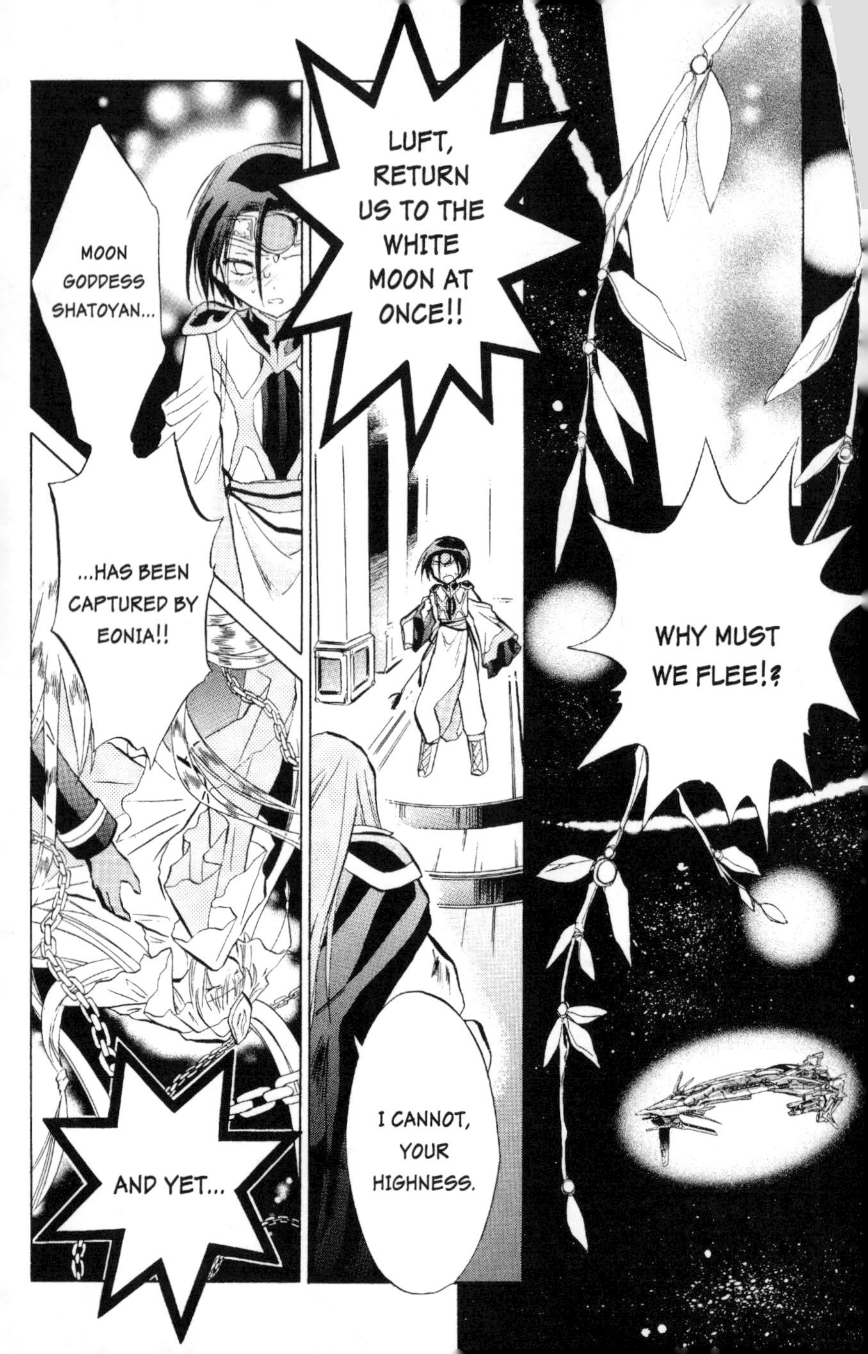
WHY MUST WE FLEE!?
LUFT, RETURN US TO THE WHITE MOON AT ONCE!!
I CANNOT, YOUR HIGHNESS.
MOON GODDESS SHATOYAN...
...HAS BEEN CAPTURED BY EONIA!!
AND YET...

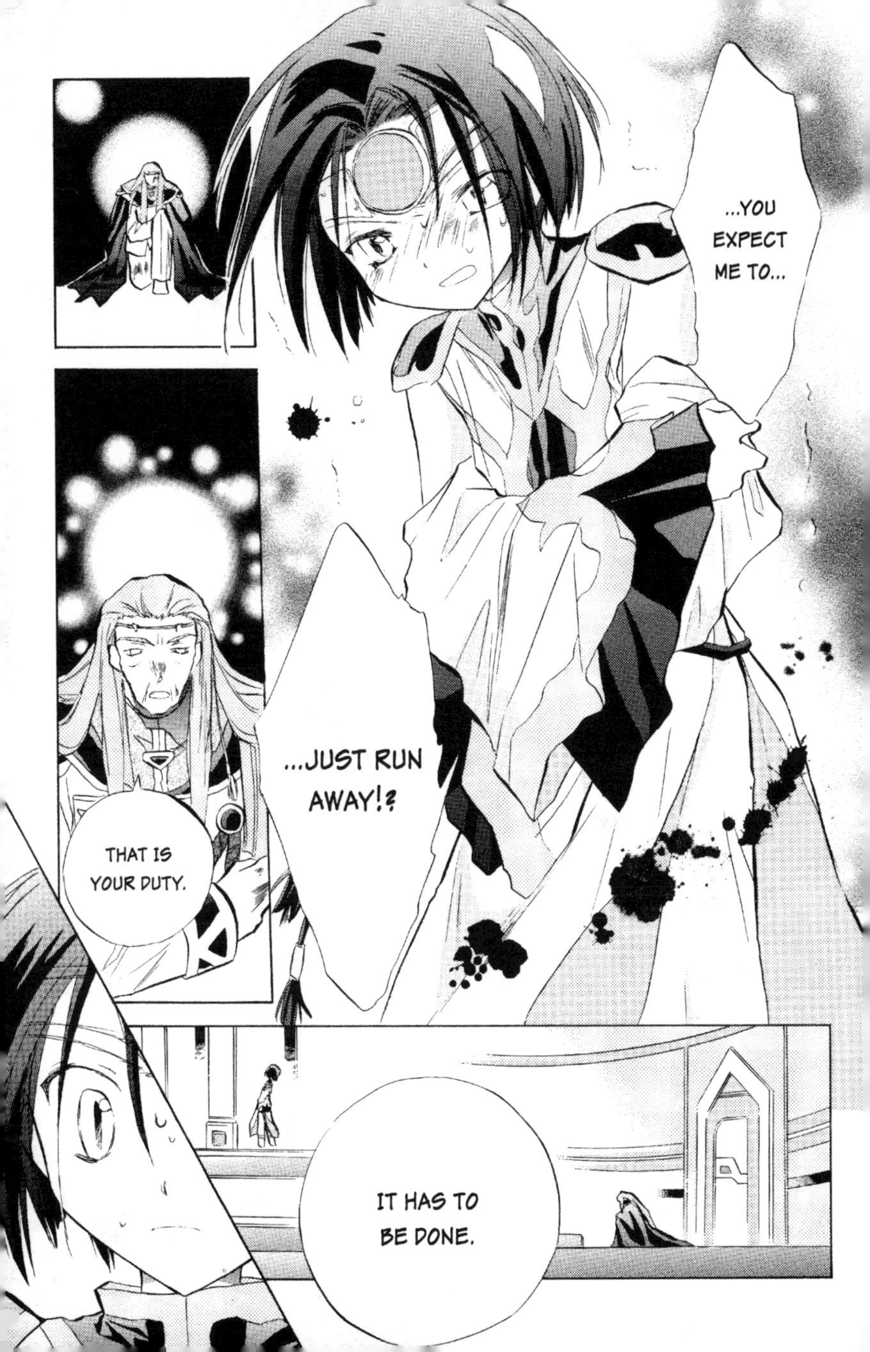
...YOU EXPECT ME TO...
...JUST RUN AWAY!?
THAT IS YOUR DUTY.
IT HAS TO BE DONE.

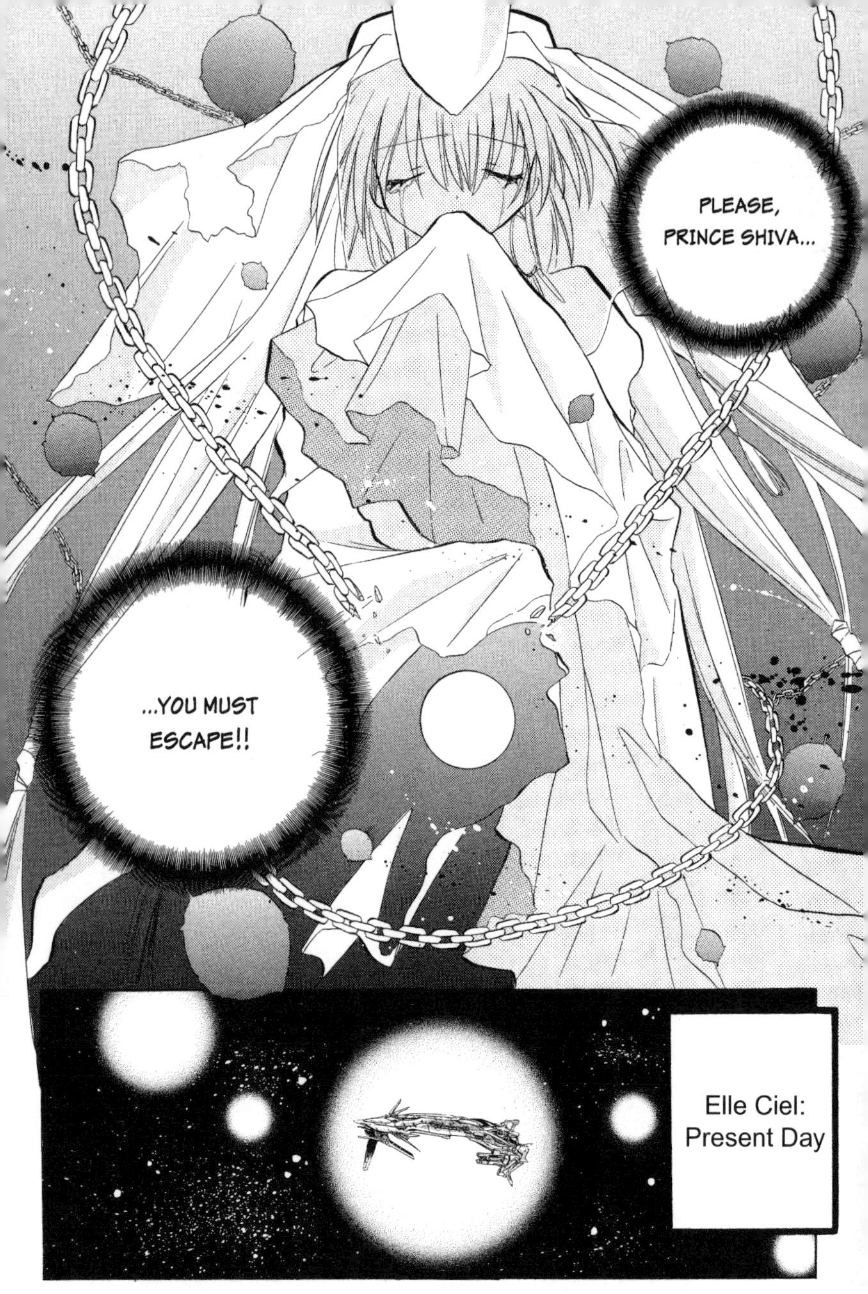
PLEASE, PRINCE SHIVA...
...YOU MUST ESCAPE!!
Elle Ciel: Present Day

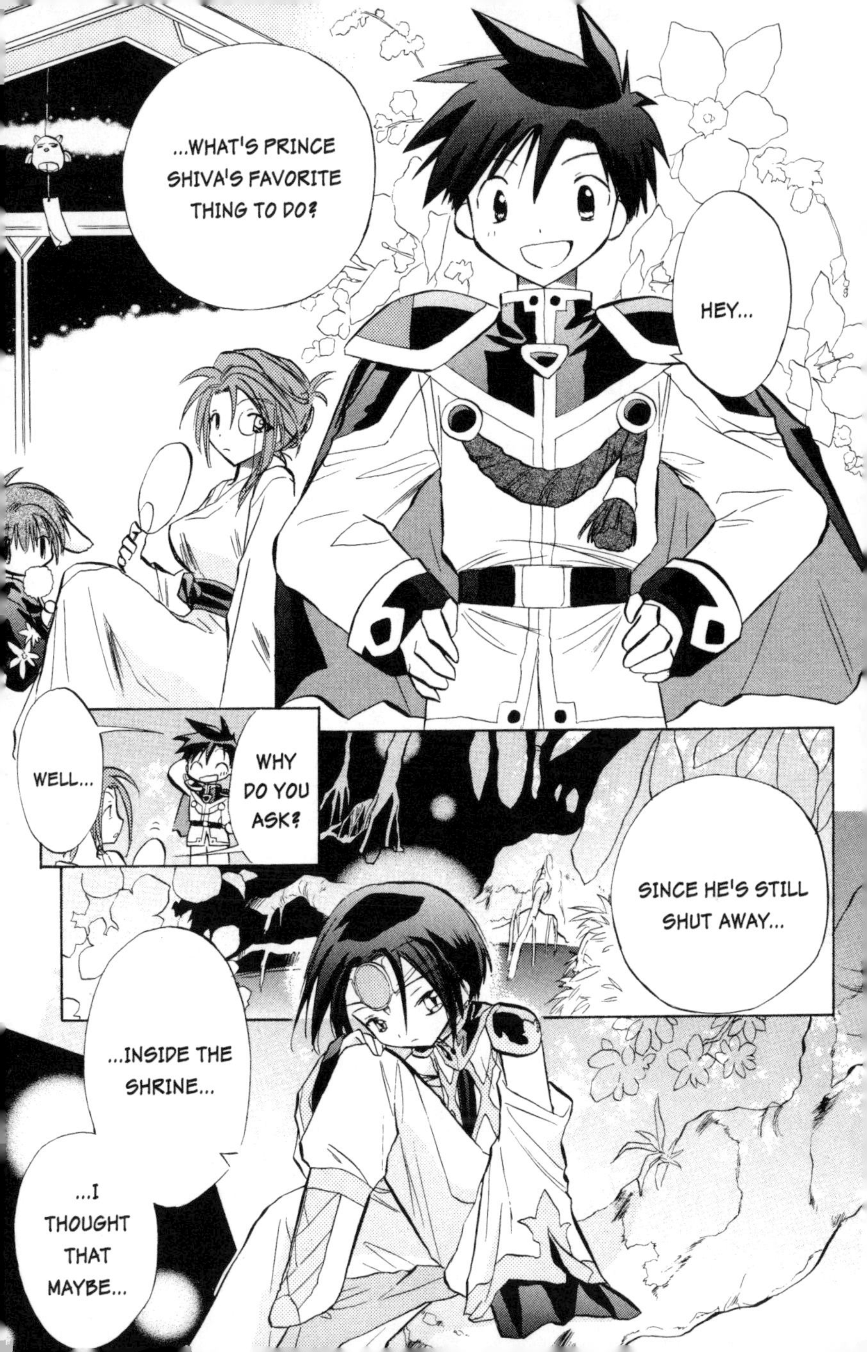
HEY...
...WHAT'S PRINCE SHIVA'S FAVORITE THING TO DO?
WHY DO YOU ASK?
WELL...
SINCE HE'S STILL SHUT AWAY...
...INSIDE THE SHRINE...
...I THOUGHT THAT MAYBE...

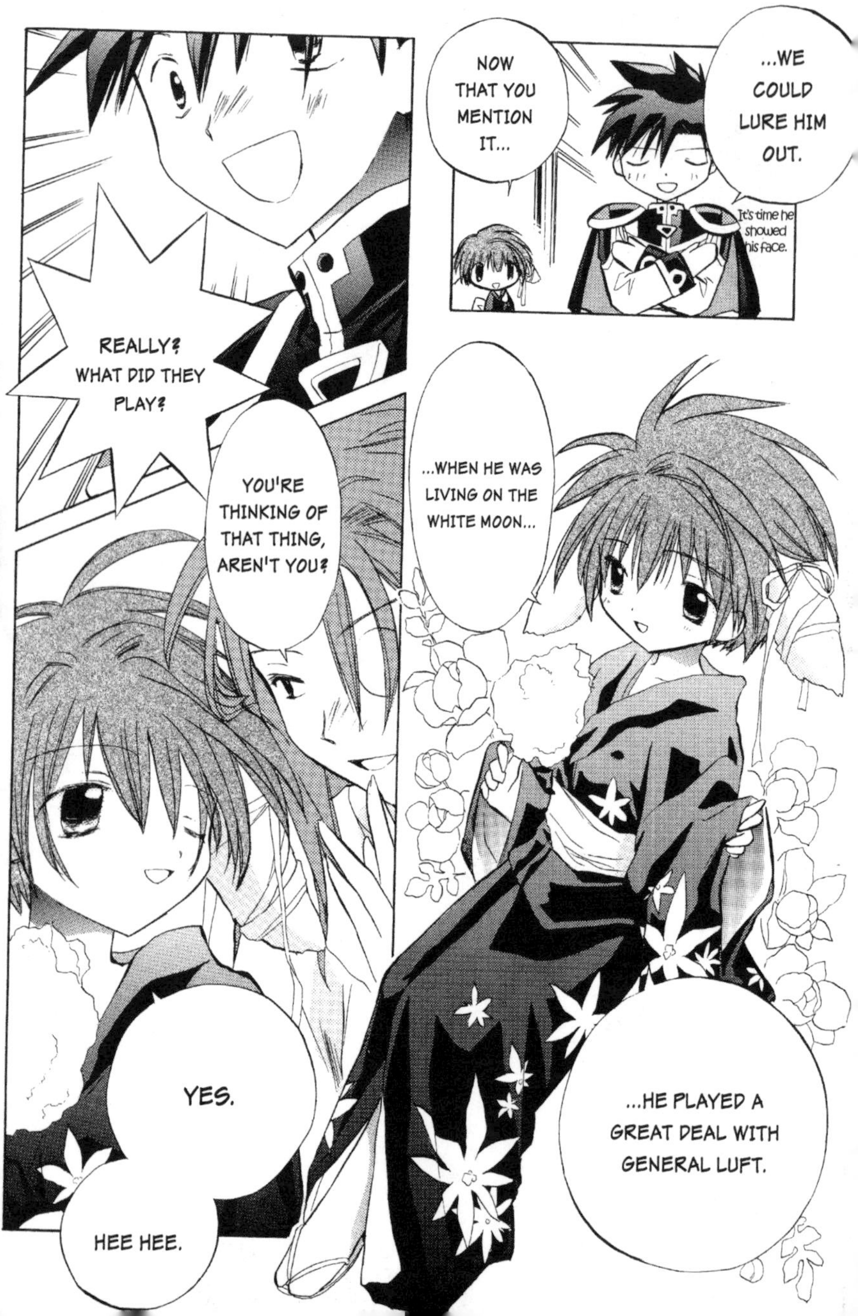
...WE COULD LURE HIM OUT.
NOW THAT YOU MENTION IT...
It's time he showed his face.
REALLY? WHAT DID THEY PLAY?
...WHEN HE WAS LIVING ON THE WHITE MOON...
...HE PLAYED A GREAT DEAL WITH GENERAL LUFT.
YOU'RE THINKING OF THAT THING, AREN'T YOU?
YES.
HEE HEE.

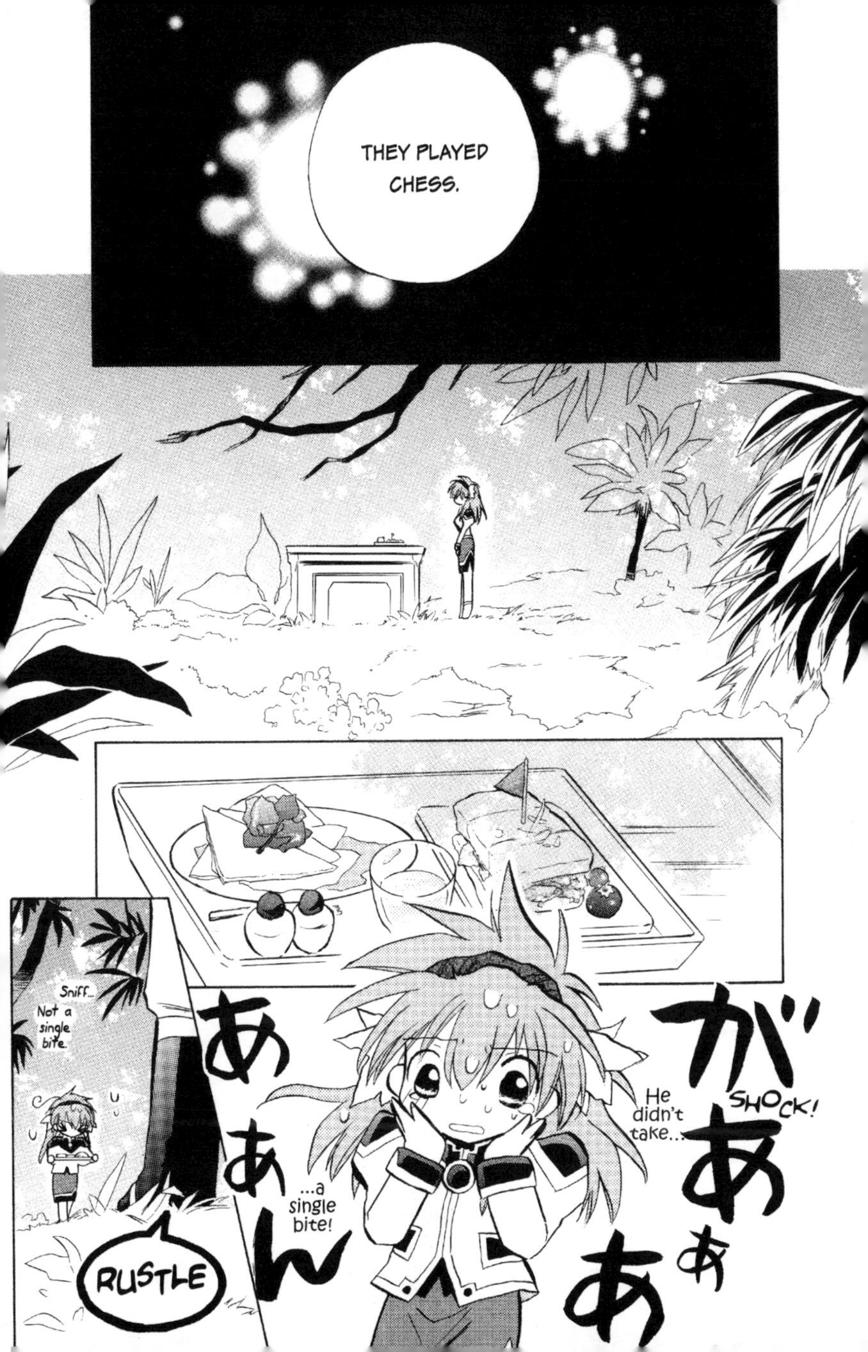
THEY PLAYED CHESS.
があぁあ
SHOCK!
He didn't take...
...a single bite!
ああん
Sniff...
Not a single bite.
RUSTLE

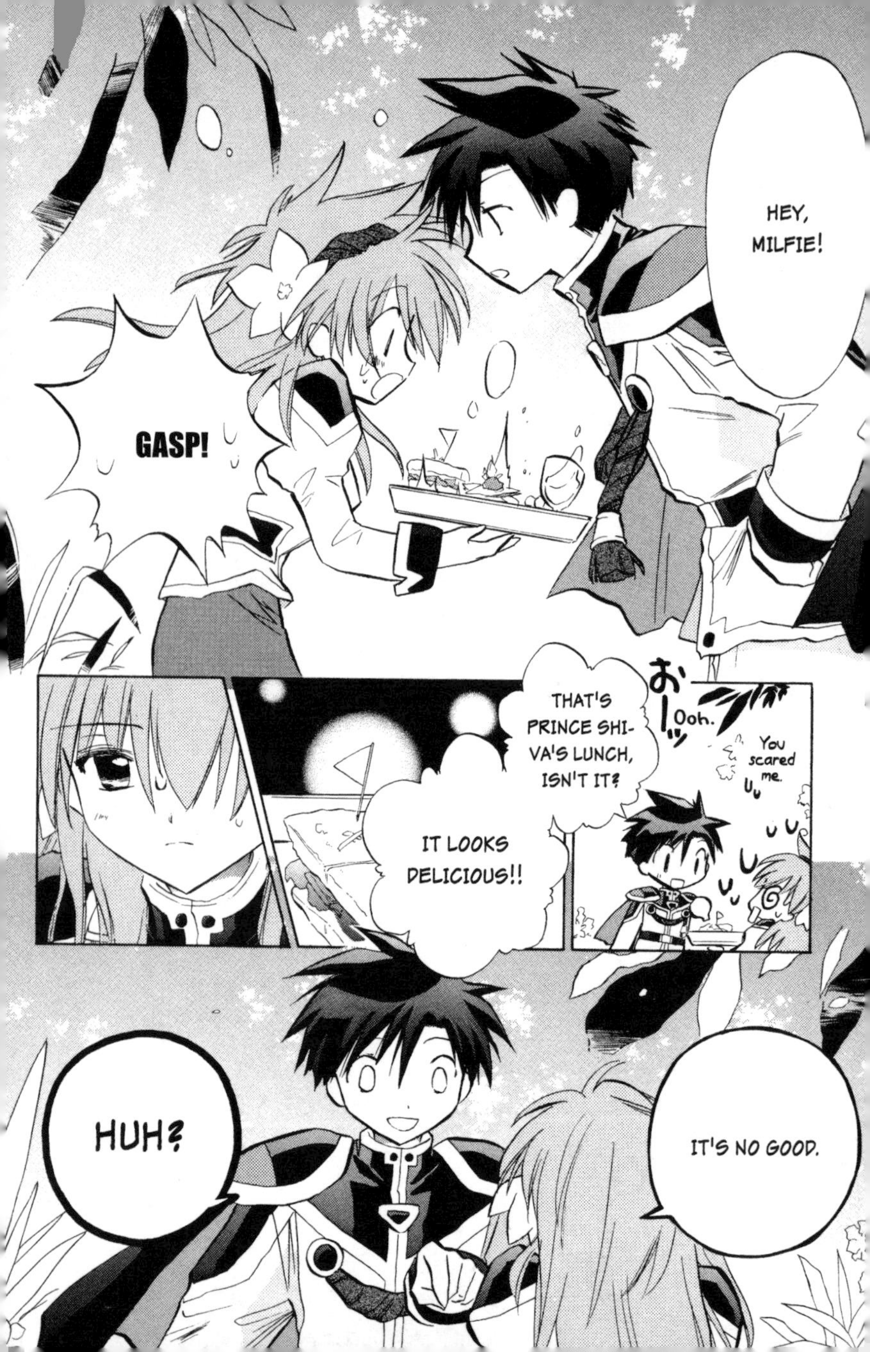
HEY, MILFIE!
GASP!
おーッ
Ooh.
You scared me.
THAT'S PRINCE SHIVA'S LUNCH, ISN'T IT?
IT LOOKS DELICIOUS!!
IT'S NO GOOD.
HUH?

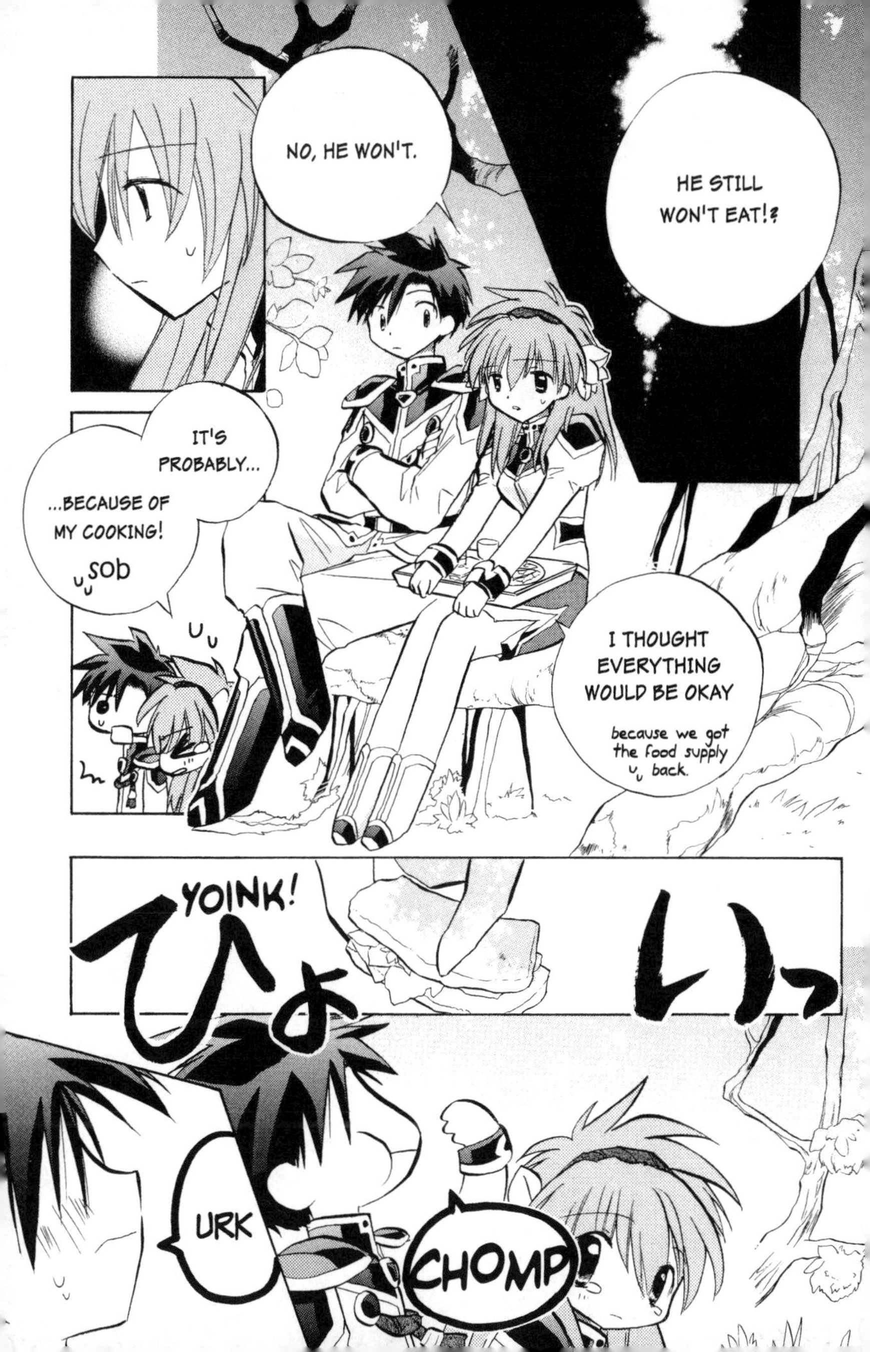
HE STILL WON'T EAT!?
NO, HE WON'T.
I THOUGHT EVERYTHING WOULD BE OKAY
because we got the food supply back.
IT'S PROBABLY...
...BECAUSE OF MY COOKING!
sob
YOINK!
ひょいっ
CHOMP
URK

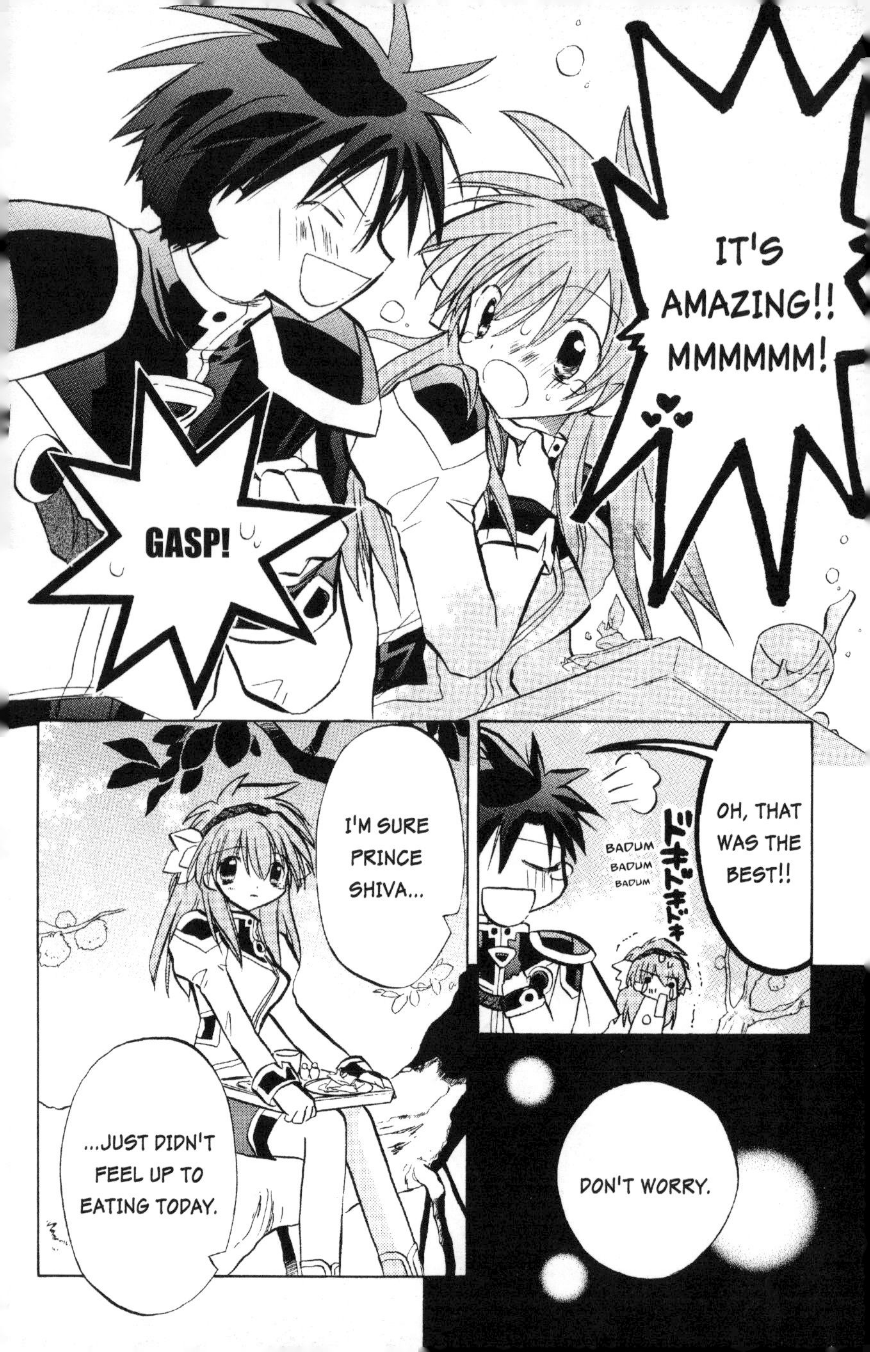
IT'S AMAZING!! MMMMMM!
GASP!
OH, THAT WAS THE BEST!!
BADUM BADUM BADUM
DON'T WORRY.
I'M SURE PRINCE SHIVA...
...JUST DIDN'T FEEL UP TO EATING TODAY.

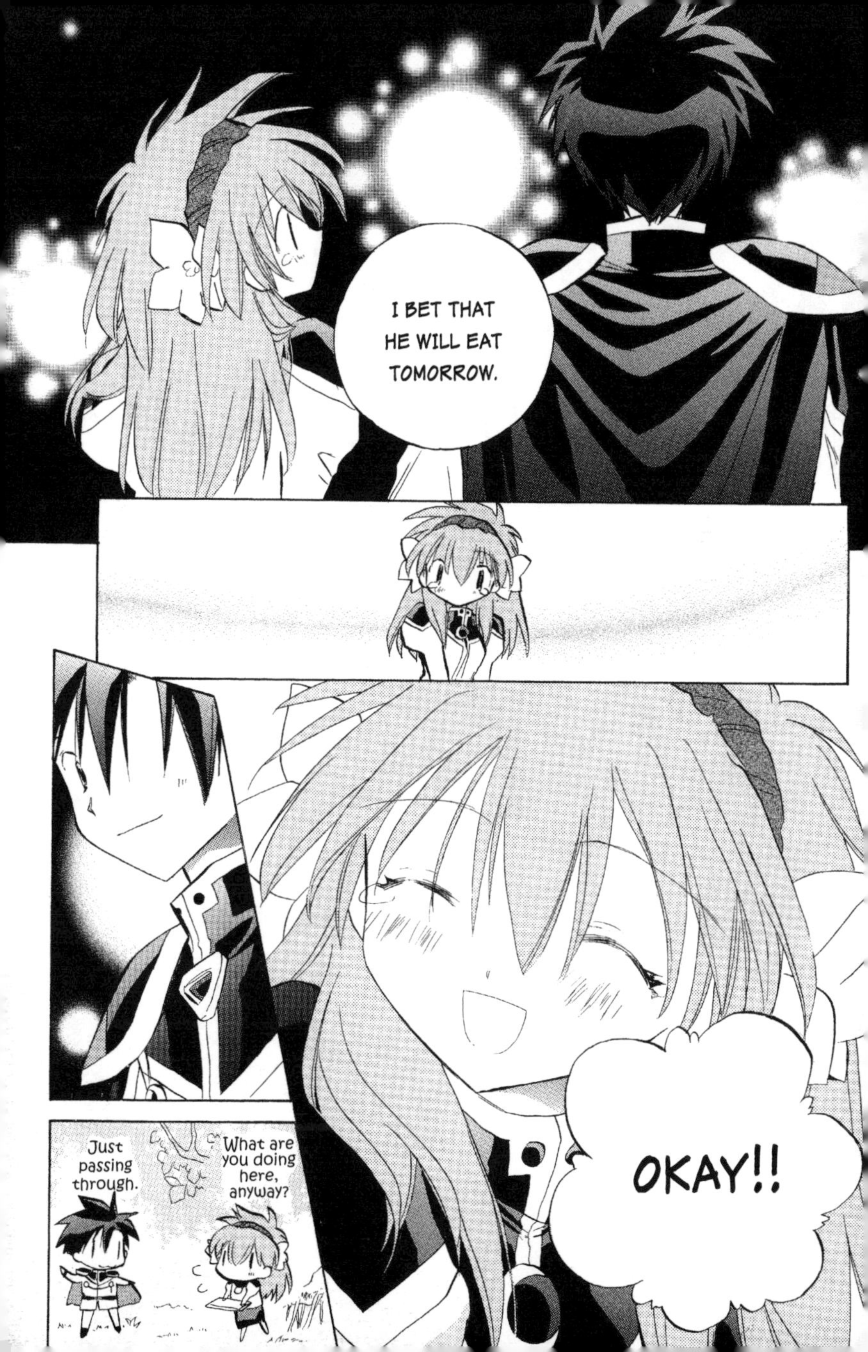
I BET THAT HE WILL EAT TOMORROW.
OKAY!!
What are you doing here, anyway?
Just passing through.

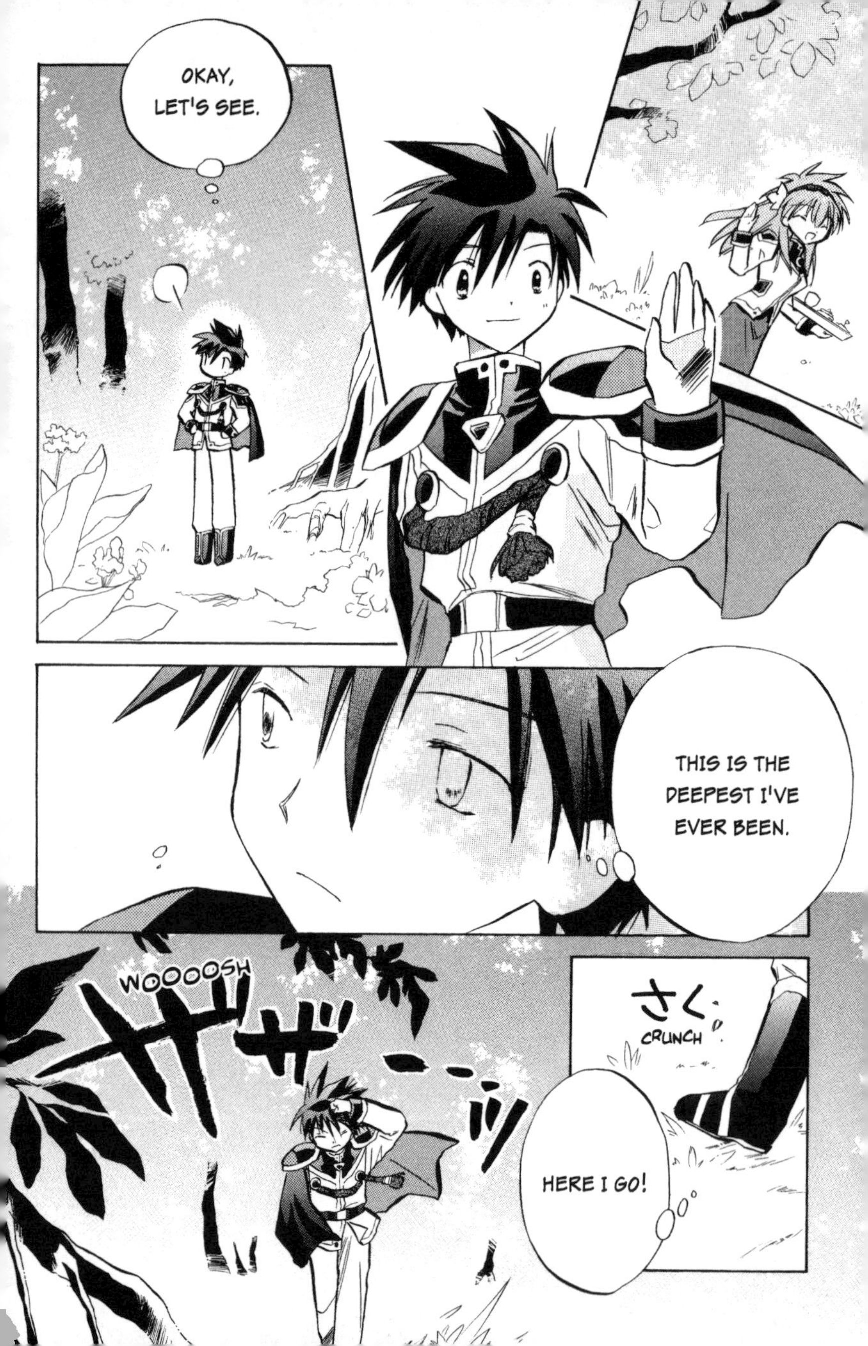
OKAY, LET'S SEE.
THIS IS THE DEEPEST I'VE EVER BEEN.
さく
CRUNCH
HERE I GO!
WOOOOSH
ザザーッ

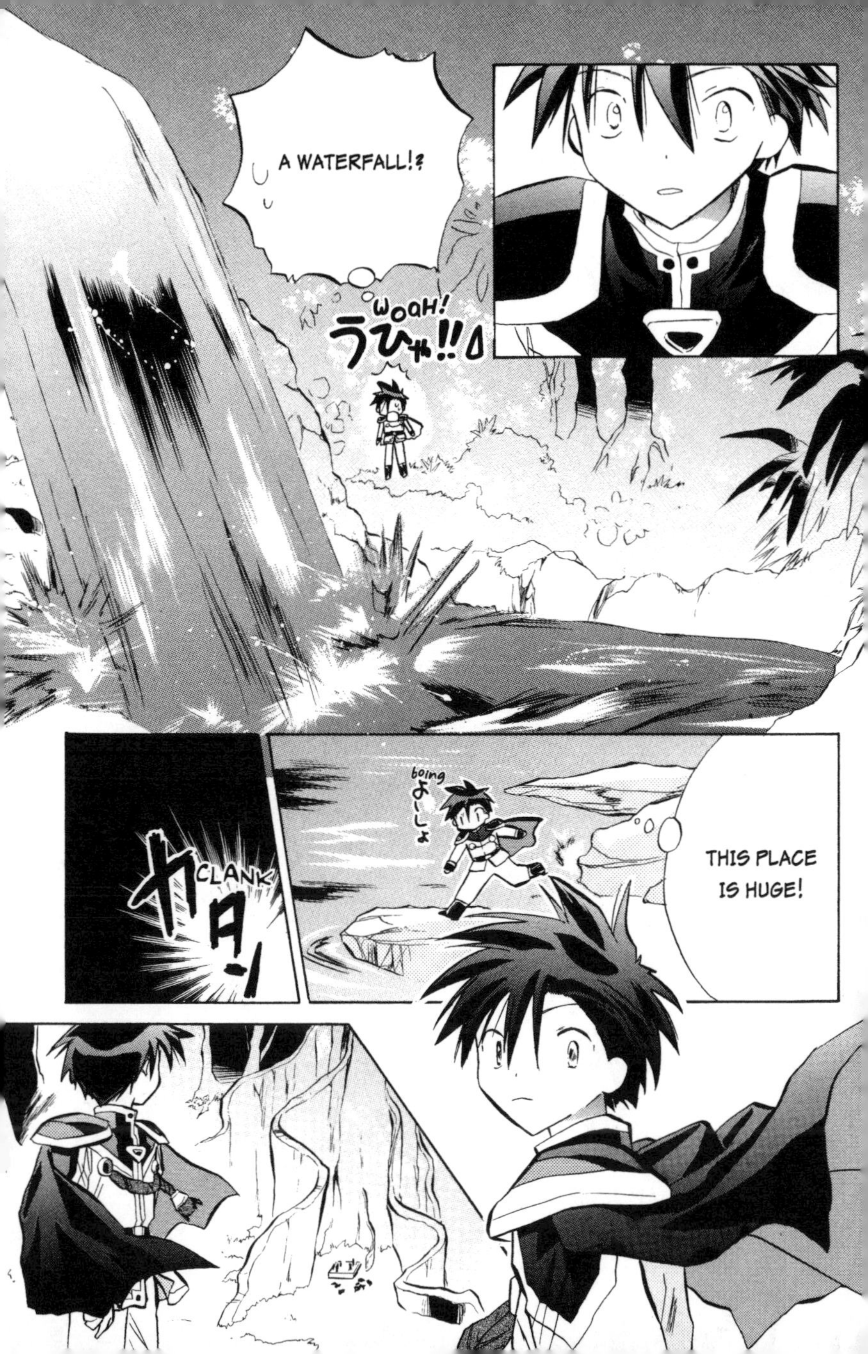
A WATERFALL!?
WOAH!
うひゃ!!
THIS PLACE IS HUGE!
boing
よいしょ
CLANK
カタ!

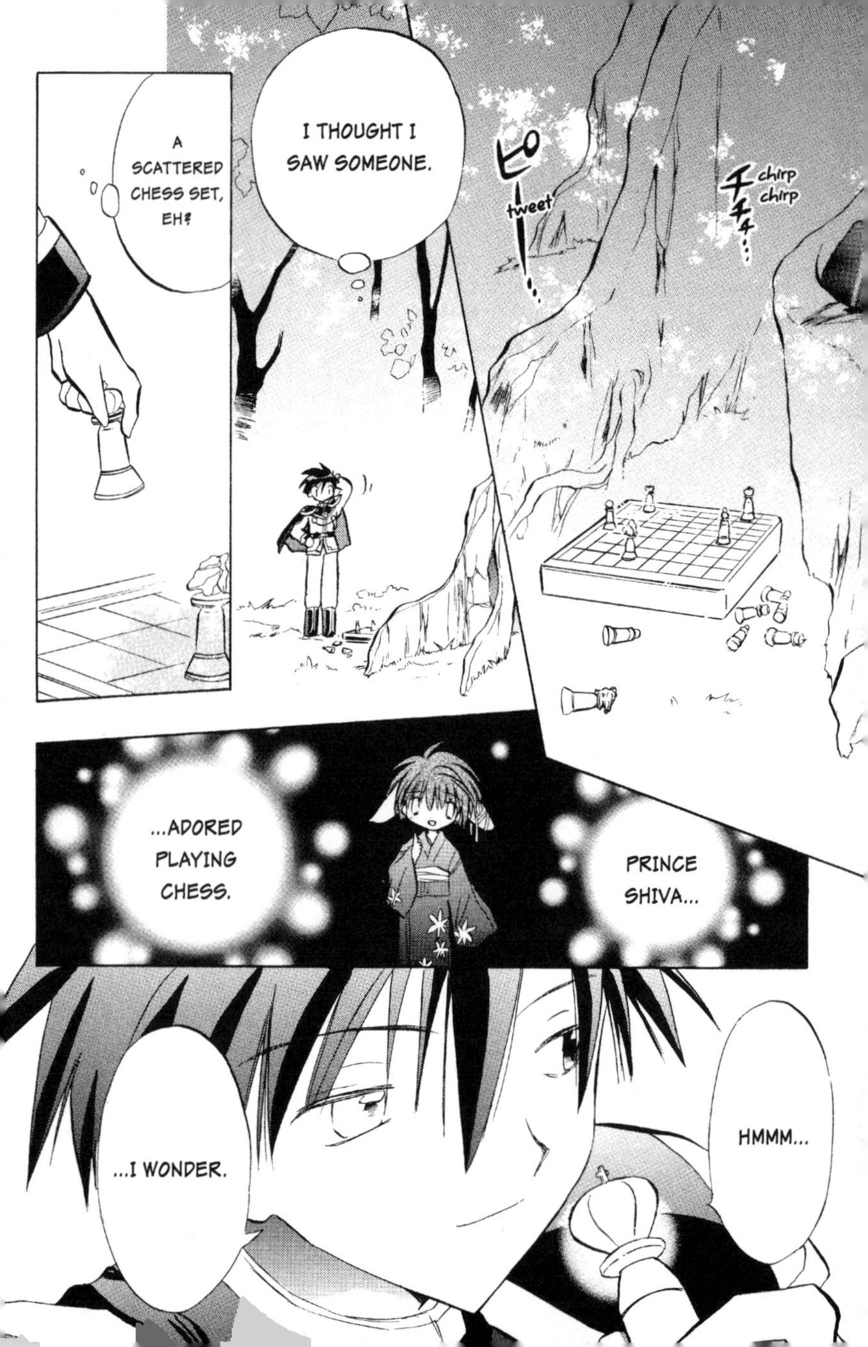
チチチ...
chirp chirp
ピ
tweet
I THOUGHT I SAW SOMEONE.
A SCATTERED CHESS SET, EH?
PRINCE SHIVA...
...ADORED PLAYING CHESS.
HMMM...
...I WONDER.

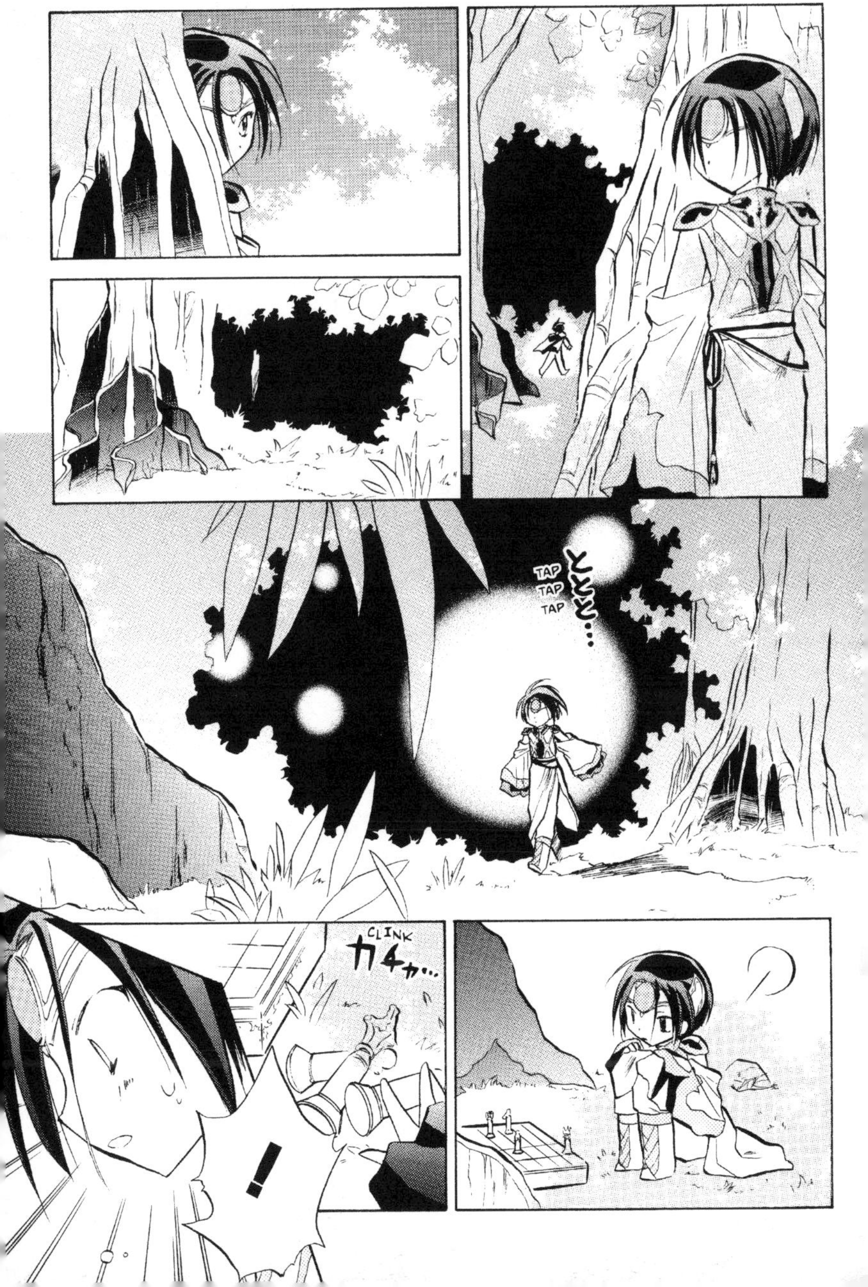

とととと...
TAP
TAP
TAP
カチャ...
CLINK
!

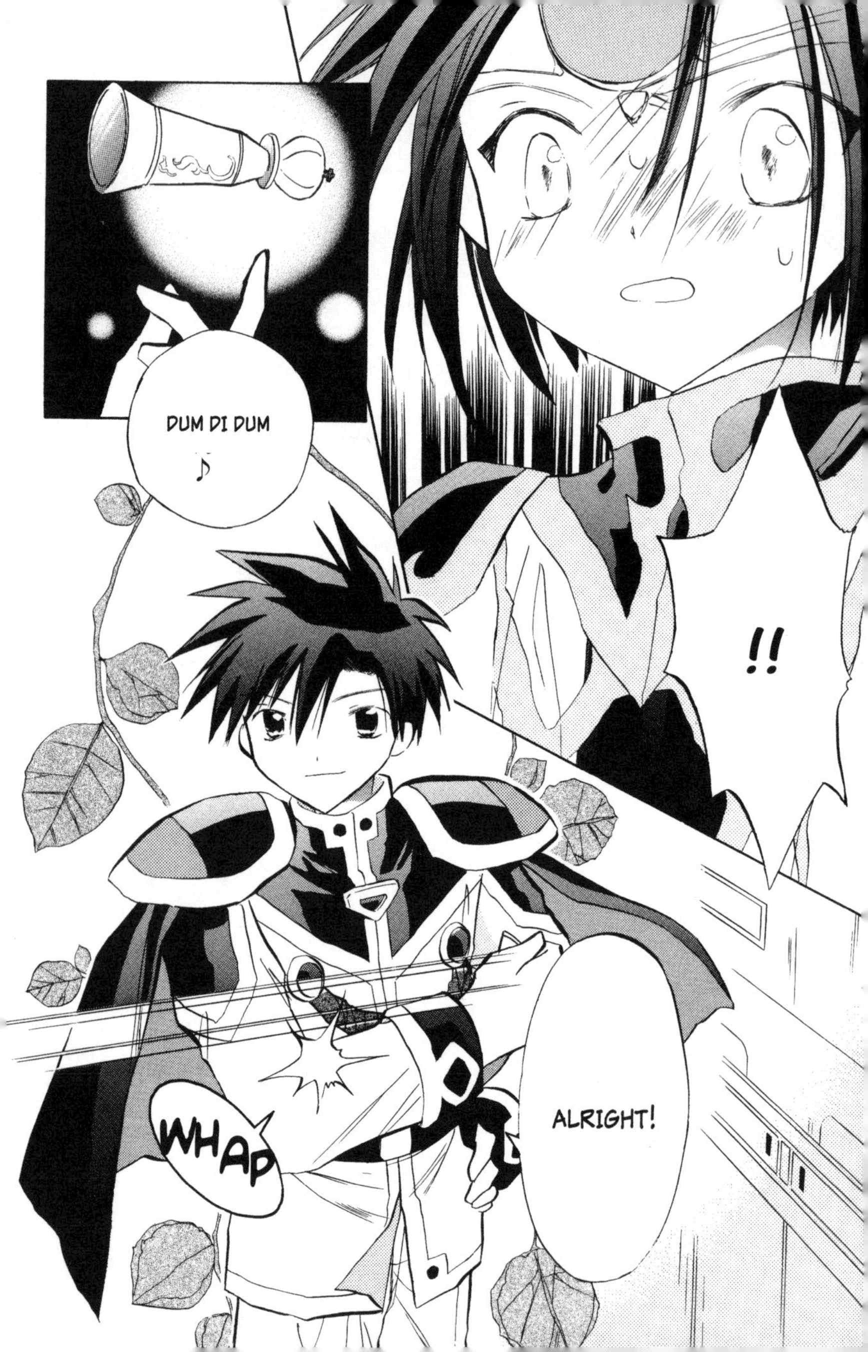

!!
DUM DI DUM ♪
ALRIGHT!
WHAP

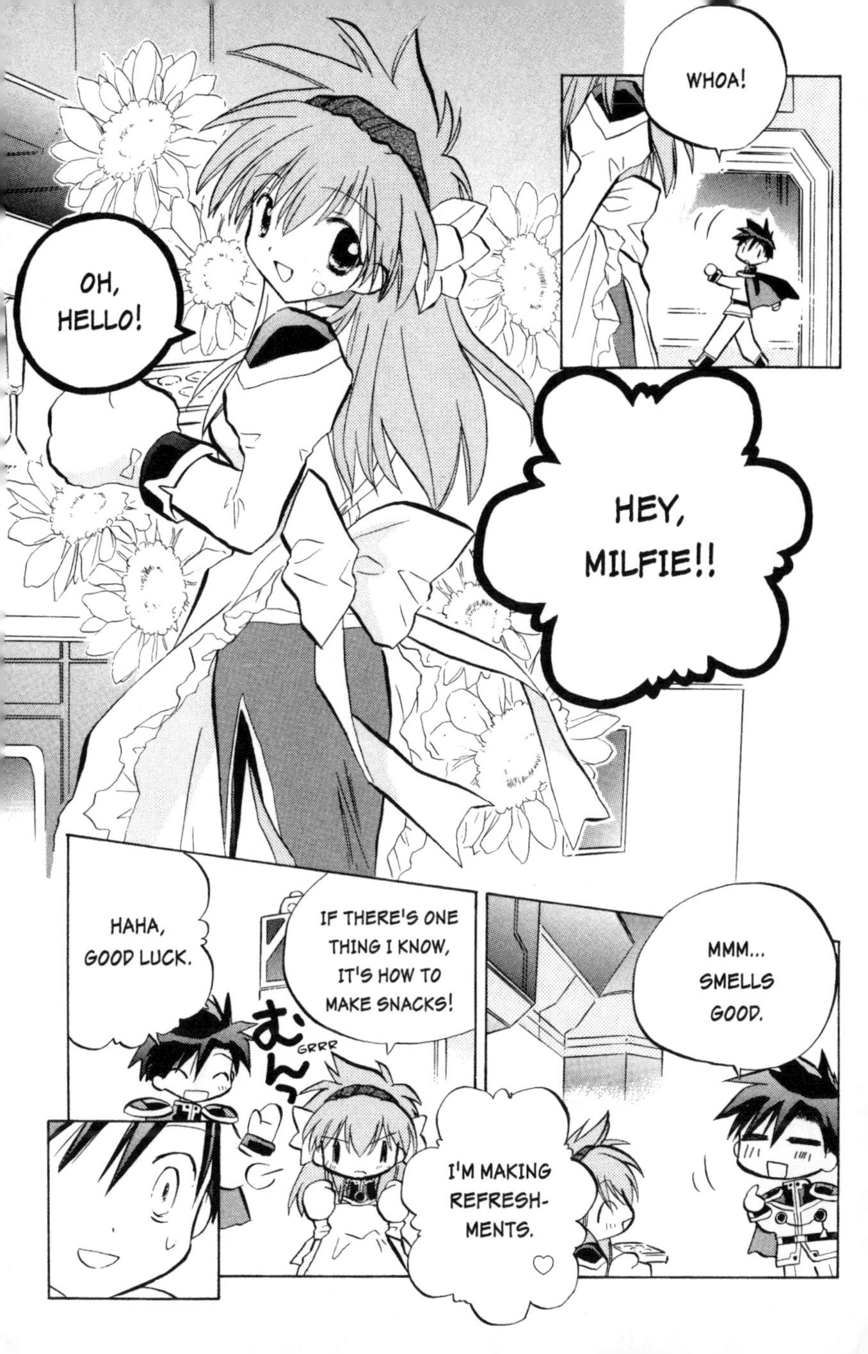
WHOA!
HEY, MILFIE!!
OH, HELLO!
MMM... SMELLS GOOD.
I'M MAKING REFRESH- MENTS.
HAHA, GOOD LUCK.
IF THERE'S ONE THING I KNOW, IT'S HOW TO MAKE SNACKS!
むんっ
GRRR

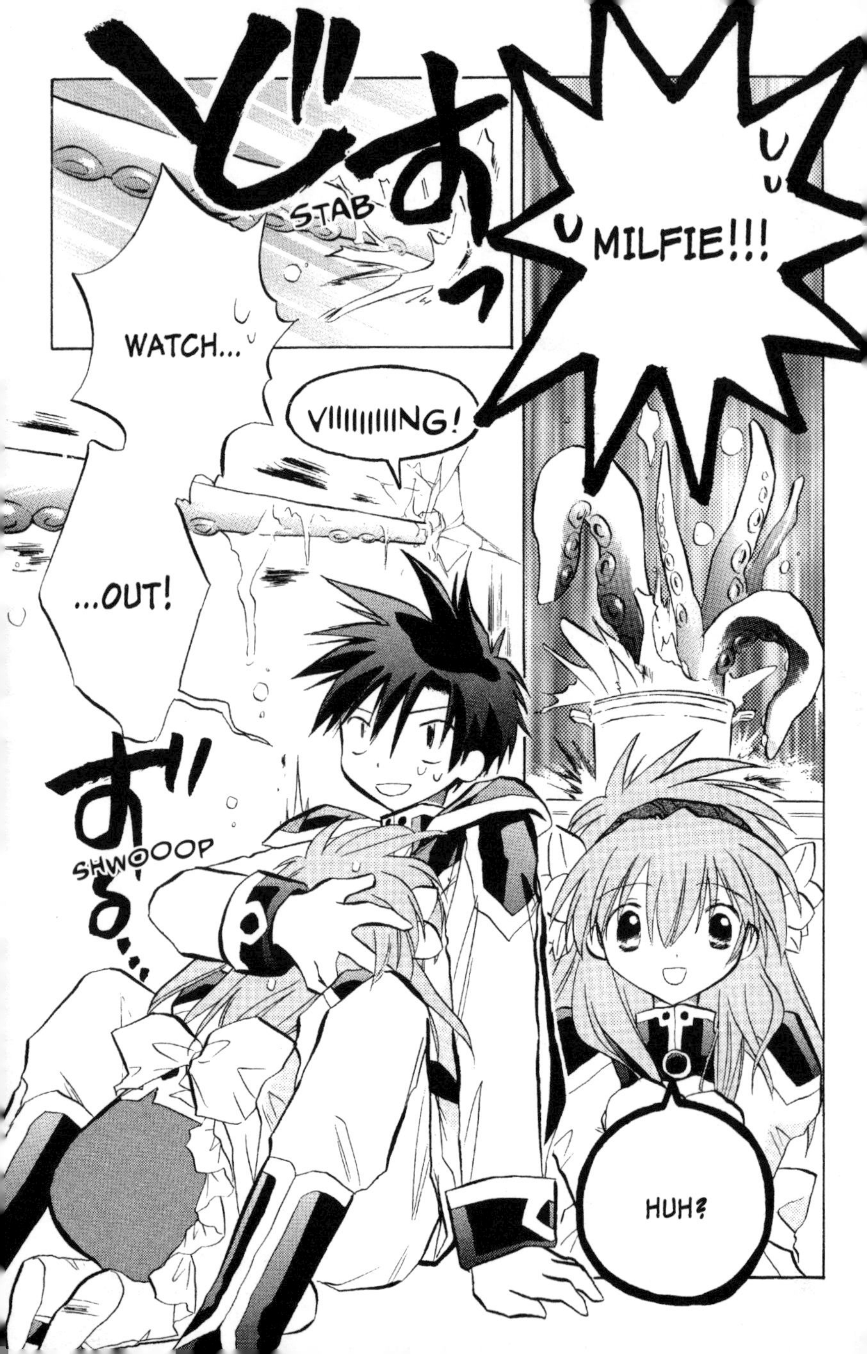
MILFIE!!!
どおっ
STAB
VIIIIIIIIING!
WATCH...
...OUT!
おろ...
SHWOOOP
HUH?

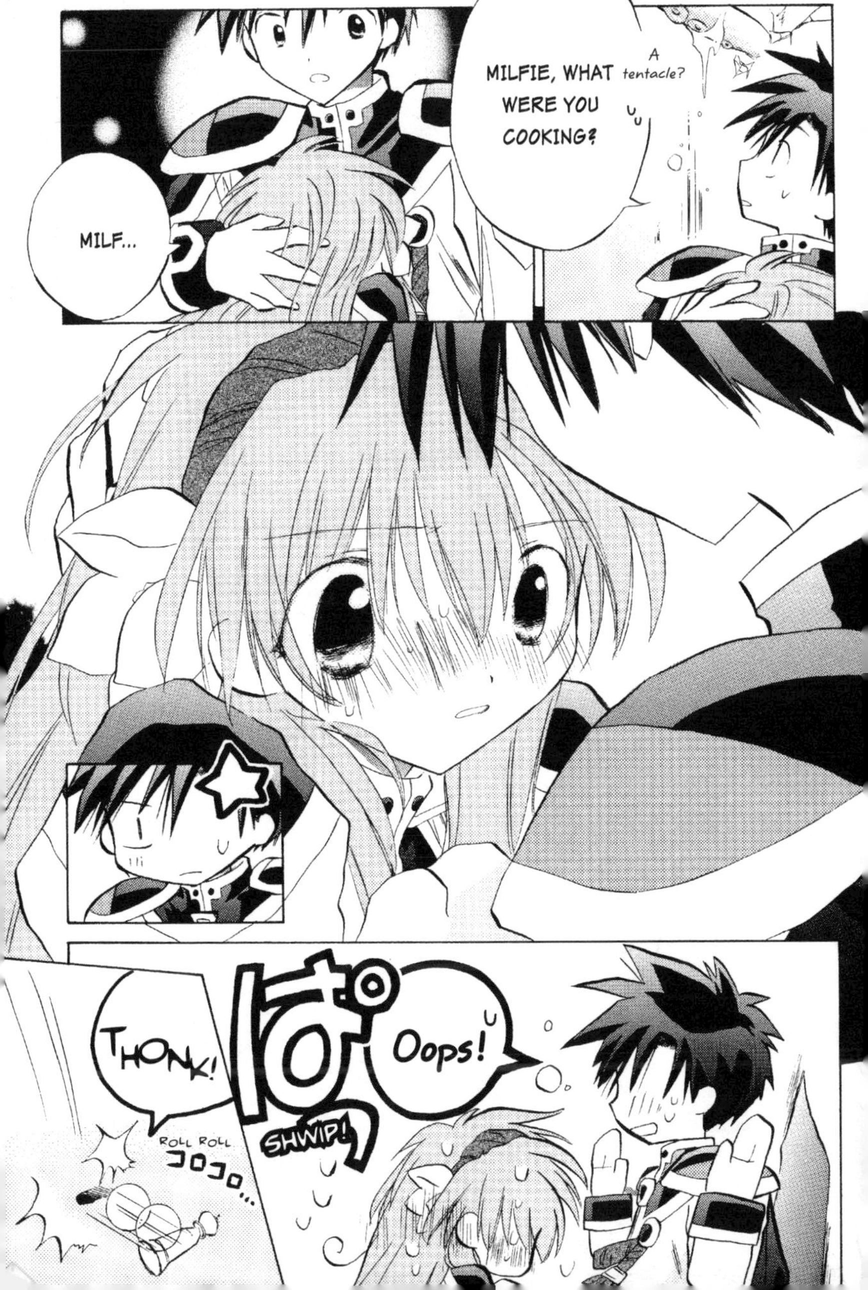
A tentacle?
MILFIE, WHAT WERE YOU COOKING?
MILF...
Oops!
ぱっ
SHWIP!
THONK!
ROLL ROLL
コロコロ...

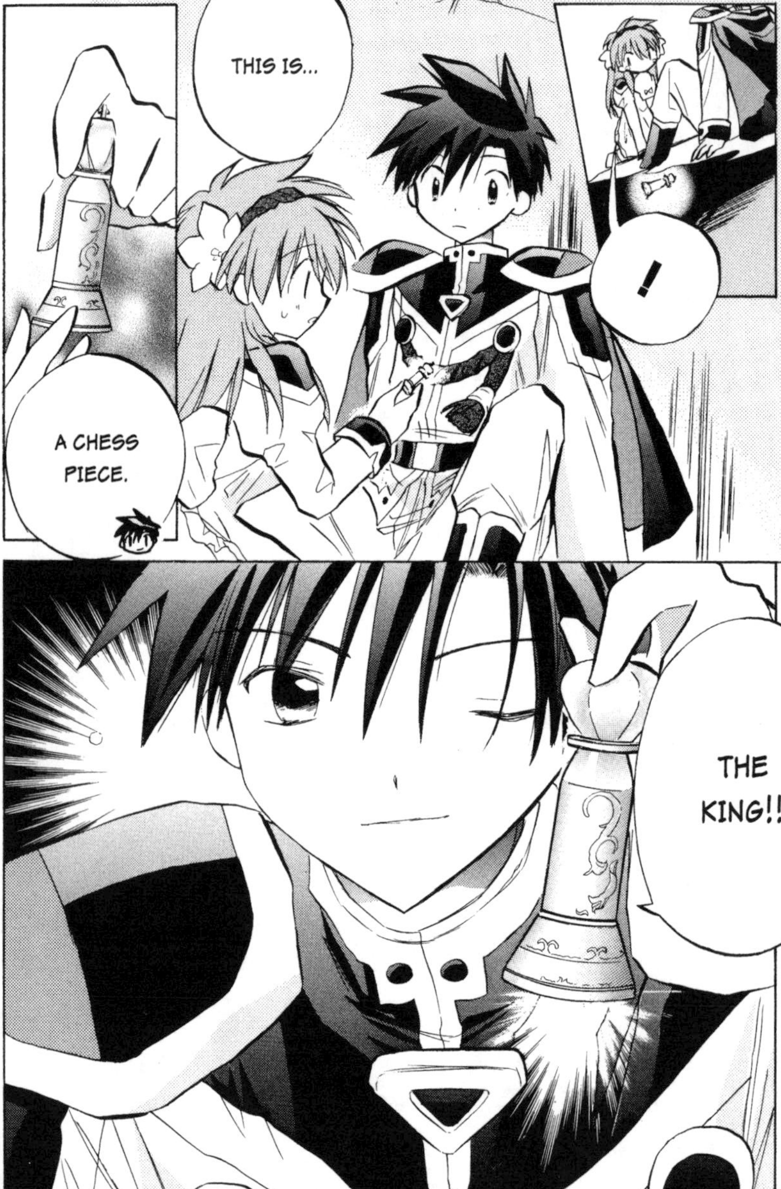
!
THIS IS...
A CHESS PIECE.
THE KING!!

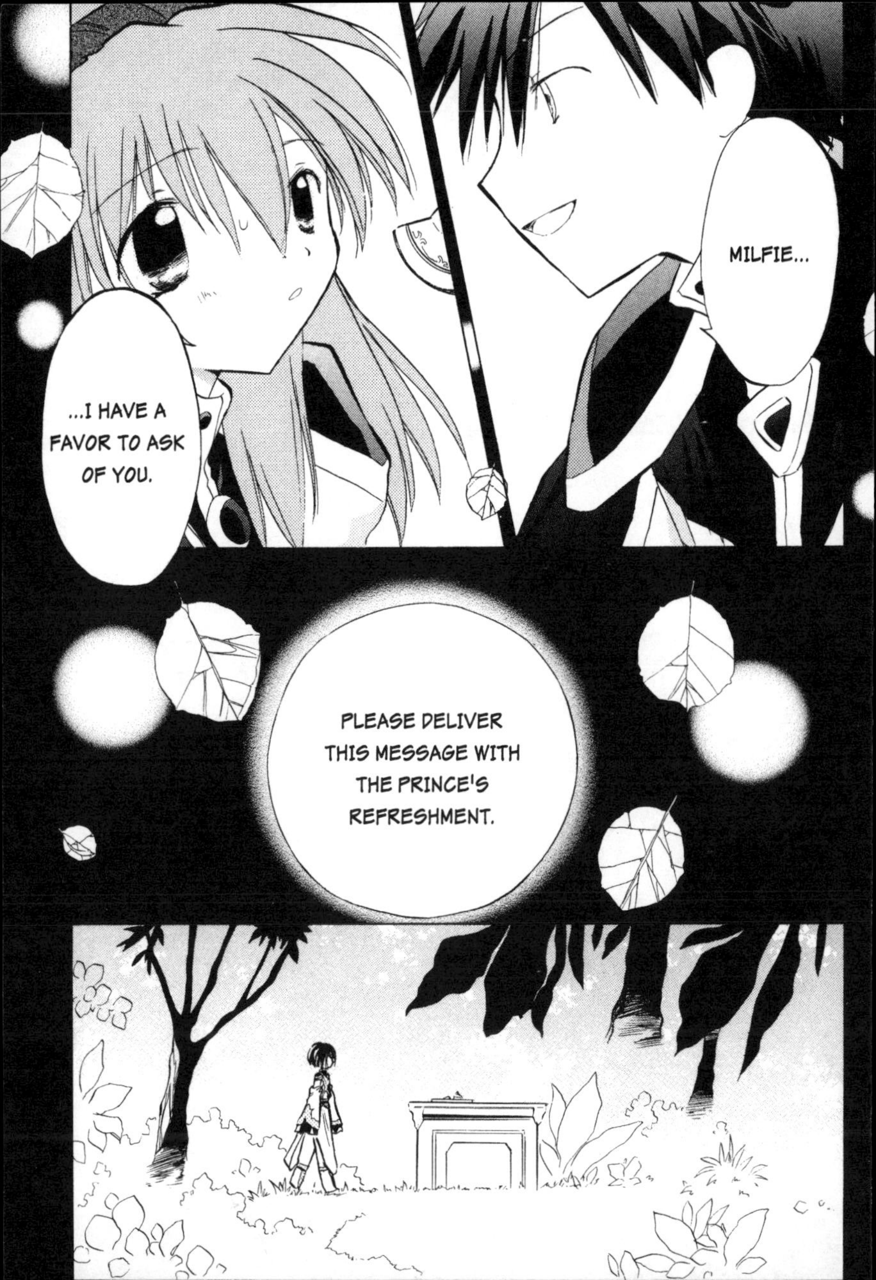
MILFIE...
...I HAVE A FAVOR TO ASK OF YOU.
PLEASE DELIVER THIS MESSAGE WITH THE PRINCE'S REFRESHMENT.

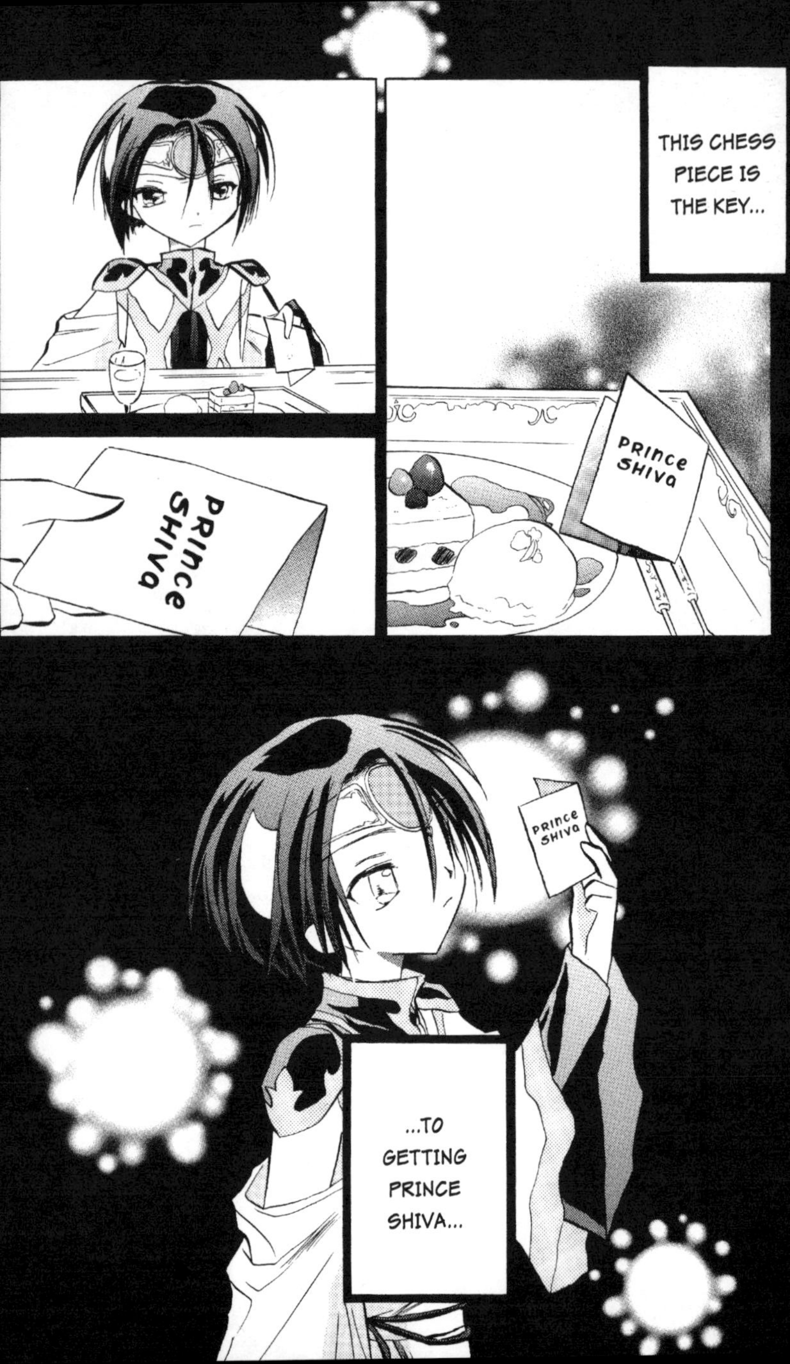
THIS CHESS PIECE IS THE KEY...
PRINCE SHIVA
PRINCE SHIVA
PRINCE SHIVA
...TO GETTING PRINCE SHIVA...

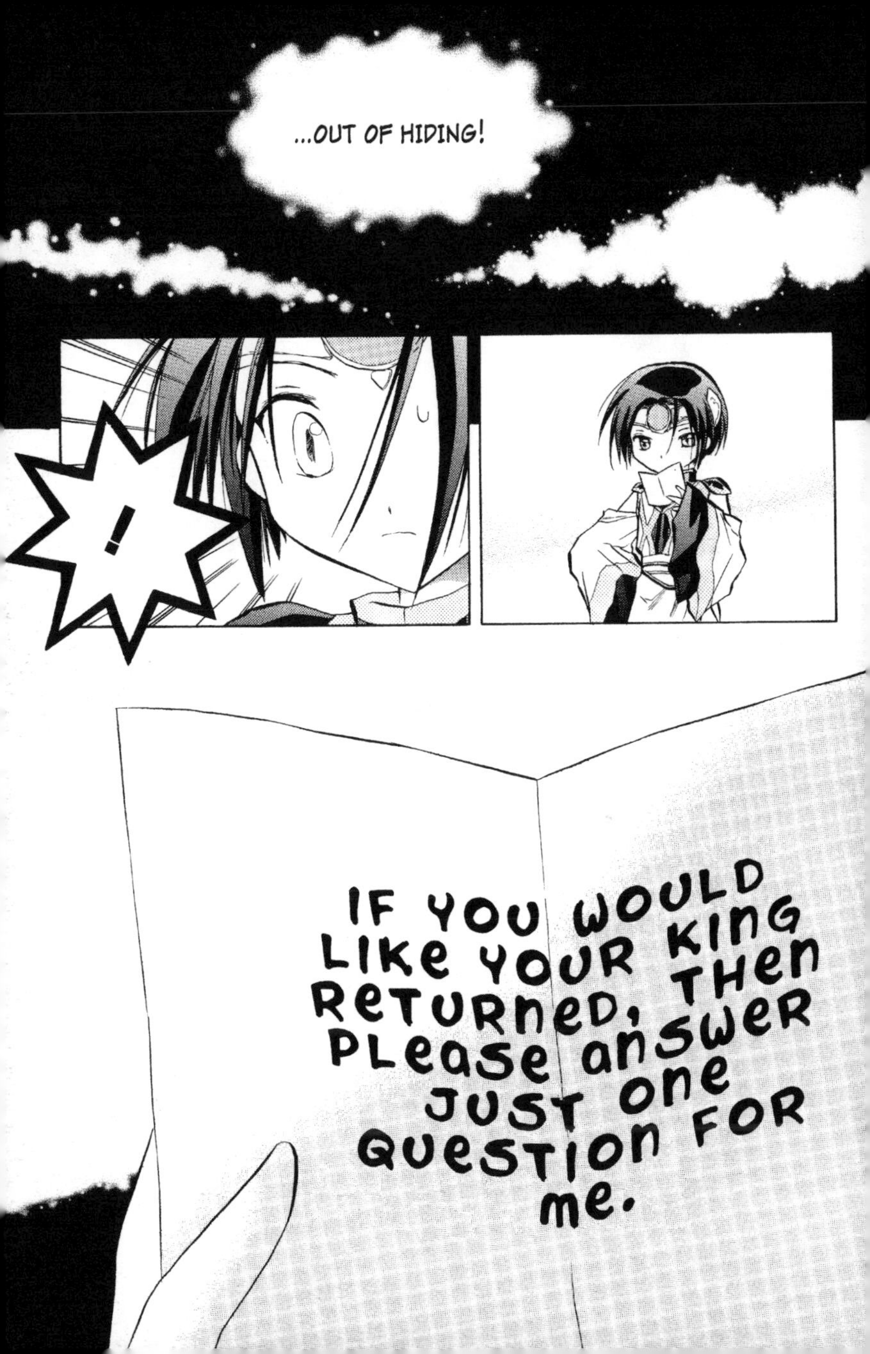
...OUT OF HIDING!
!
IF YOU WOULD LIKE YOUR KING RETURNED, THEN PLEASE ANSWER JUST ONE QUESTION FOR ME.

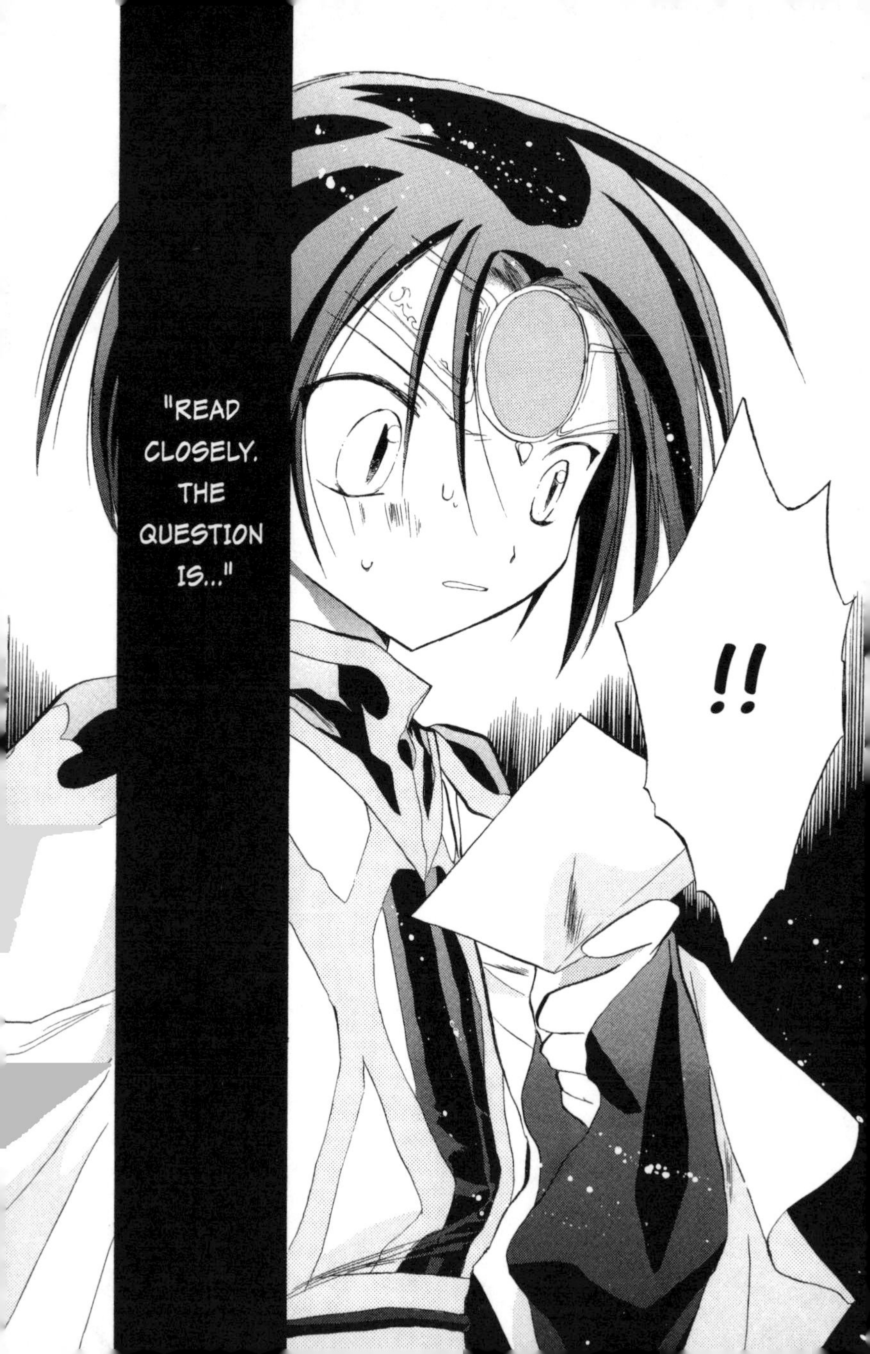
!!
"READ CLOSELY. THE QUESTION IS..."

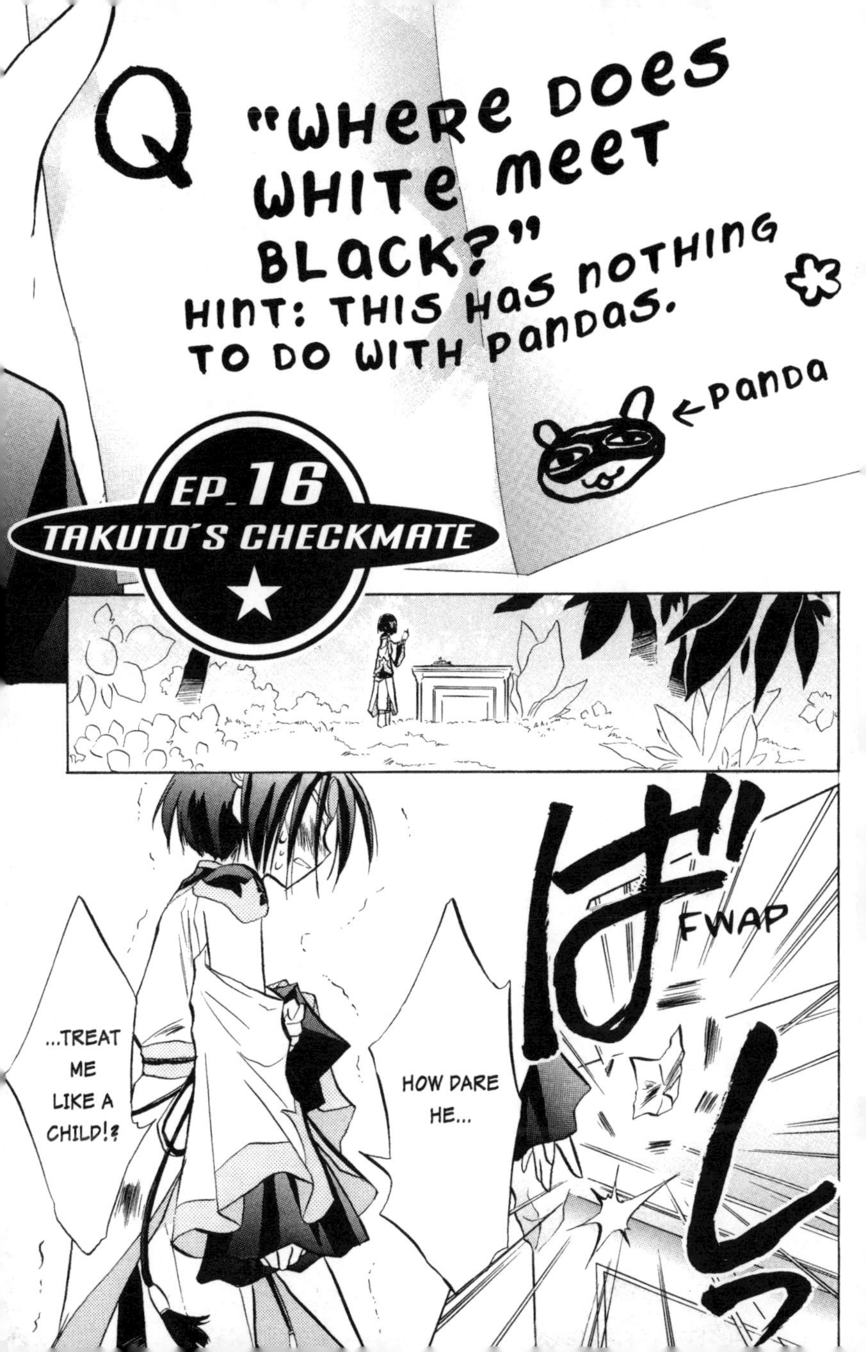
Q "WHERE DOES WHITE MEET BLACK?"
HINT: THIS HAS NOTHING TO DO WITH PANDAS.
←PANDA
EP_16
TAKUTO'S CHECKMATE
ばしっ
FWAP
HOW DARE HE...
...TREAT ME LIKE A CHILD!?

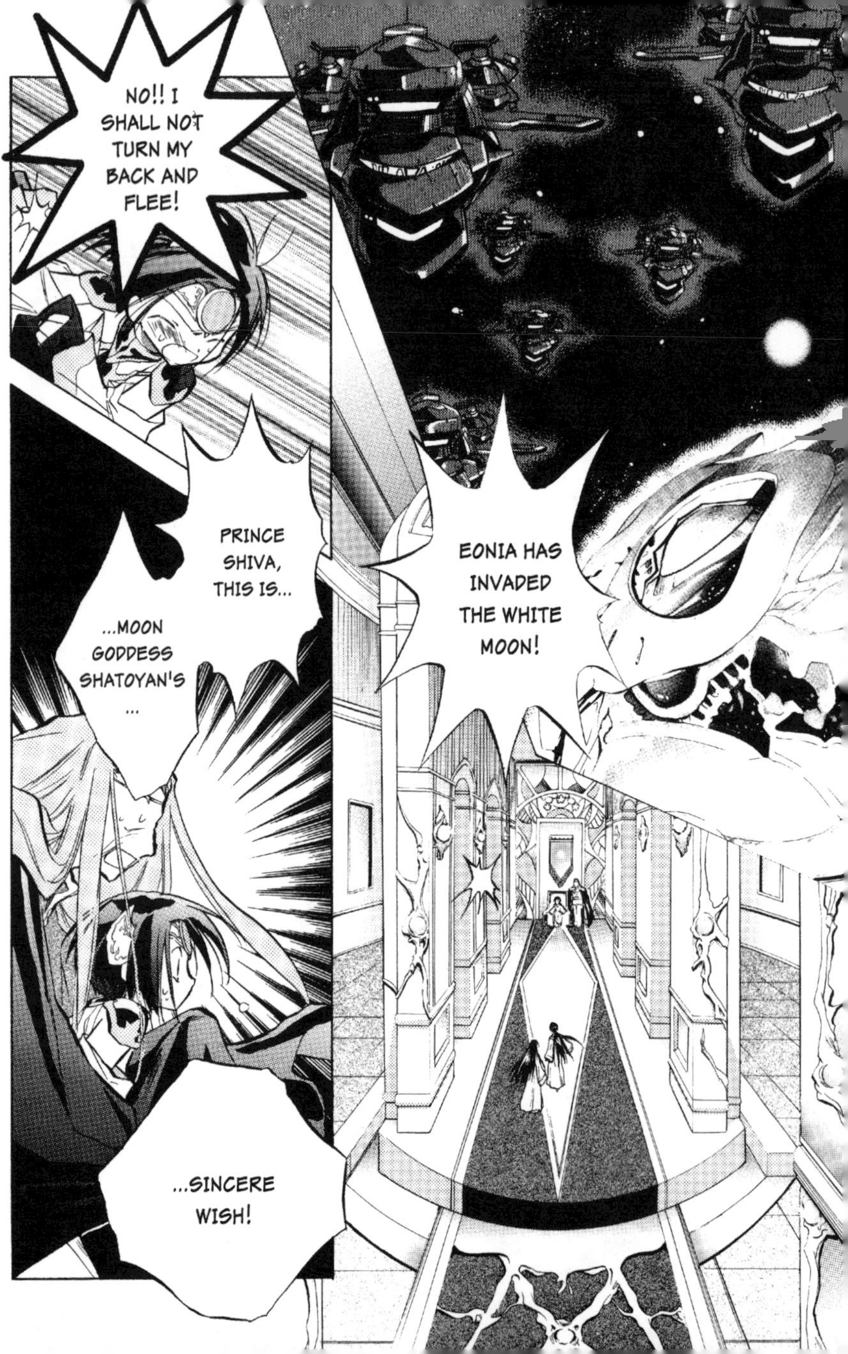
EONIA HAS INVADED THE WHITE MOON!
NO!! I SHALL NOT TURN MY BACK AND FLEE!
PRINCE SHIVA, THIS IS...
...MOON GODDESS SHATOYAN'S ...
...SINCERE WISH!

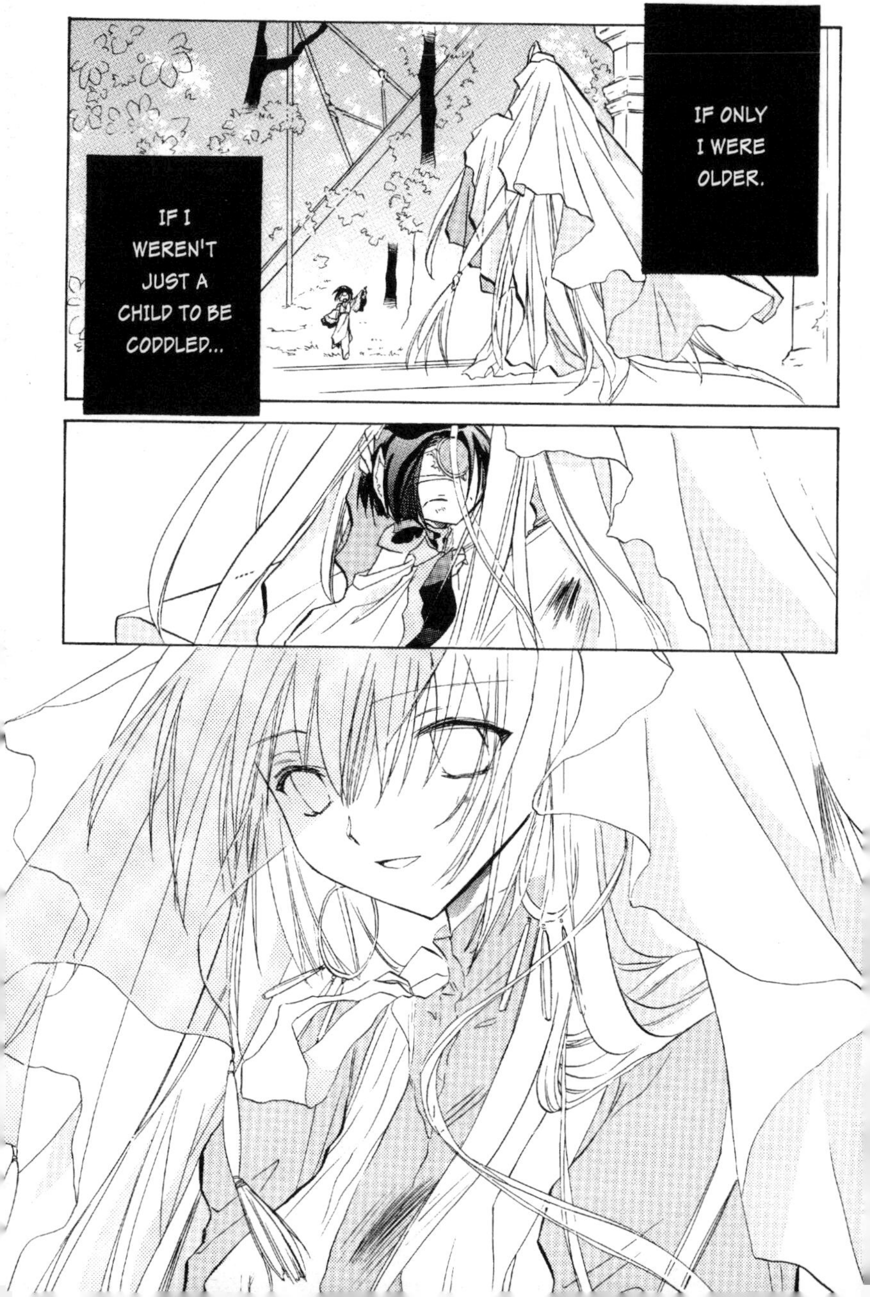
IF ONLY I WERE OLDER.
IF I WEREN'T JUST A CHILD TO BE CODDLED...

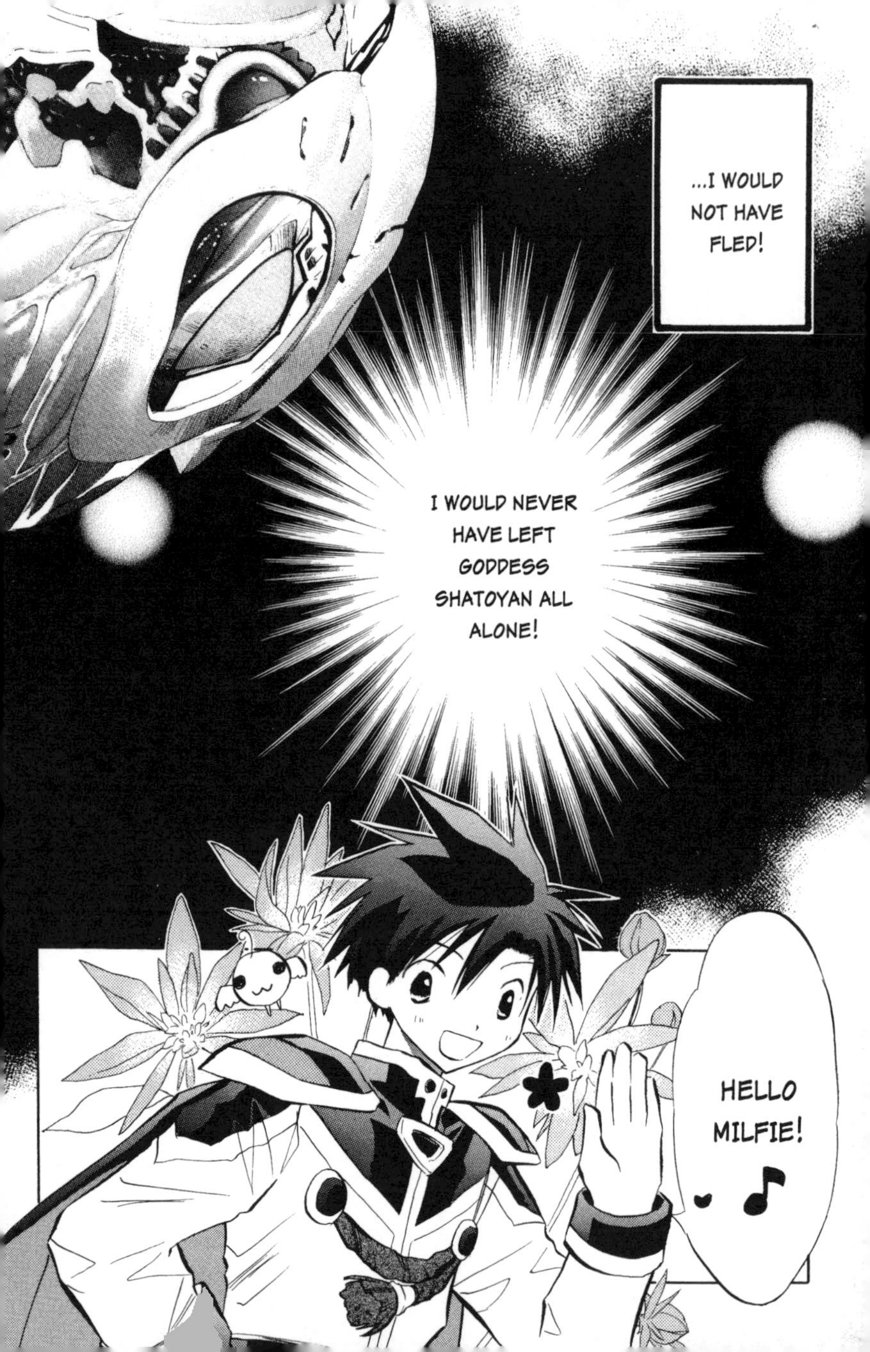
...I WOULD NOT HAVE FLED!
I WOULD NEVER HAVE LEFT GODDESS SHATOYAN ALL ALONE!
HELLO MILFIE!

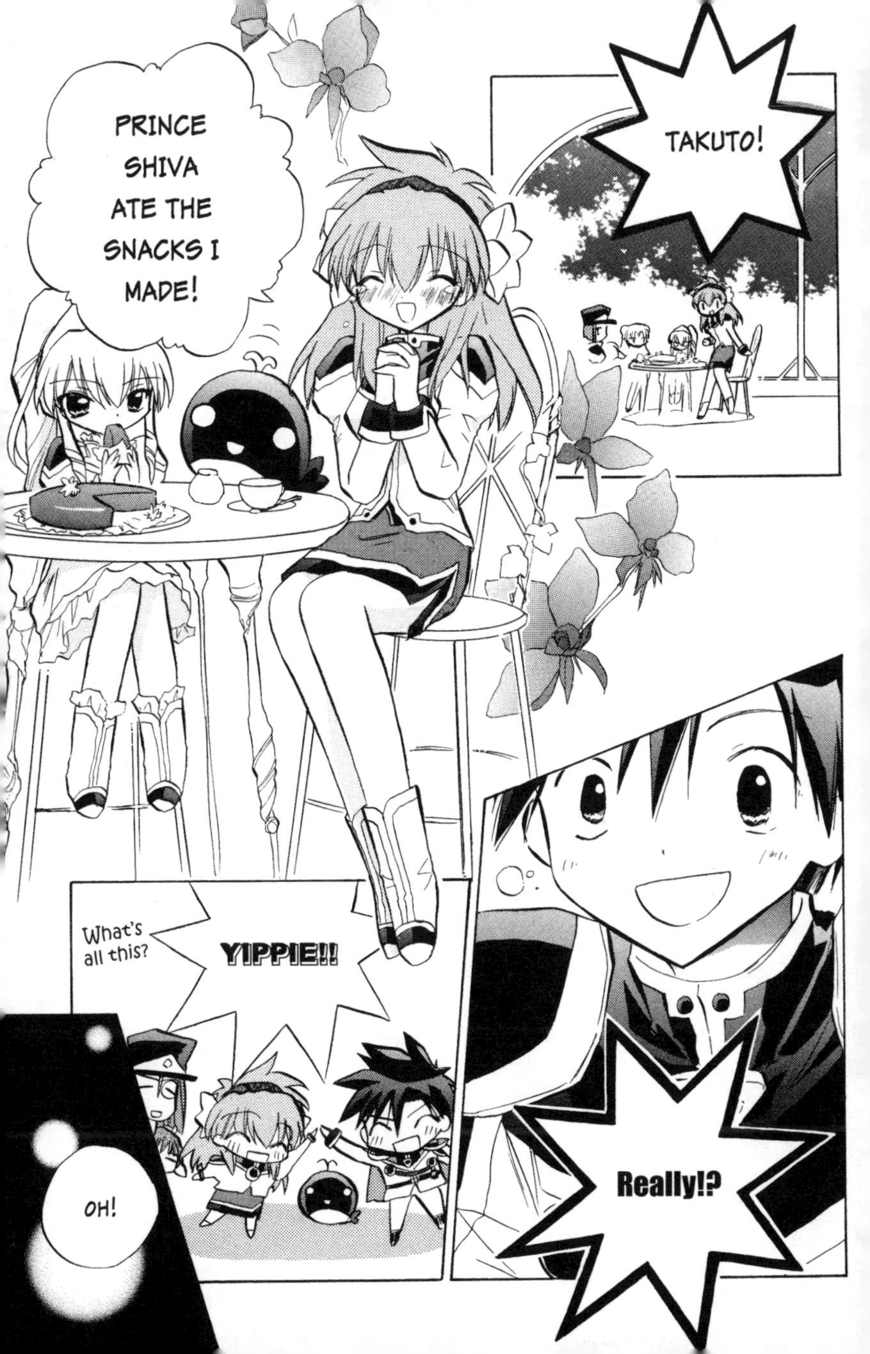
TAKUTO!
PRINCE SHIVA ATE THE SNACKS I MADE!
Really!?
YIPPIE!!
What's all this?
OH!

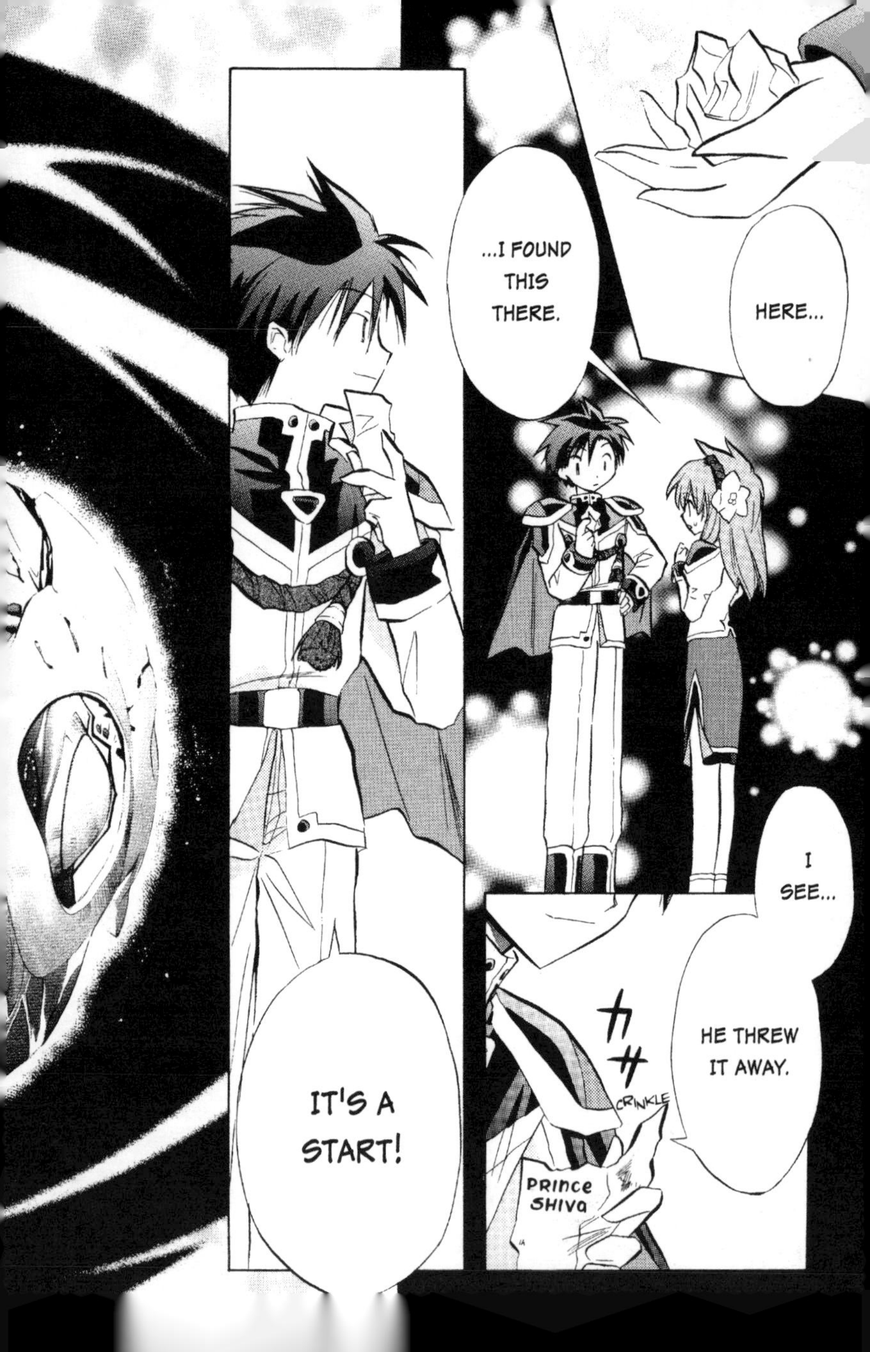
HERE...
...I FOUND THIS THERE.
I SEE...
HE THREW IT AWAY.
CRINKLE
Prince SHIVA
IT'S A START!

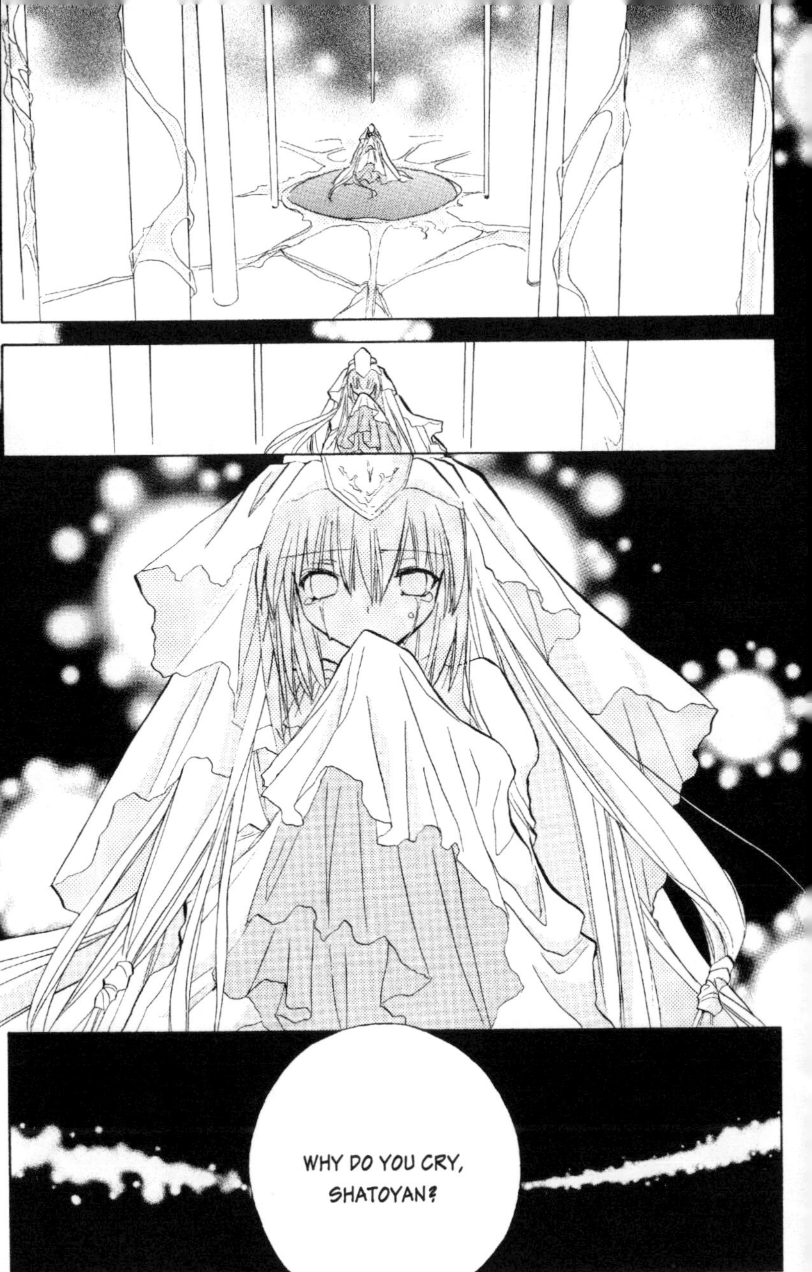
WHY DO YOU CRY, SHATOYAN?

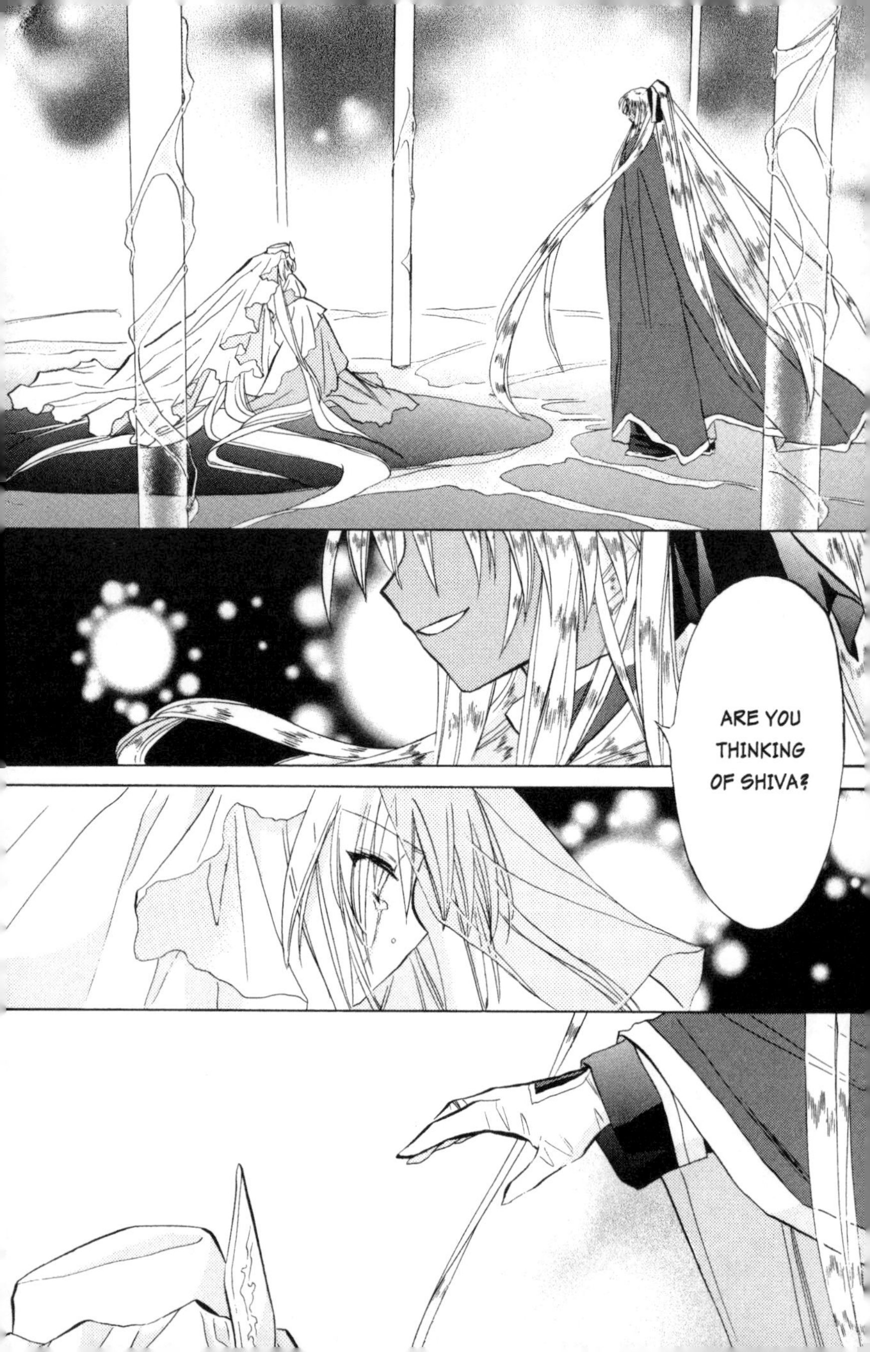
ARE YOU THINKING OF SHIVA?

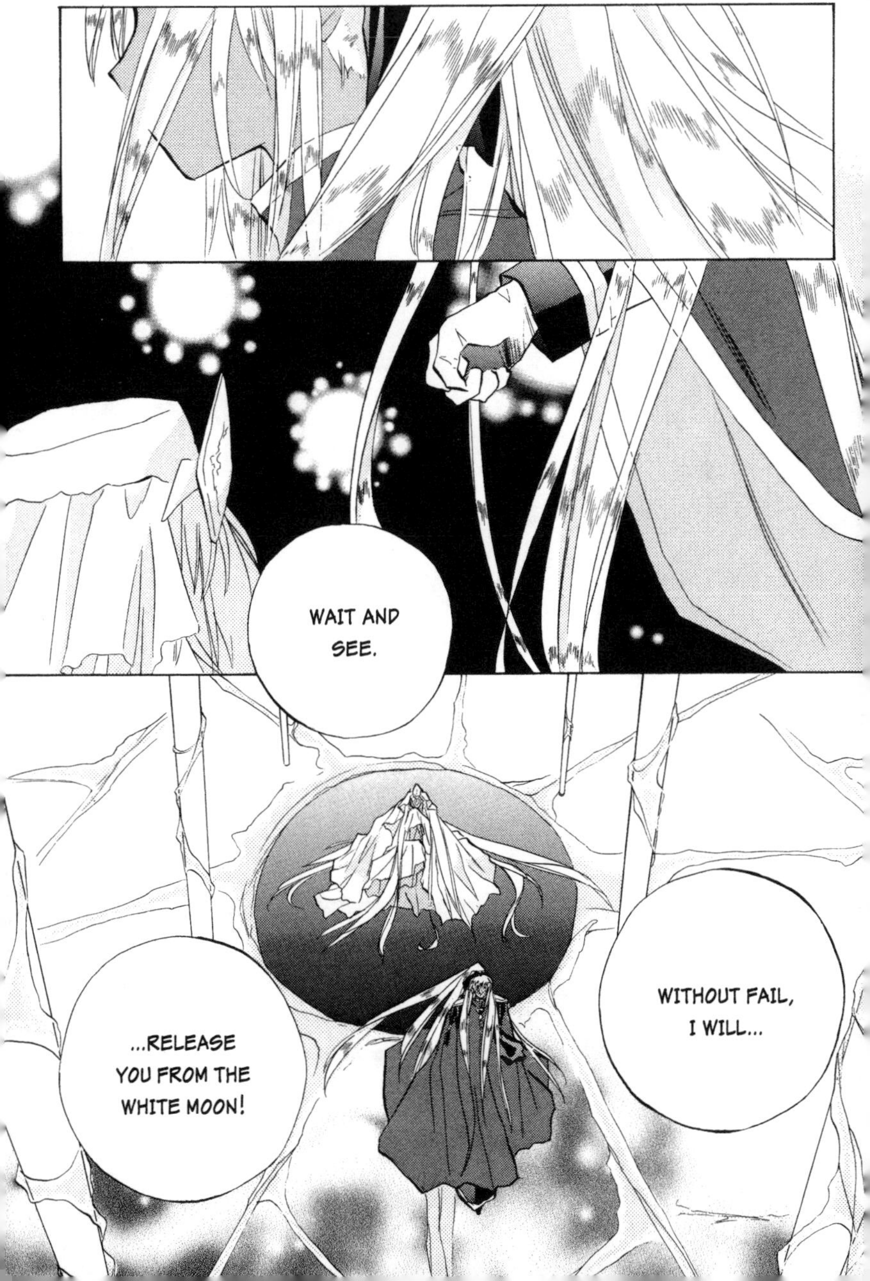
WAIT AND SEE.
WITHOUT FAIL, I WILL...
...RELEASE YOU FROM THE WHITE MOON!

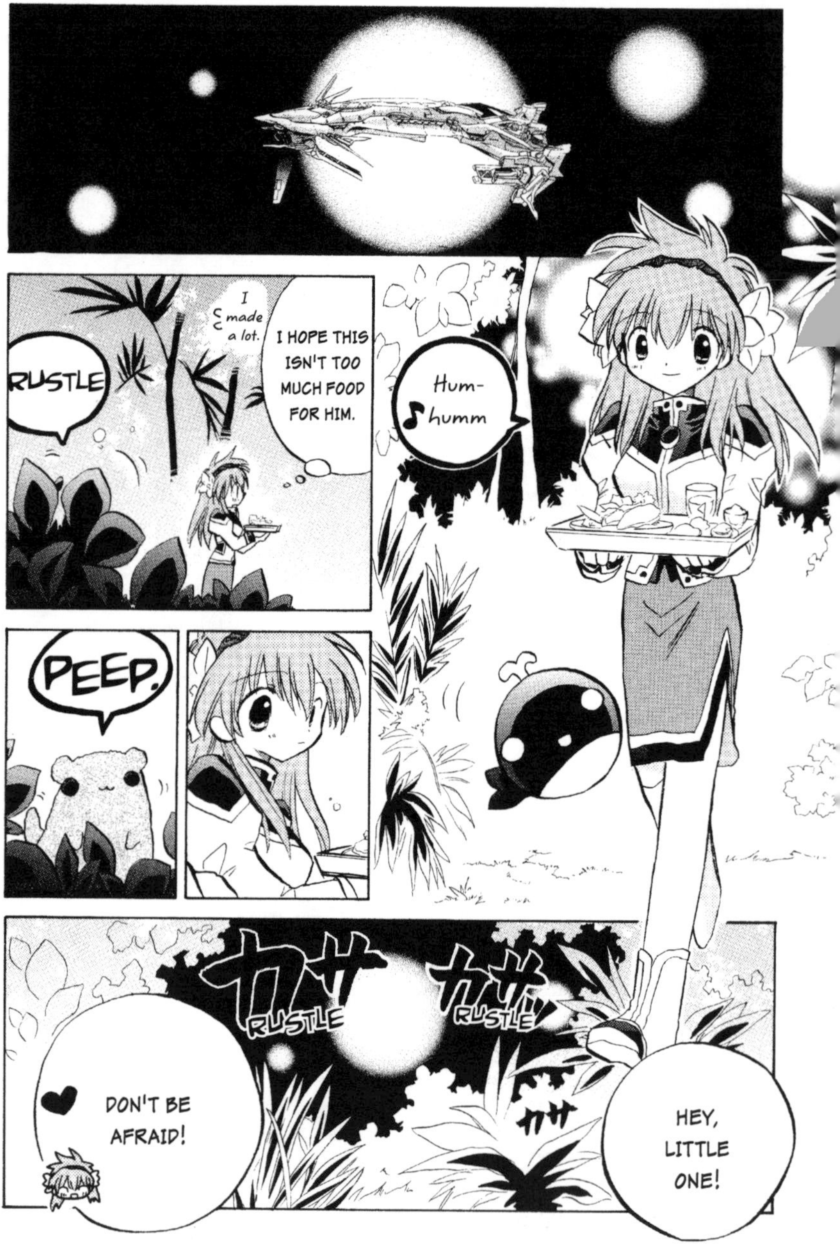
Hum- humm
I HOPE THIS ISN'T TOO MUCH FOOD FOR HIM.
I made a lot.
RUSTLE
PEEP.
カサ RUSTLE
カサ RUSTLE
HEY, LITTLE ONE!
カサ
DON'T BE AFRAID!

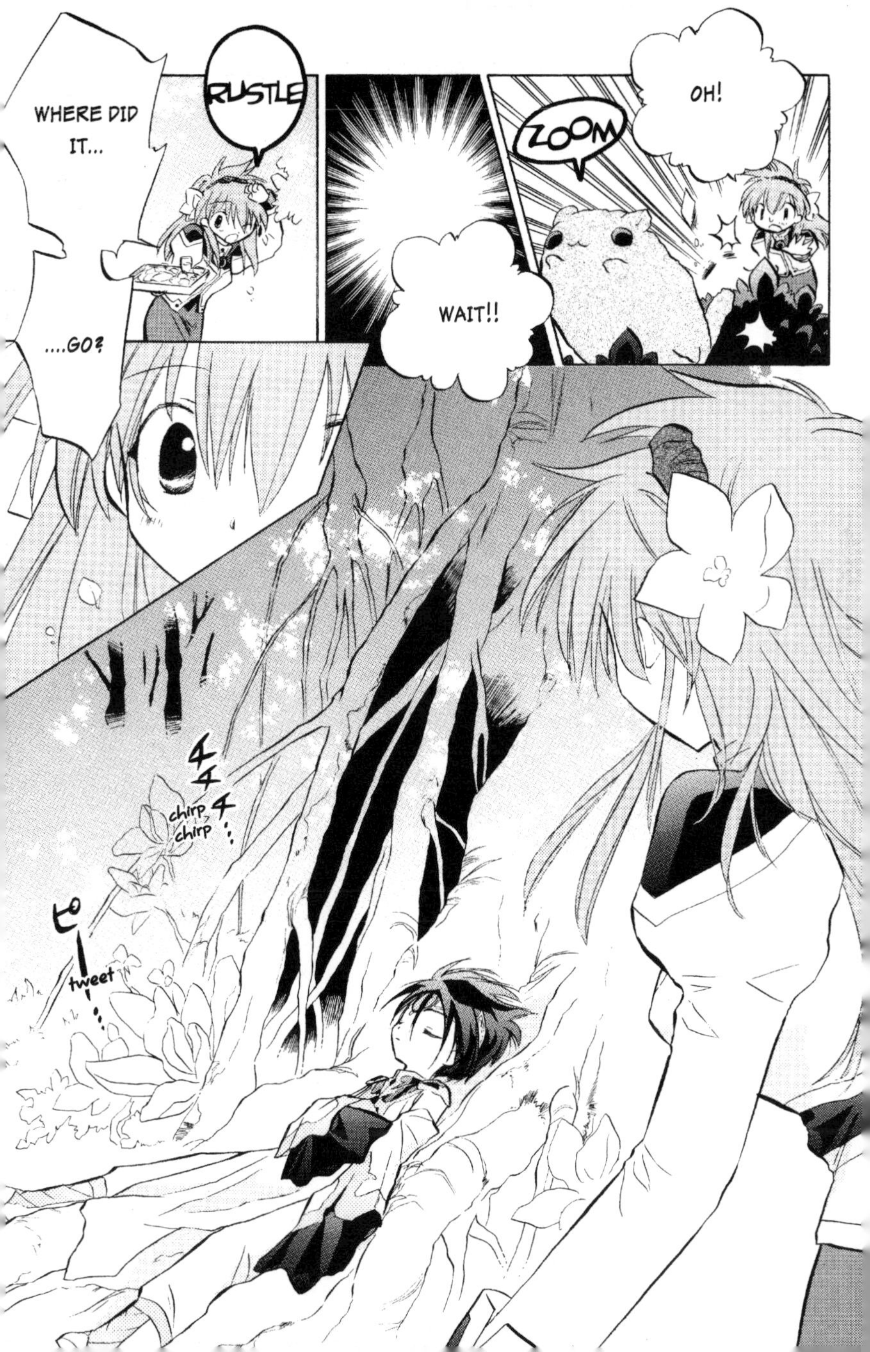
OH!
ZOOM
WAIT!!
RUSTLE
WHERE DID IT...
....GO?
chirp chirp
tweet

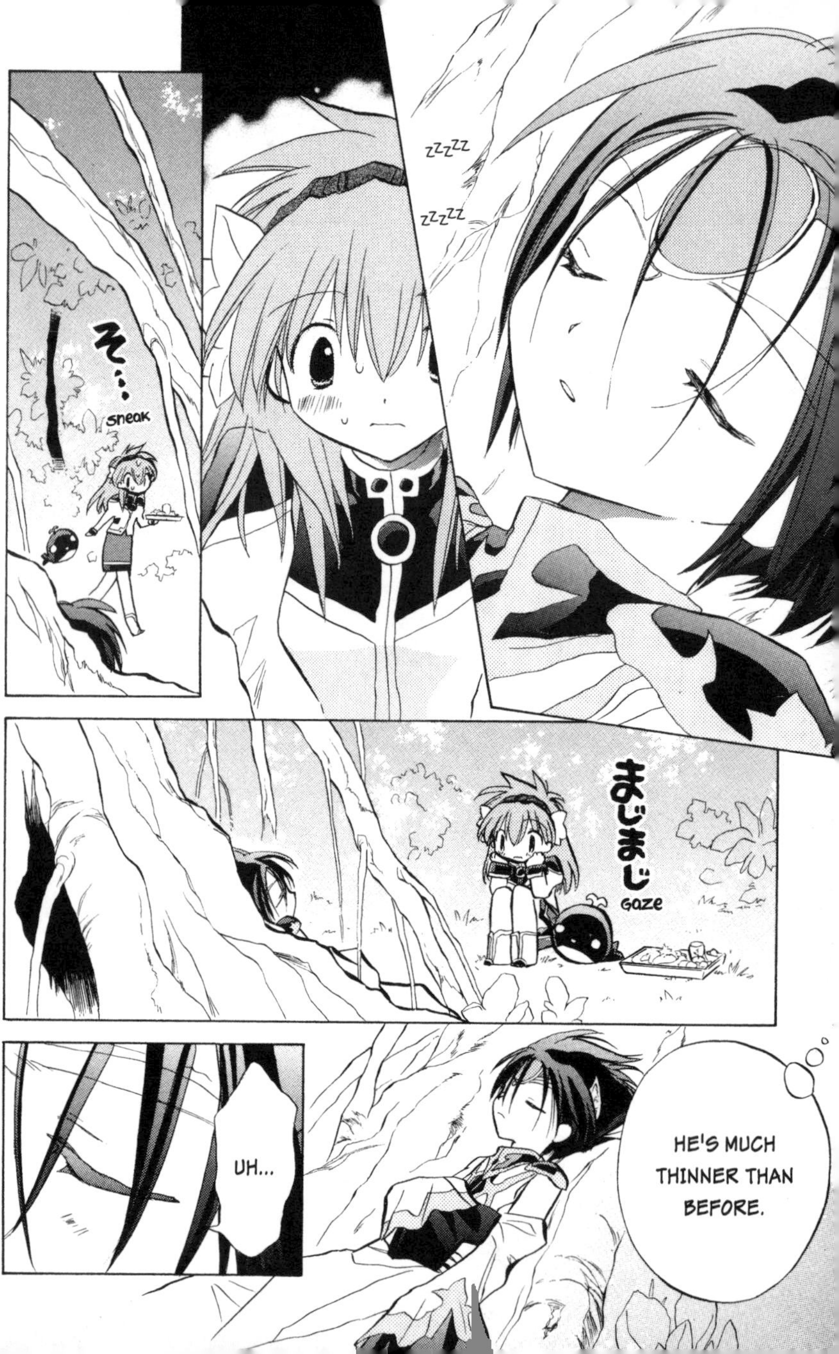
ZZZZZ
ZZZZZ
そ…
sneak
まじまじ
gaze
HE'S MUCH THINNER THAN BEFORE.
UH...

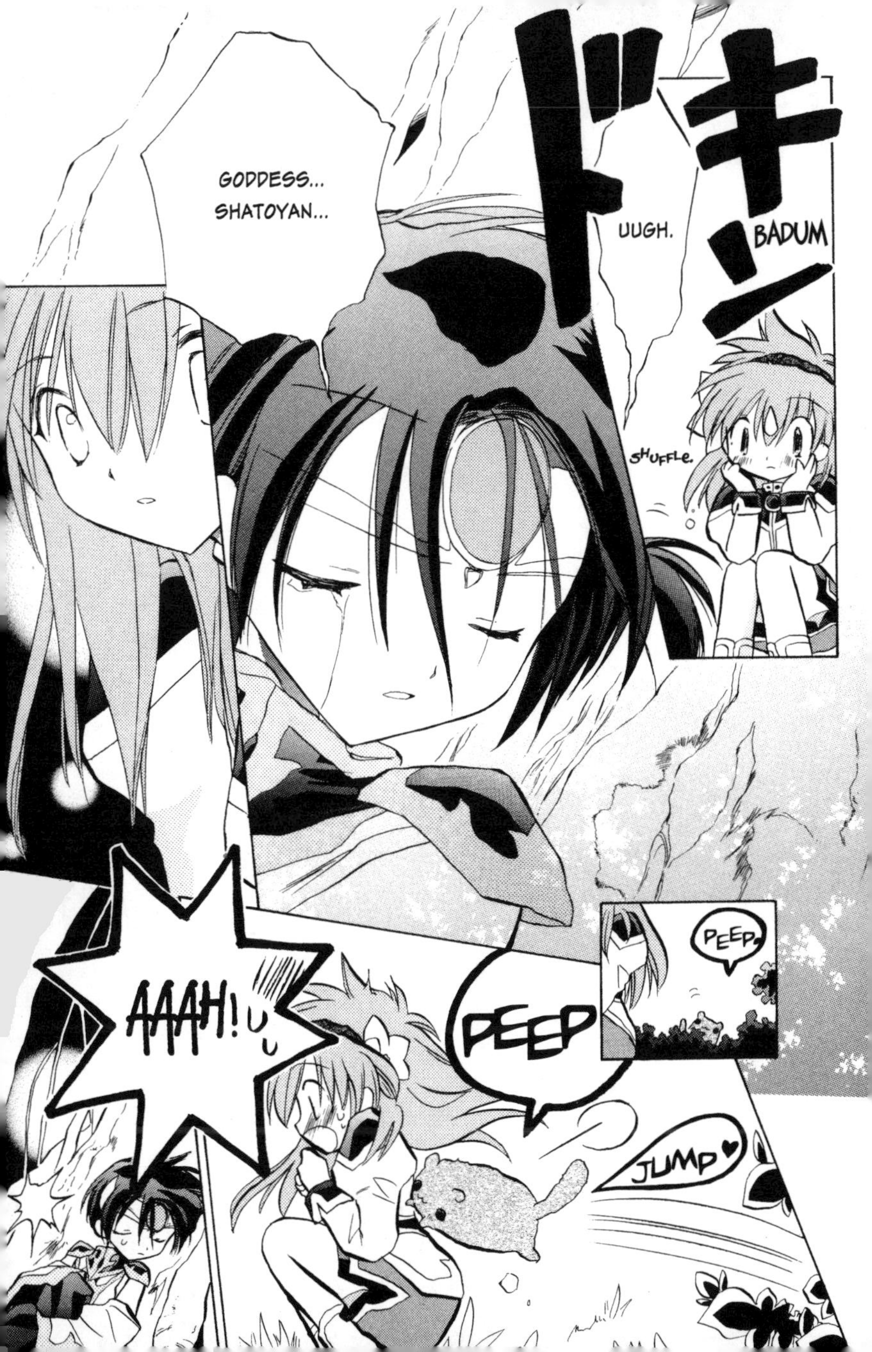
ドキン
BADUM
UUGH.
SHUFFLE.
GODDESS...
SHATOYAN...
PEEP.
PEEP
AAAH!
JUMP♥

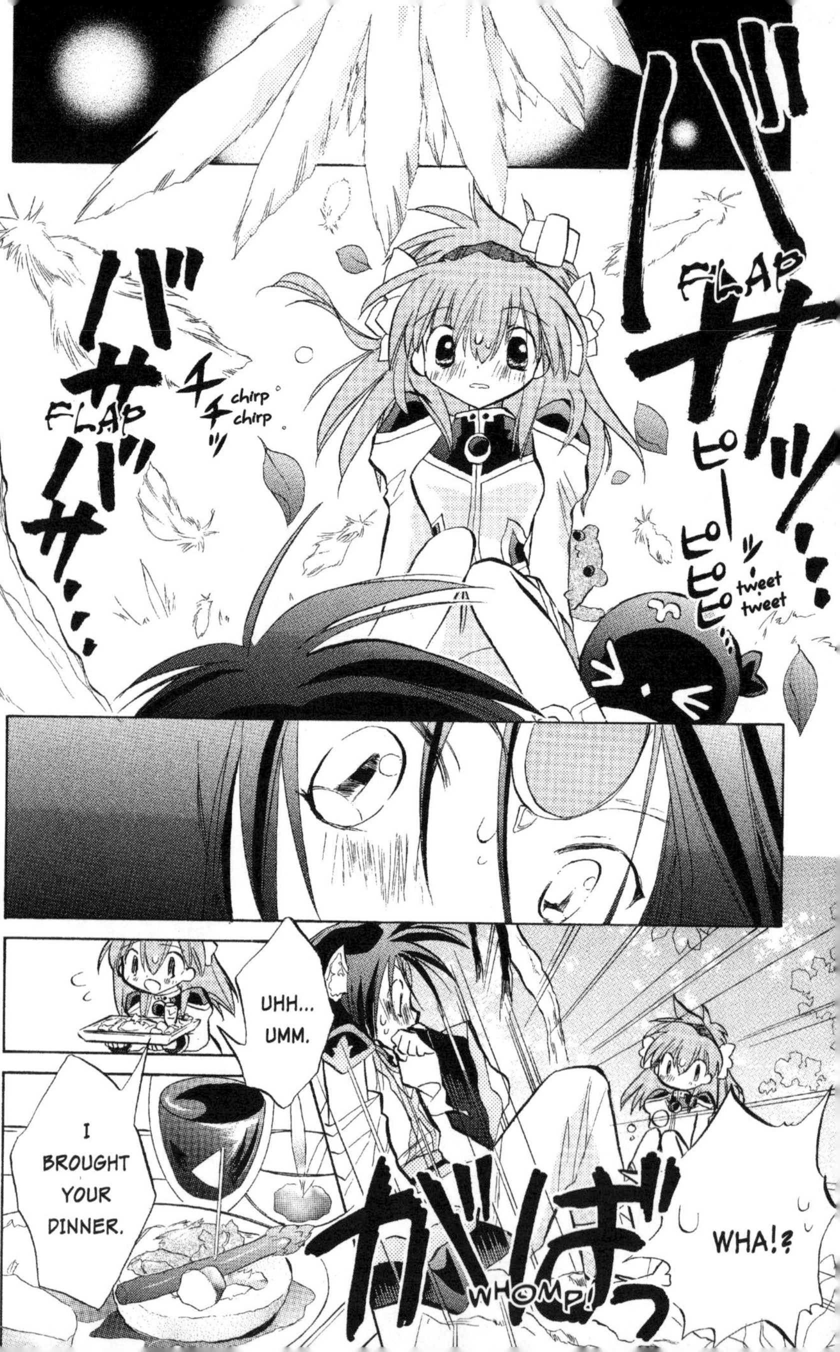
バサッ
FLAP
ピーピッピピ…
tweet tweet
バサバサ…
FLAP
チチッ
chirp chirp
WHA!?
WHOMP!
UHH... UMM.
I BROUGHT YOUR DINNER.

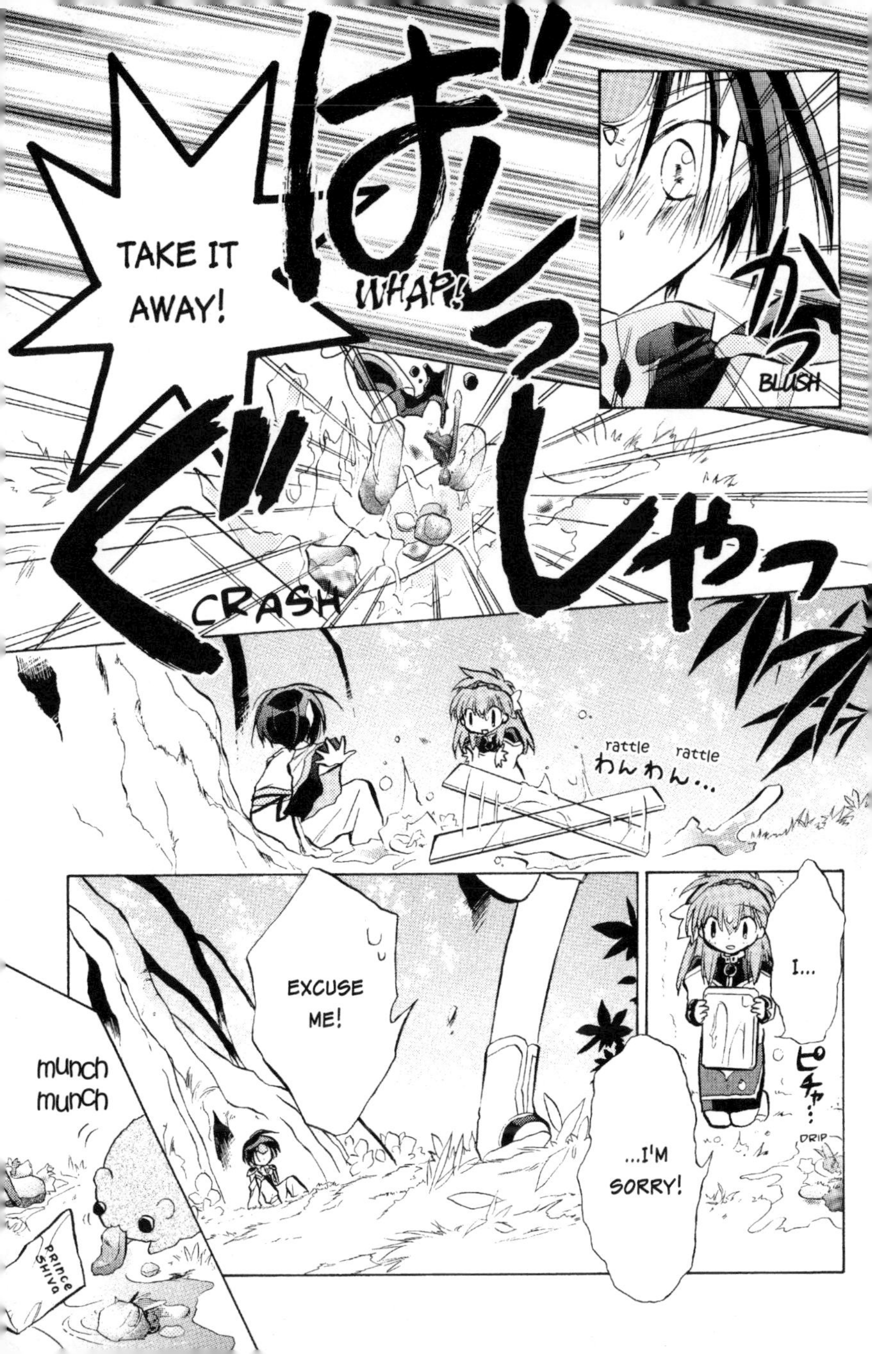
BLUSH
TAKE IT AWAY!
WHAP!
ぐしゃっ
CRASH
rattle rattle
わんわん...
I...
...I'M SORRY!
ピチャ...
DRIP
EXCUSE ME!
munch munch
Prince Shiva

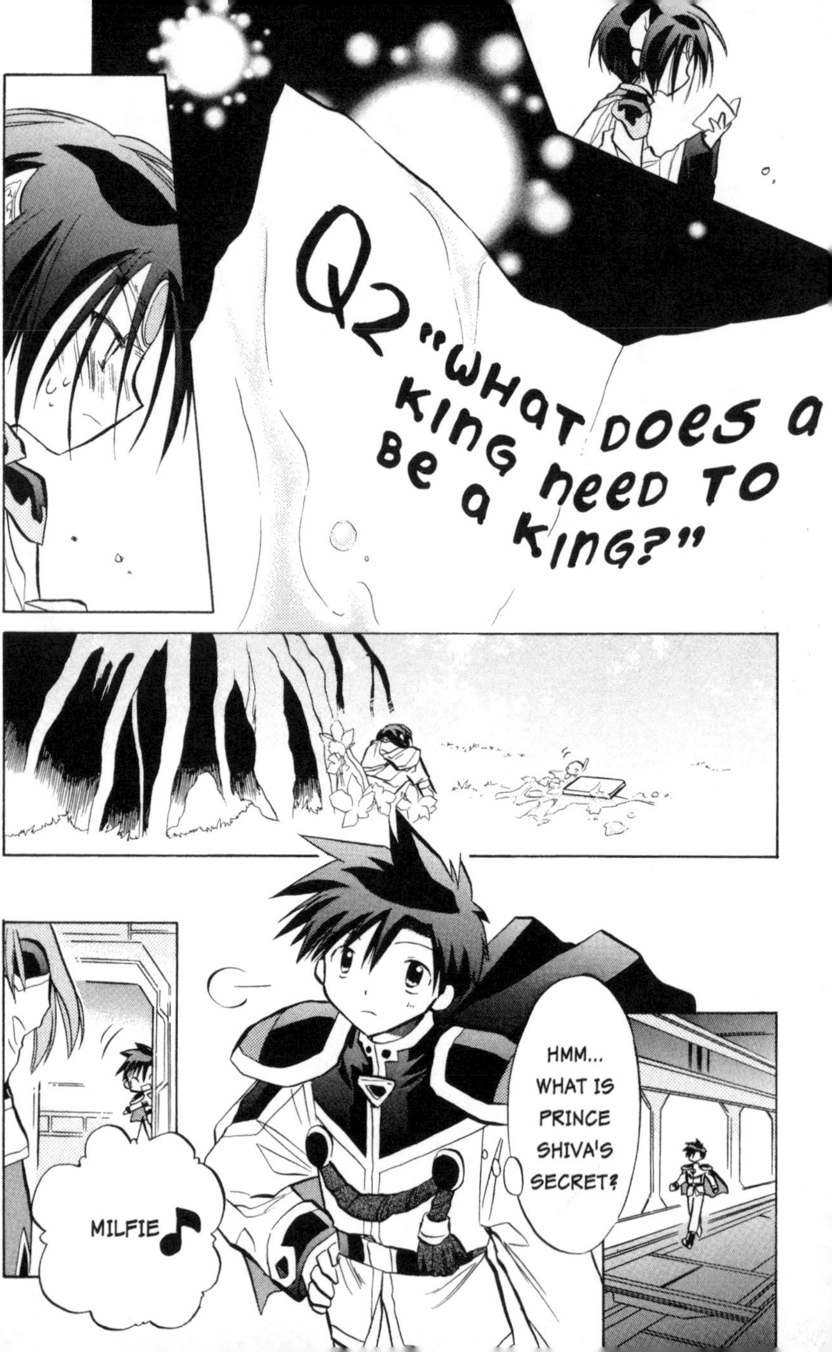
Q2 "WHAT DOES A KING NEED TO BE A KING?"
HMM... WHAT IS PRINCE SHIVA'S SECRET?
MILFIE♪

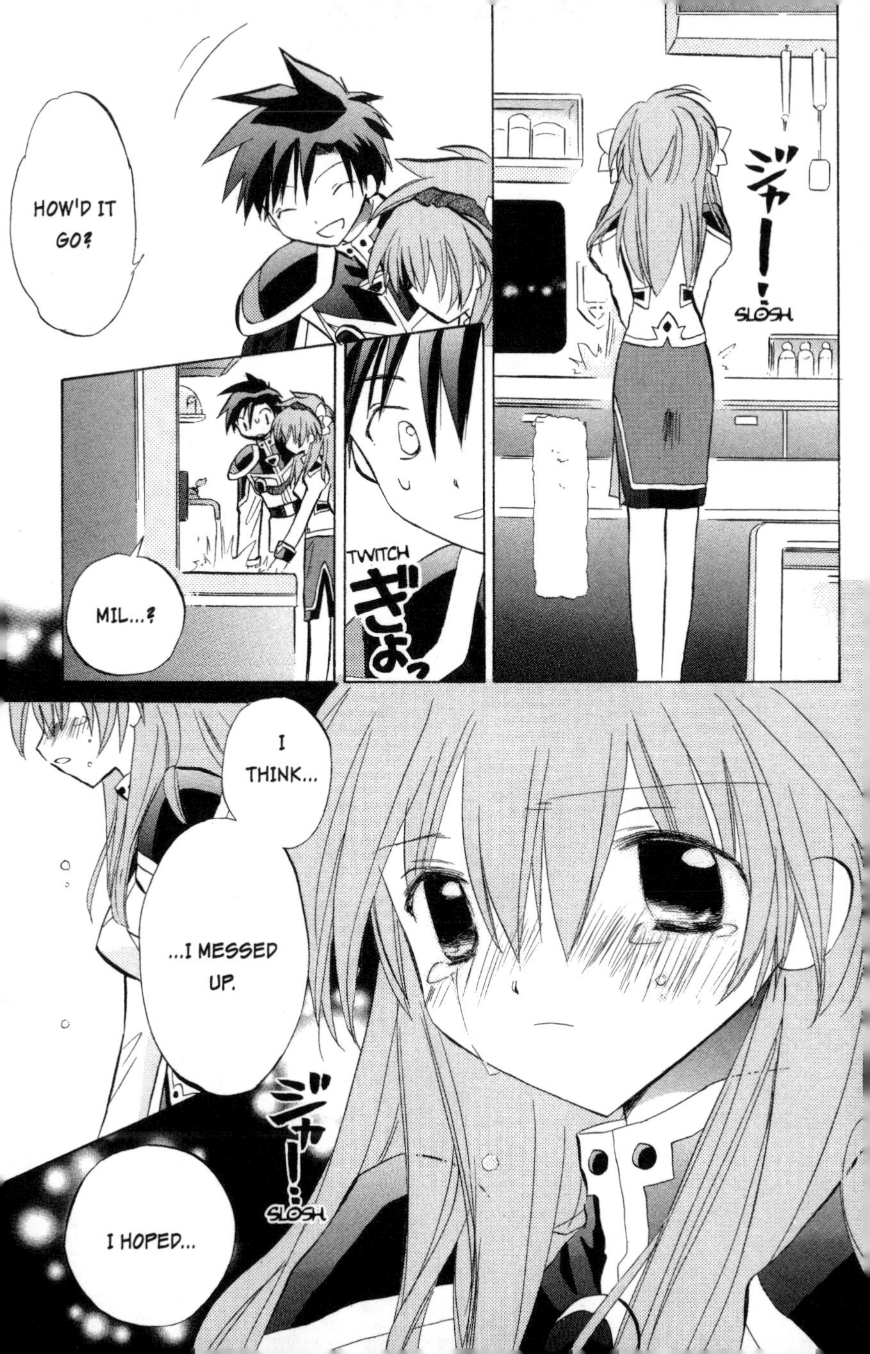
ジャー!!
SLOSH
HOW'D IT GO?
TWITCH
ぎょっ
MIL...?
I THINK...
...I MESSED UP.
ジャー!!
SLOSH
I HOPED...

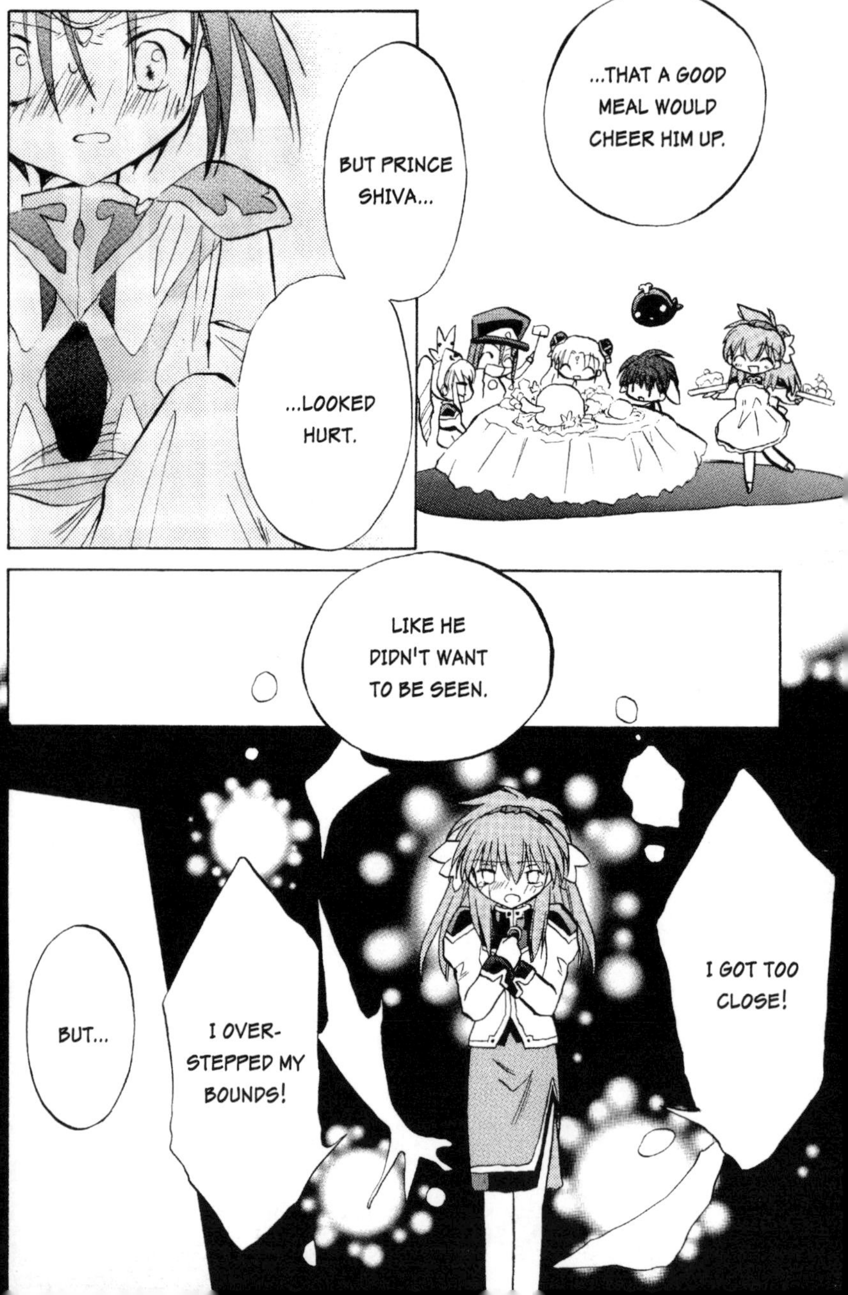
...THAT A GOOD MEAL WOULD CHEER HIM UP.
BUT PRINCE SHIVA...
...LOOKED HURT.
LIKE HE DIDN'T WANT TO BE SEEN.
I GOT TOO CLOSE!
I OVER-STEPPED MY BOUNDS!
BUT...

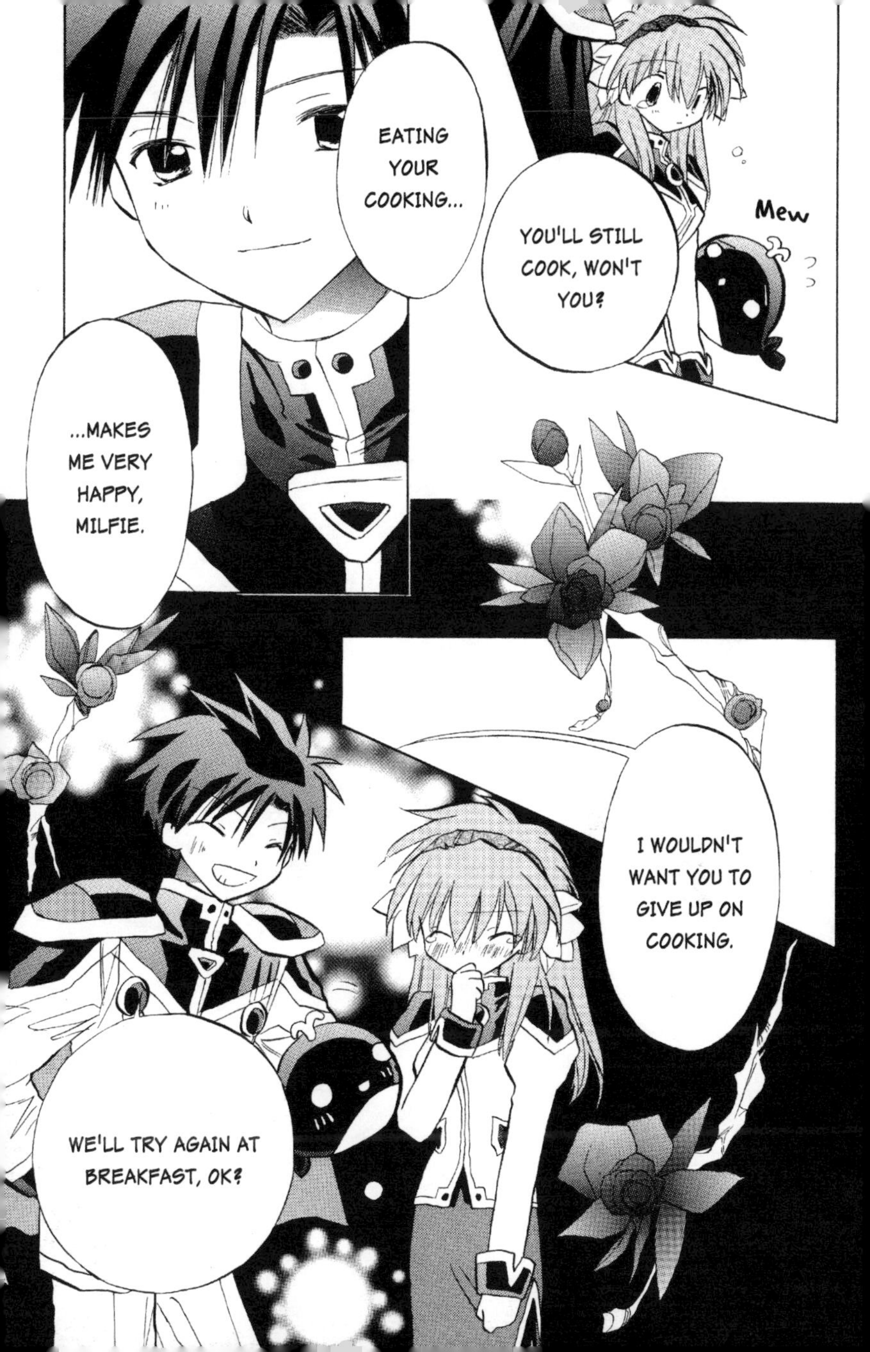
Mew
YOU'LL STILL COOK, WON'T YOU?
EATING YOUR COOKING...
...MAKES ME VERY HAPPY, MILFIE.
I WOULDN'T WANT YOU TO GIVE UP ON COOKING.
WE'LL TRY AGAIN AT BREAKFAST, OK?

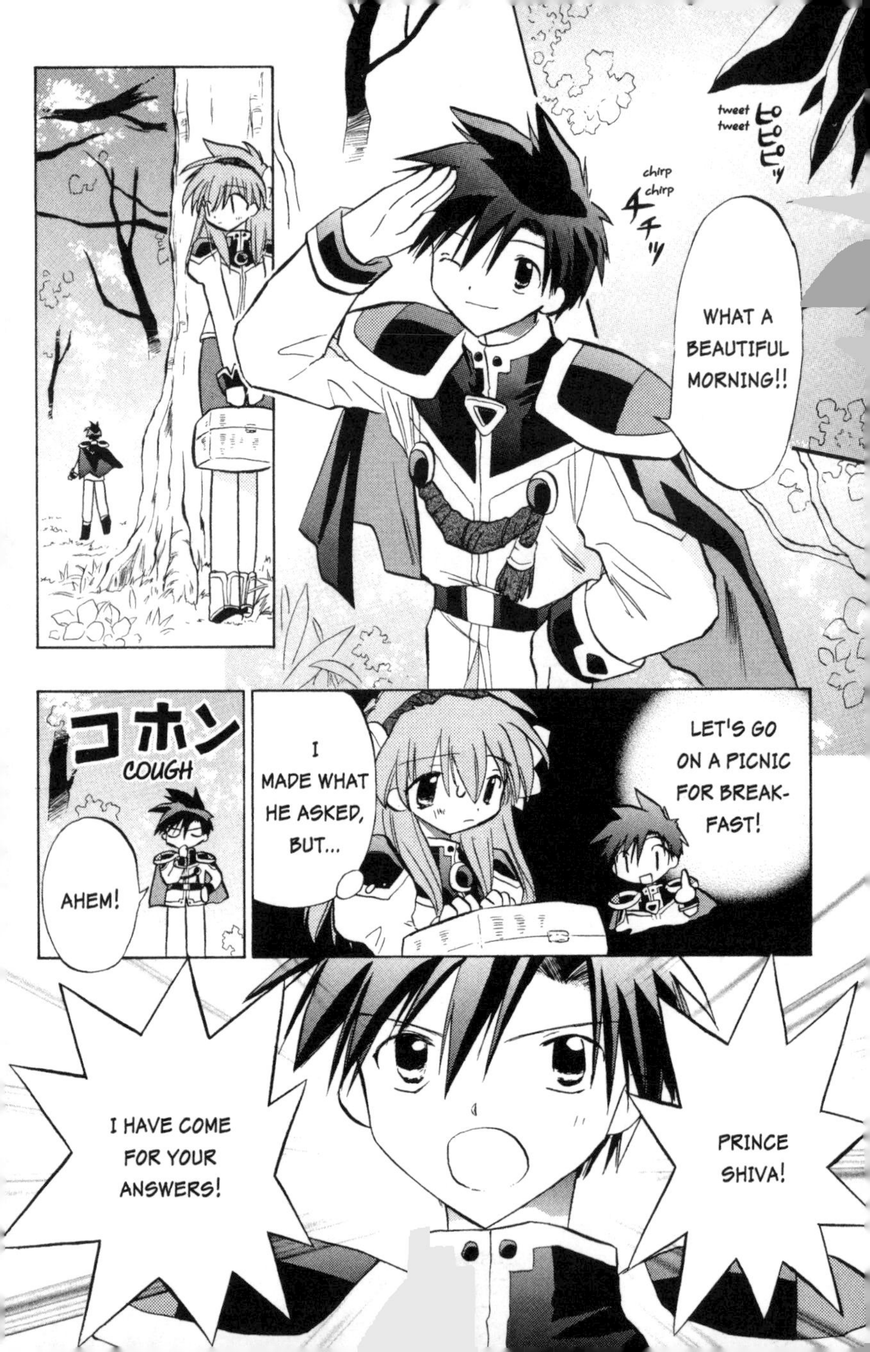
tweet tweet
ピピピッ
chirp chirp
チチッ
WHAT A BEAUTIFUL MORNING!!
LET'S GO ON A PICNIC FOR BREAK-FAST!
I MADE WHAT HE ASKED, BUT...
コホン
COUGH
AHEM!
PRINCE SHIVA!
I HAVE COME FOR YOUR ANSWERS!

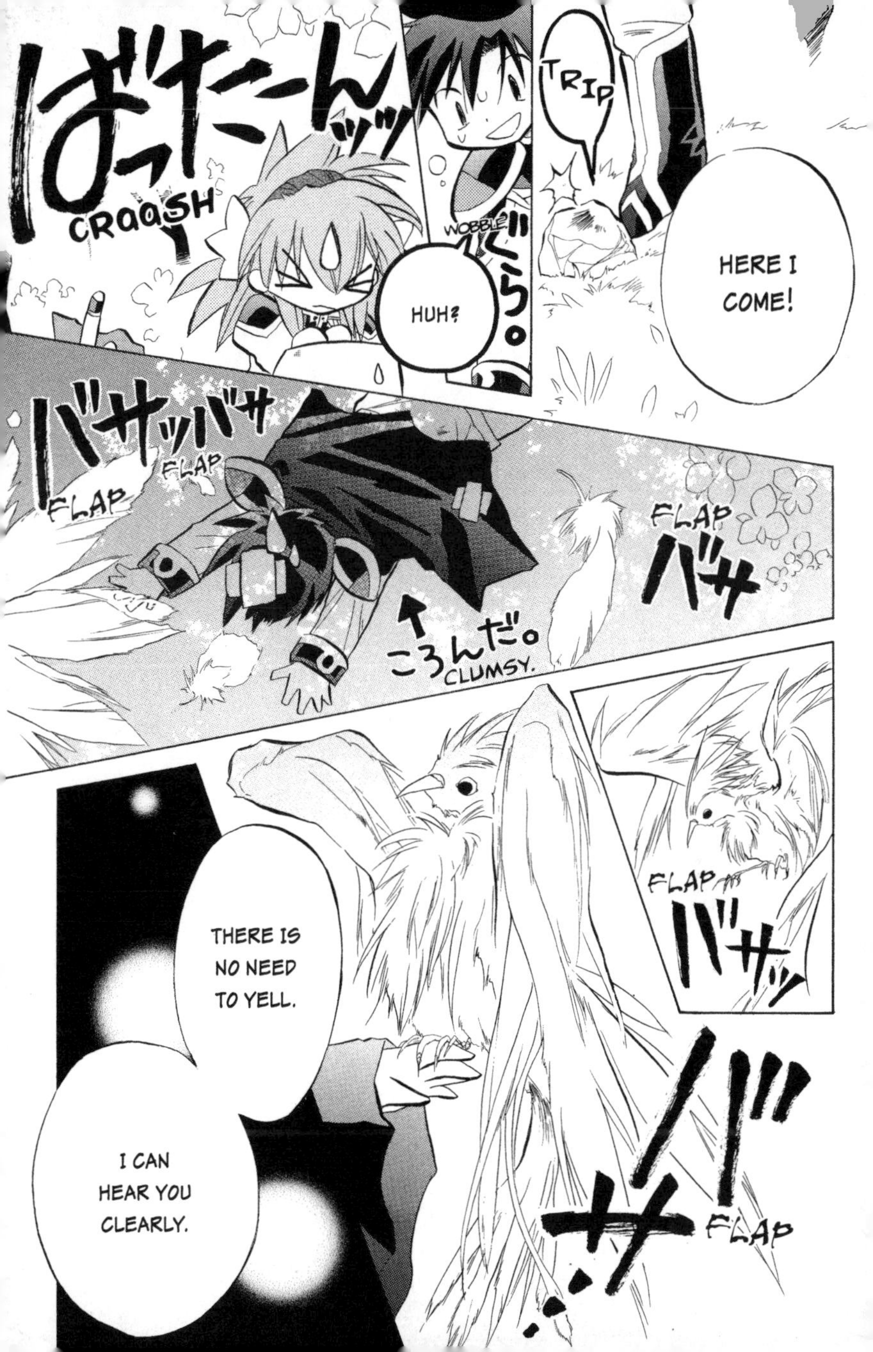
HERE I COME!
TRIP
WOBBLE
ぐら。
HUH?
ばったーんッッ
CRAASH
バサッバサ
FLAP
FLAP
バサ
FLAP
ころんだ。
CLUMSY.
バサッ
FLAP
THERE IS NO NEED TO YELL.
I CAN HEAR YOU CLEARLY.
バサ
FLAP

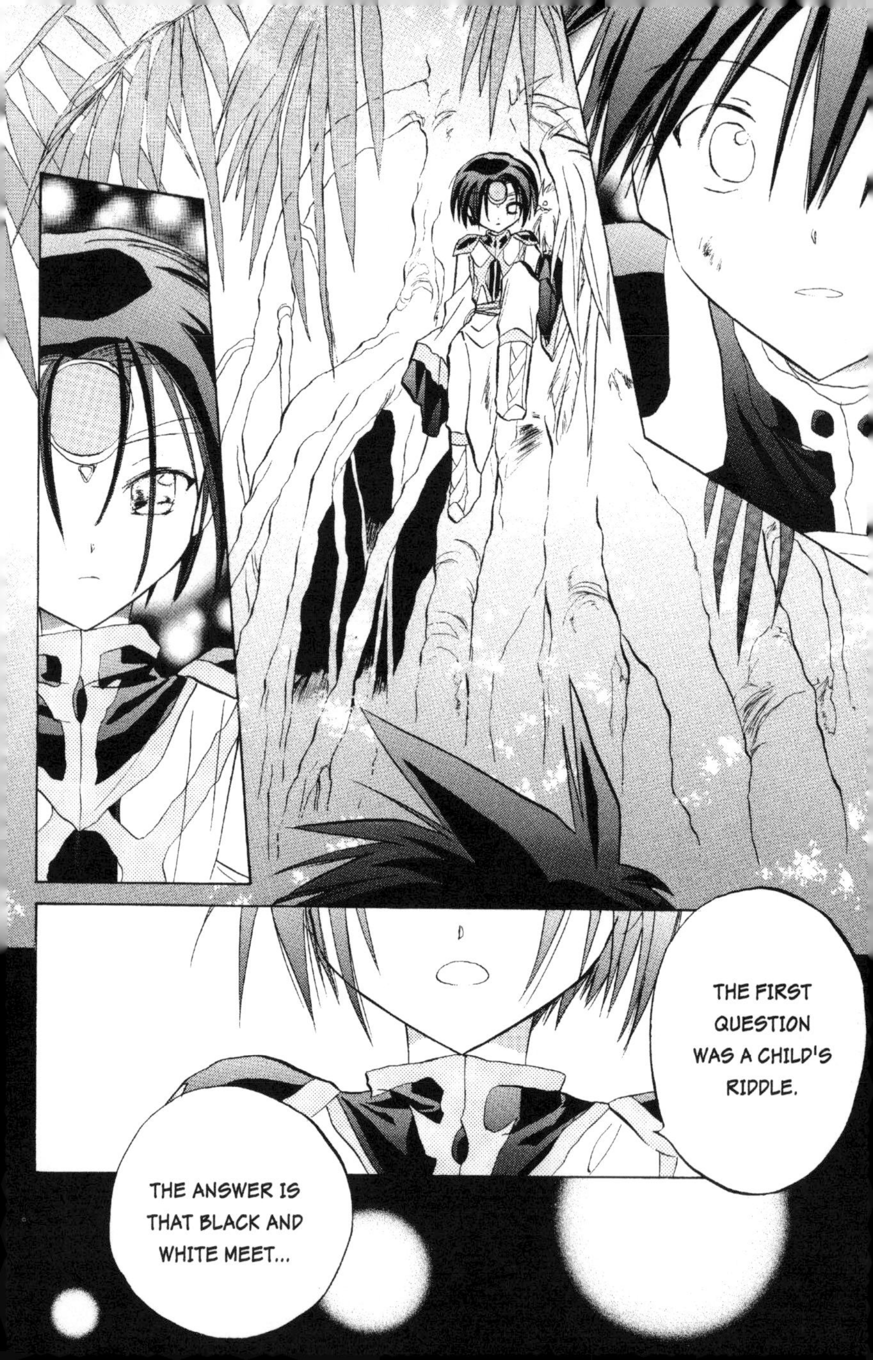
THE FIRST QUESTION WAS A CHILD'S RIDDLE.
THE ANSWER IS THAT BLACK AND WHITE MEET...

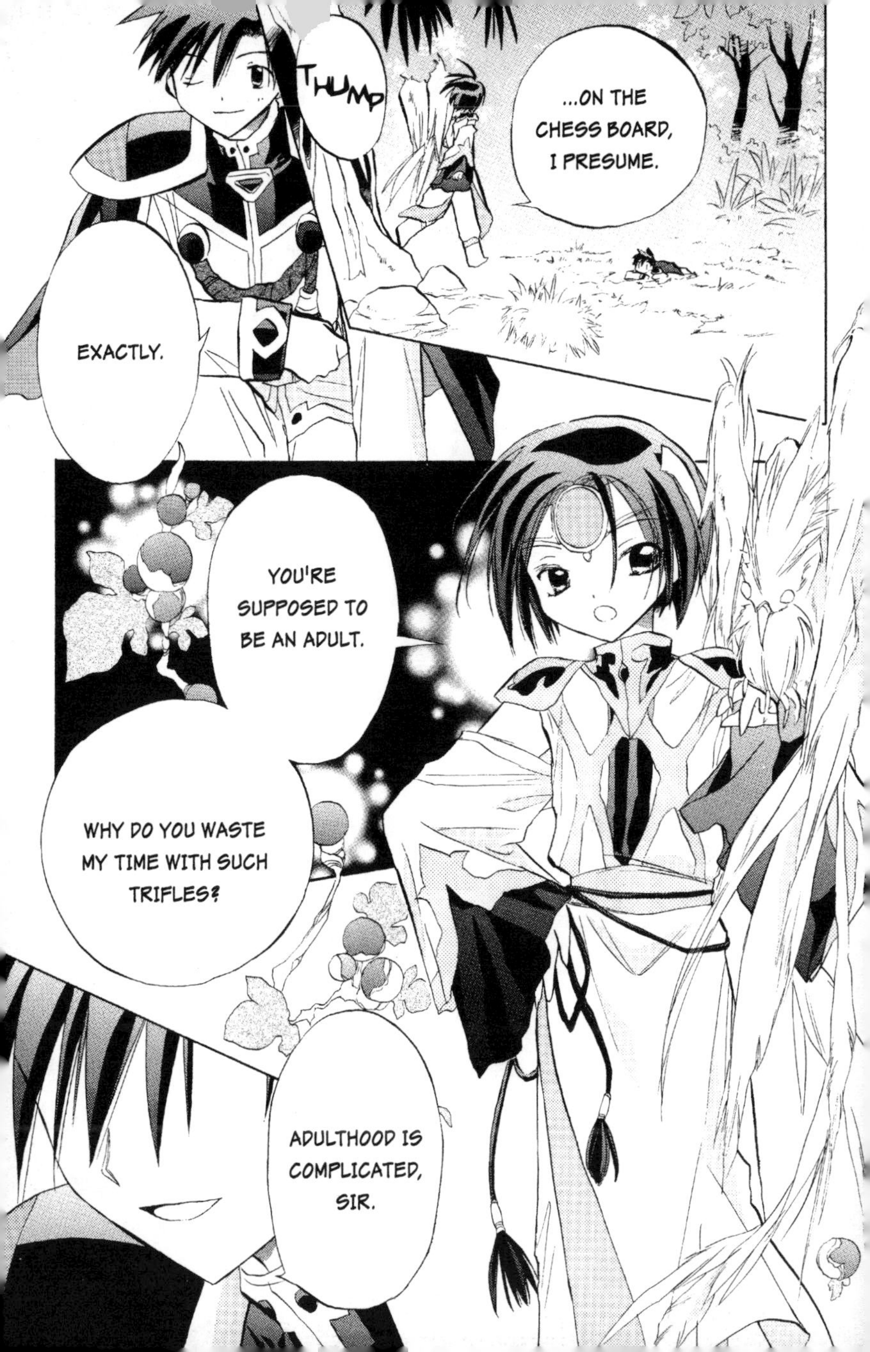
...ON THE CHESS BOARD, I PRESUME.
THUMP
EXACTLY.
YOU'RE SUPPOSED TO BE AN ADULT.
WHY DO YOU WASTE MY TIME WITH SUCH TRIFLES?
ADULTHOOD IS COMPLICATED, SIR.

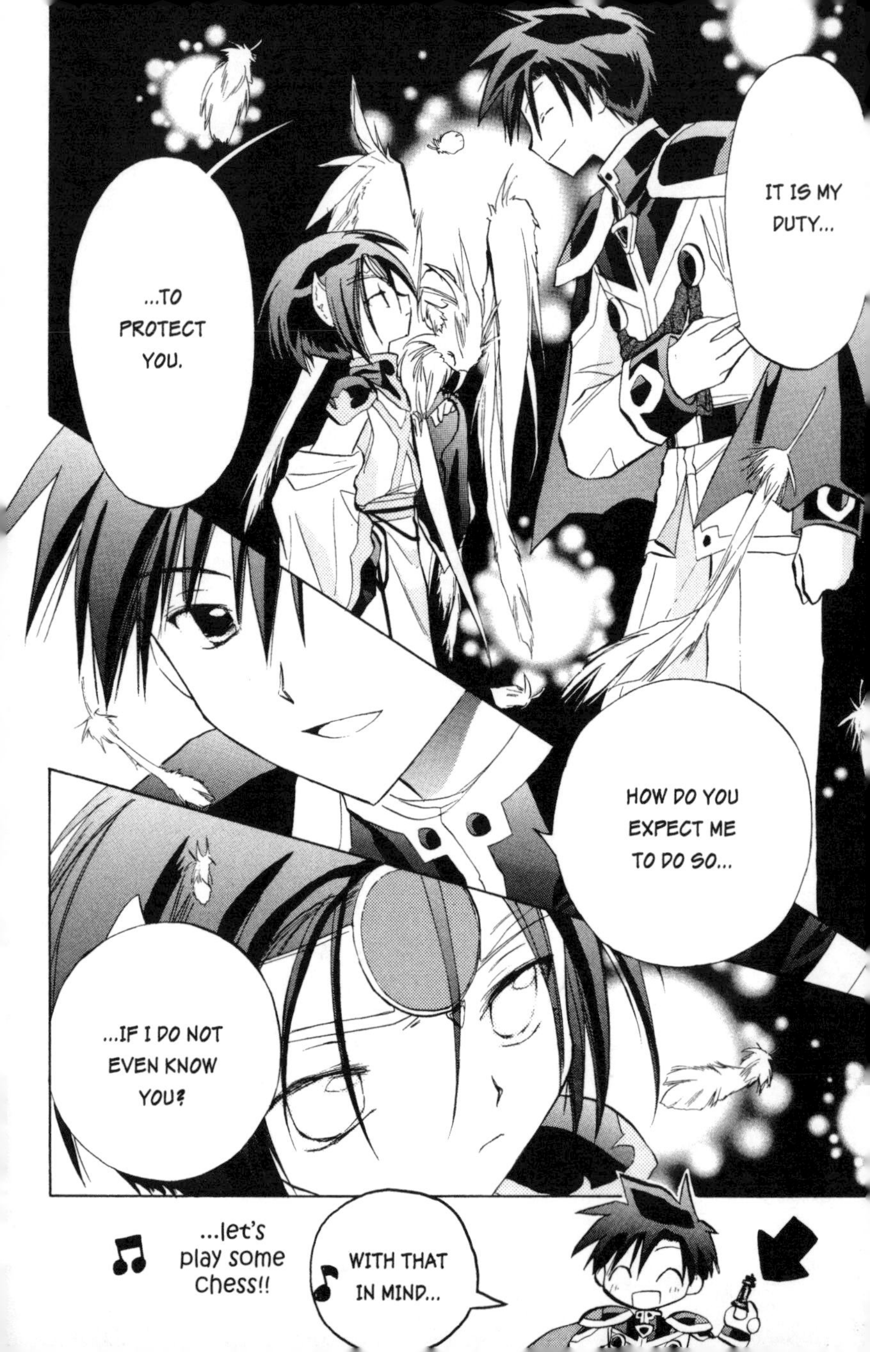
IT IS MY DUTY...
...TO PROTECT YOU.
HOW DO YOU EXPECT ME TO DO SO...
...IF I DO NOT EVEN KNOW YOU?
WITH THAT IN MIND...
...let's play some chess!!

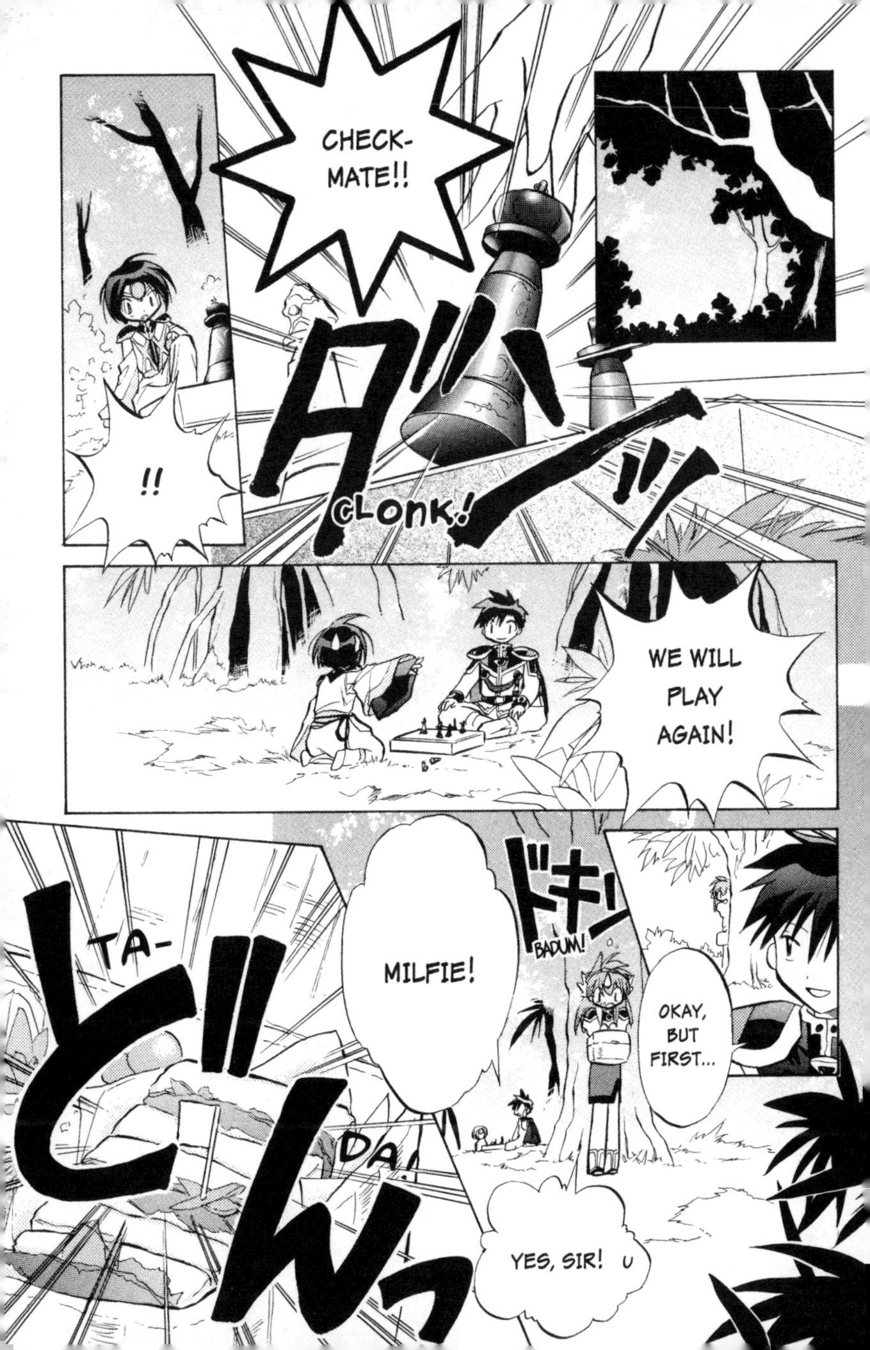
CHECK-
MATE!!
CLONK!
!!
WE WILL PLAY AGAIN!
BADUM!
MILFIE!
OKAY, BUT FIRST...
YES, SIR!
TA-
DA!

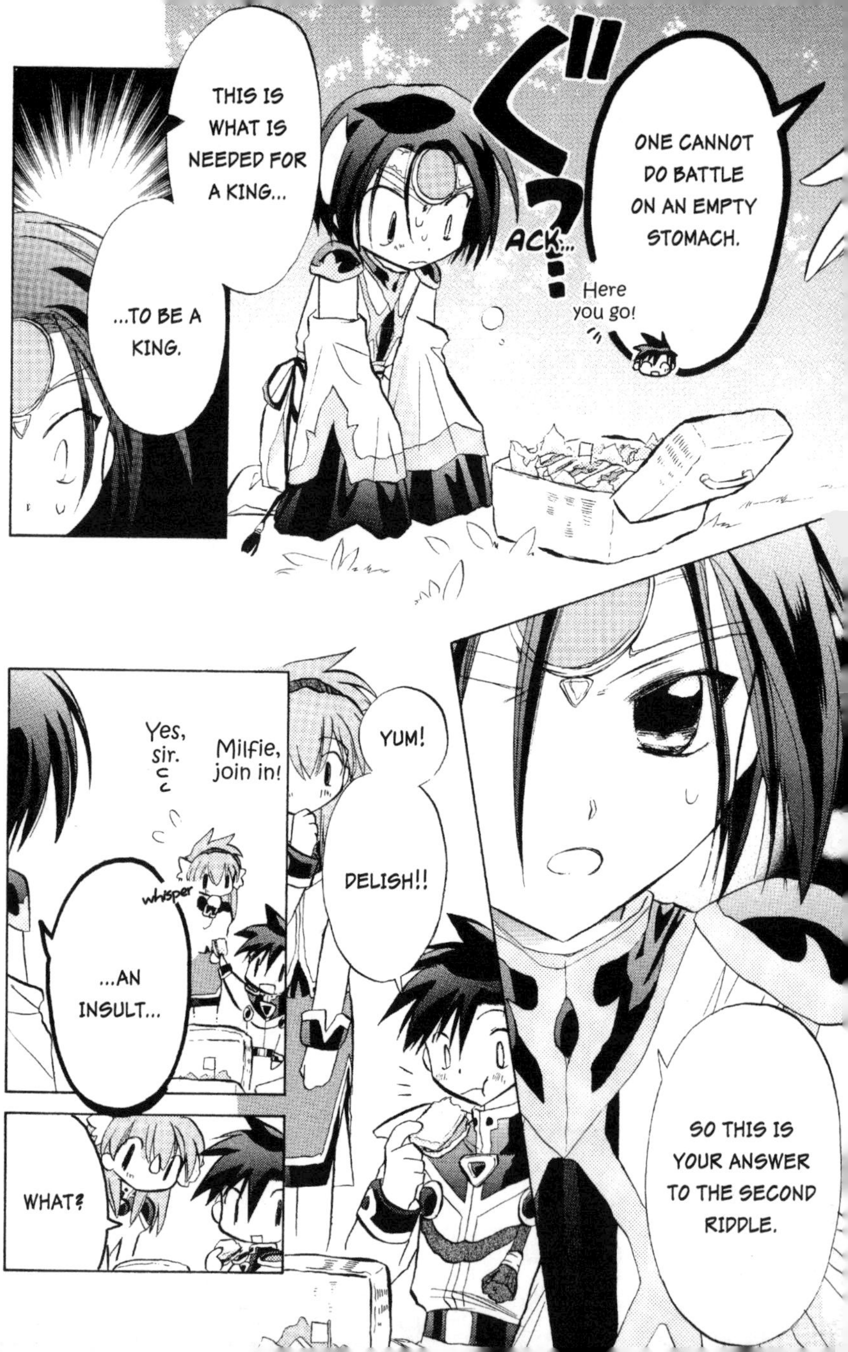
ONE CANNOT DO BATTLE ON AN EMPTY STOMACH.
ACK...
Here you go!
THIS IS WHAT IS NEEDED FOR A KING...
...TO BE A KING.
SO THIS IS YOUR ANSWER TO THE SECOND RIDDLE.
YUM!
DELISH!!
Milfie, join in!
Yes, sir.
whisper
...AN INSULT...
WHAT?

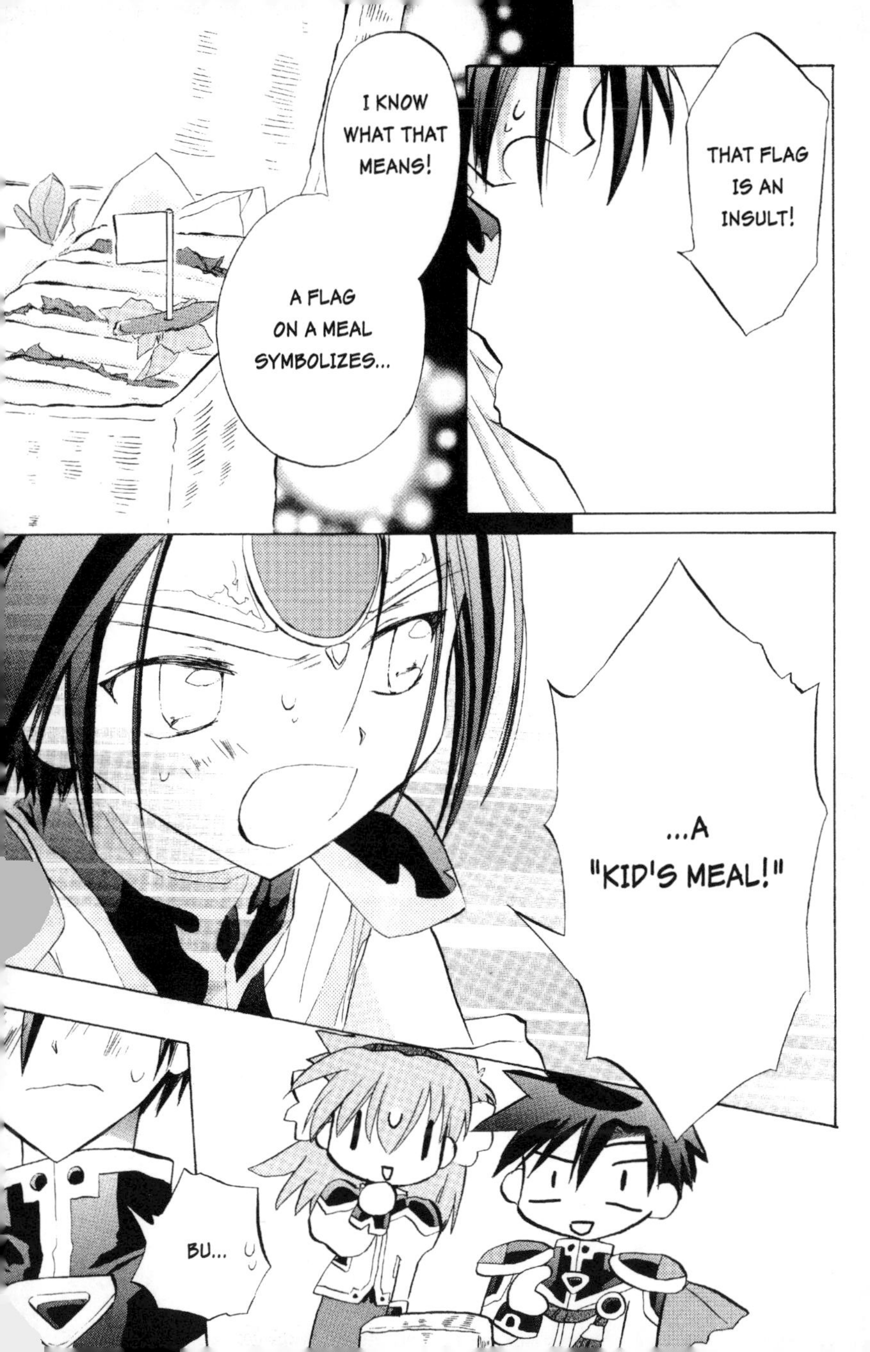
THAT FLAG IS AN INSULT!
I KNOW WHAT THAT MEANS!
A FLAG ON A MEAL SYMBOLIZES...
...A "KID'S MEAL!"
BU...

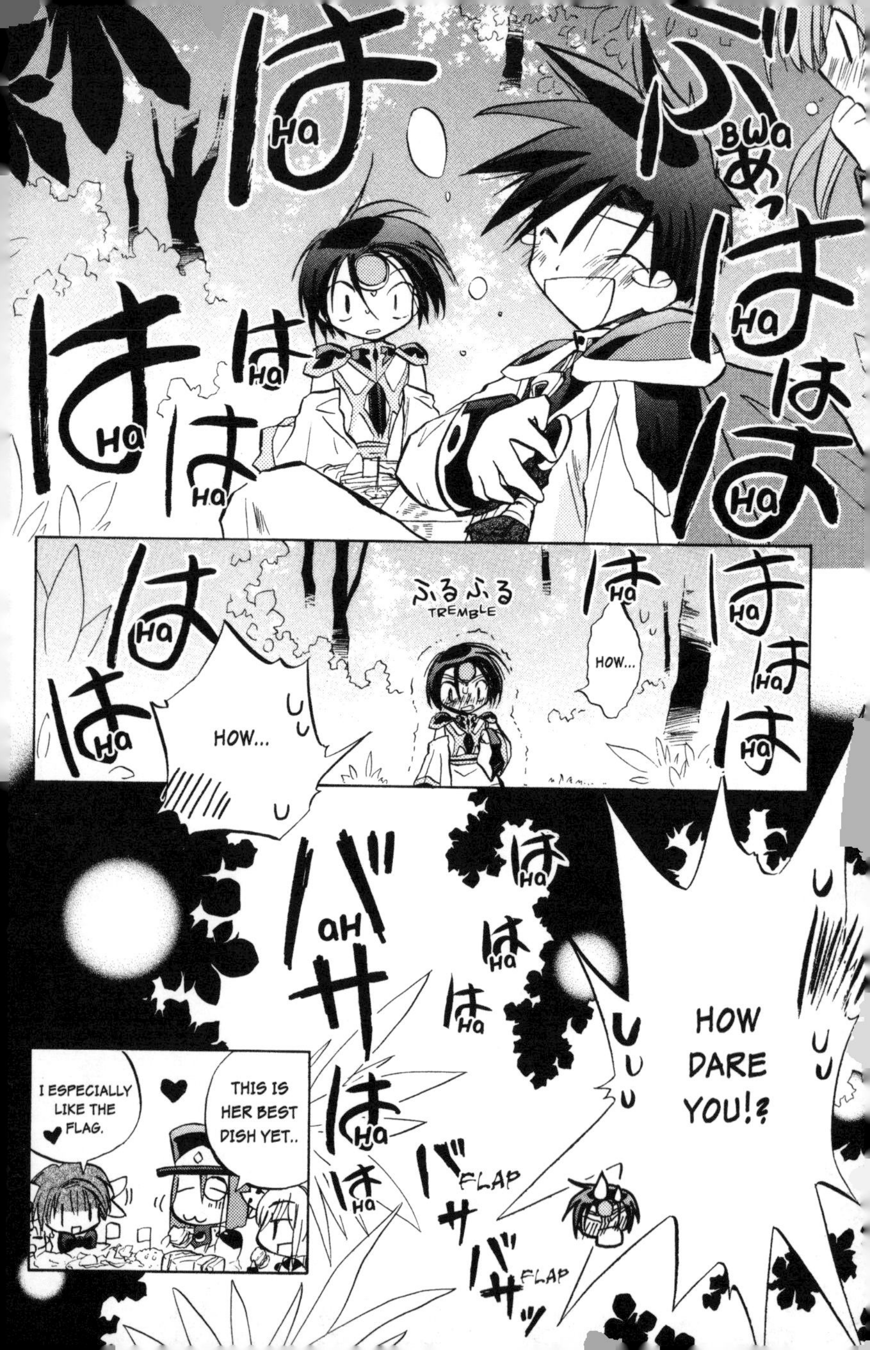
ぶぁっ BWA
はは Ha Ha
ははは Ha Ha Ha
ははは Ha Ha Ha
ははは Ha Ha Ha
ははは Ha Ha
ふるふる TREMBLE
HOW...
HOW...
HOW DARE YOU!?
ははは Ha Ha Ha
バサ aH
はは Ha Ha
THIS IS HER BEST DISH YET..
I ESPECIALLY LIKE THE FLAG.
バサ FLAP
バサッ FLAP

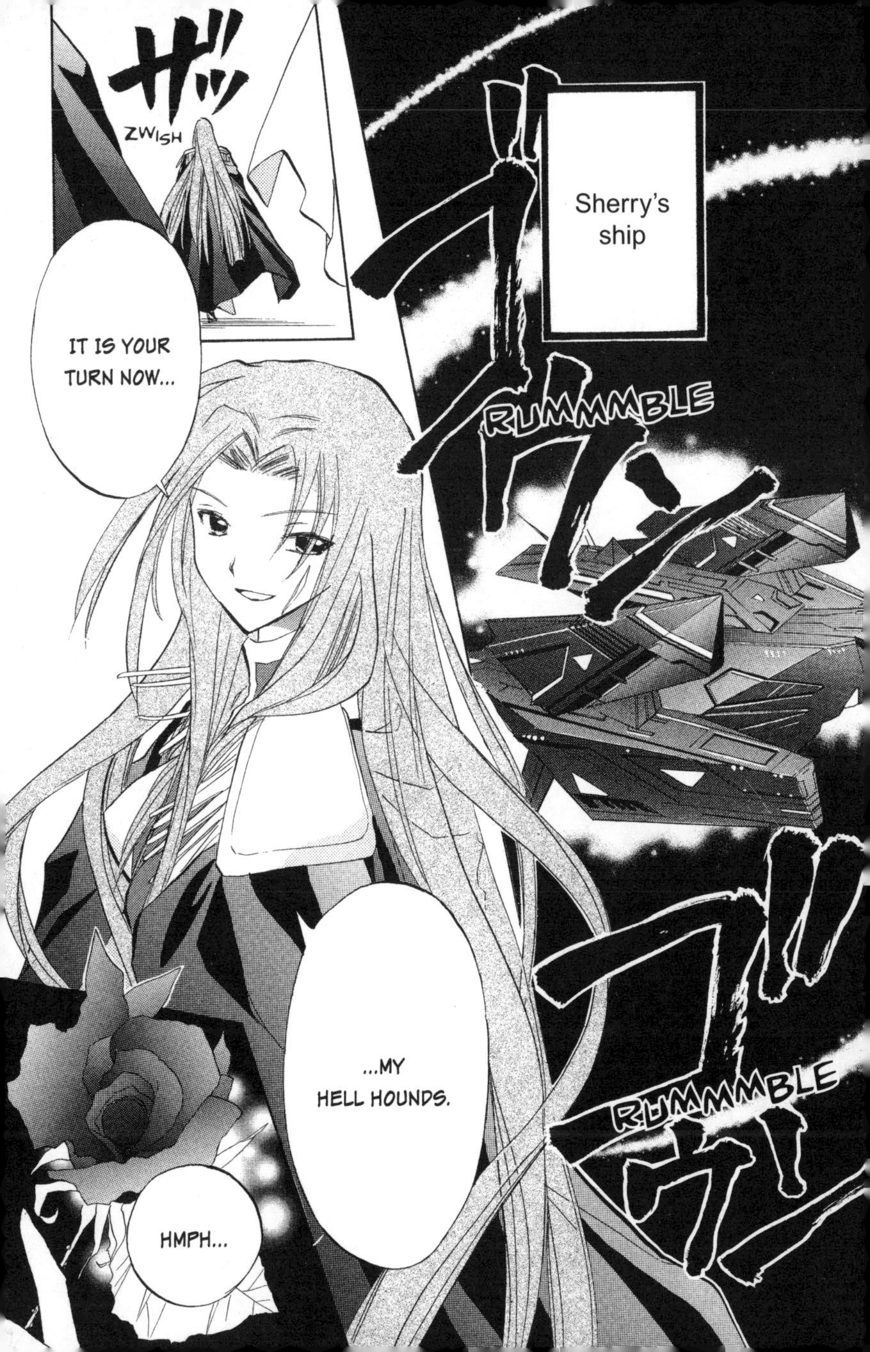
Sherry's ship
RUMMMBLE
RUMMMBLE
ZWISH
IT IS YOUR TURN NOW...
...MY HELL HOUNDS.
HMPH...

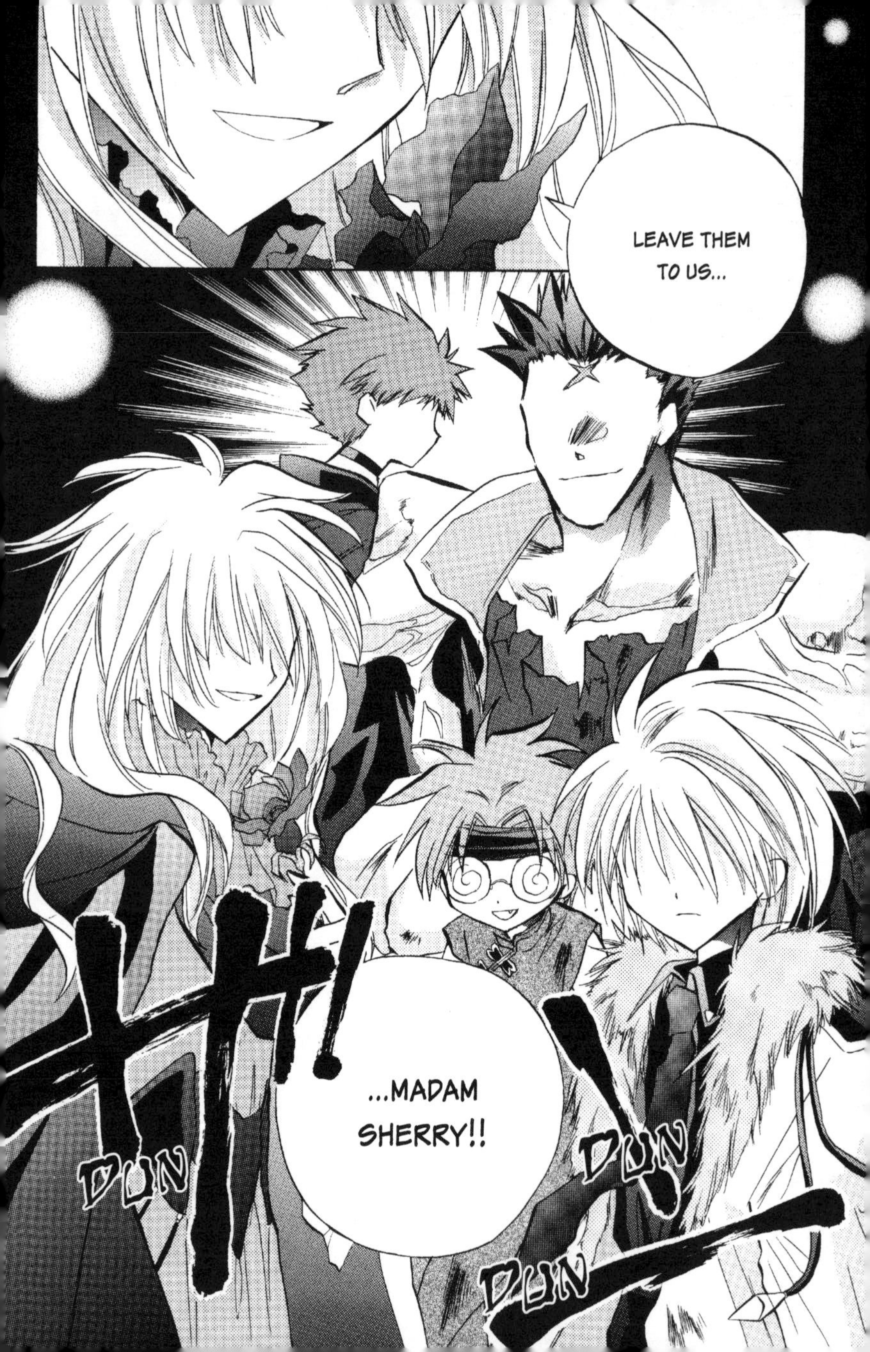
LEAVE THEM TO US...
...MADAM SHERRY!!
DUN
DUN
DUN

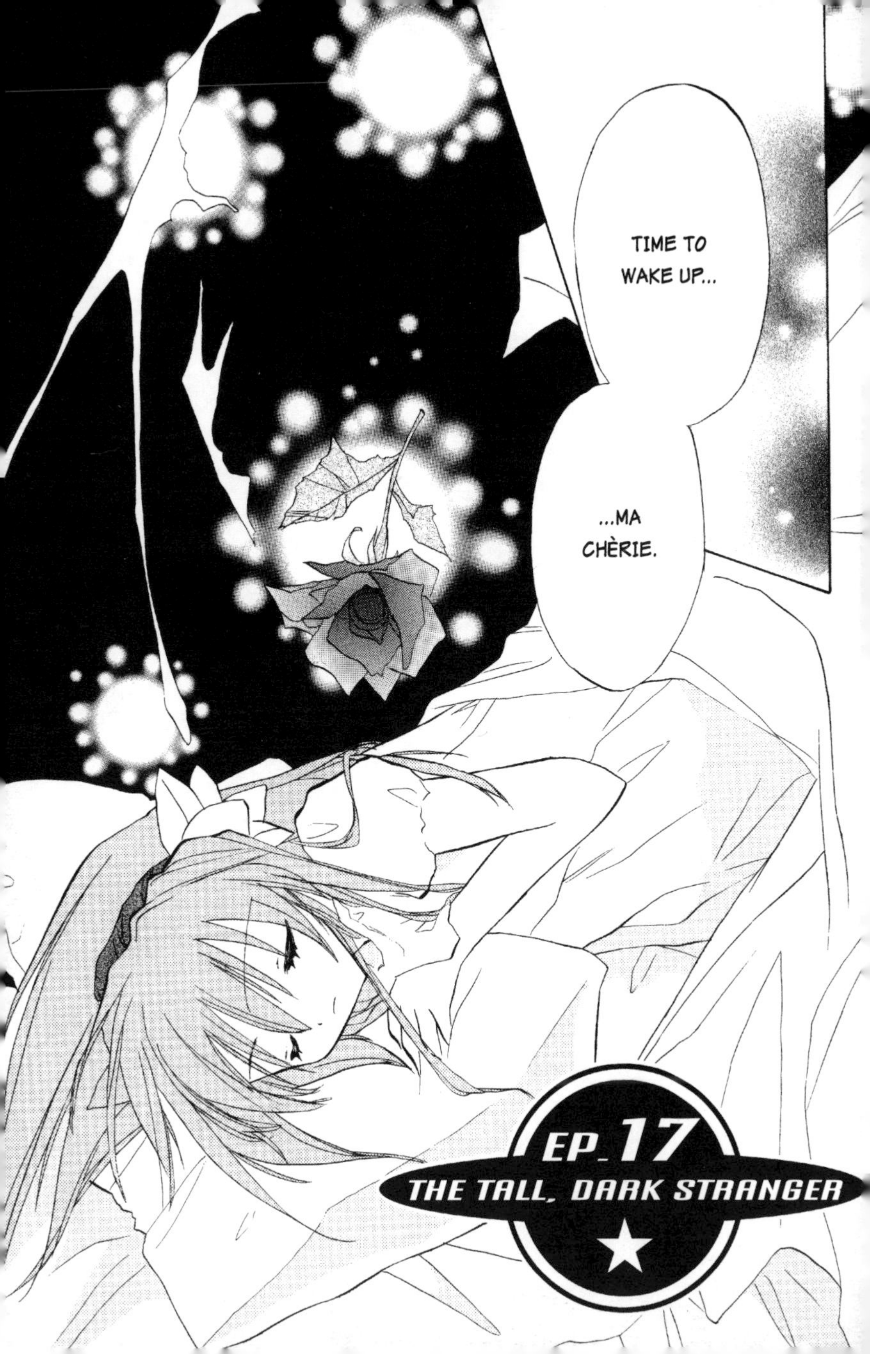
TIME TO WAKE UP...
...MA CHÈRIE.
EP_17
THE TALL, DARK STRANGER

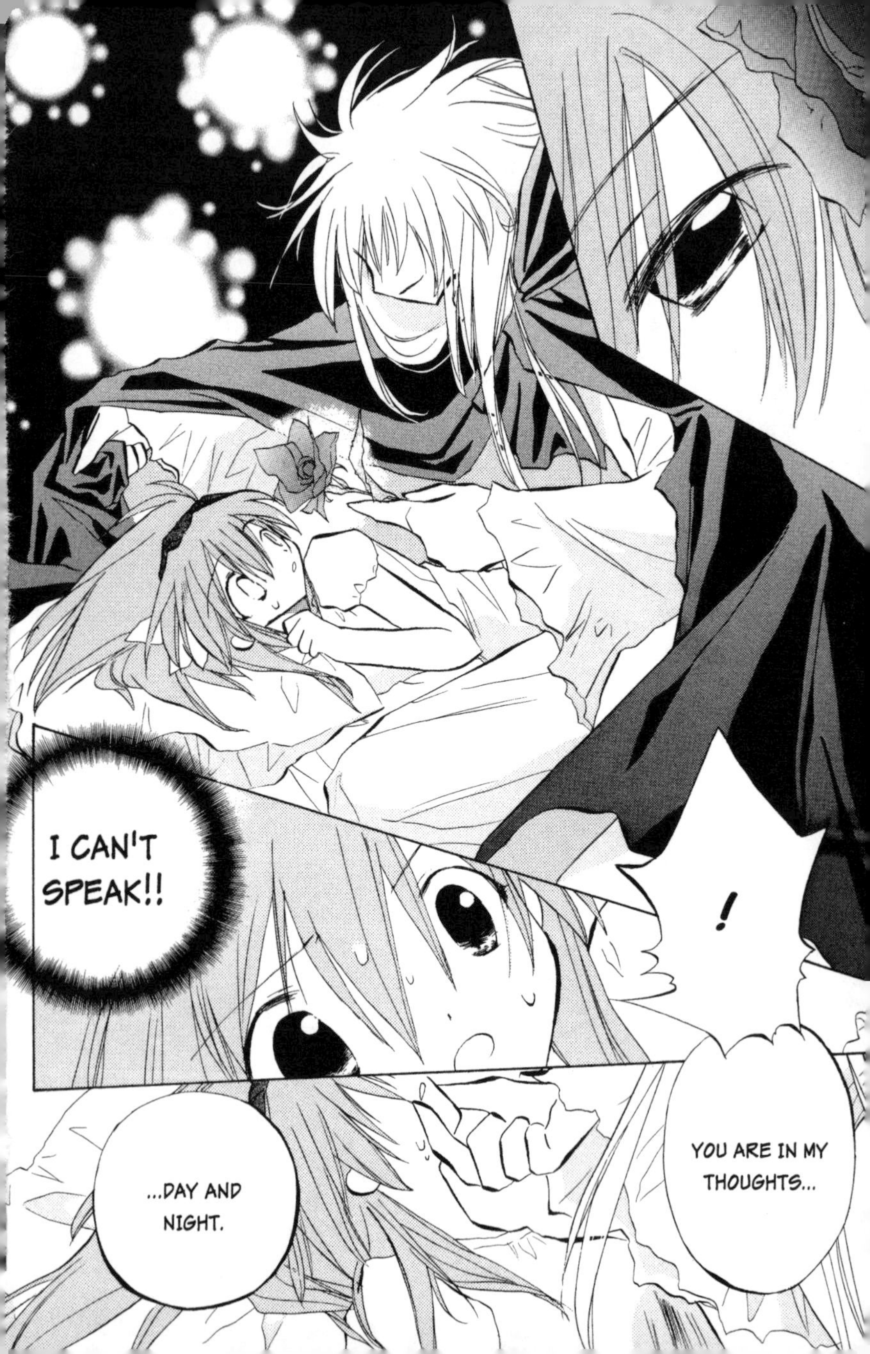
!
I CAN'T SPEAK!!
YOU ARE IN MY THOUGHTS...
...DAY AND NIGHT.

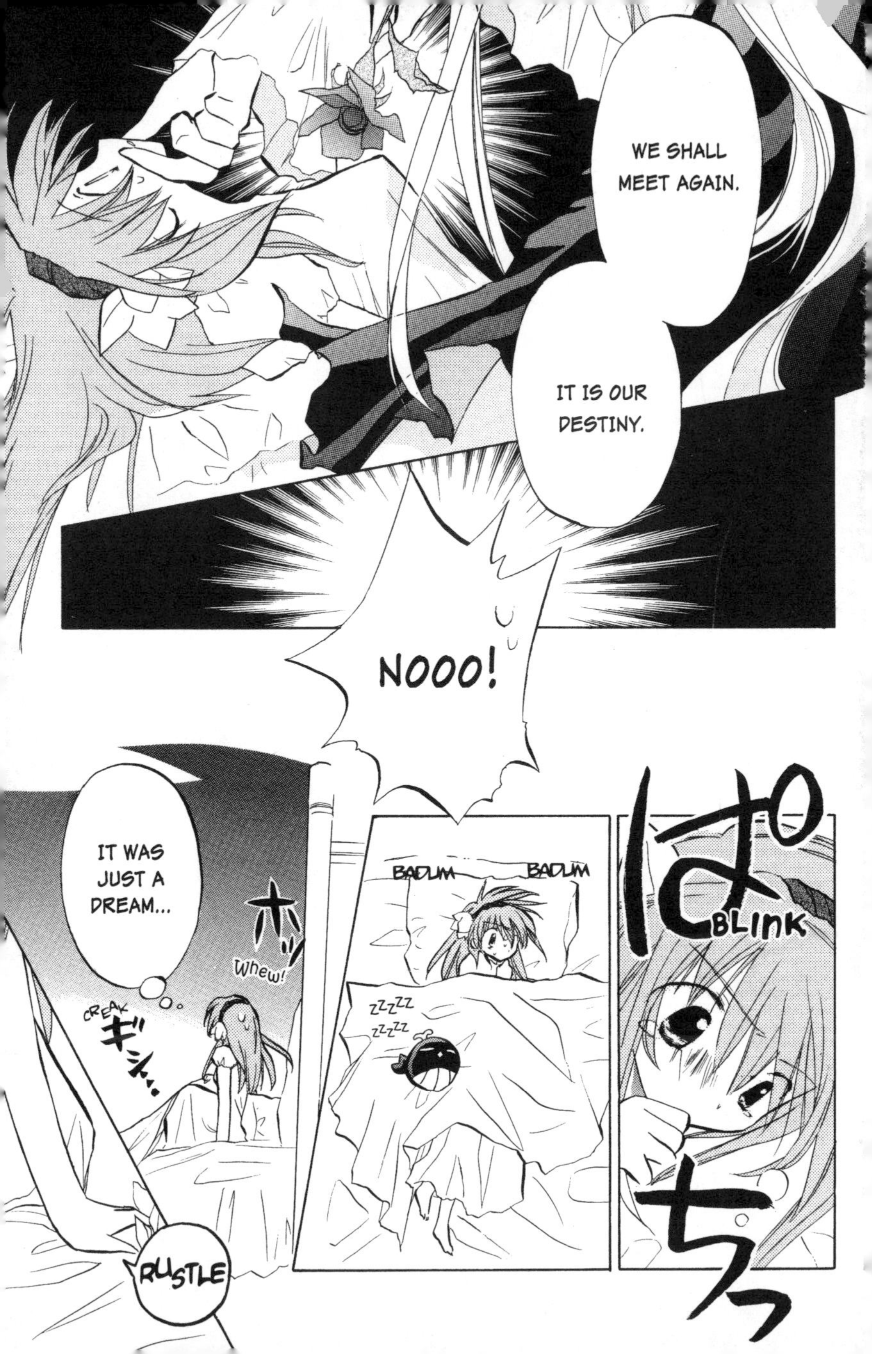
WE SHALL MEET AGAIN.
IT IS OUR DESTINY.
NOOO!
ぱちっ
BLINK
BADUM
BADUM
ZZZZZ
ZZZZZ
ホッ
Whew!
IT WAS JUST A DREAM...
CREAK
ギシ…
RUSTLE

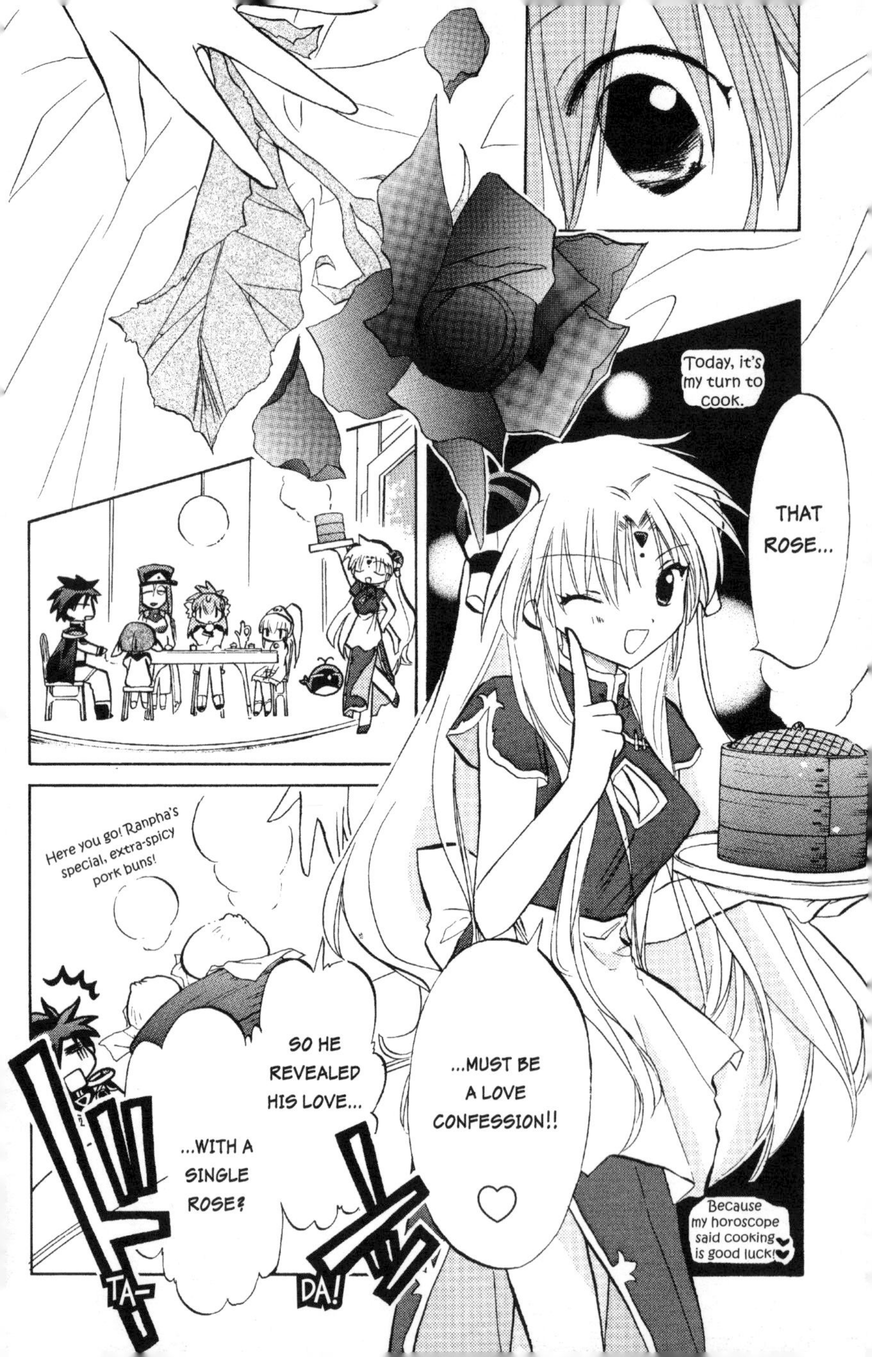
Today, it's my turn to cook.
THAT ROSE...
...MUST BE A LOVE CONFESSION!!
♡
Because my horoscope said cooking is good luck!♥
Here you go! Ranpha's special, extra-spicy pork buns!
SO HE REVEALED HIS LOVE...
...WITH A SINGLE ROSE?
TA-
DA!

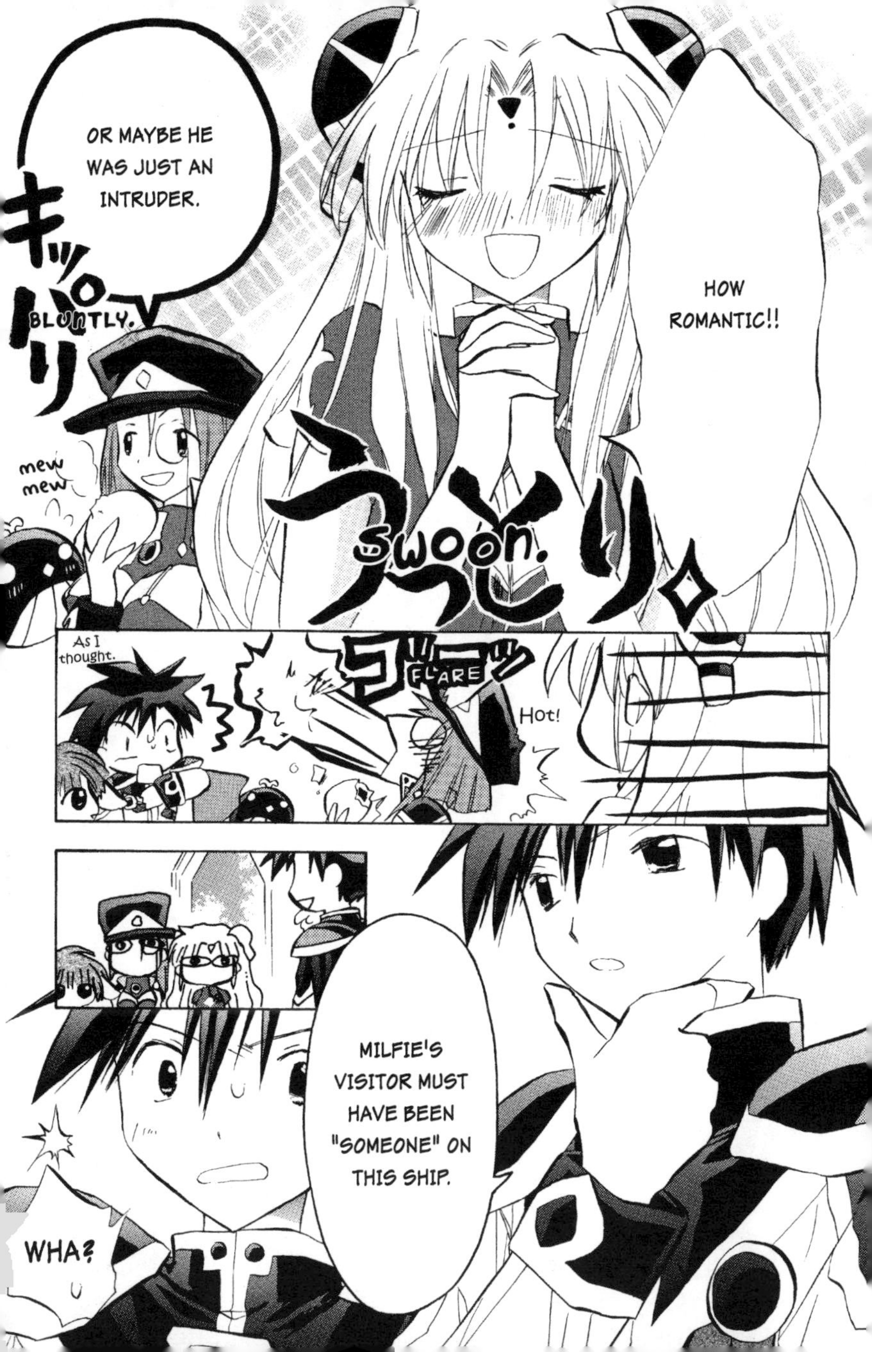
HOW ROMANTIC!!
うっとり
swoon.
OR MAYBE HE WAS JUST AN INTRUDER.
キッパリ
BLUNTLY.
mew mew
Hot!
FLARE
As I thought.
MILFIE'S VISITOR MUST HAVE BEEN "SOMEONE" ON THIS SHIP.
WHA?

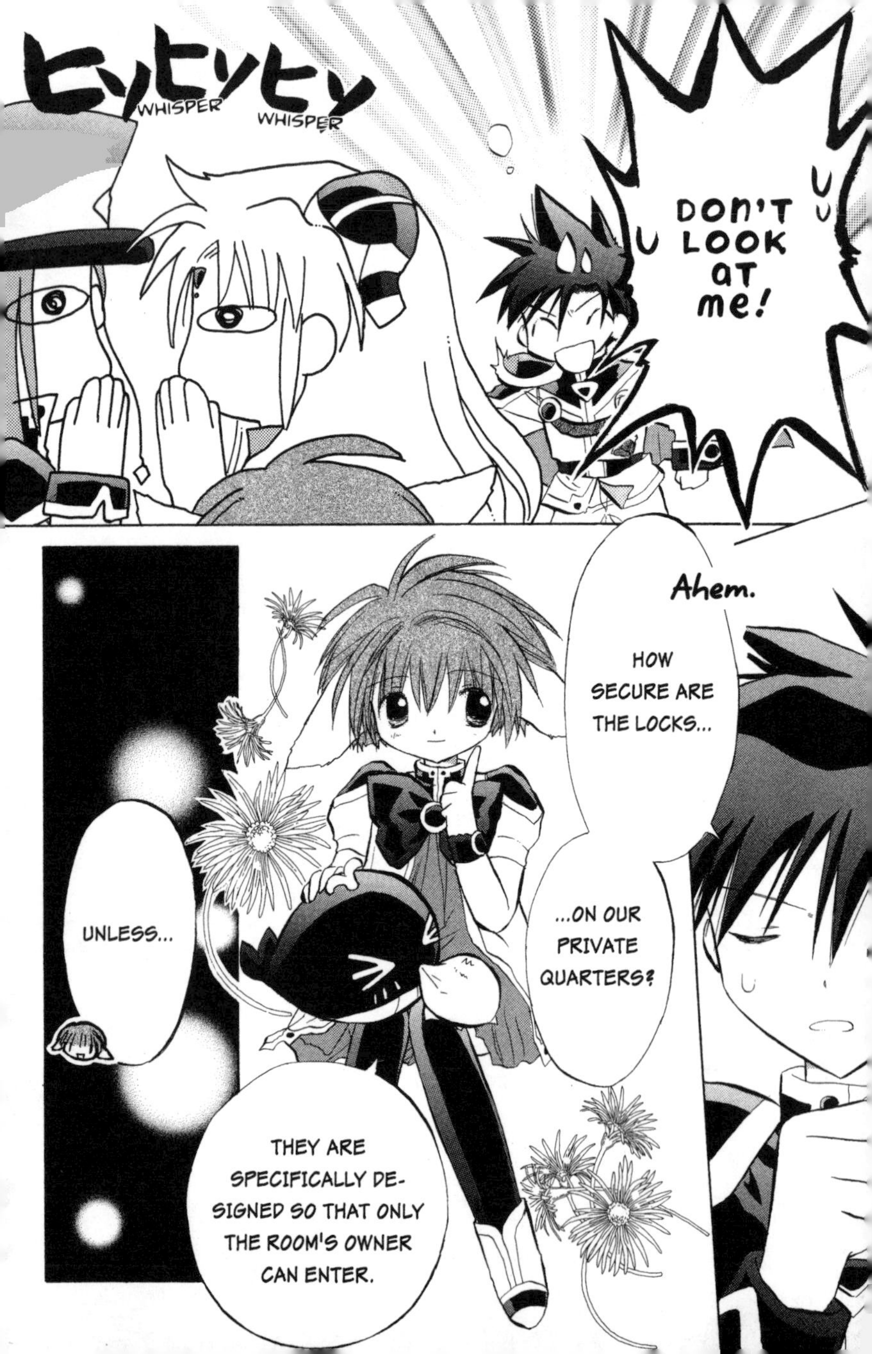
DON'T LOOK AT ME!
ヒソヒソヒソ
WHISPER
WHISPER
Ahem.
HOW SECURE ARE THE LOCKS...
...ON OUR PRIVATE QUARTERS?
THEY ARE SPECIFICALLY DE-SIGNED SO THAT ONLY THE ROOM'S OWNER CAN ENTER.
UNLESS...

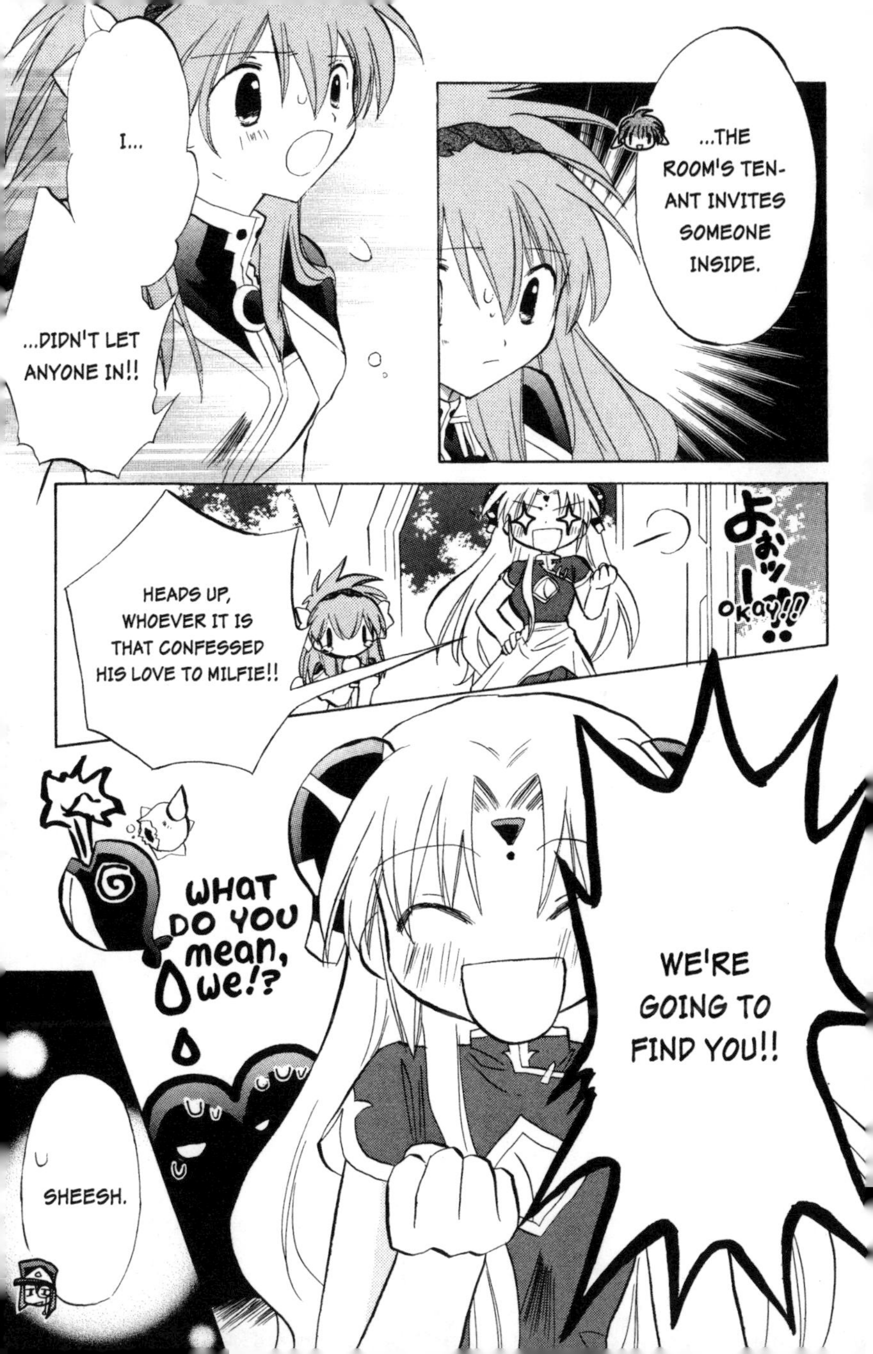
...THE ROOM'S TEN-ANT INVITES SOMEONE INSIDE.
I...
...DIDN'T LET ANYONE IN!!
よぉッし OKAY!!
HEADS UP, WHOEVER IT IS THAT CONFESSED HIS LOVE TO MILFIE!!
WE'RE GOING TO FIND YOU!!
WHAT DO YOU mean, we!?
SHEESH.

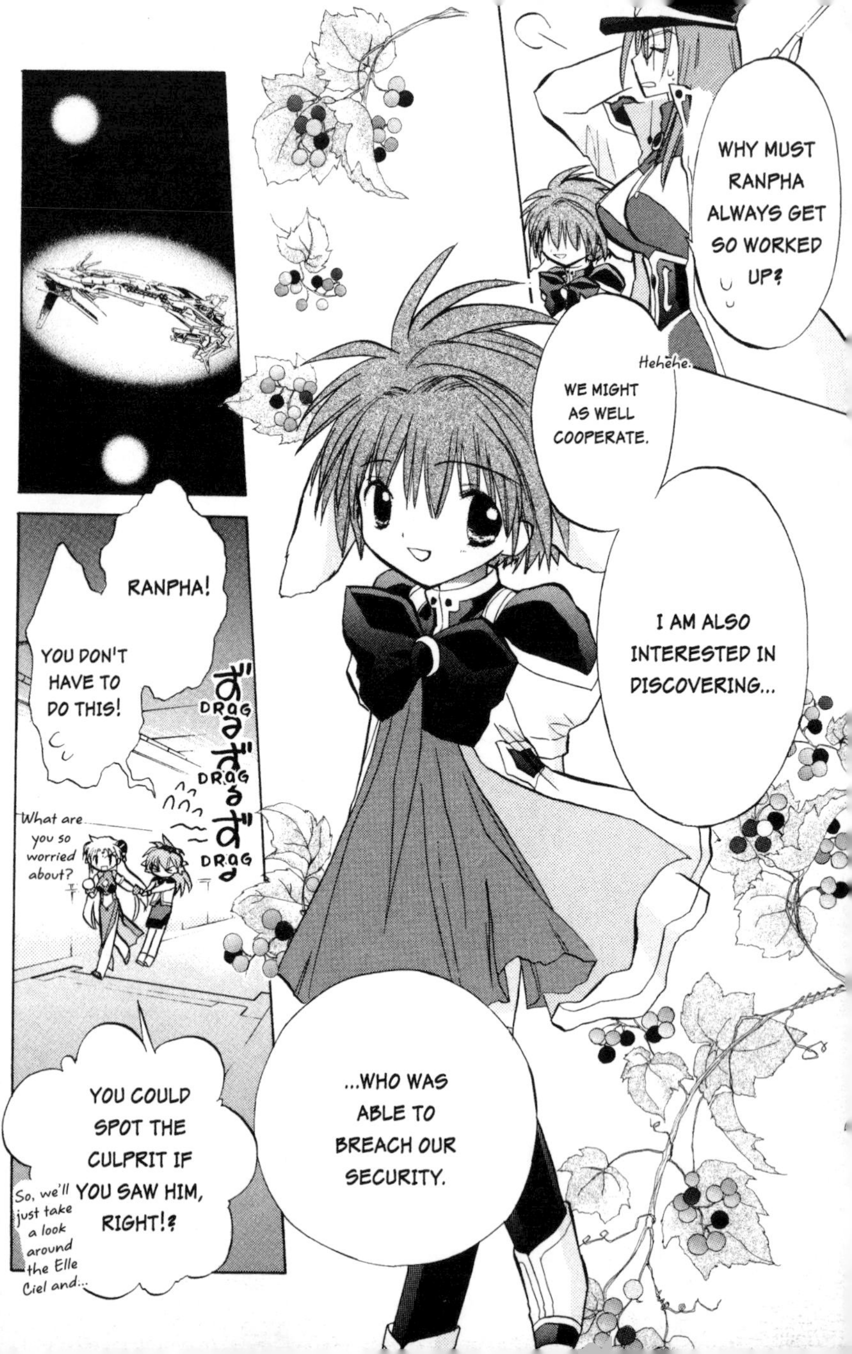
WHY MUST RANPHA ALWAYS GET SO WORKED UP?
Hehehe.
WE MIGHT AS WELL COOPERATE.
I AM ALSO INTERESTED IN DISCOVERING...
...WHO WAS ABLE TO BREACH OUR SECURITY.
RANPHA!
YOU DON'T HAVE TO DO THIS!
ずるずるず
DRAG DRAG DRAG
What are you so worried about?
YOU COULD SPOT THE CULPRIT IF YOU SAW HIM, RIGHT!?
So, we'll just take a look around the Elle Ciel and...

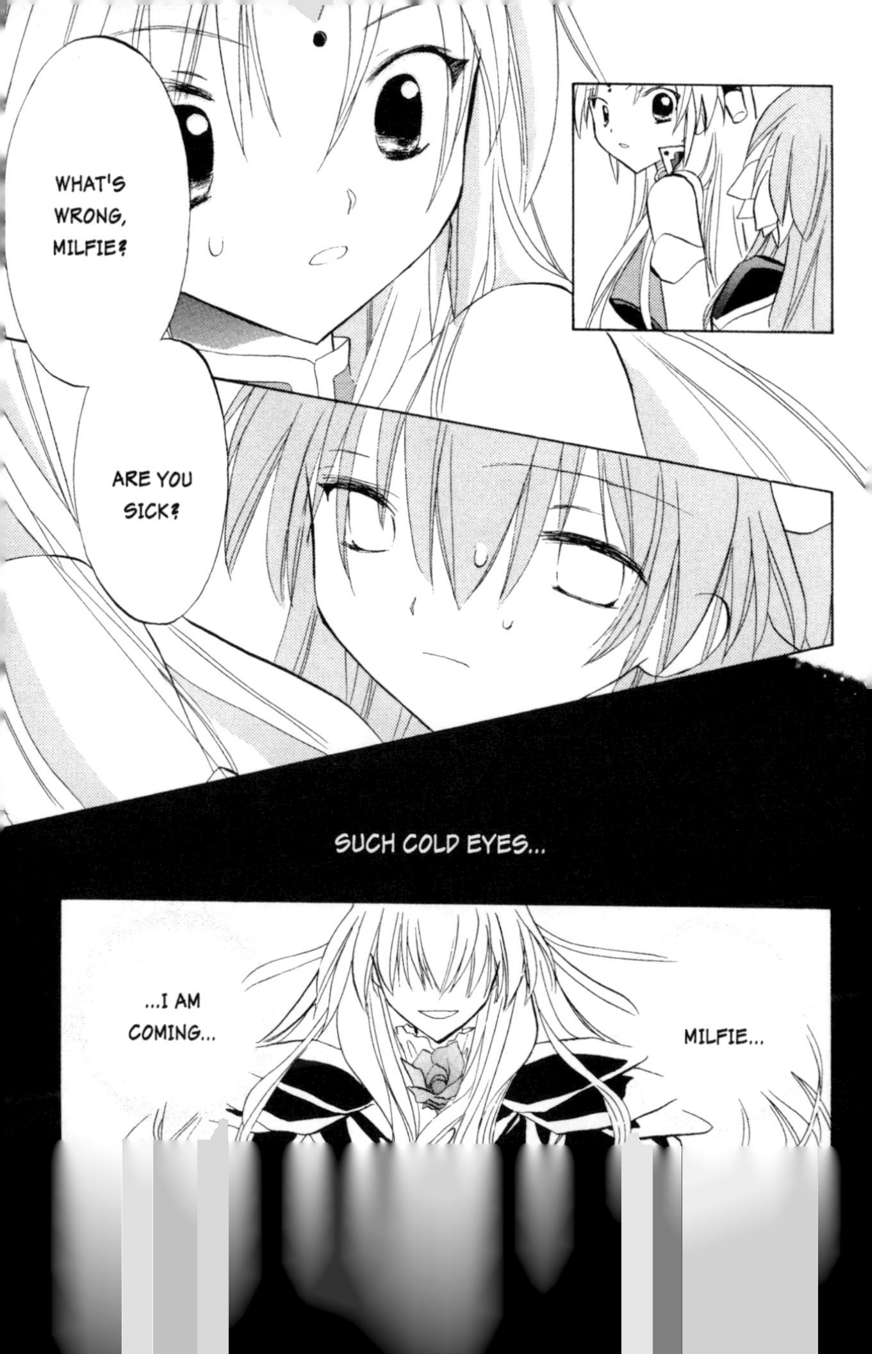
WHAT'S WRONG, MILFIE?
ARE YOU SICK?
SUCH COLD EYES...
...I AM COMING...
MILFIE...

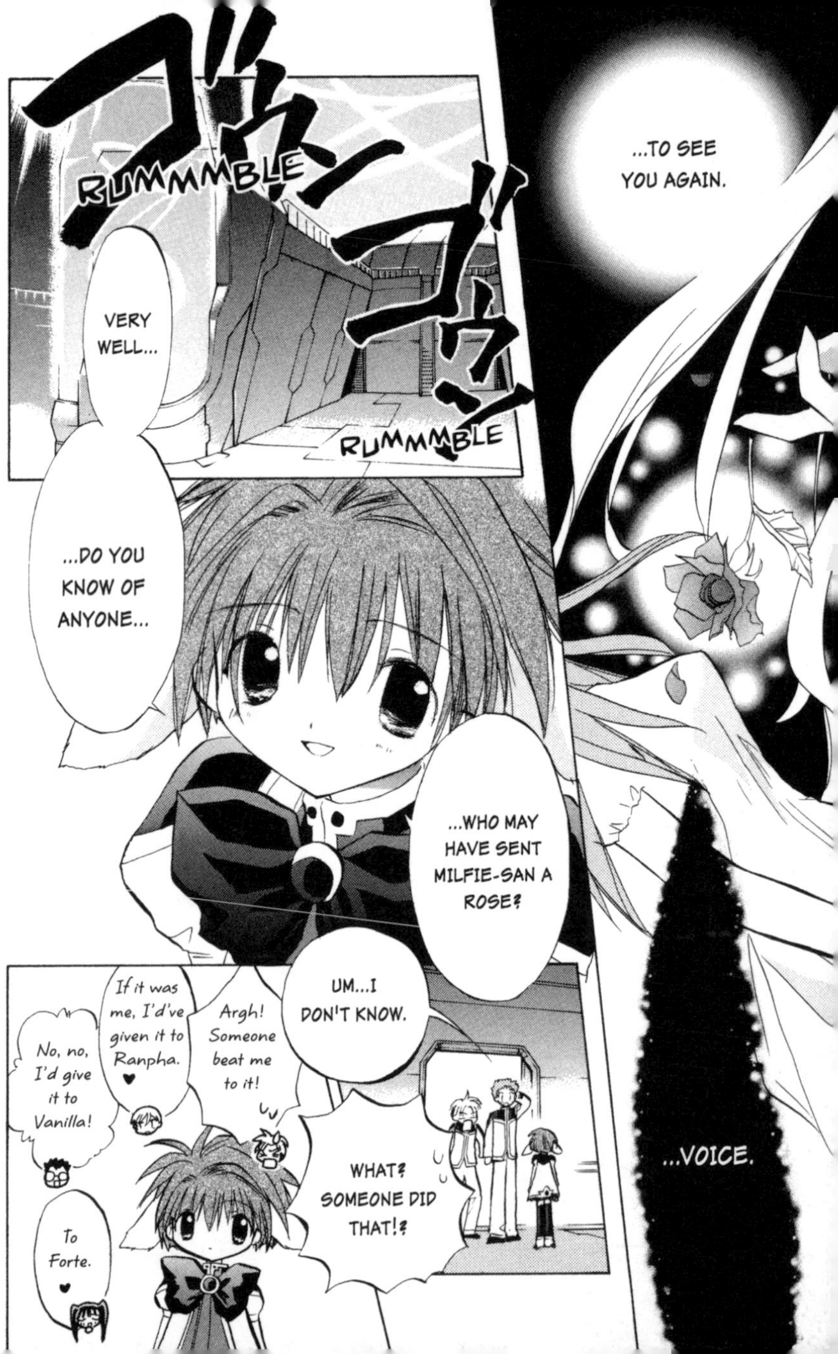
...TO SEE YOU AGAIN.
...VOICE.
RUMMMBLE
RUMMMBLE
VERY WELL...
...DO YOU KNOW OF ANYONE...
...WHO MAY HAVE SENT MILFIE-SAN A ROSE?
UM...I DON'T KNOW.
WHAT? SOMEONE DID THAT!?
Argh! Someone beat me to it!
If it was me, I'd've given it to Ranpha. ♥
No, no, I'd give it to Vanilla!
To Forte. ♥

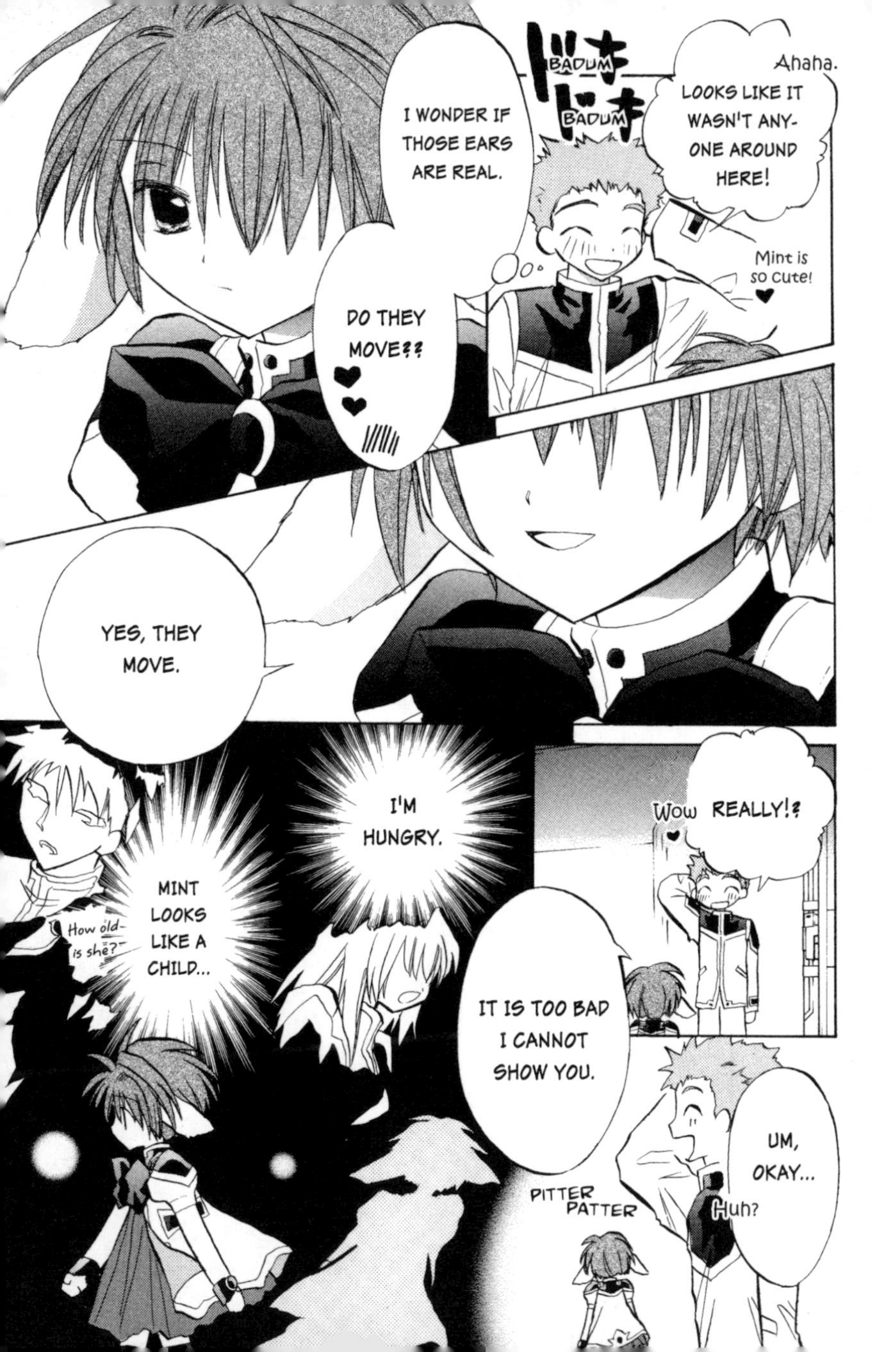
BADUM
BADUM
Ahaha.
LOOKS LIKE IT WASN'T ANY-ONE AROUND HERE!
Mint is so cute!
I WONDER IF THOSE EARS ARE REAL.
DO THEY MOVE??
YES, THEY MOVE.
Wow
REALLY!?
IT IS TOO BAD I CANNOT SHOW YOU.
UM, OKAY...
Huh?
PITTER PATTER
I'M HUNGRY.
MINT LOOKS LIKE A CHILD...
How old is she?

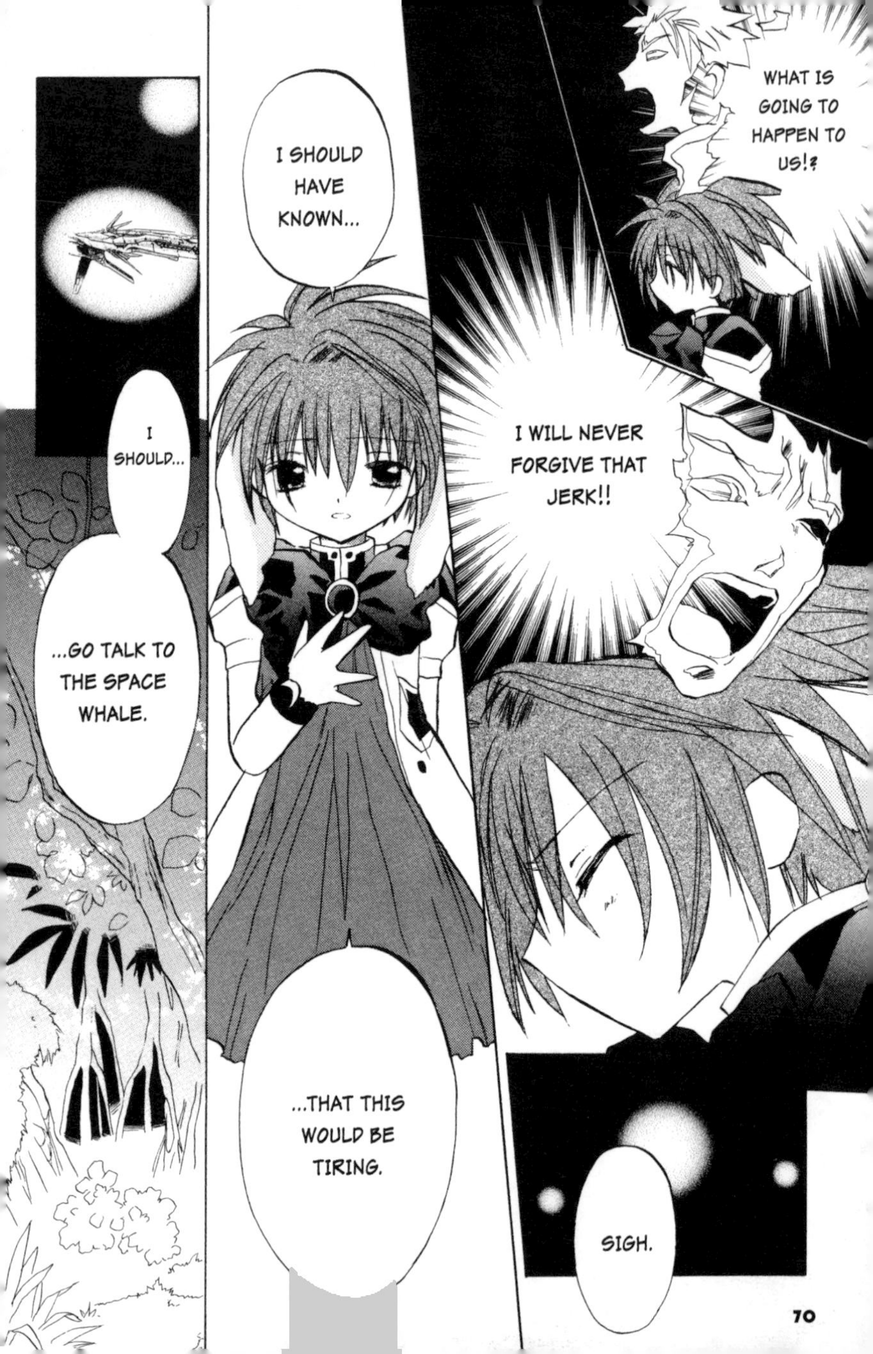
WHAT IS GOING TO HAPPEN TO US!?
I WILL NEVER FORGIVE THAT JERK!!
SIGH.
I SHOULD HAVE KNOWN...
...THAT THIS WOULD BE TIRING.
I SHOULD...
...GO TALK TO THE SPACE WHALE.

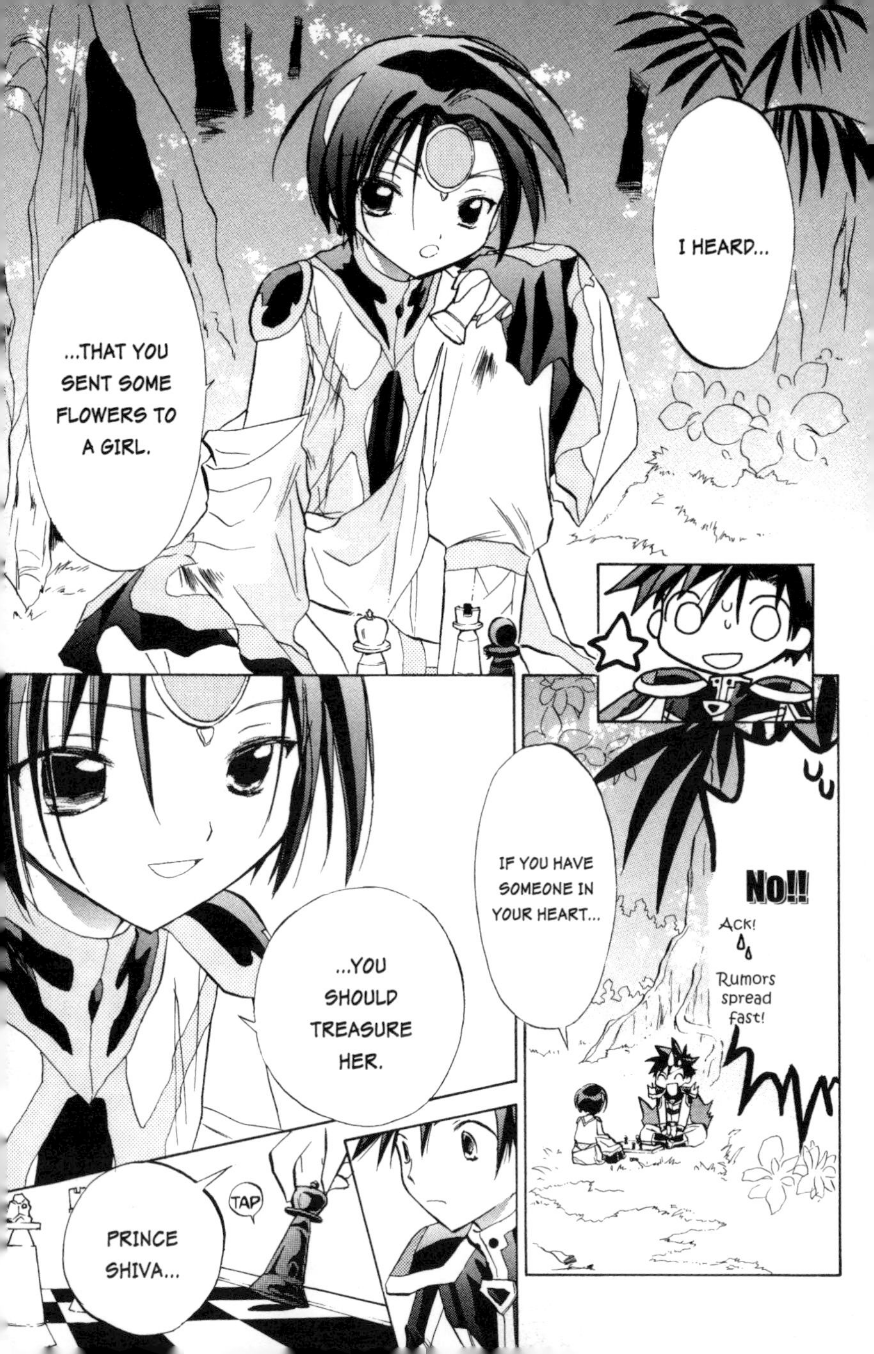
I HEARD...
...THAT YOU SENT SOME FLOWERS TO A GIRL.
No!!
Ack!
Rumors spread fast!
IF YOU HAVE SOMEONE IN YOUR HEART...
...YOU SHOULD TREASURE HER.
TAP
PRINCE SHIVA...

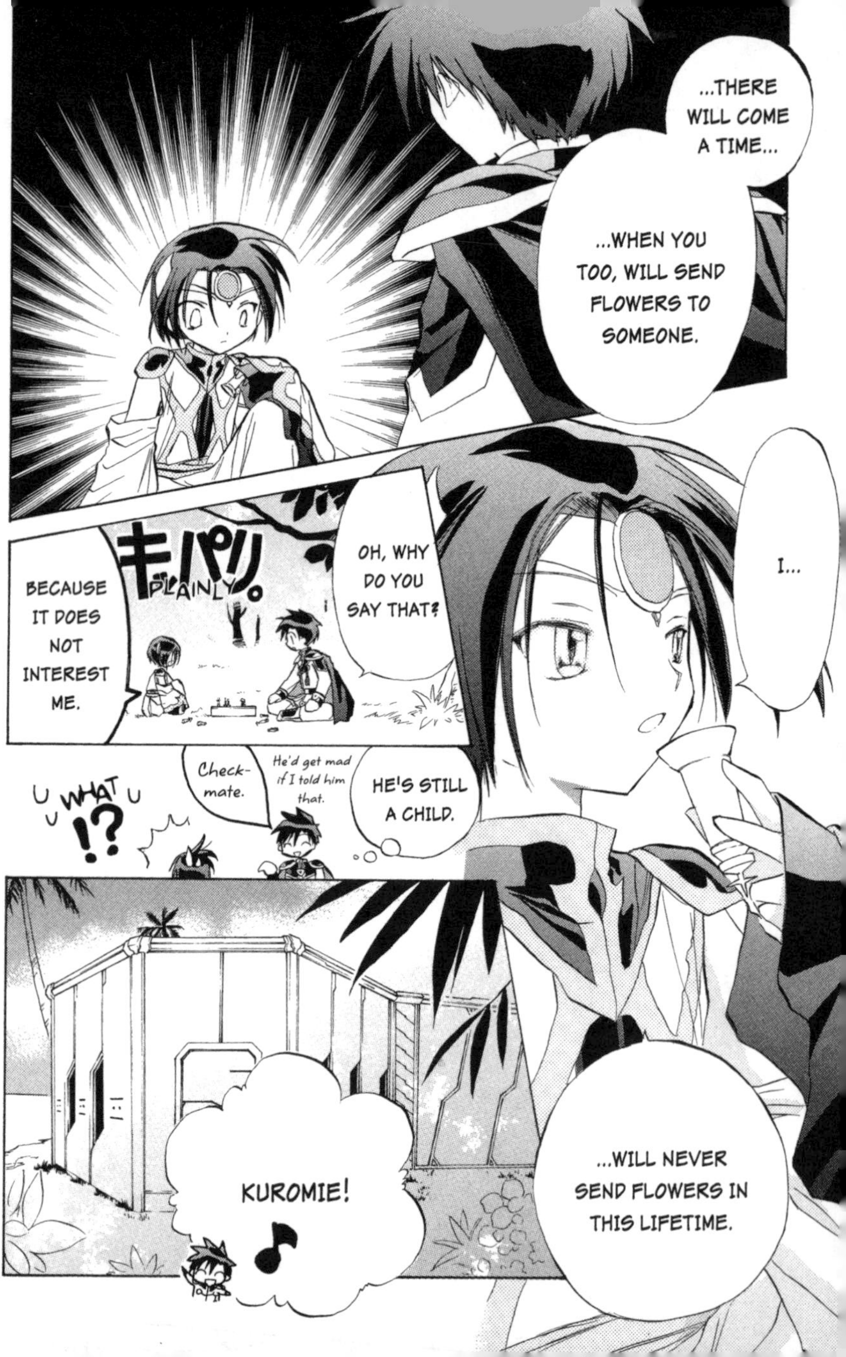
...THERE WILL COME A TIME...
...WHEN YOU TOO, WILL SEND FLOWERS TO SOMEONE.
I...
...WILL NEVER SEND FLOWERS IN THIS LIFETIME.
OH, WHY DO YOU SAY THAT?
キッパリ
PLAINLY
BECAUSE IT DOES NOT INTEREST ME.
HE'S STILL A CHILD.
He'd get mad if I told him that.
Check-mate.
WHAT !?
KUROMIE!

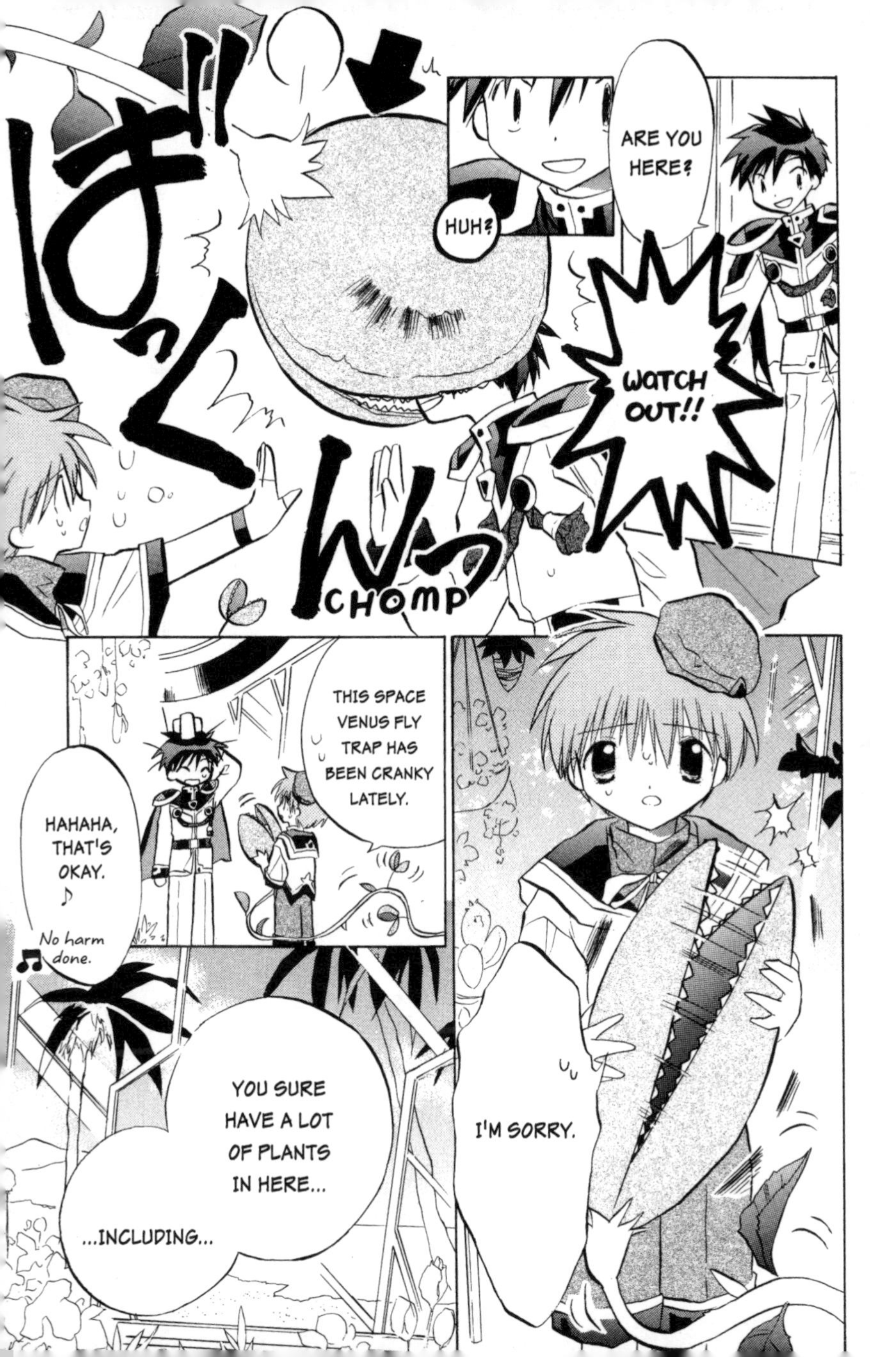
ARE YOU HERE?
HUH?
WATCH OUT!!
ぱっくんっ
CHOMP
I'M SORRY.
THIS SPACE VENUS FLY TRAP HAS BEEN CRANKY LATELY.
HAHAHA, THAT'S OKAY. ♪
No harm done.
YOU SURE HAVE A LOT OF PLANTS IN HERE...
...INCLUDING...

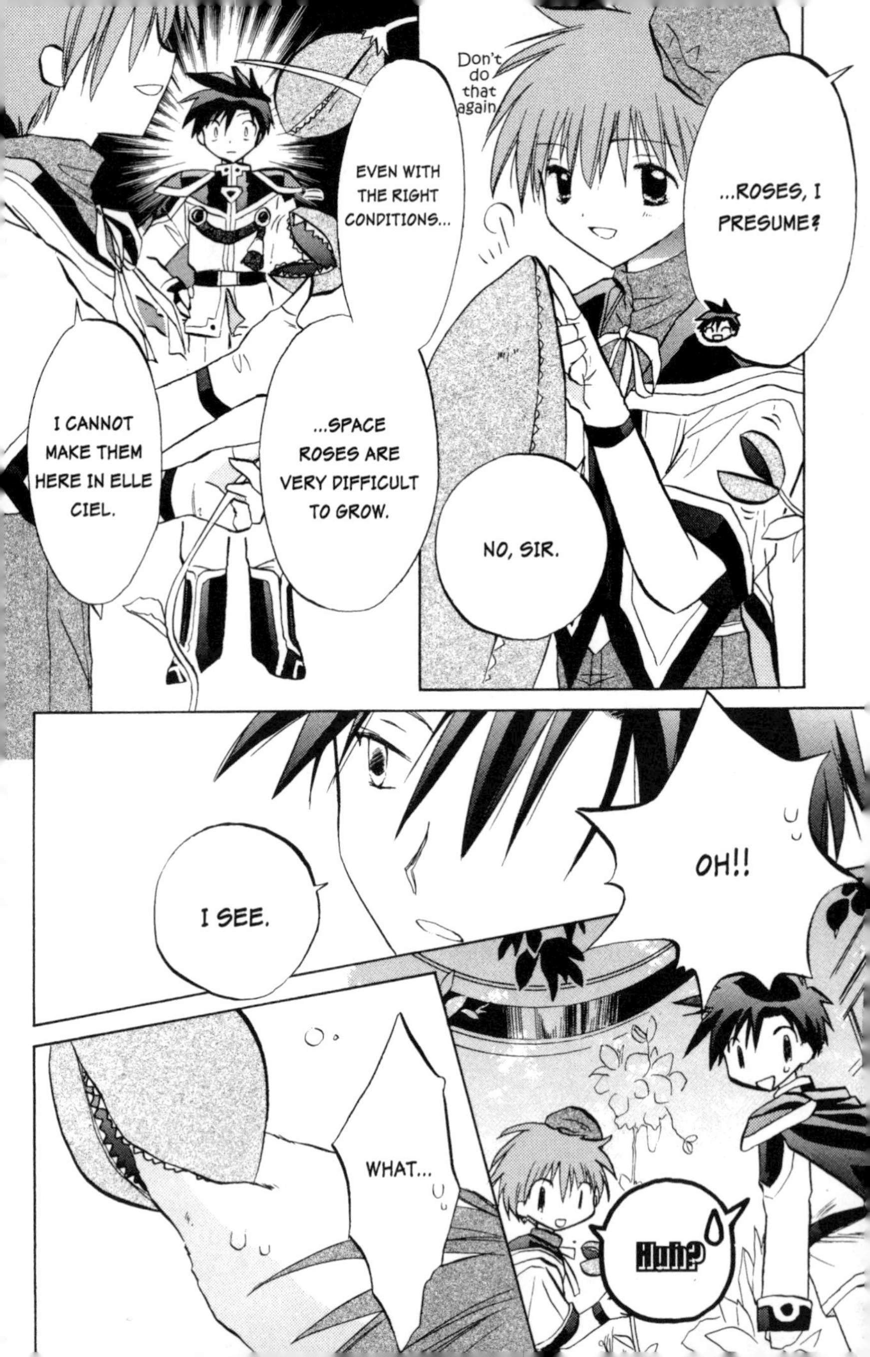
...ROSES, I PRESUME?
Don't do that again
NO, SIR.
EVEN WITH THE RIGHT CONDITIONS...
...SPACE ROSES ARE VERY DIFFICULT TO GROW.
I CANNOT MAKE THEM HERE IN ELLE CIEL.
OH!!
I SEE.
Huh?
WHAT...

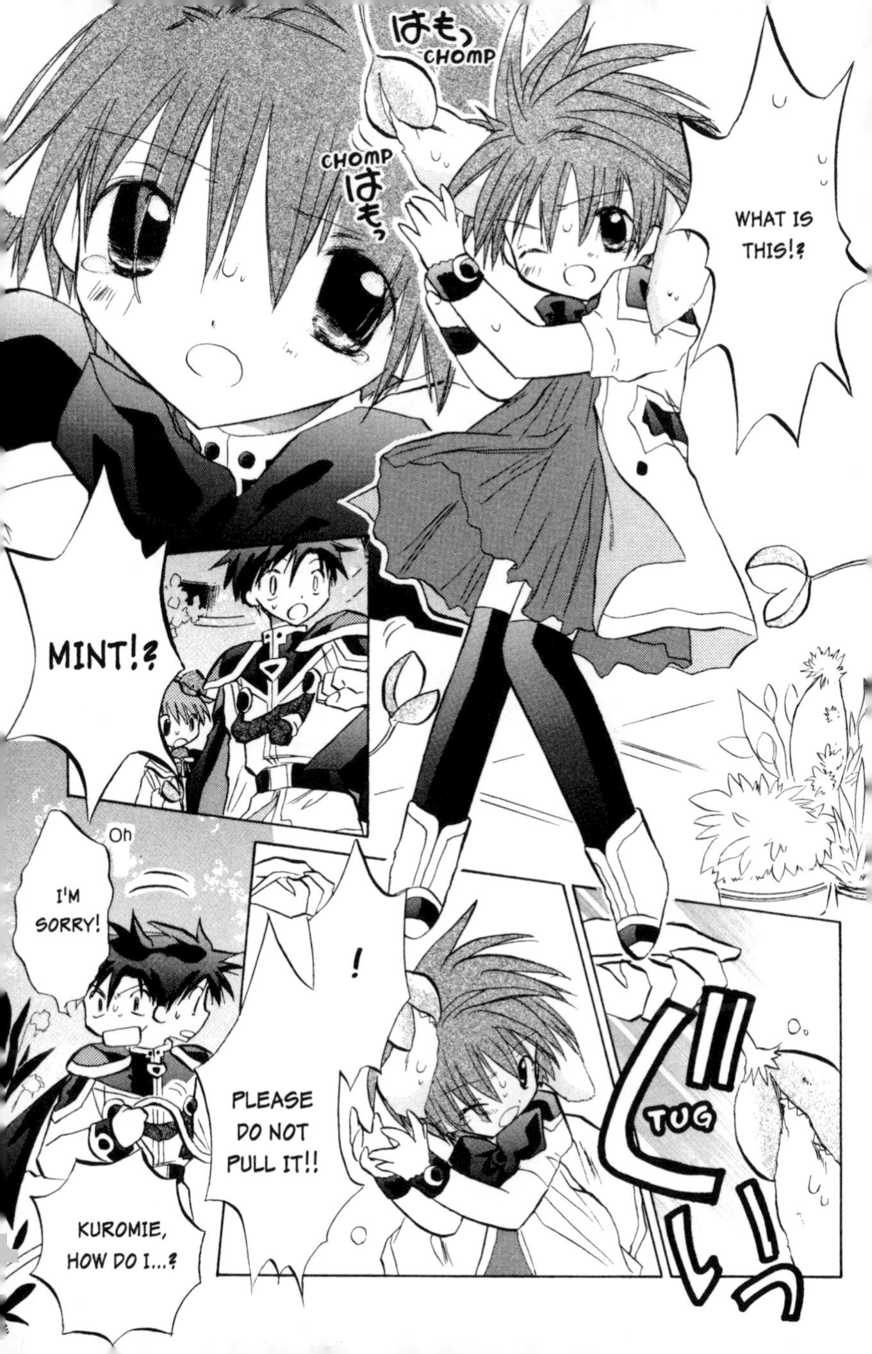
はもっ
CHOMP
WHAT IS THIS!?
CHOMP
はもっ
MINT!?
くいーっ
TUG
!
PLEASE DO NOT PULL IT!!
Oh
I'M SORRY!
KUROMIE, HOW DO I...?

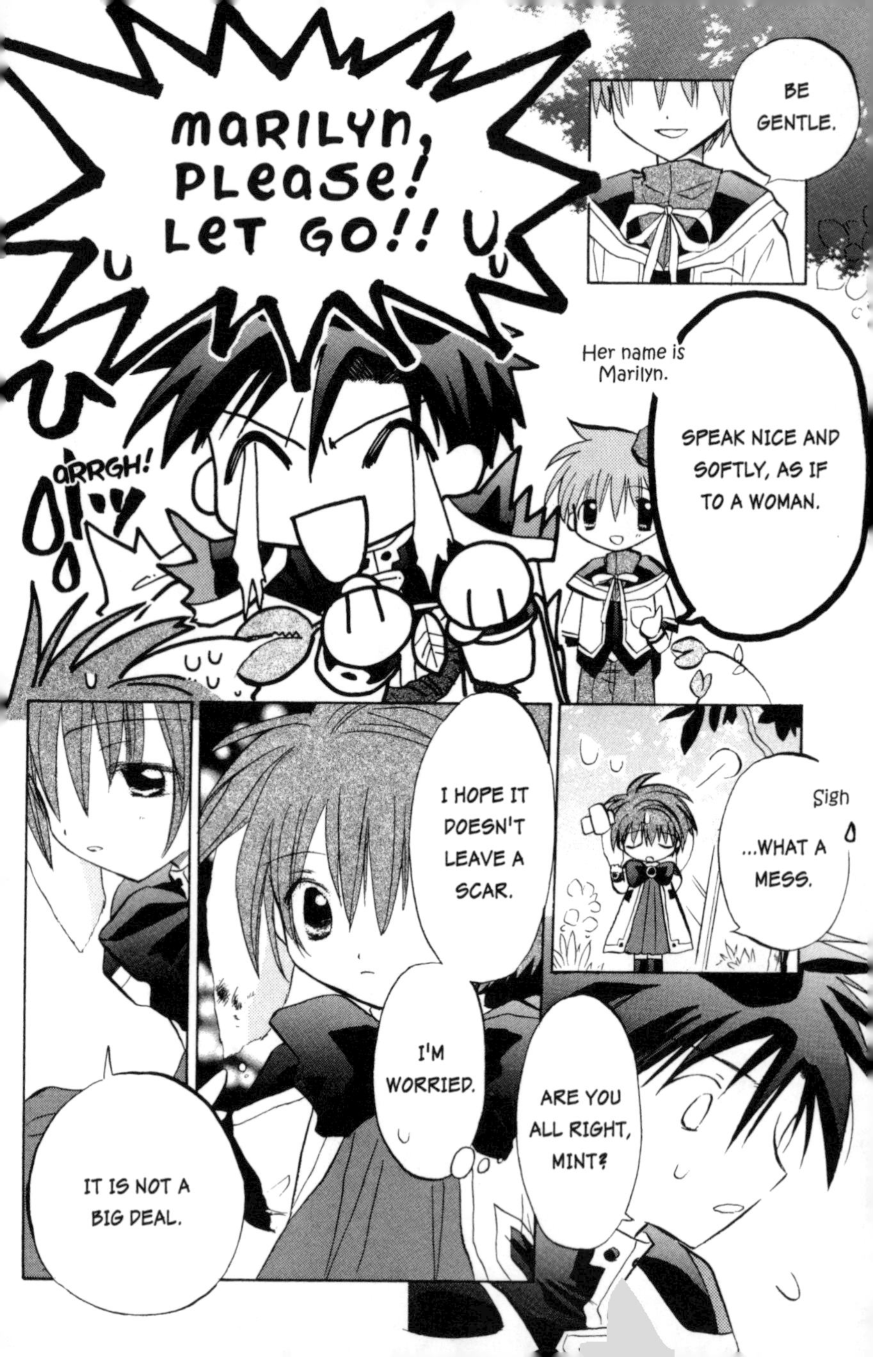
BE GENTLE.
Her name is Marilyn.
SPEAK NICE AND SOFTLY, AS IF TO A WOMAN.
MARILYN, PLEASE! LET GO!!
ARRGH!
Sigh
...WHAT A MESS.
ARE YOU ALL RIGHT, MINT?
I HOPE IT DOESN'T LEAVE A SCAR.
I'M WORRIED.
IT IS NOT A BIG DEAL.

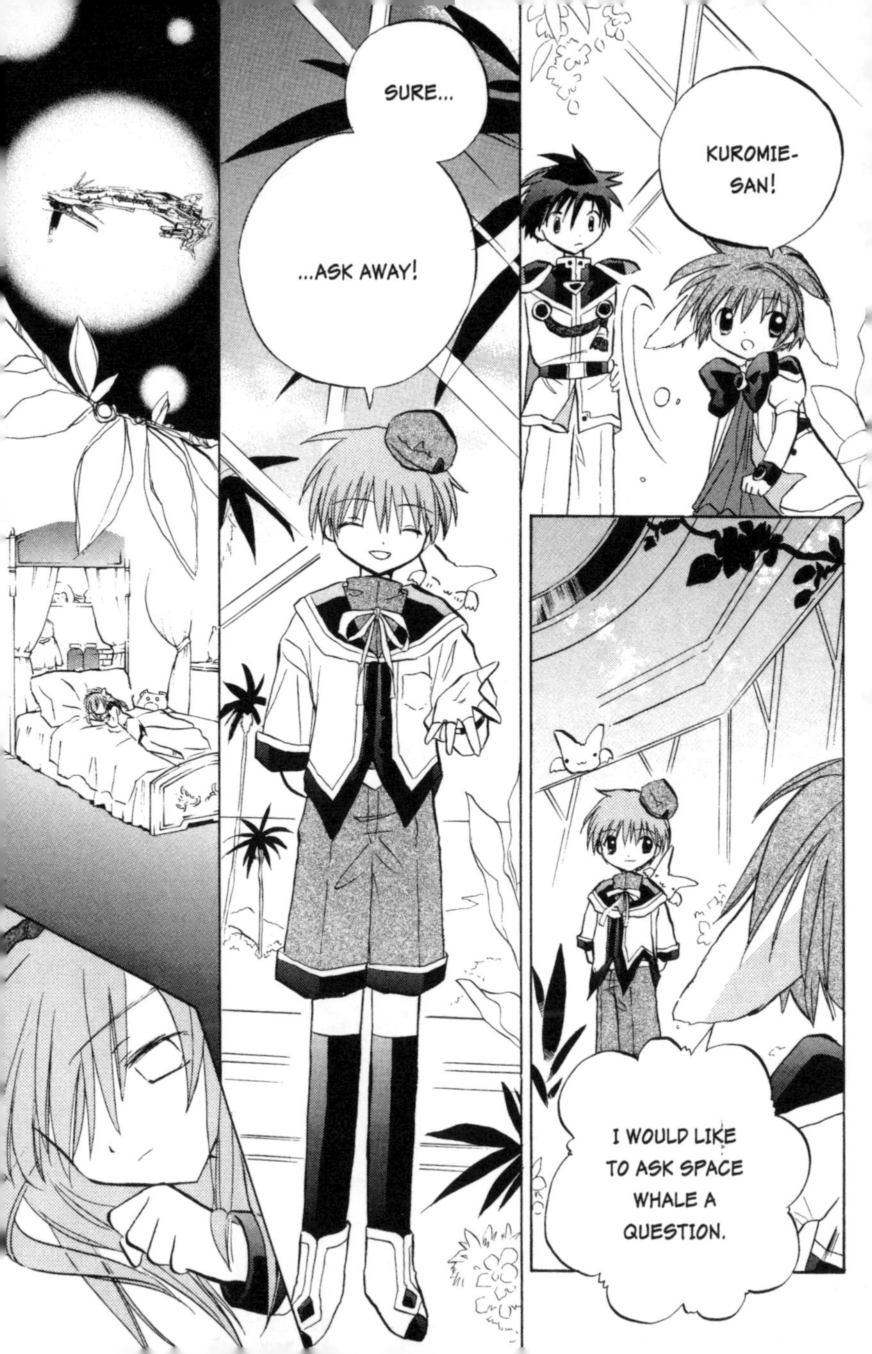
KUROMIE-SAN!
I WOULD LIKE TO ASK SPACE WHALE A QUESTION.
SURE...
...ASK AWAY!

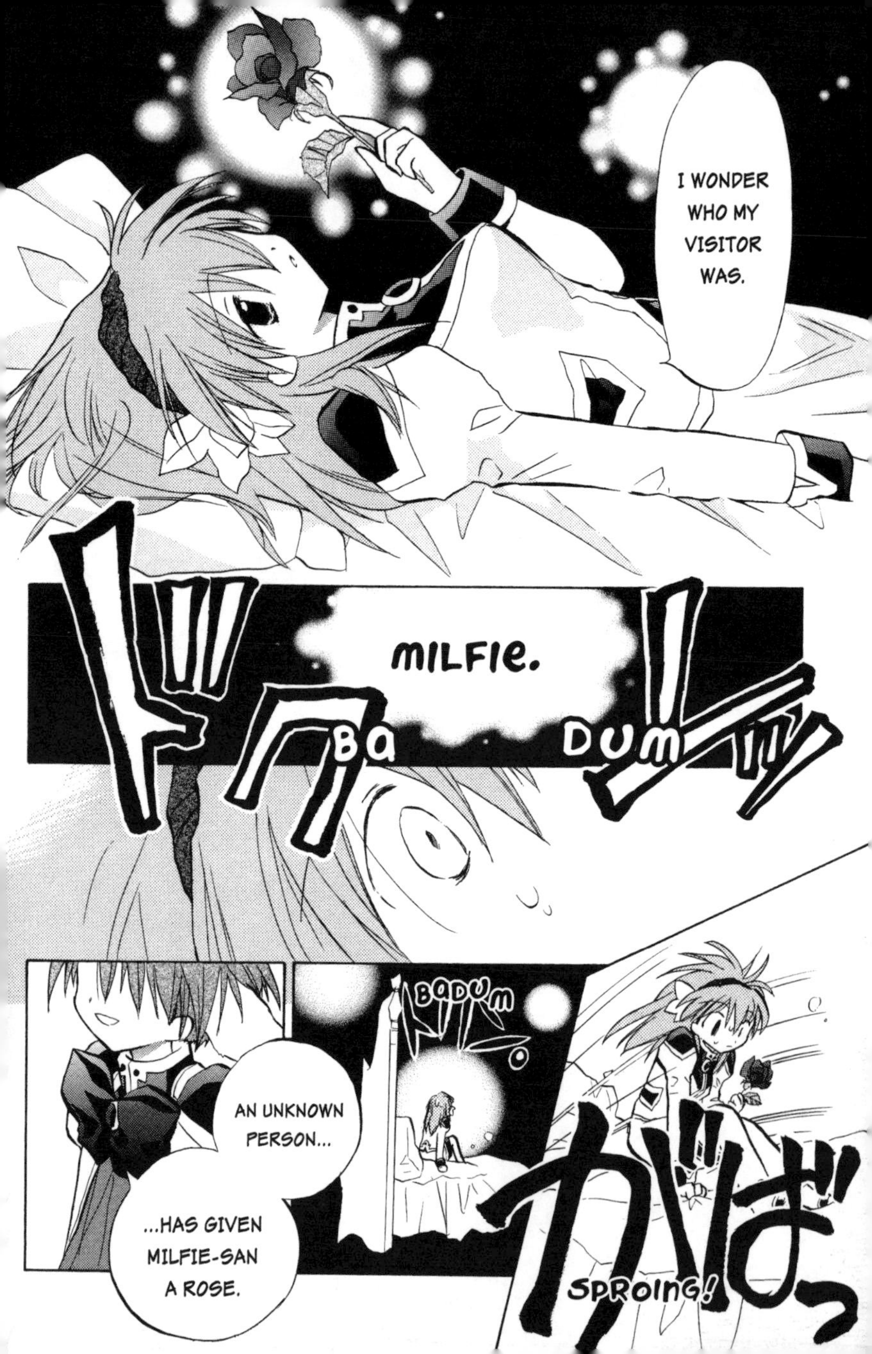
I WONDER WHO MY VISITOR WAS.
MILFIE.
BA DUM
SPROING!
BADUM
AN UNKNOWN PERSON...
...HAS GIVEN MILFIE-SAN A ROSE.

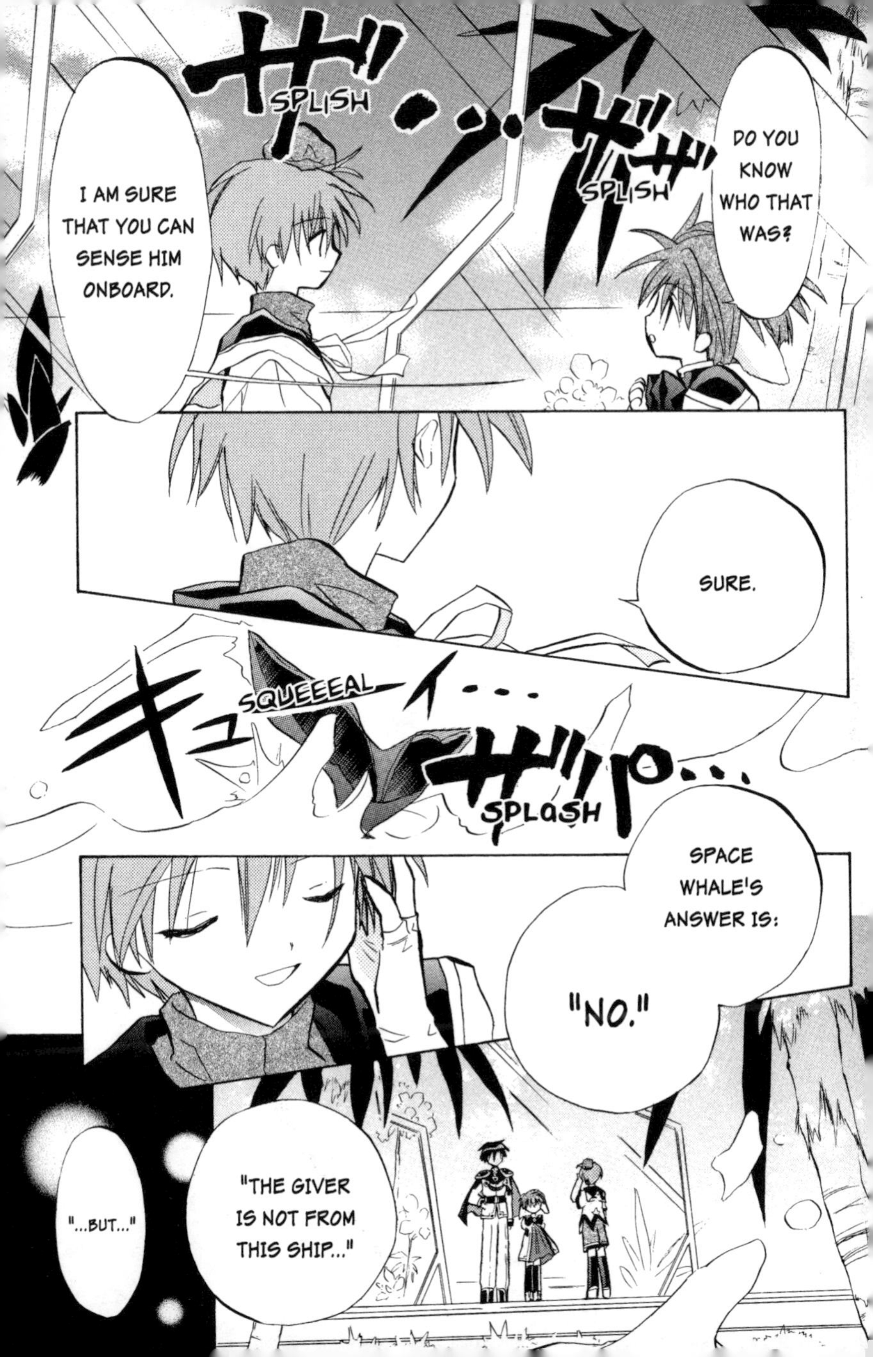
DO YOU KNOW WHO THAT WAS?
SPLISH
SPLISH
I AM SURE THAT YOU CAN SENSE HIM ONBOARD.
SURE.
SQUEEEAL
SPLASH
SPACE WHALE'S ANSWER IS:
"NO."
"THE GIVER IS NOT FROM THIS SHIP..."
"...BUT..."

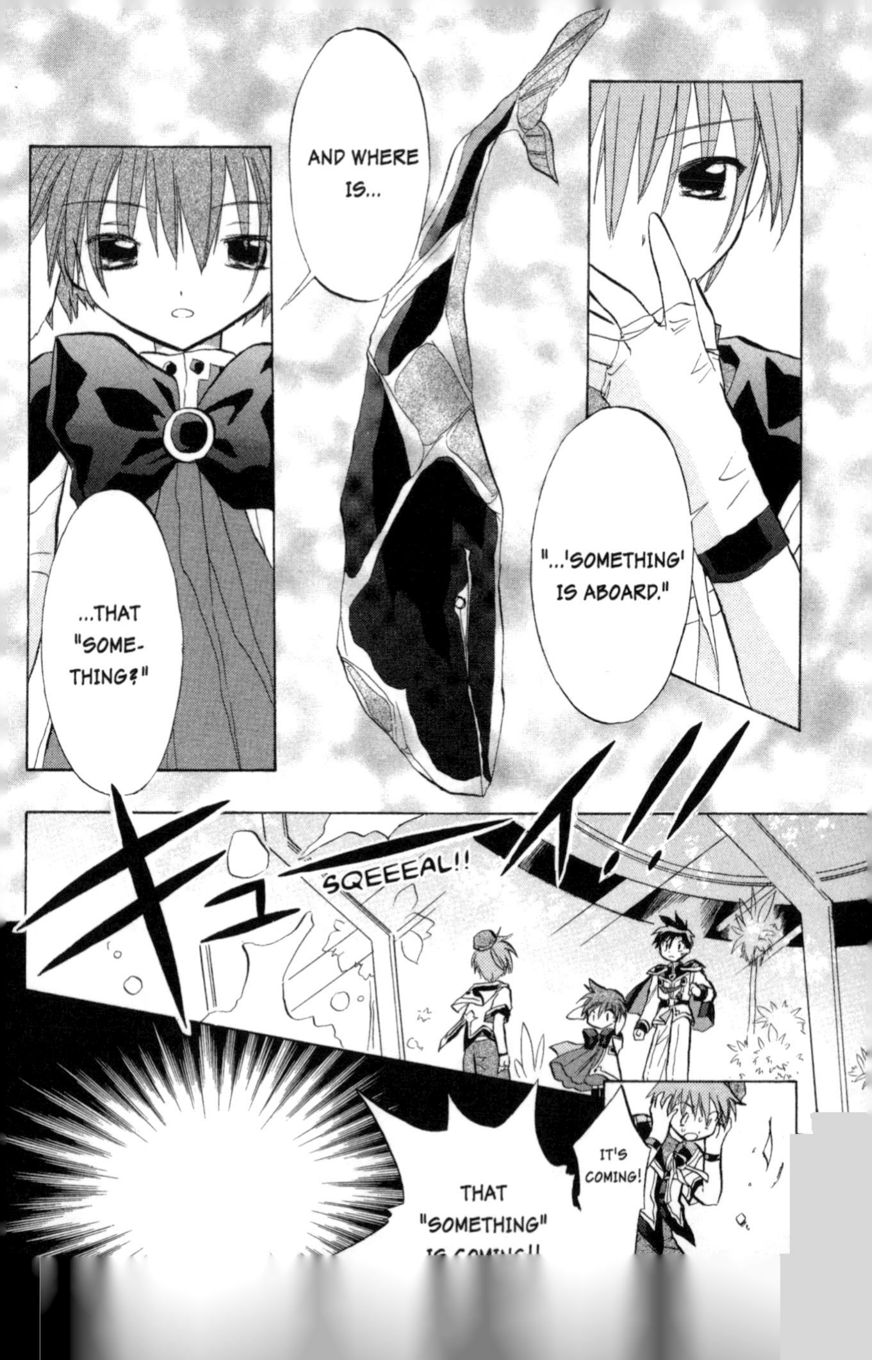

"...'SOMETHING' IS ABOARD."
AND WHERE IS...
...THAT "SOME-THING?"
キューィ!!
SQEEEAL!!
IT'S COMING!
THAT "SOMETHING"

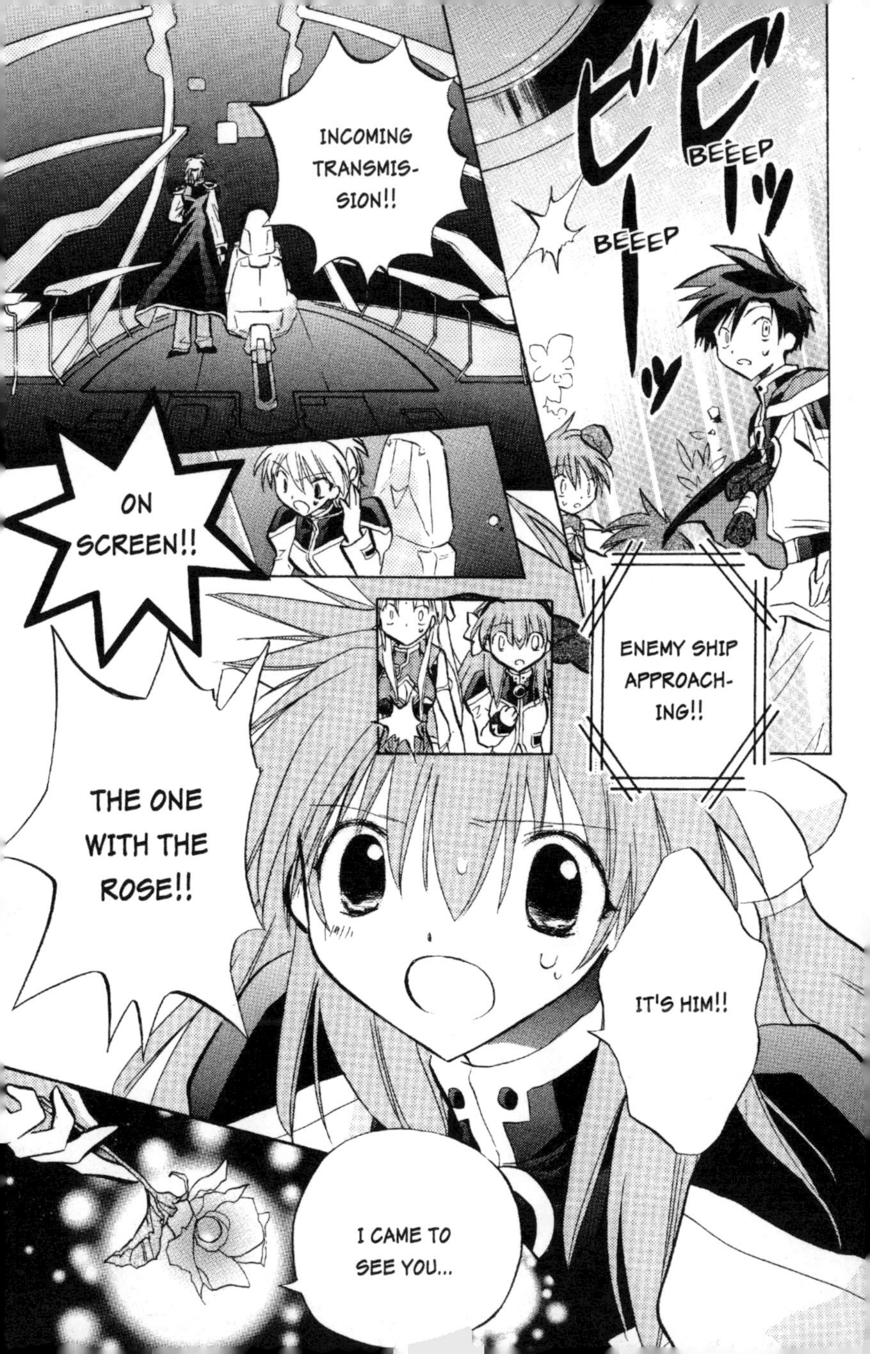

BEEEP
BEEEP
ENEMY SHIP APPROACH-ING!!
INCOMING TRANSMIS-SION!!
ON SCREEN!!
IT'S HIM!!
THE ONE WITH THE ROSE!!
I CAME TO SEE YOU...

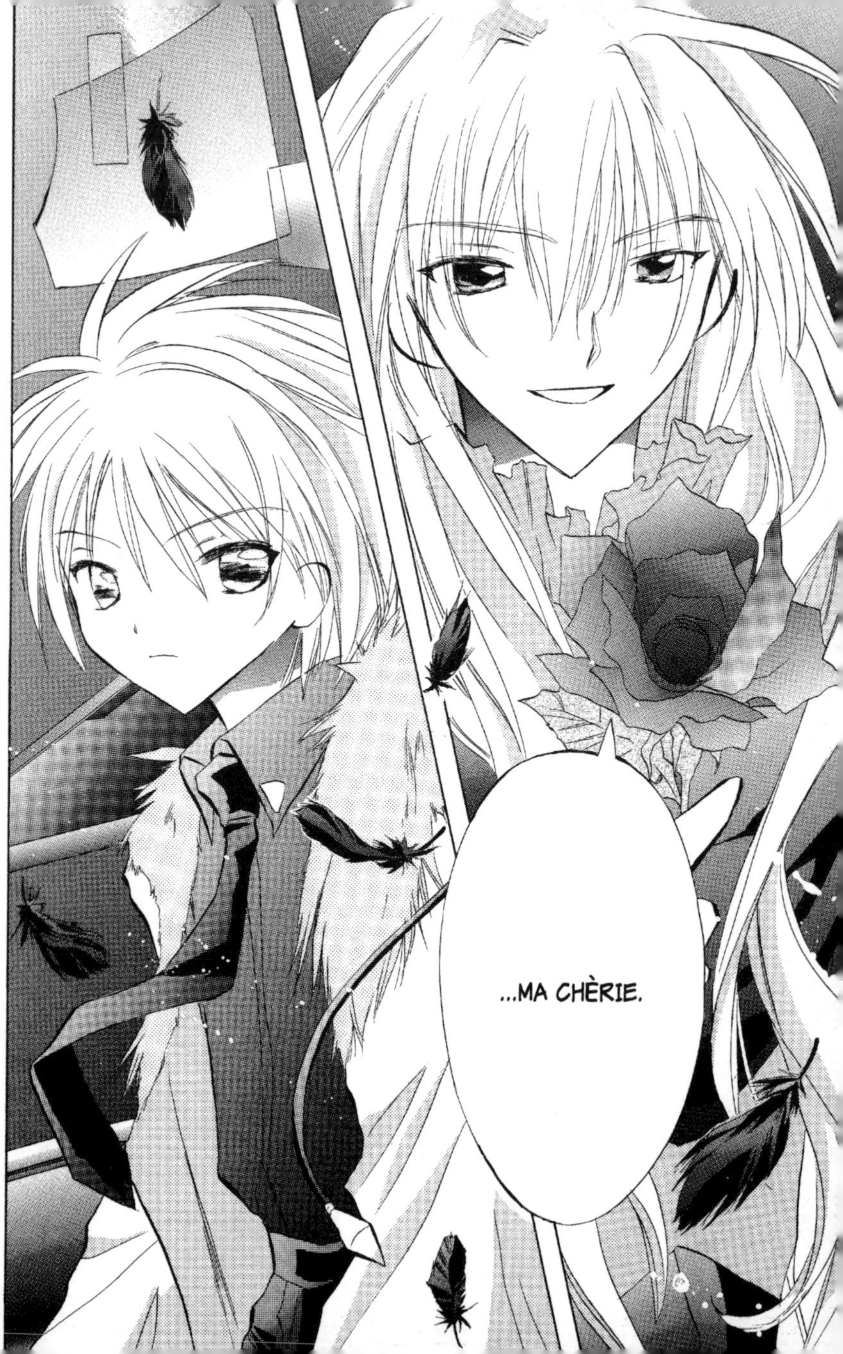
...MA CHÈRIE.

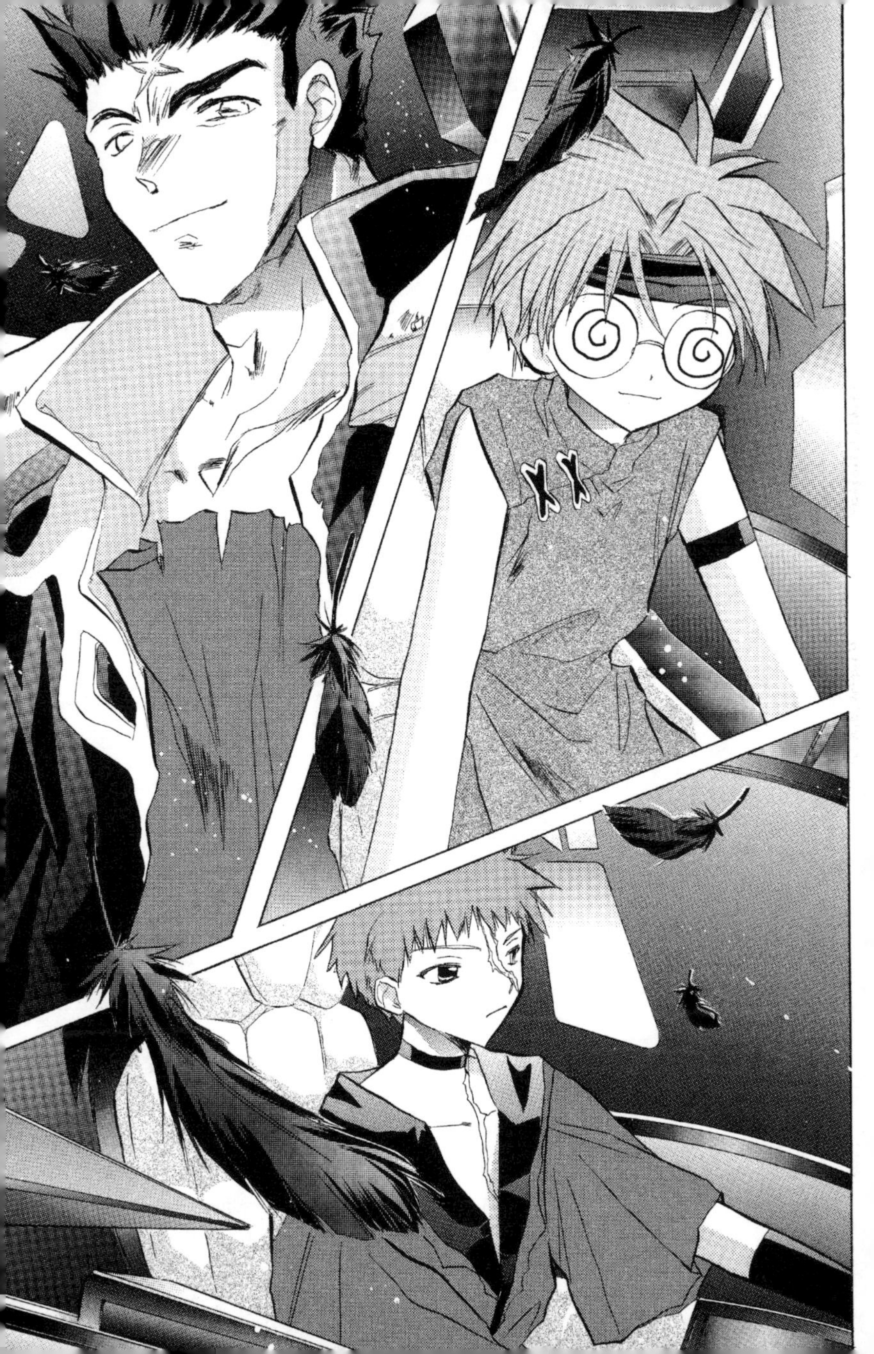

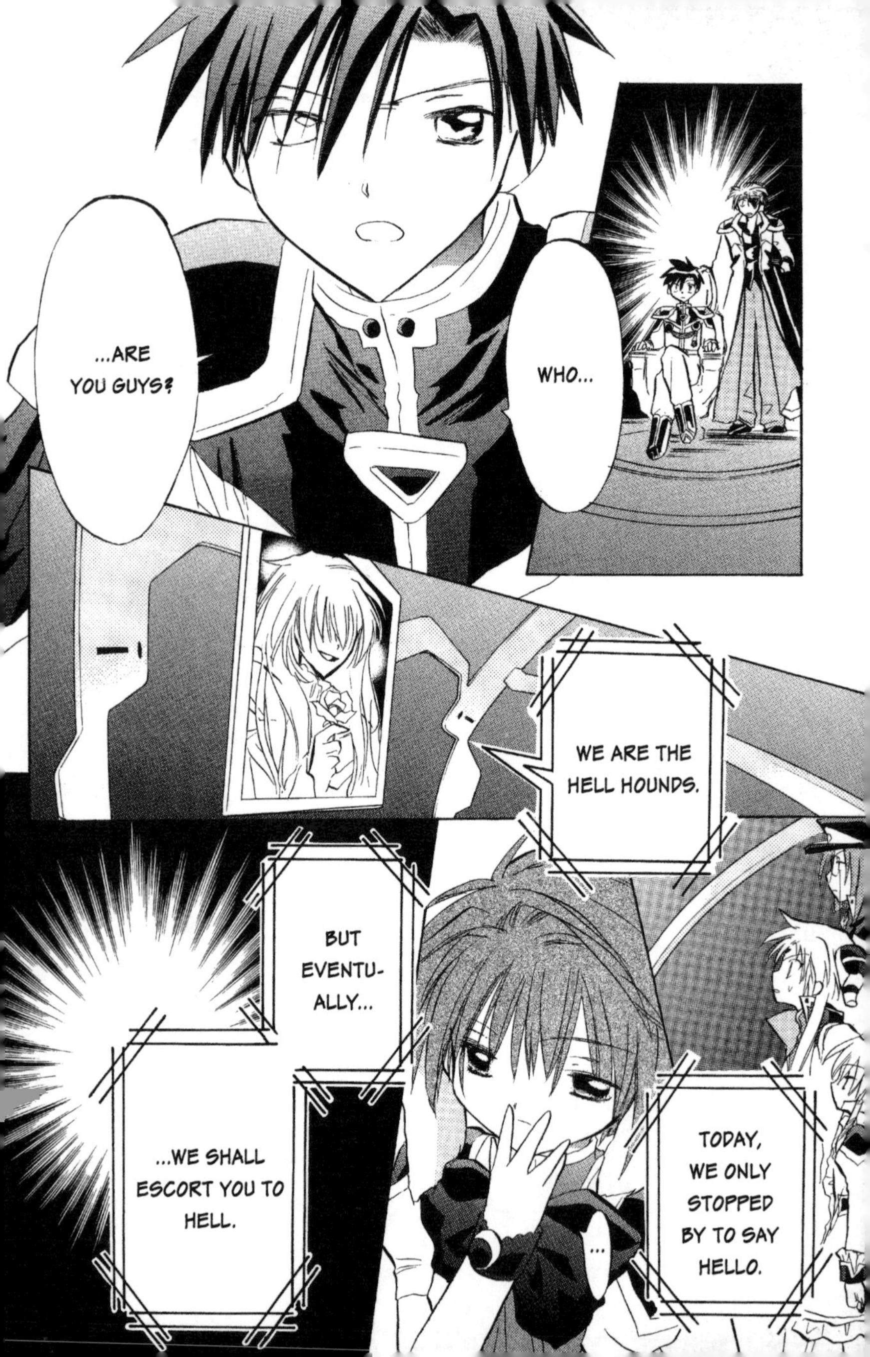
WHO...
...ARE YOU GUYS?
WE ARE THE HELL HOUNDS.
TODAY, WE ONLY STOPPED BY TO SAY HELLO.
...
BUT EVENTU-ALLY...
...WE SHALL ESCORT YOU TO HELL.

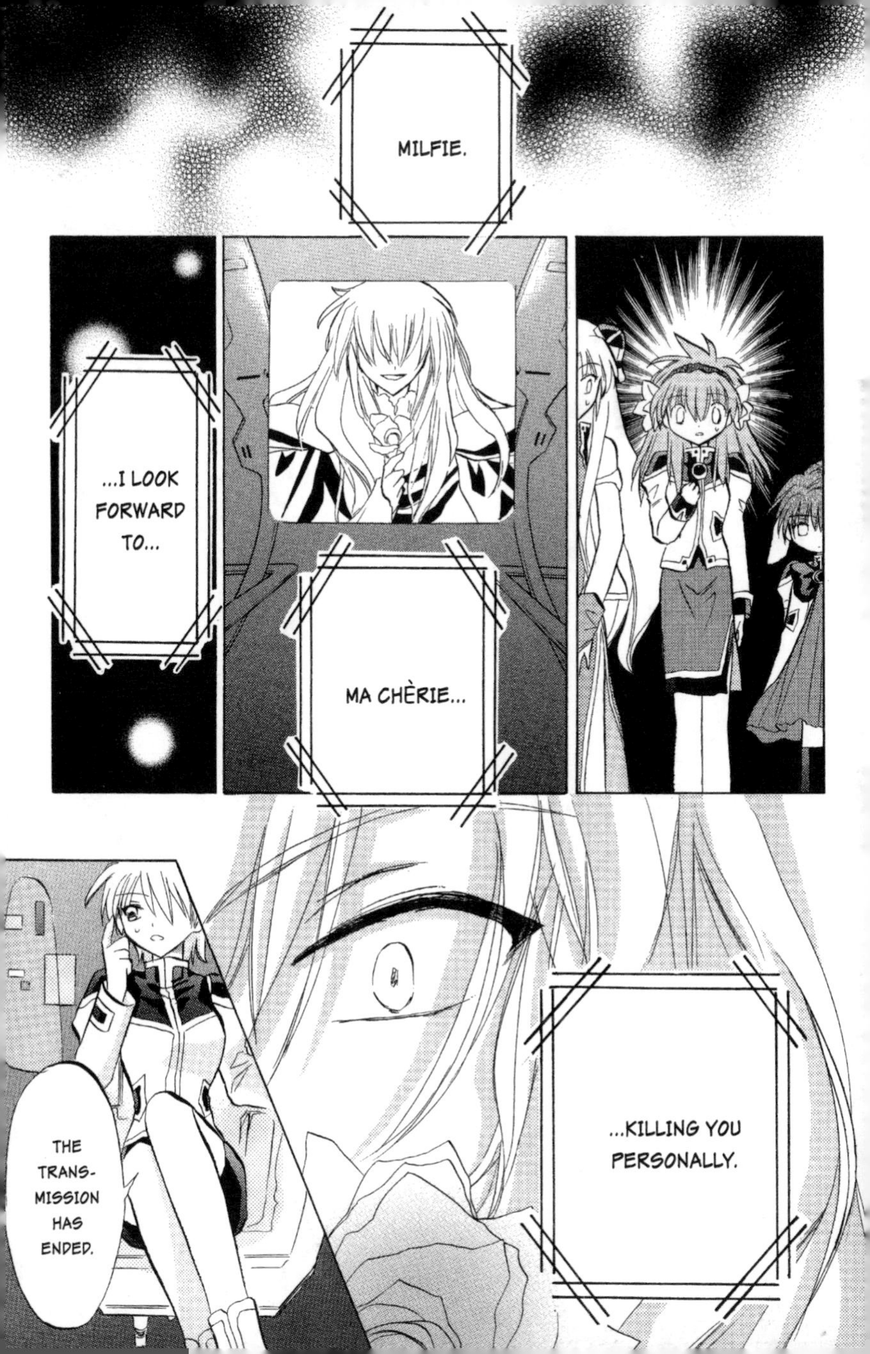
MILFIE.
MA CHÈRIE...
...I LOOK FORWARD TO...
...KILLING YOU PERSONALLY.
THE TRANS-MISSION HAS ENDED.

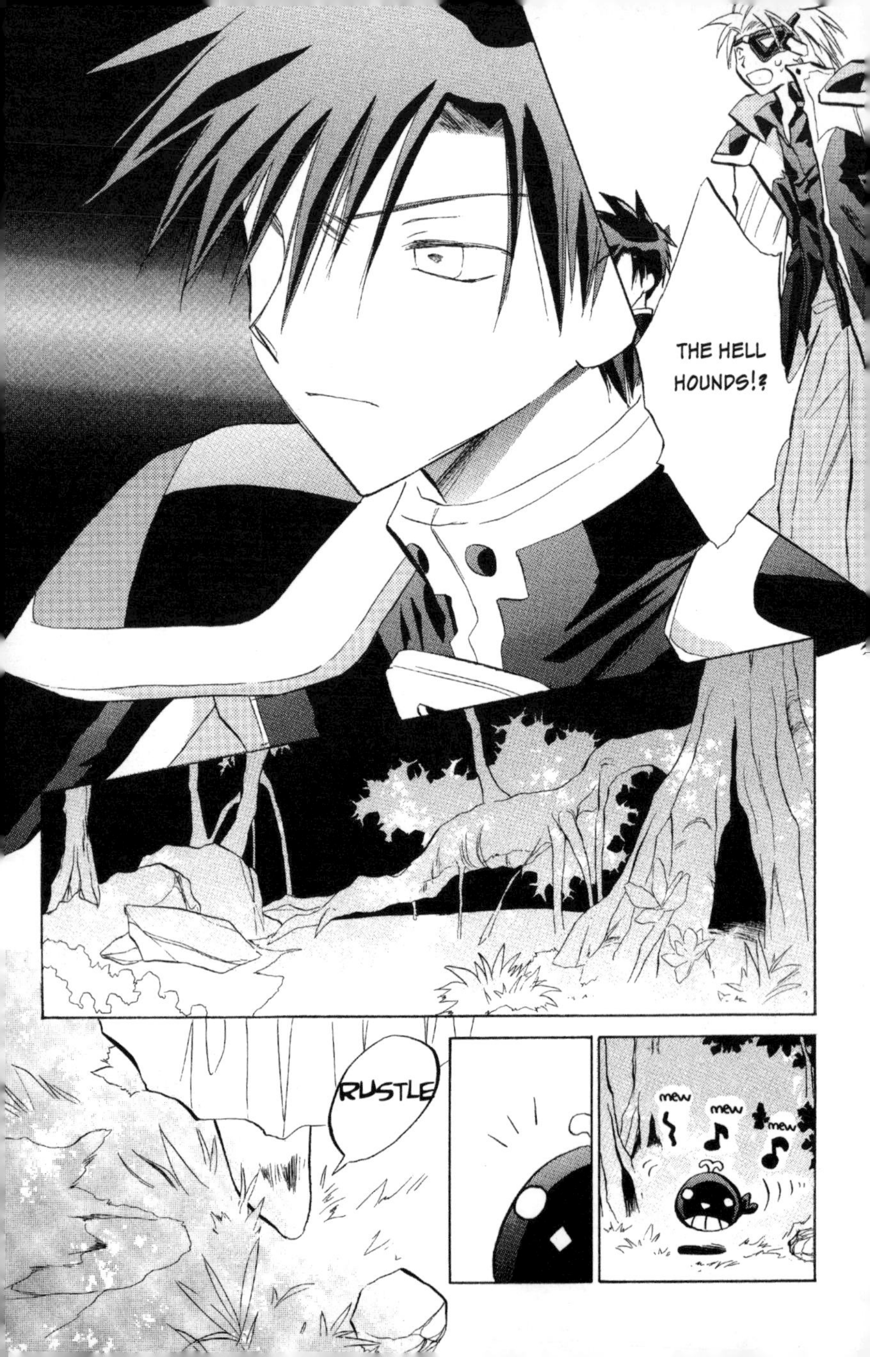
THE HELL HOUNDS!?
RUSTLE
mew
mew
mew

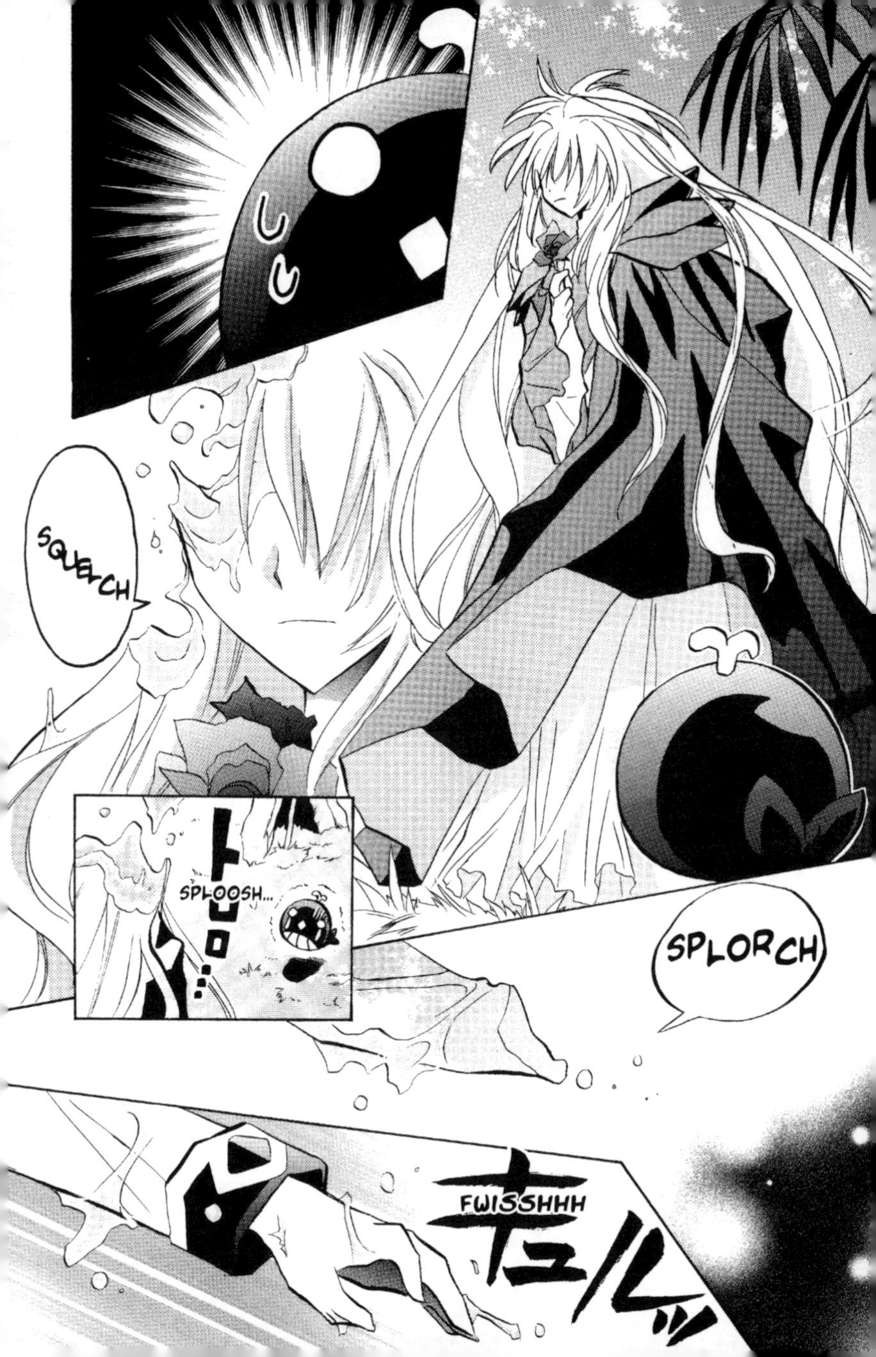
SQUELCH
SPLORCH
SPLOOSH...
FWISSHHH

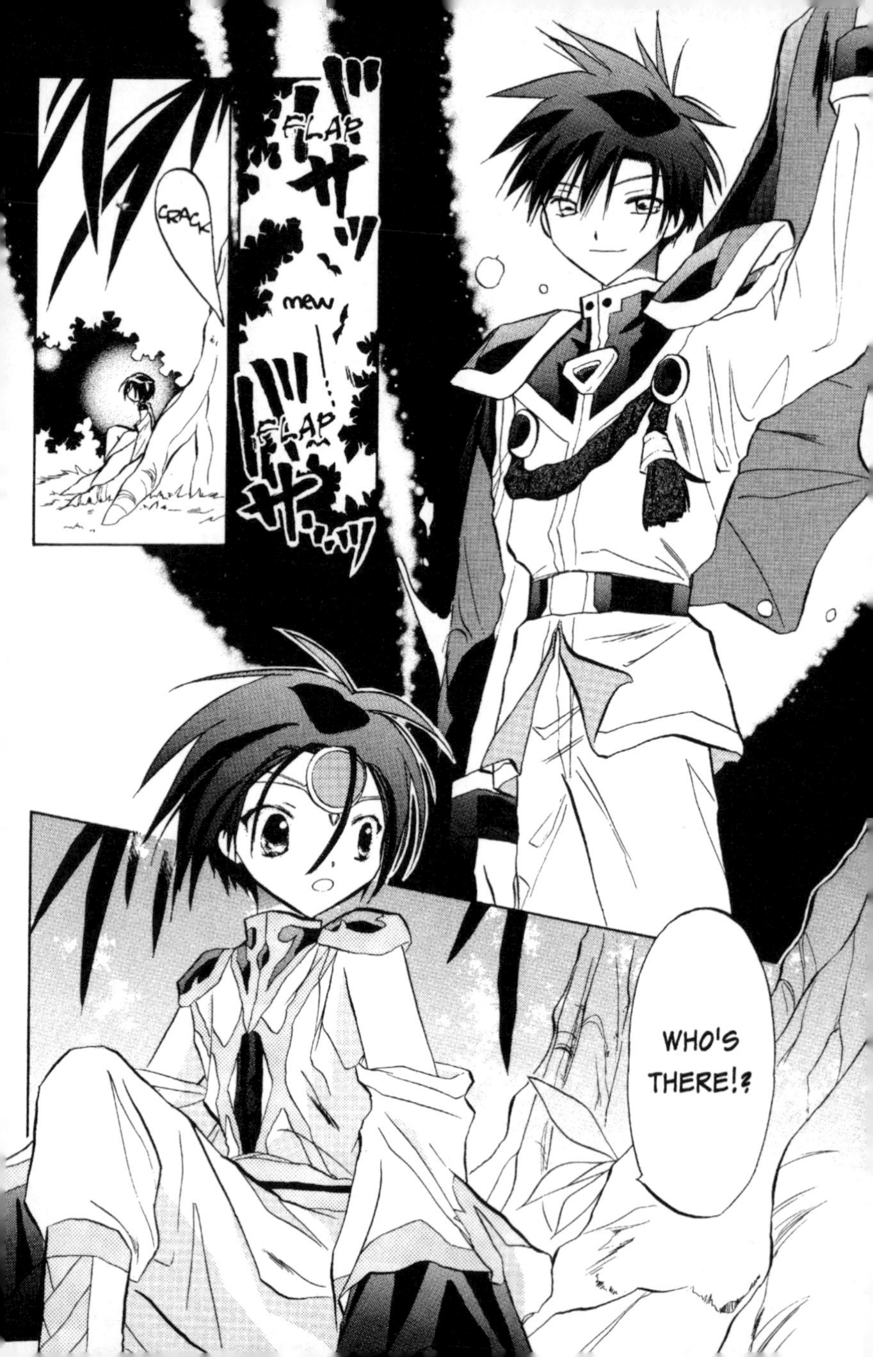
FLAP
mew
FLAP
CRACK
WHO'S THERE!?

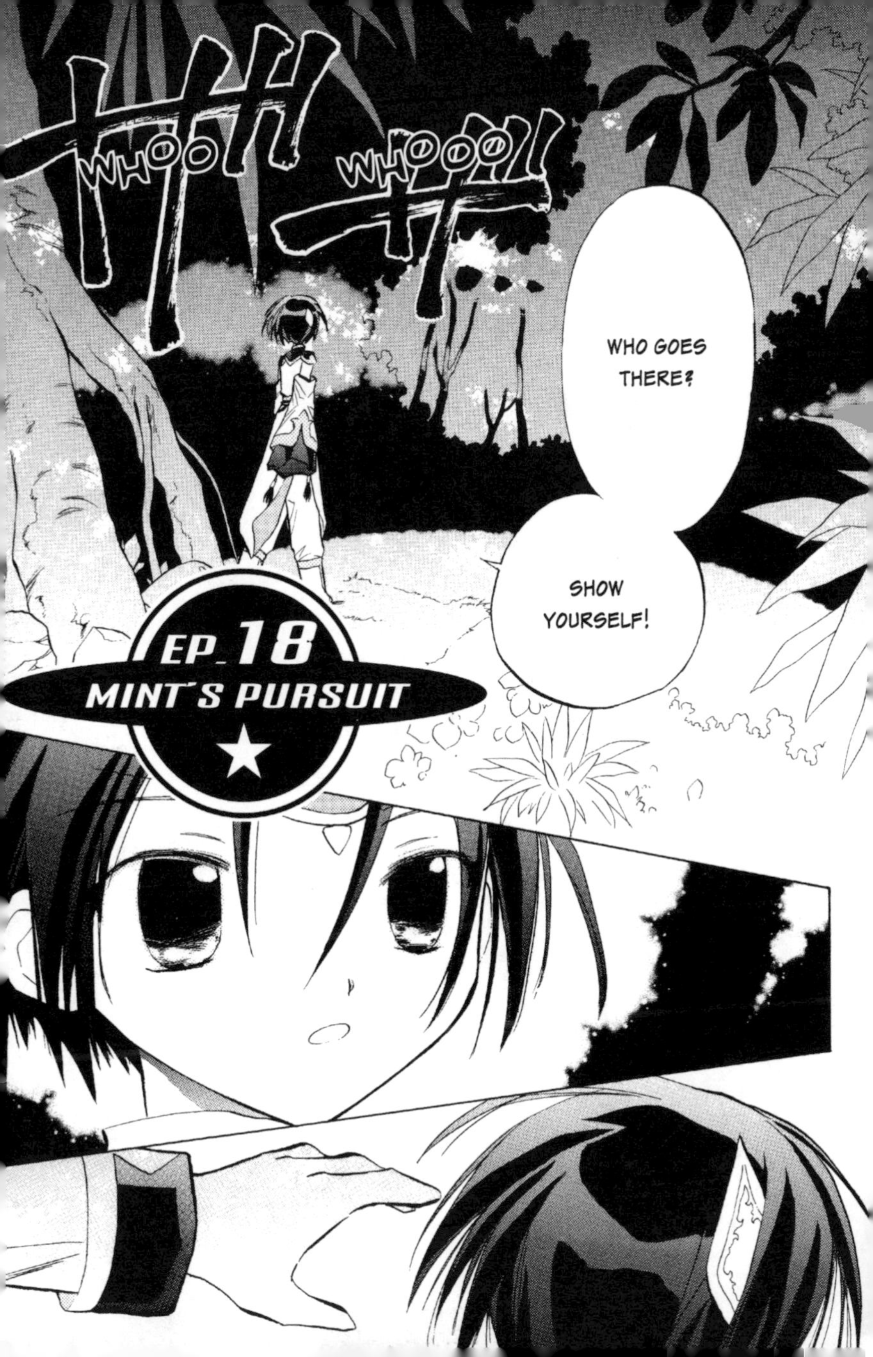
WHOOOO
WHOOO
WHO GOES THERE?
SHOW YOURSELF!
EP. 18
MINT'S PURSUIT

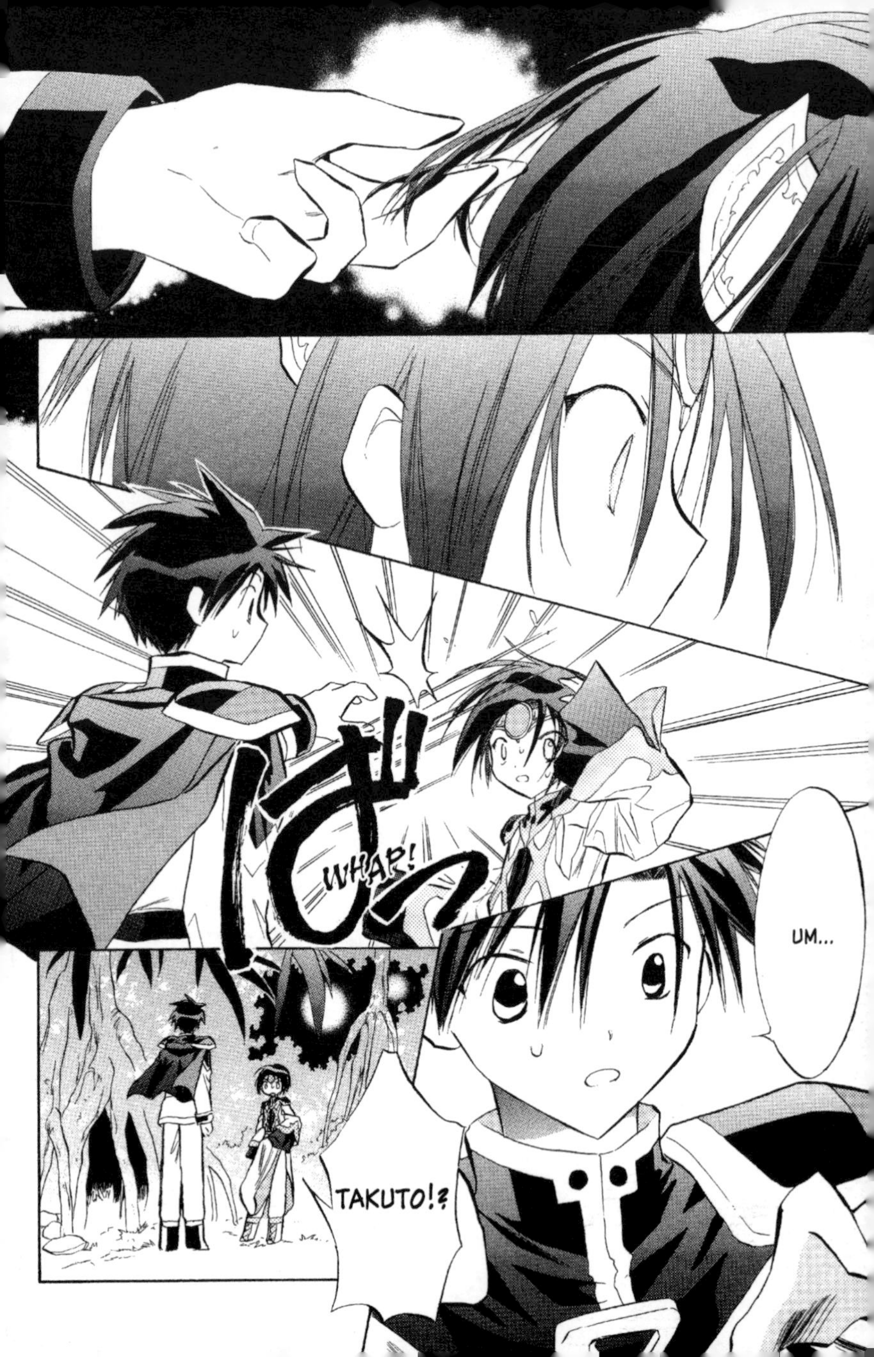
ぱっ
WHAP!
UM...
TAKUTO!?

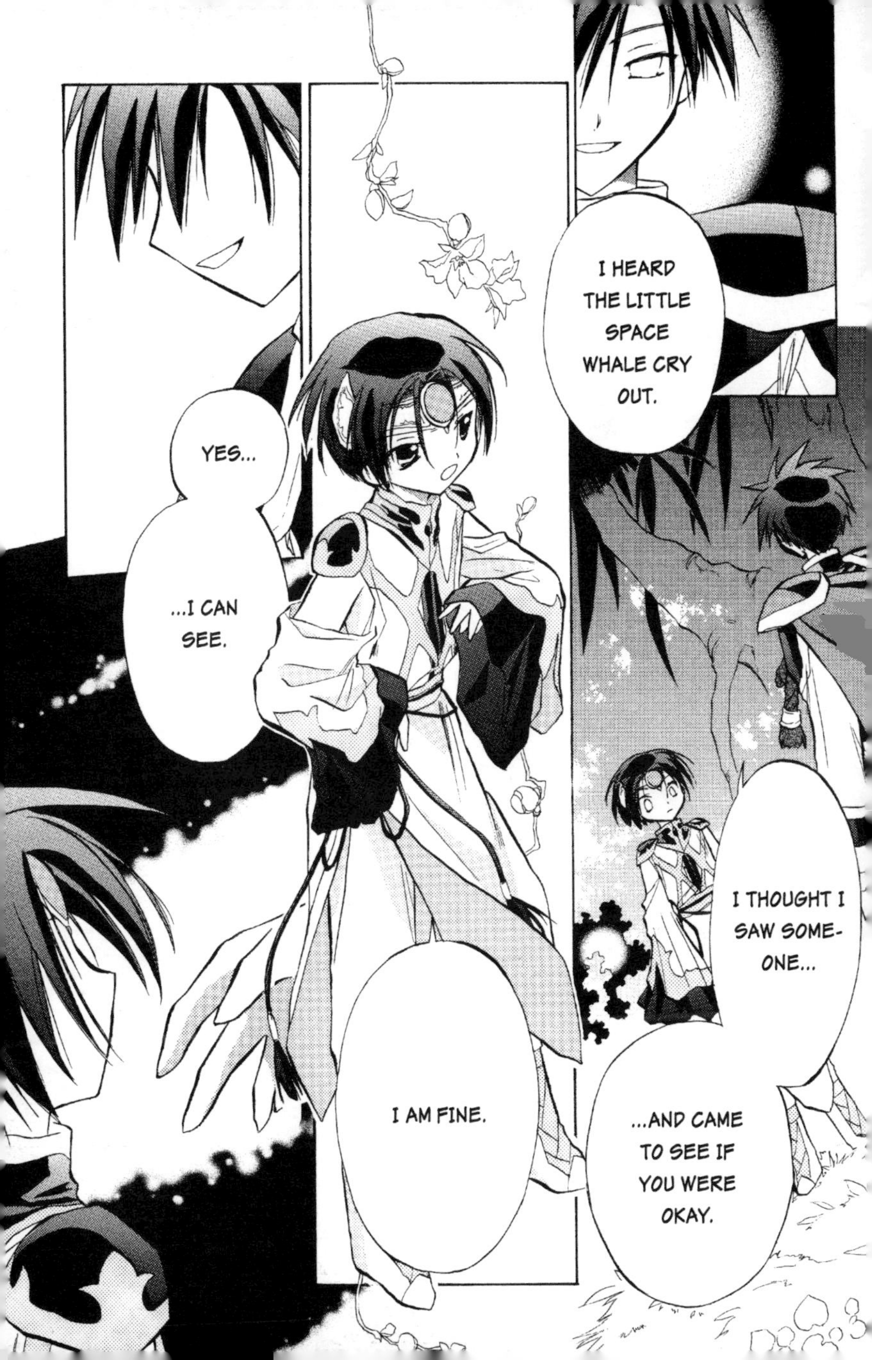
I HEARD THE LITTLE SPACE WHALE CRY OUT.
I THOUGHT I SAW SOME-ONE...
...AND CAME TO SEE IF YOU WERE OKAY.
YES...
...I CAN SEE.
I AM FINE.

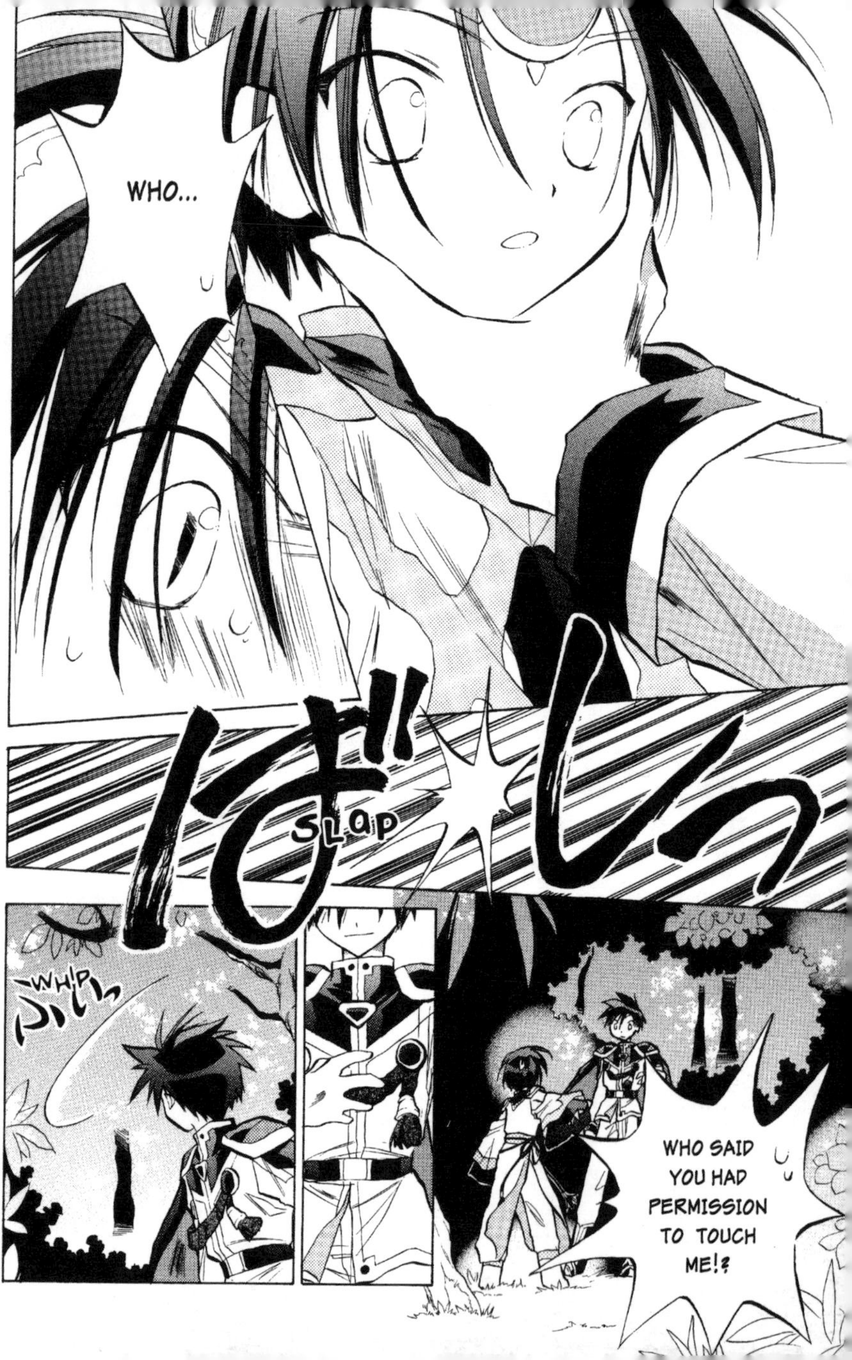
WHO...
ぱしっ
SLAP
WHO SAID YOU HAD PERMISSION TO TOUCH ME!?
ふいっ
WHIP

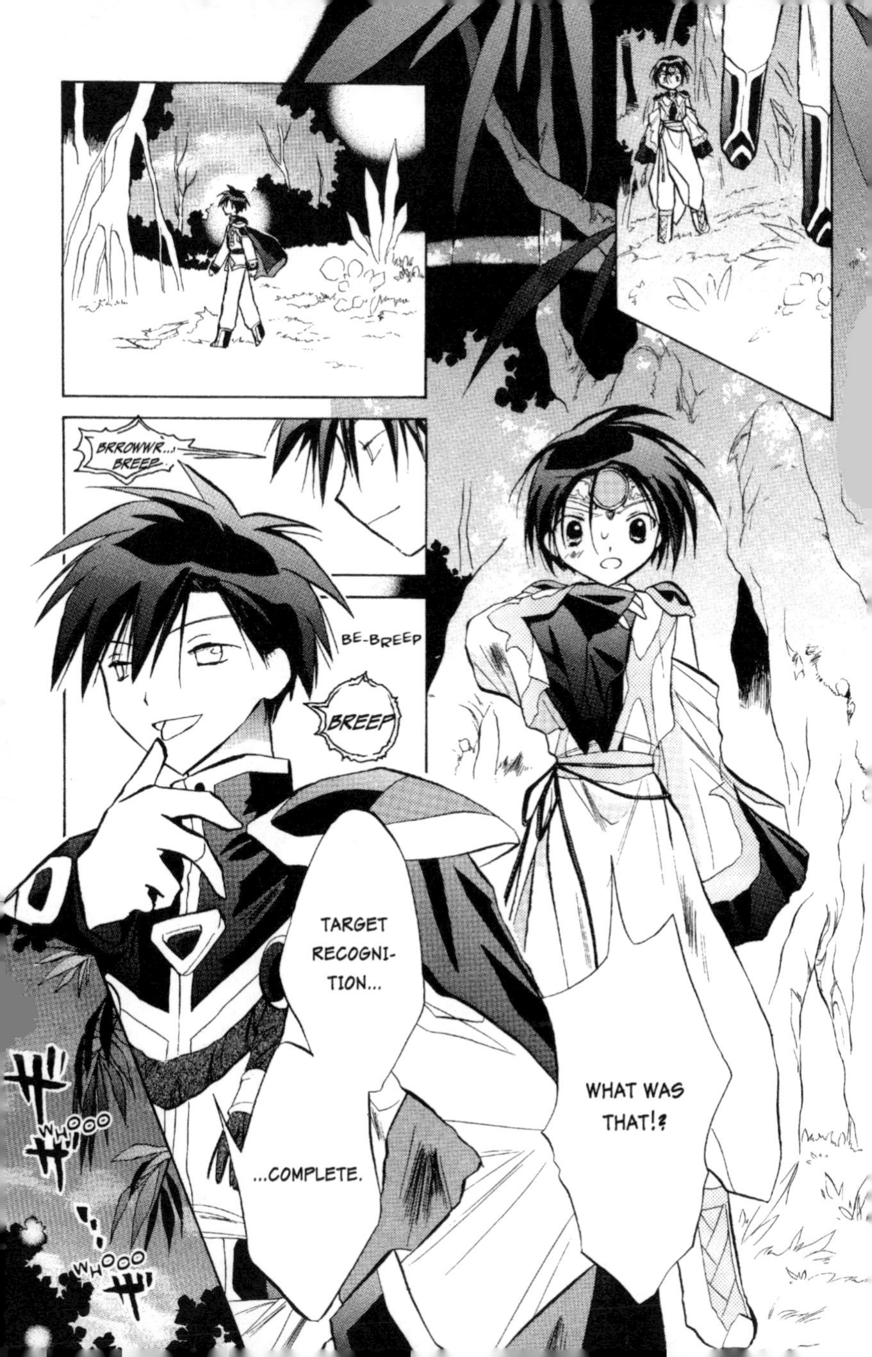
WHAT WAS THAT!?
BRROWWR... BREEP
BE-BREEP
BREEP
TARGET RECOGNITION...
...COMPLETE.
WHOOO
WHOOO

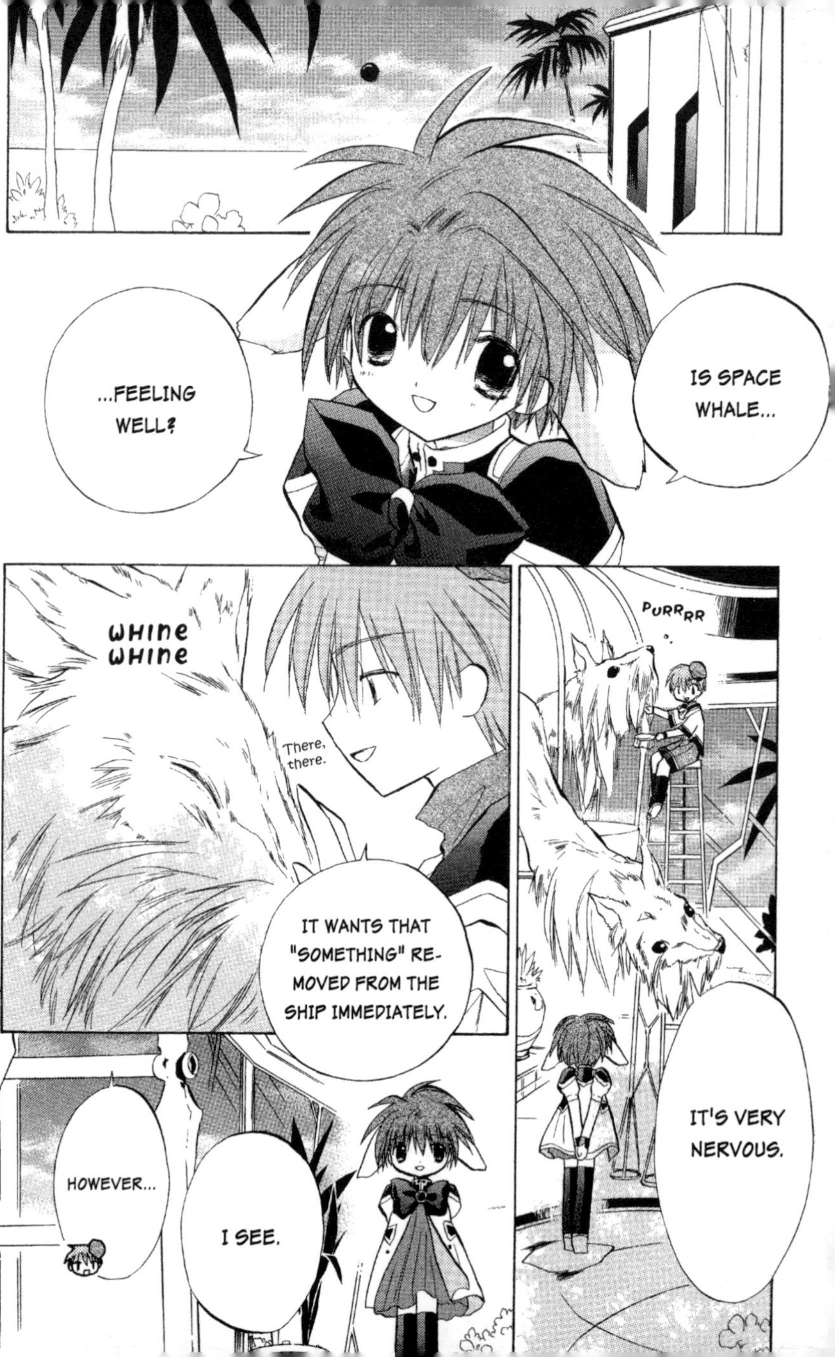
IS SPACE WHALE...
...FEELING WELL?
PURRRR
IT'S VERY NERVOUS.
WHINE WHINE
There, there.
IT WANTS THAT "SOMETHING" RE-MOVED FROM THE SHIP IMMEDIATELY.
I SEE.
HOWEVER...

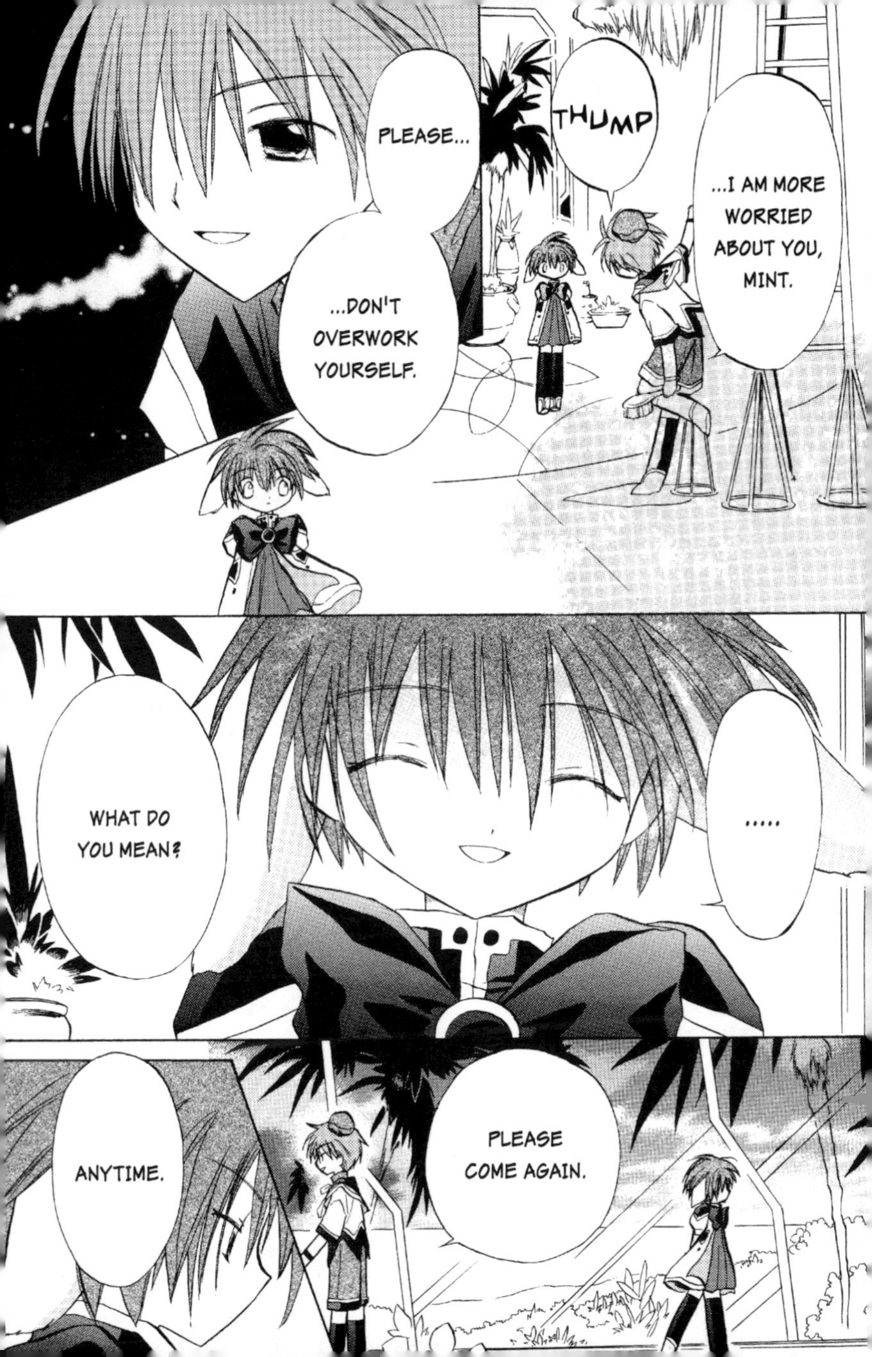
THUMP
...I AM MORE WORRIED ABOUT YOU, MINT.
PLEASE...
...DON'T OVERWORK YOURSELF.
.....
WHAT DO YOU MEAN?
PLEASE COME AGAIN.
ANYTIME.

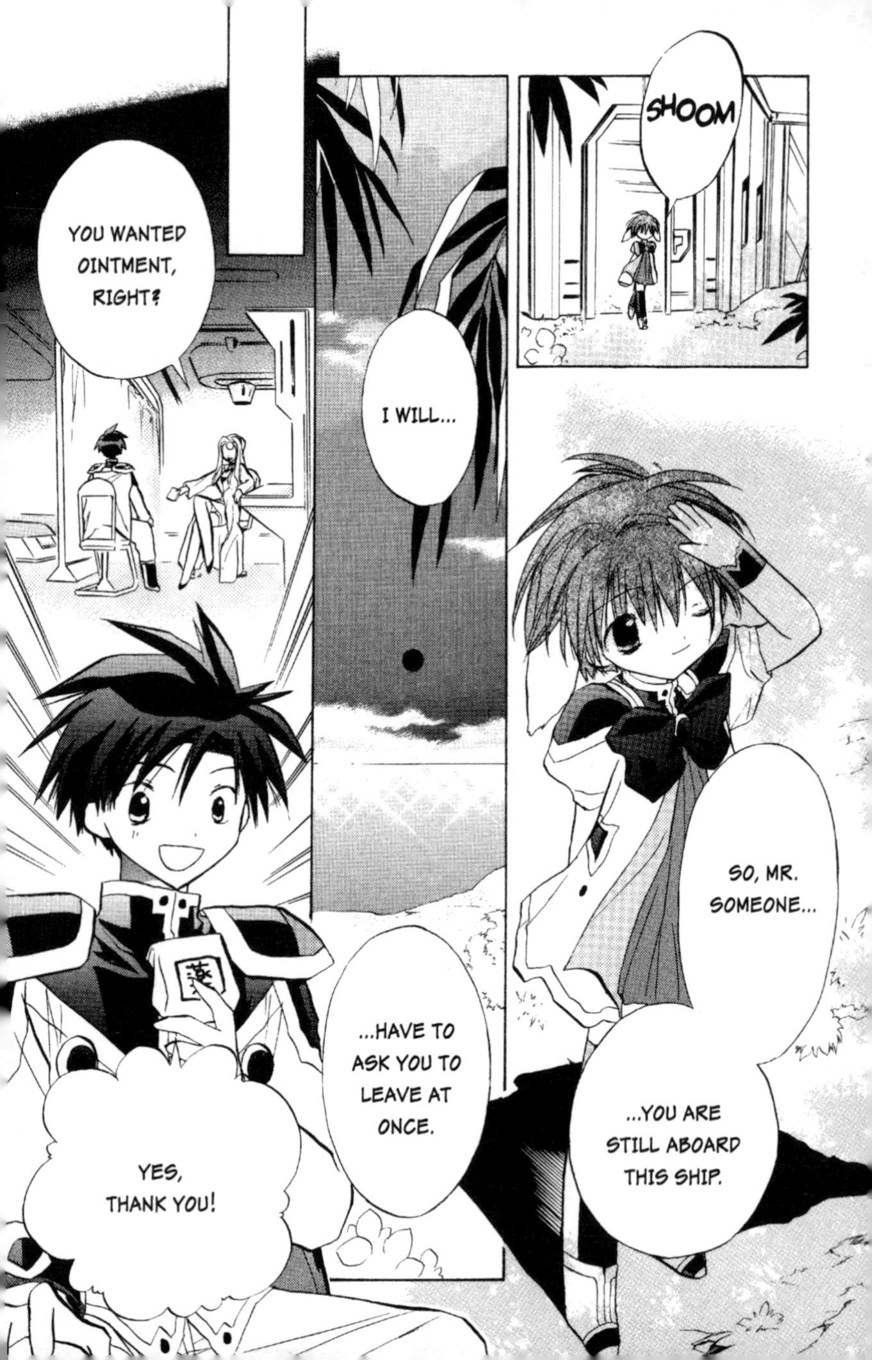
SHOOM
SO, MR. SOMEONE...
...YOU ARE STILL ABOARD THIS SHIP.
I WILL...
...HAVE TO ASK YOU TO LEAVE AT ONCE.
YOU WANTED OINTMENT, RIGHT?
YES, THANK YOU!

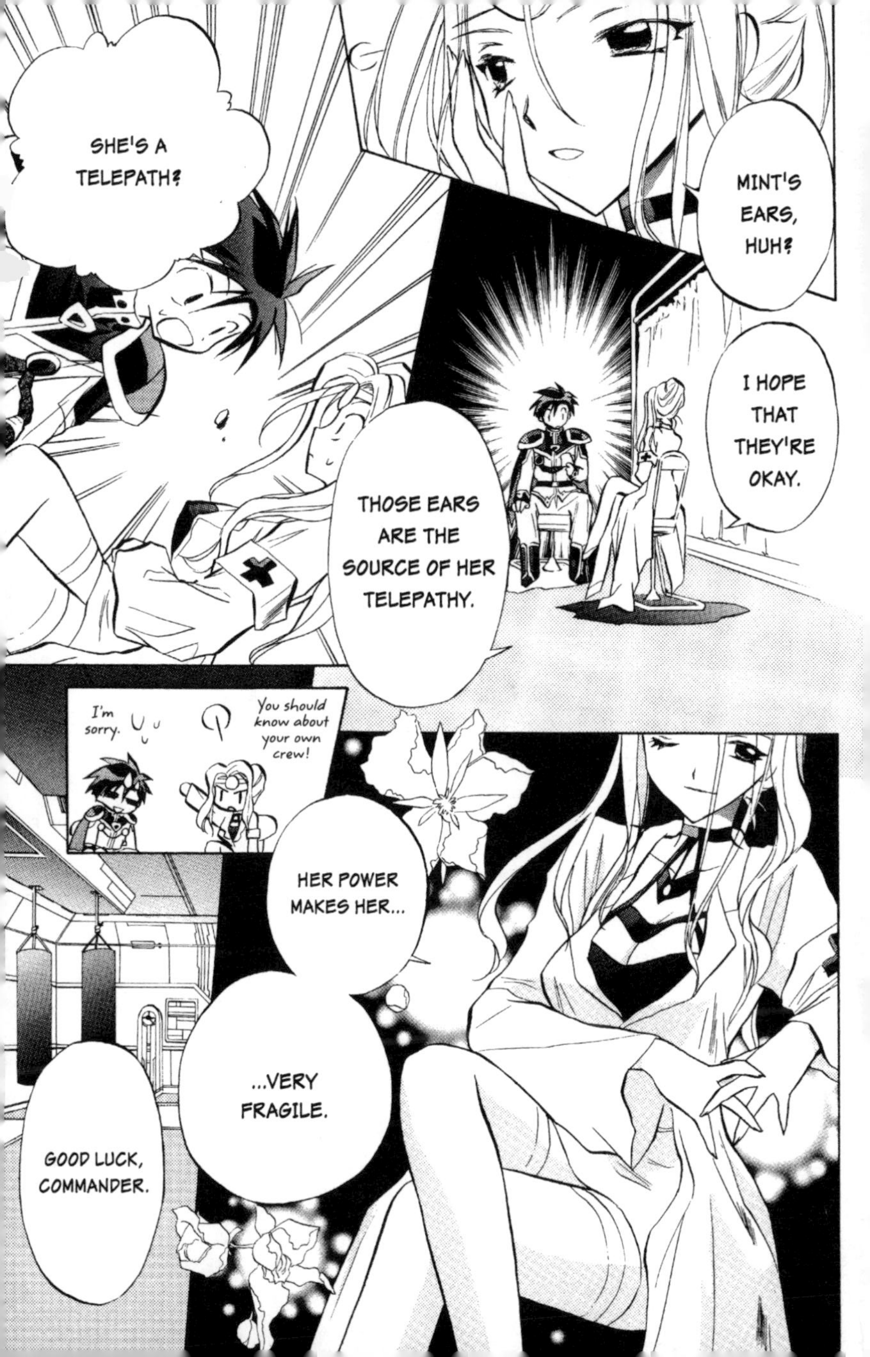
MINT'S EARS, HUH?
SHE'S A TELEPATH?
I HOPE THAT THEY'RE OKAY.
THOSE EARS ARE THE SOURCE OF HER TELEPATHY.
You should know about your own crew!
I'm sorry.
HER POWER MAKES HER...
...VERY FRAGILE.
GOOD LUCK, COMMANDER.

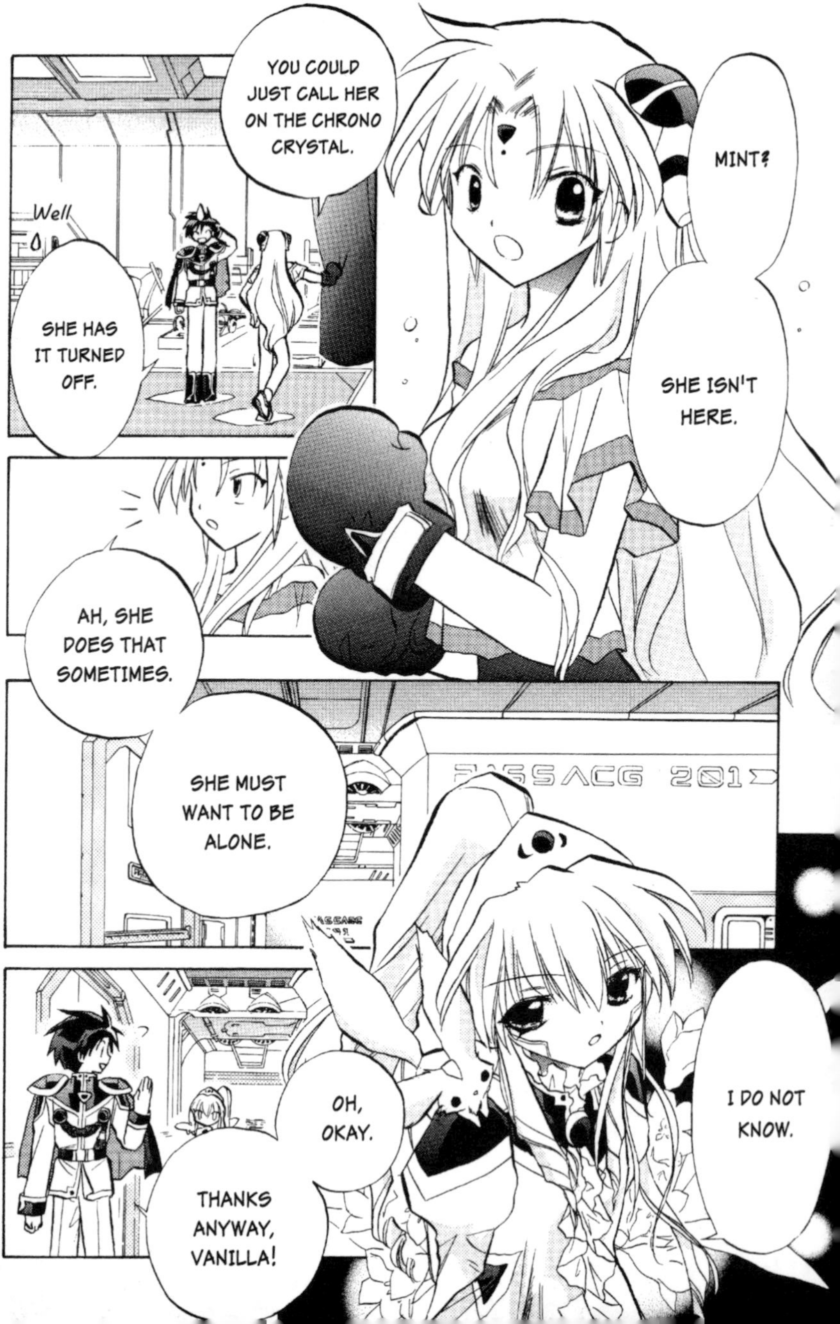
MINT?
SHE ISN'T HERE.
YOU COULD JUST CALL HER ON THE CHRONO CRYSTAL.
Well
SHE HAS IT TURNED OFF.
AH, SHE DOES THAT SOMETIMES.
SHE MUST WANT TO BE ALONE.
I DO NOT KNOW.
OH, OKAY.
THANKS ANYWAY, VANILLA!

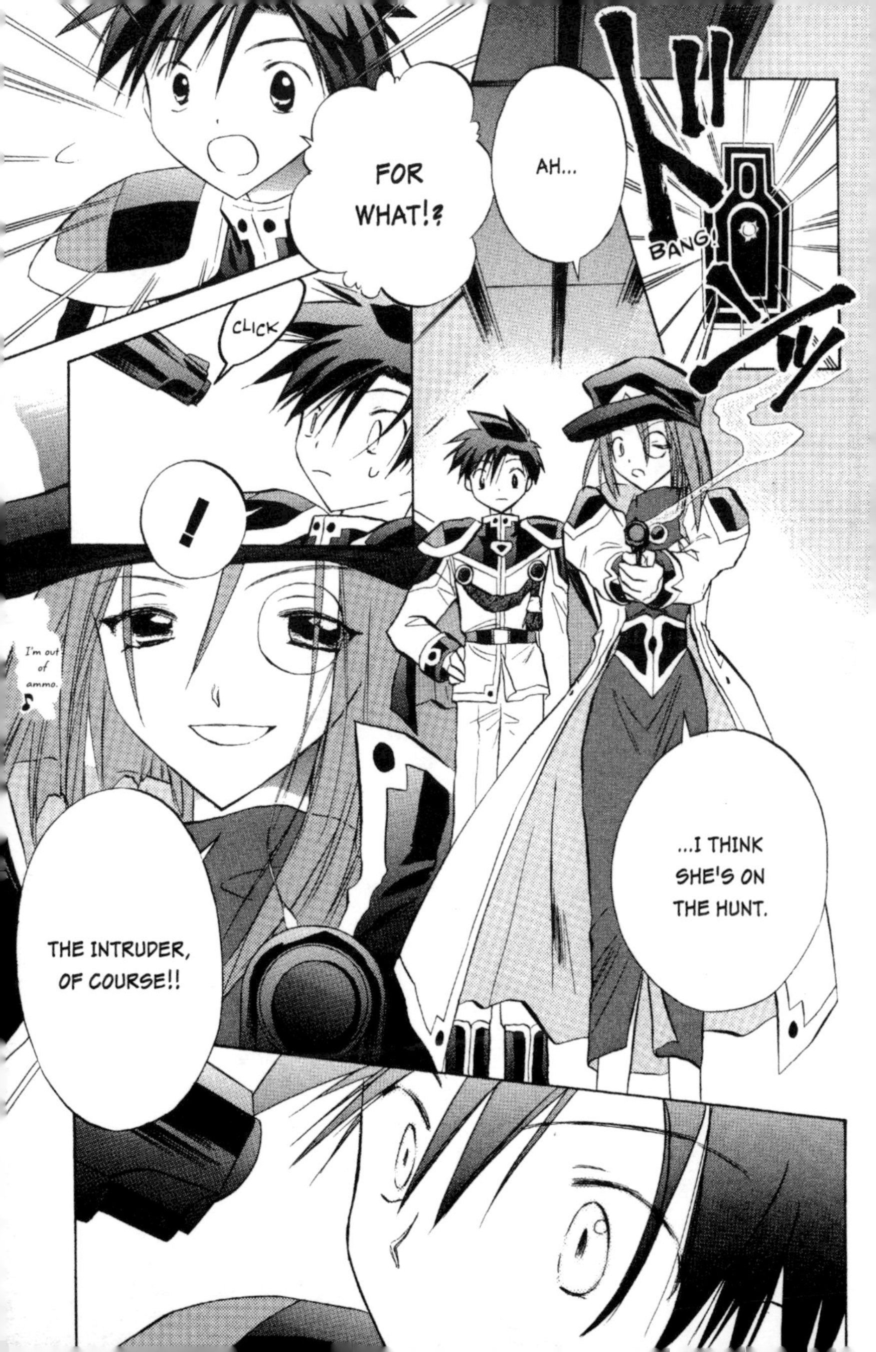
BANG!
AH...
...I THINK SHE'S ON THE HUNT.
FOR WHAT!?
CLICK
!
THE INTRUDER, OF COURSE!!
I'm out of ammo.

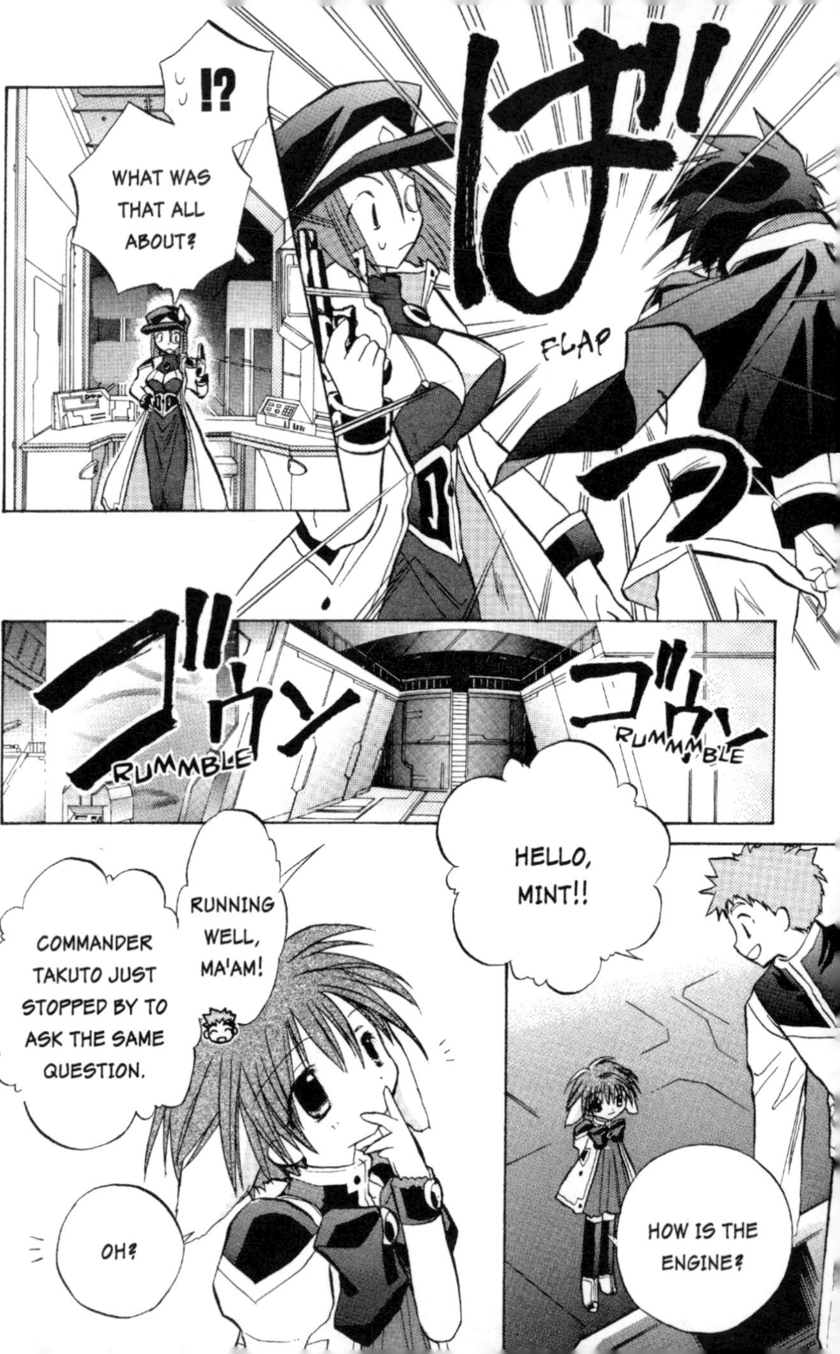
ぱっ
FLAP
!?
WHAT WAS THAT ALL ABOUT?
ゴウン
RUMMMBLE
ゴウン
RUMMBLE
HELLO, MINT!!
HOW IS THE ENGINE?
RUNNING WELL, MA'AM!
COMMANDER TAKUTO JUST STOPPED BY TO ASK THE SAME QUESTION.
OH?

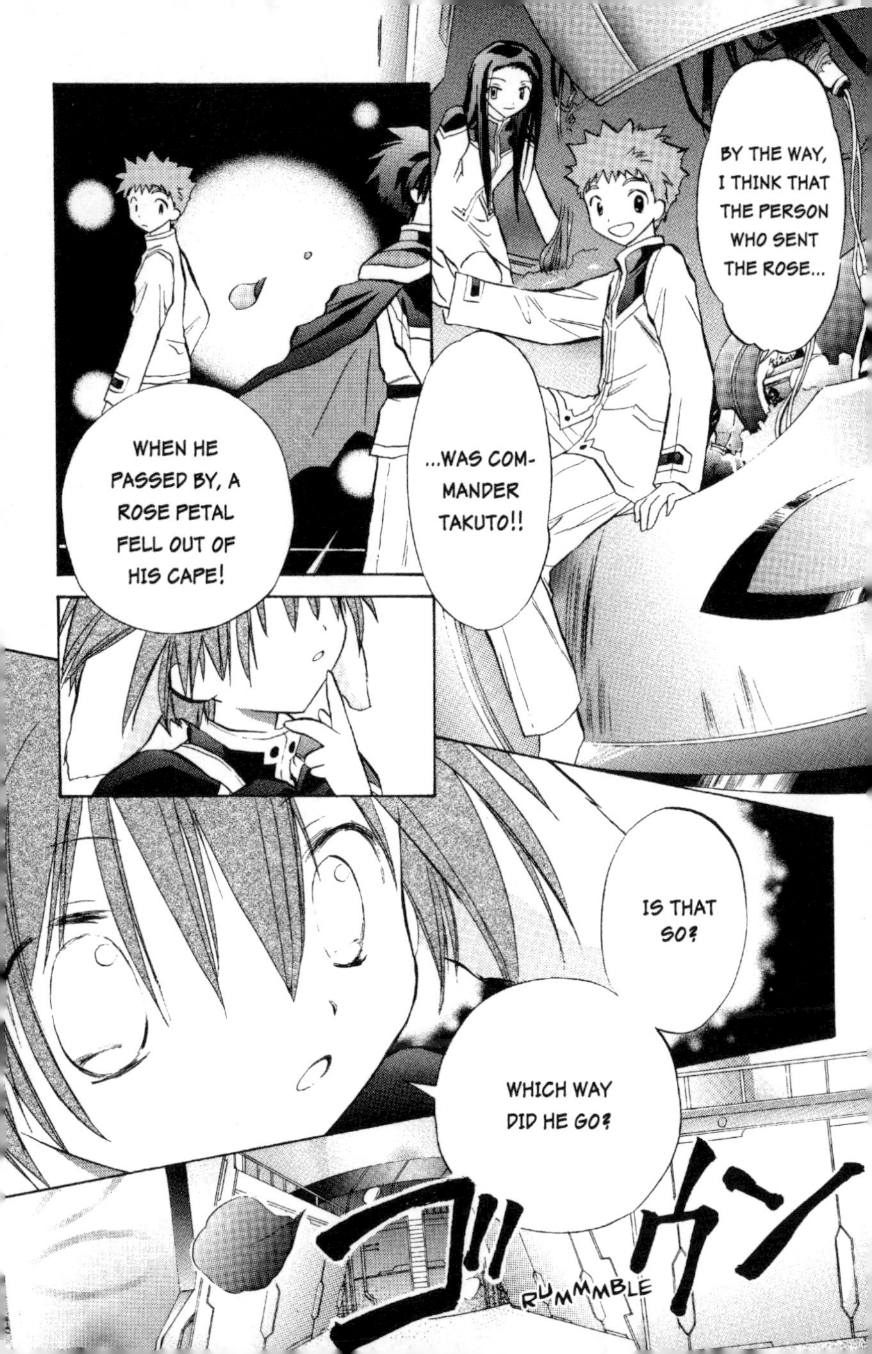
BY THE WAY, I THINK THAT THE PERSON WHO SENT THE ROSE...
...WAS COM-MANDER TAKUTO!!
WHEN HE PASSED BY, A ROSE PETAL FELL OUT OF HIS CAPE!
IS THAT SO?
WHICH WAY DID HE GO?
ゴウン
RUMMMBLE

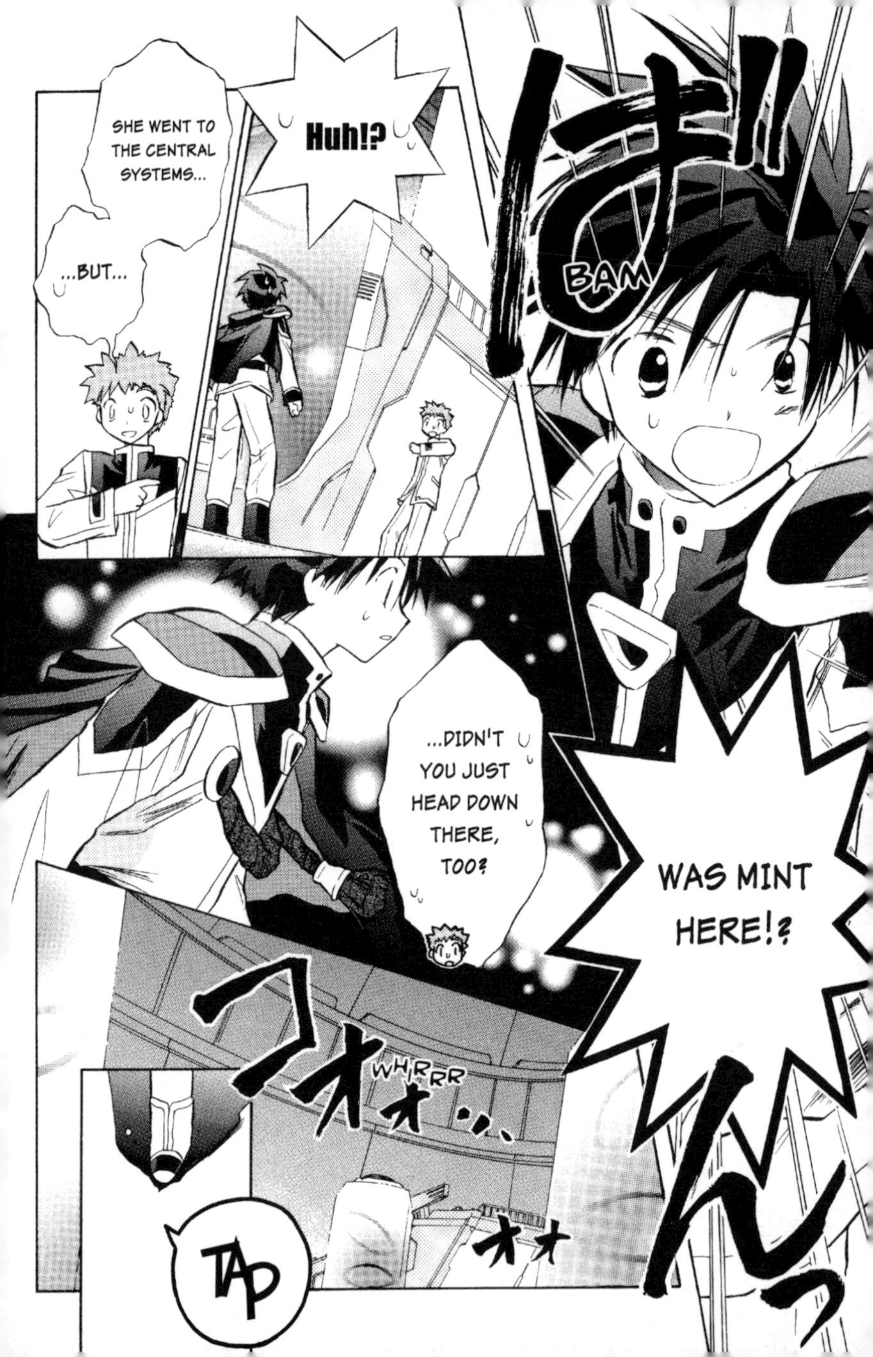
BAM
WAS MINT HERE!?
Huh!?
SHE WENT TO THE CENTRAL SYSTEMS...
...BUT...
...DIDN'T YOU JUST HEAD DOWN THERE, TOO?
WHIRRR
TAP

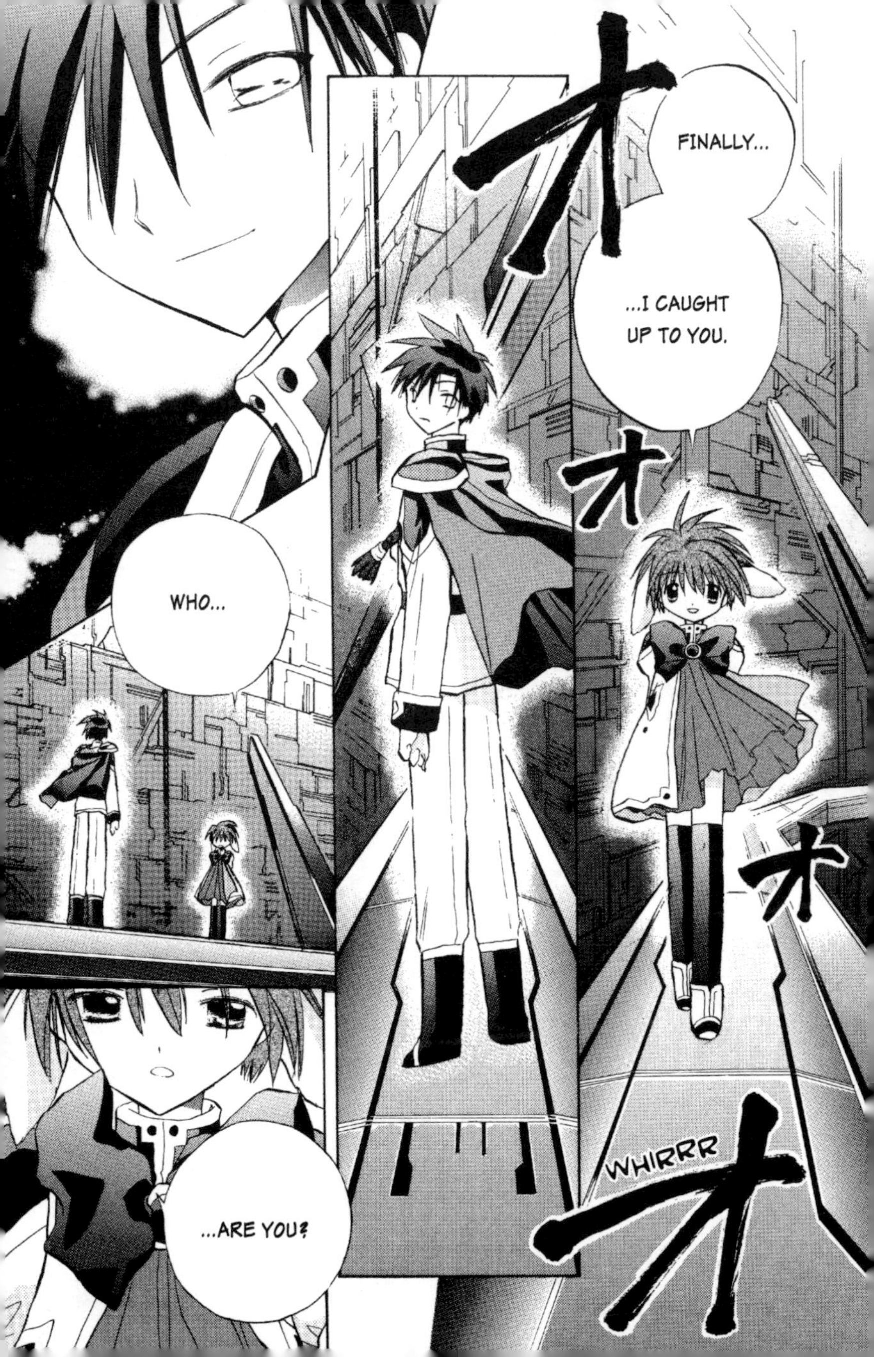
FINALLY...
...I CAUGHT UP TO YOU.
WHIRRR
WHO...
...ARE YOU?

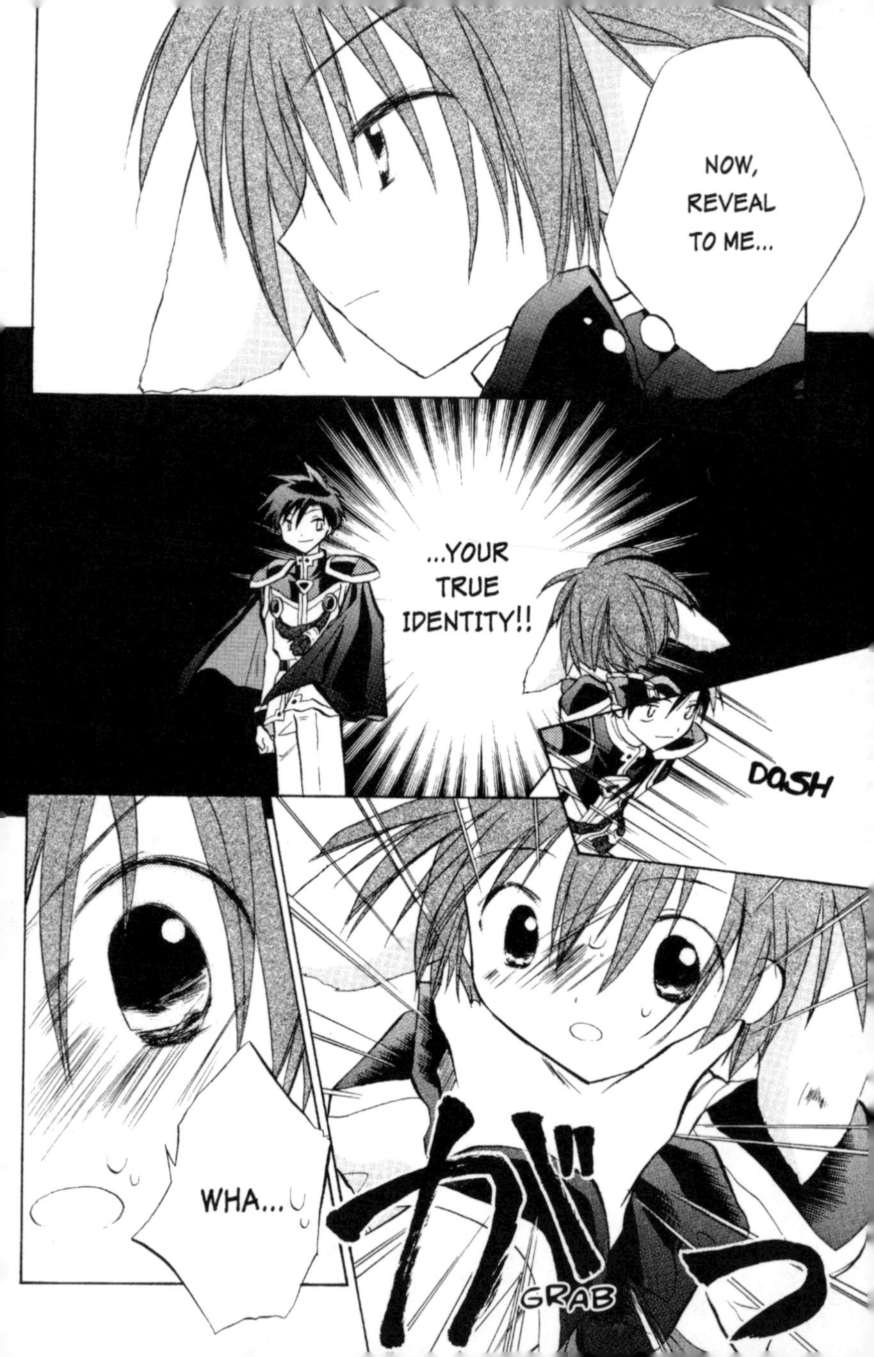
NOW, REVEAL TO ME...
...YOUR TRUE IDENTITY!!
DASH
GRAB
WHA...

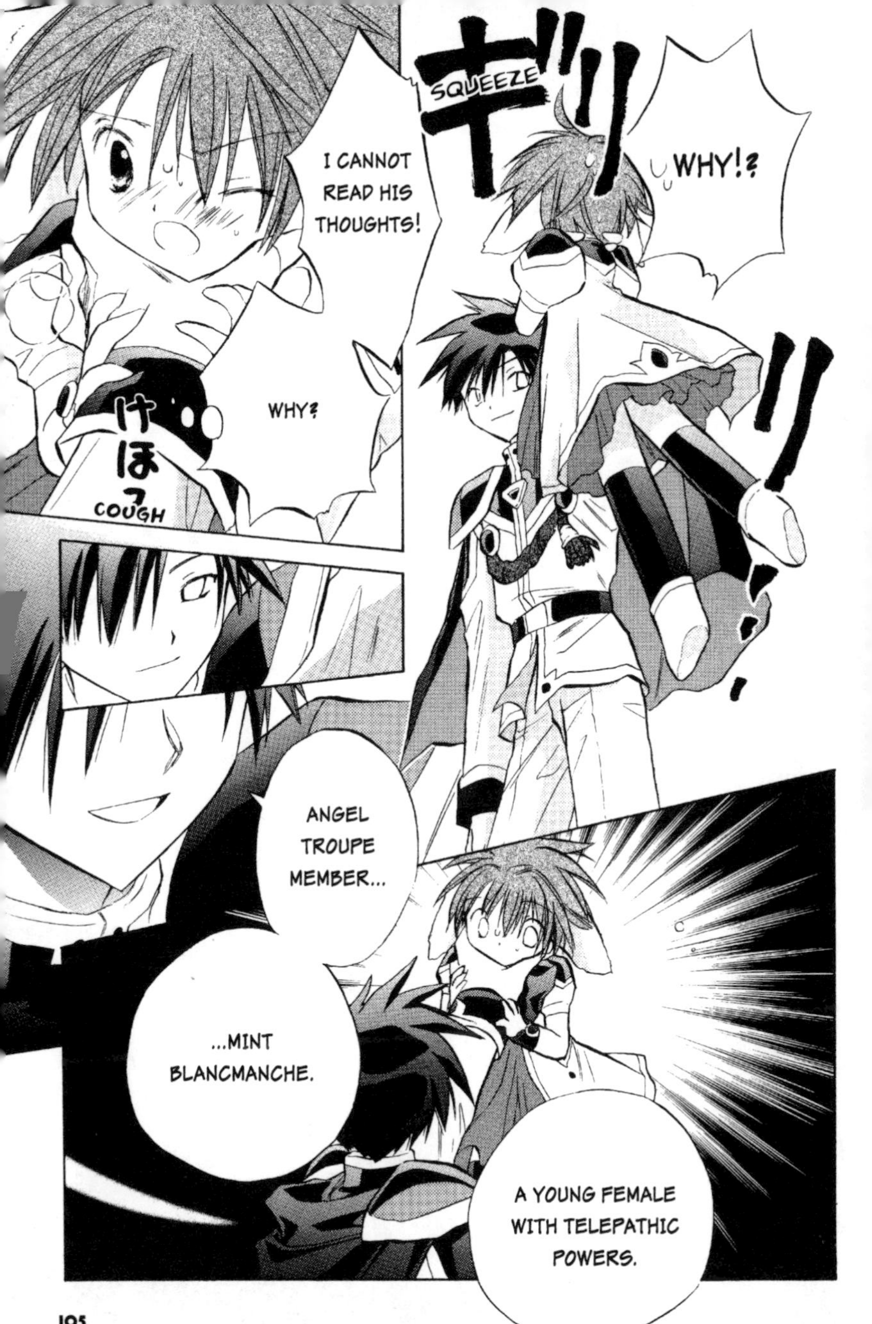
ギリ
SQUEEZE
WHY!?
I CANNOT READ HIS THOUGHTS!
WHY?
けほっ
COUGH
ANGEL TROUPE MEMBER...
...MINT BLANCMANCHE.
A YOUNG FEMALE WITH TELEPATHIC POWERS.

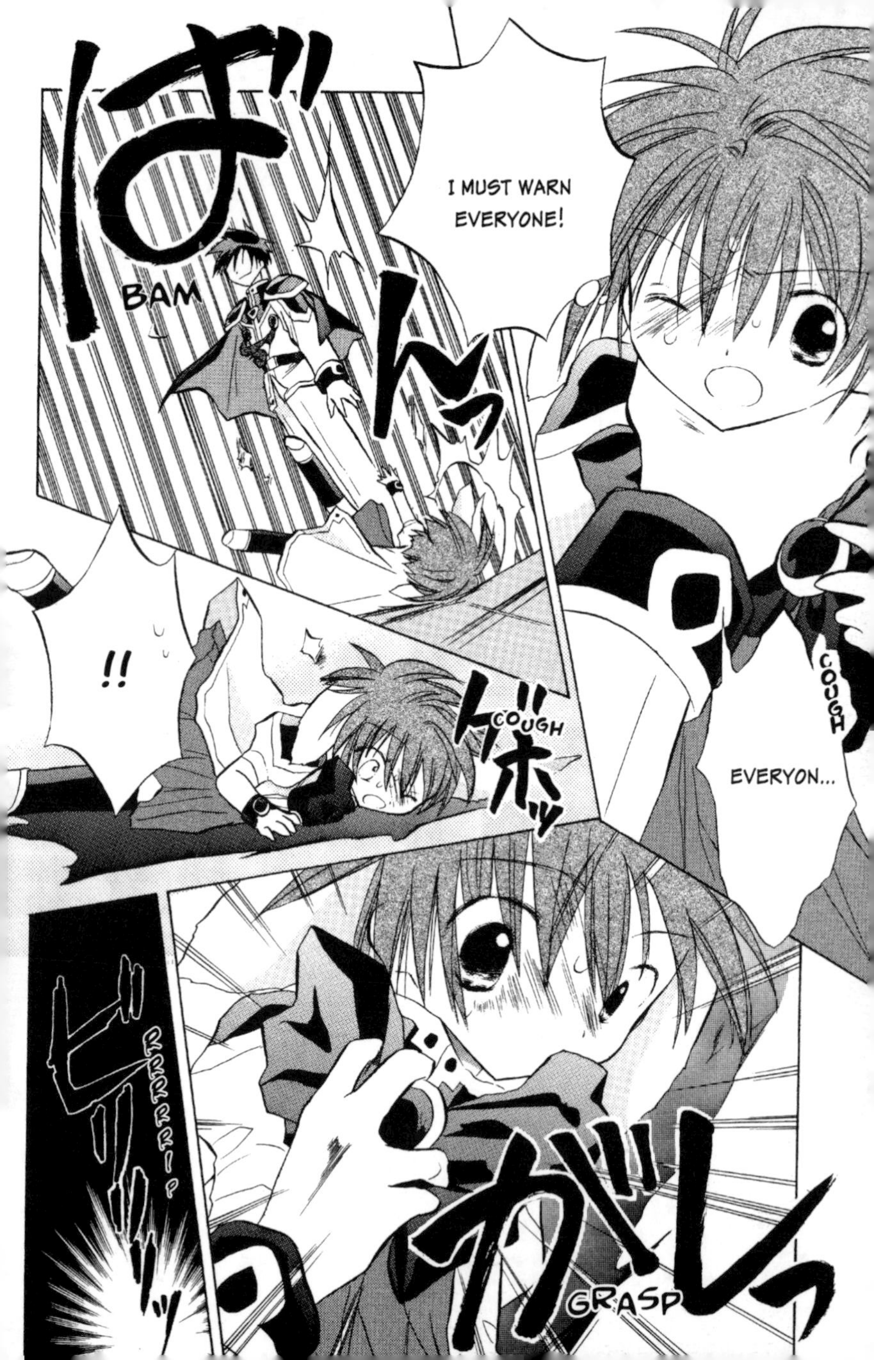
I MUST WARN EVERYONE!
COUGH
EVERYON...
ばんっ
BAM
!!
ゲホッ
COUGH
ビリッ
RRRRRIP
がしっ
GRASP

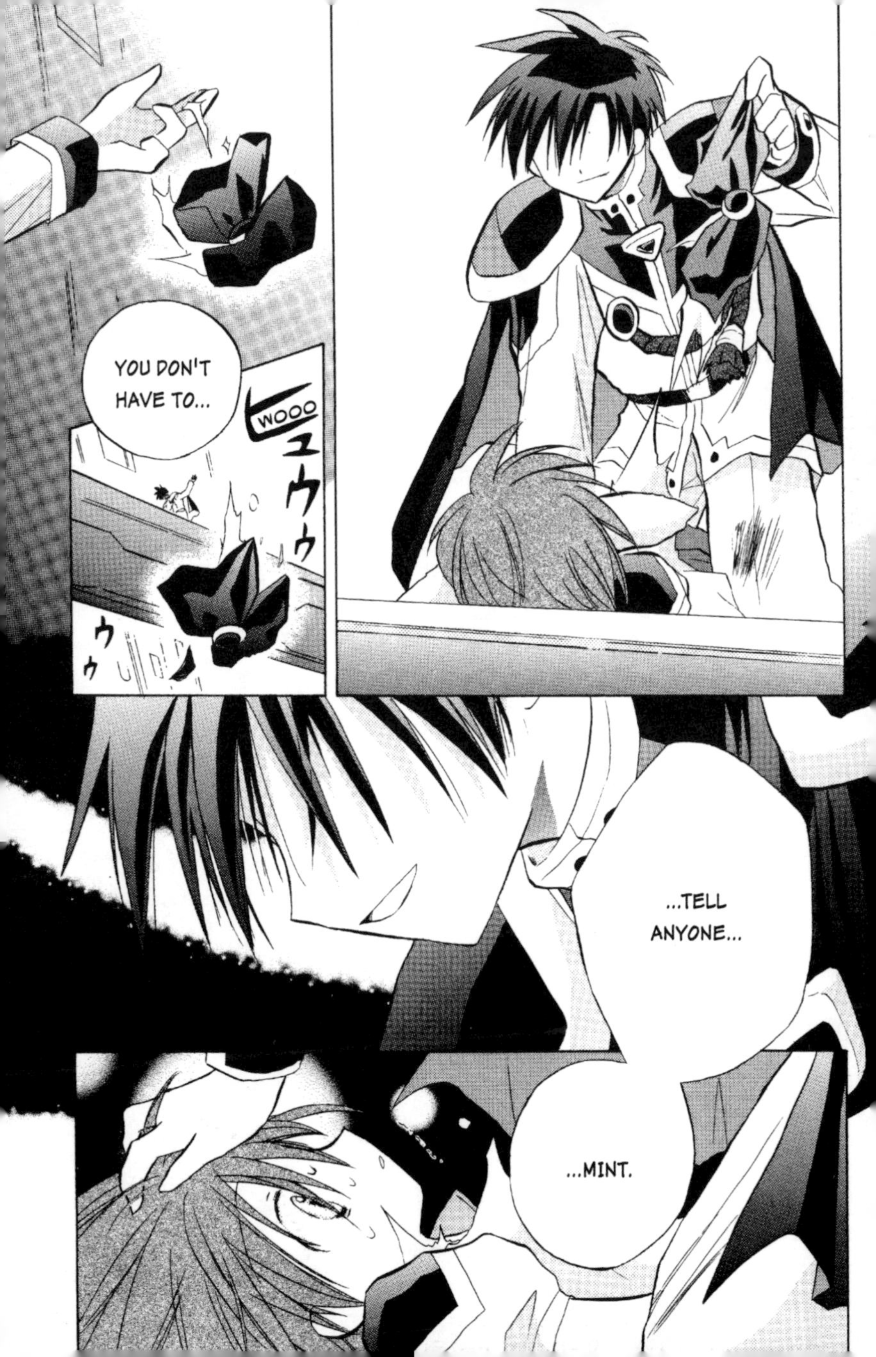
YOU DON'T HAVE TO...
WOOO
...TELL ANYONE...
...MINT.

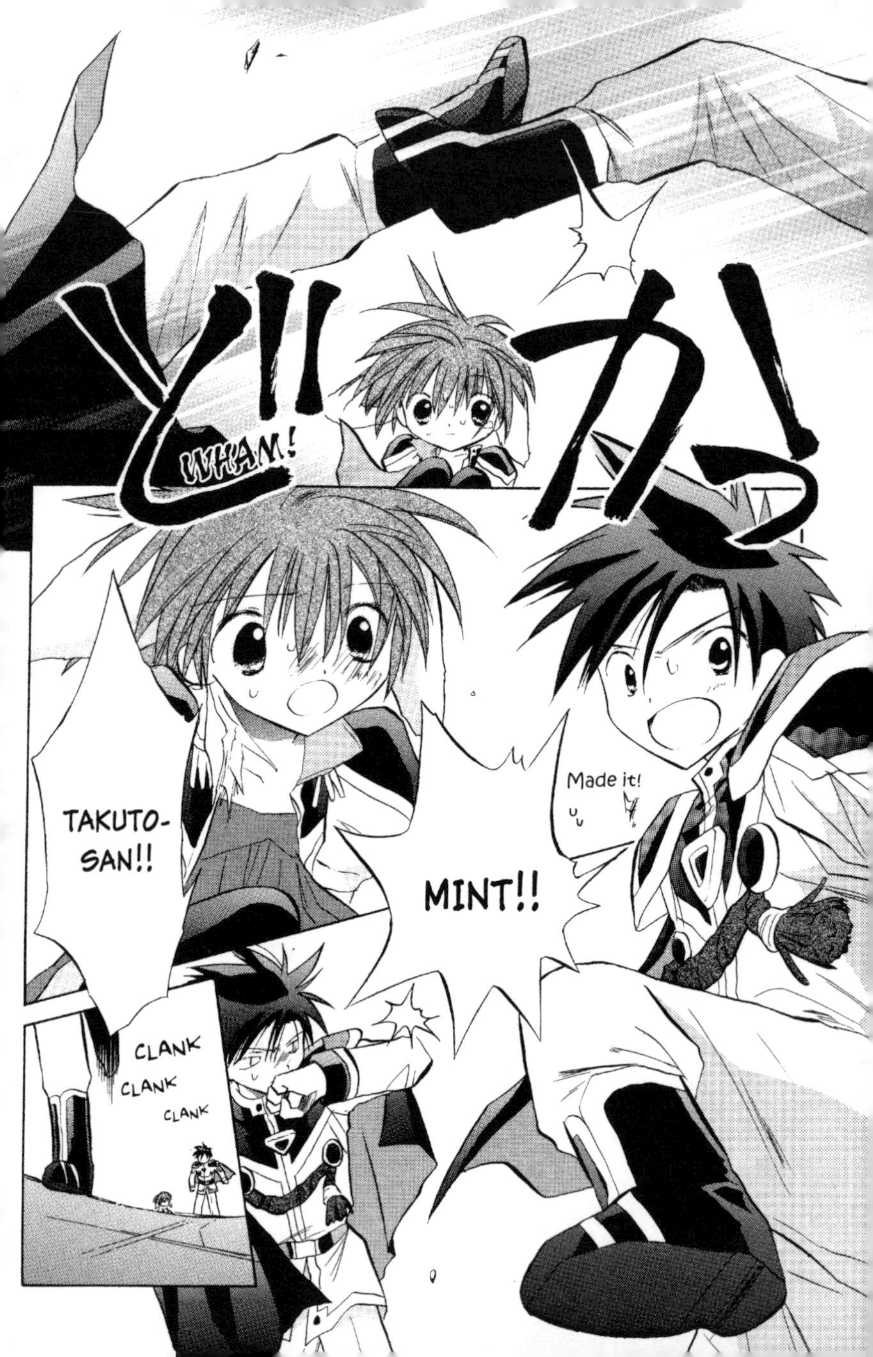
WHAM!
Made it!
MINT!!
TAKUTO-SAN!!
CLANK
CLANK
CLANK

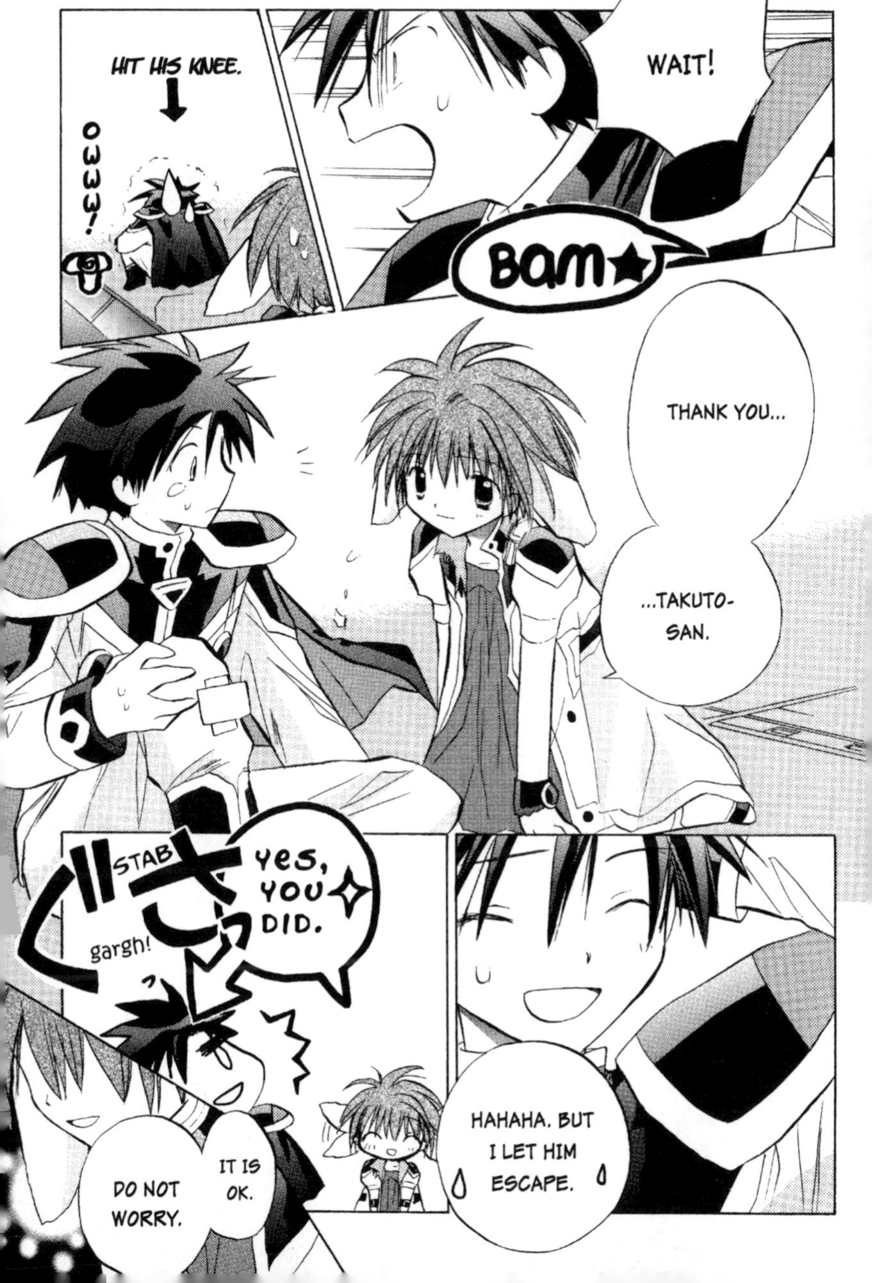
WAIT!
BAM★
HIT HIS KNEE.
OWWW!
THANK YOU...
...TAKUTO-SAN.
HAHAHA. BUT I LET HIM ESCAPE.
YES, YOU DID.
STAB
gargh!
IT IS OK.
DO NOT WORRY.

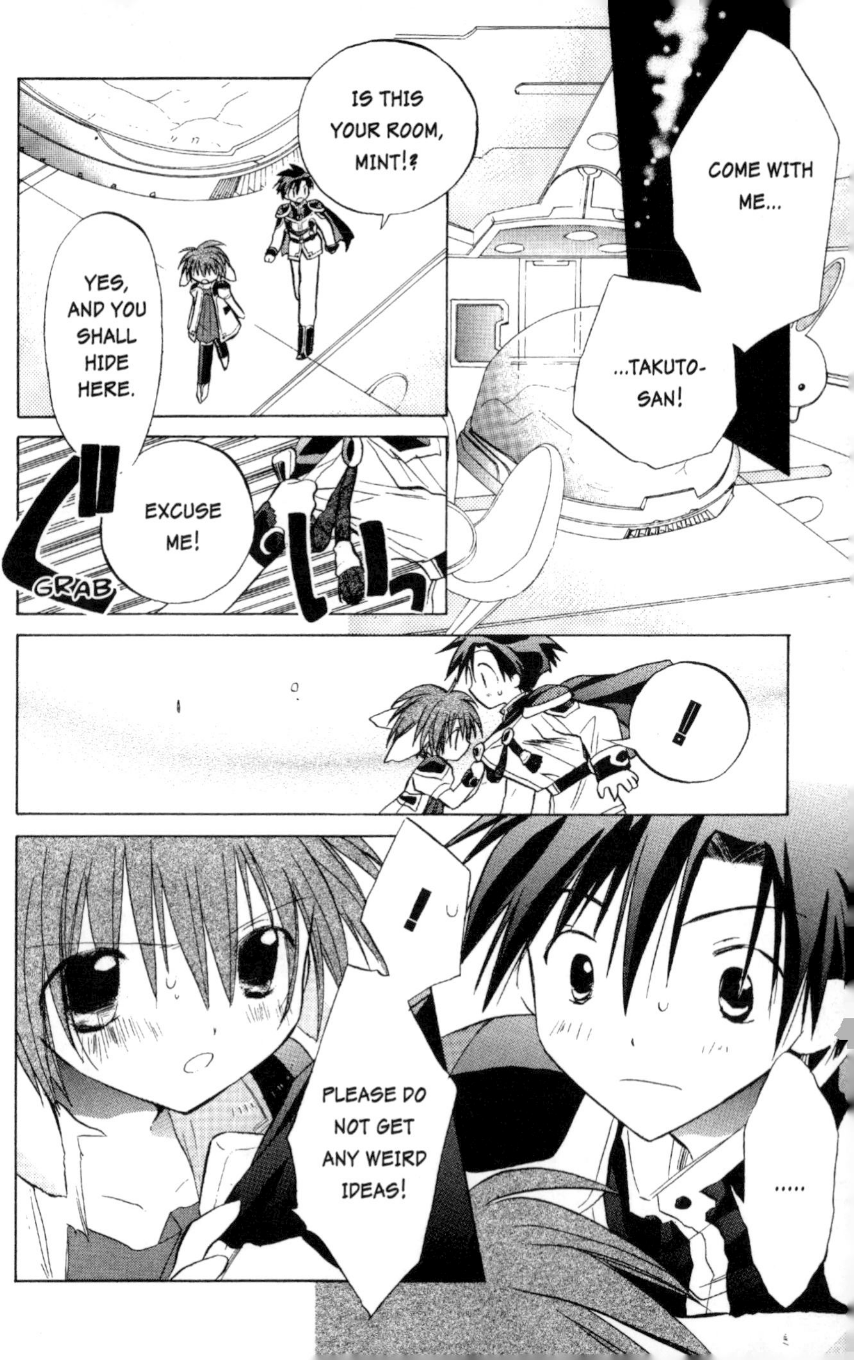
COME WITH ME...
...TAKUTO-SAN!
IS THIS YOUR ROOM, MINT!?
YES, AND YOU SHALL HIDE HERE.
EXCUSE ME!
GRAB
!
!
PLEASE DO NOT GET ANY WEIRD IDEAS!
.....

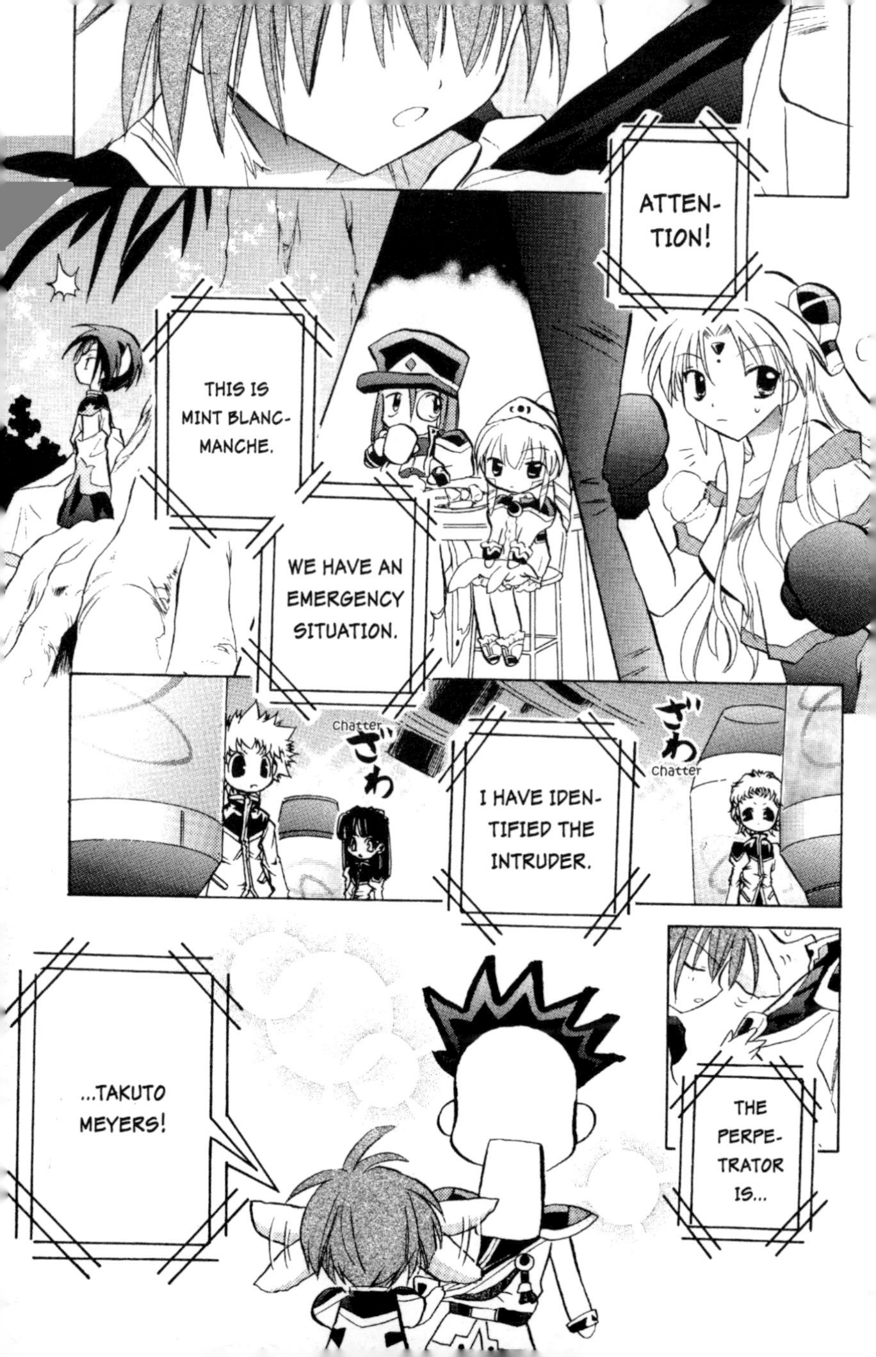
ATTEN-TION!
THIS IS MINT BLANC-MANCHE.
WE HAVE AN EMERGENCY SITUATION.
ざわ
Chatter
I HAVE IDEN-TIFIED THE INTRUDER.
Chatter
ざわ
THE PERPE-TRATOR IS...
...TAKUTO MEYERS!

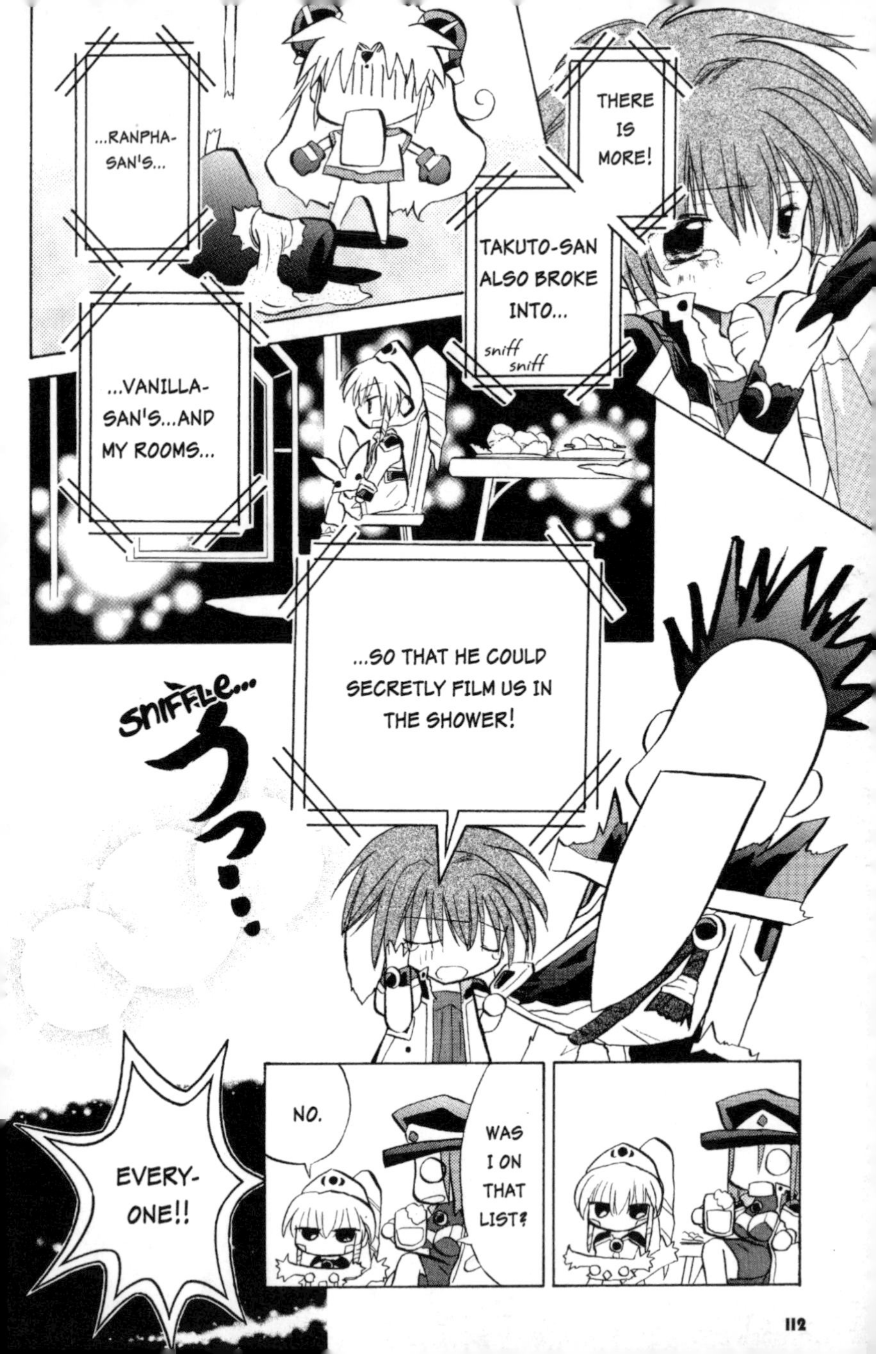
THERE IS MORE!
TAKUTO-SAN ALSO BROKE INTO...
sniff sniff
...RANPHA-SAN'S...
...VANILLA-SAN'S...AND MY ROOMS...
...SO THAT HE COULD SECRETLY FILM US IN THE SHOWER!
SNIFFLE...
う...
EVERY-ONE!!
WAS I ON THAT LIST?
NO.

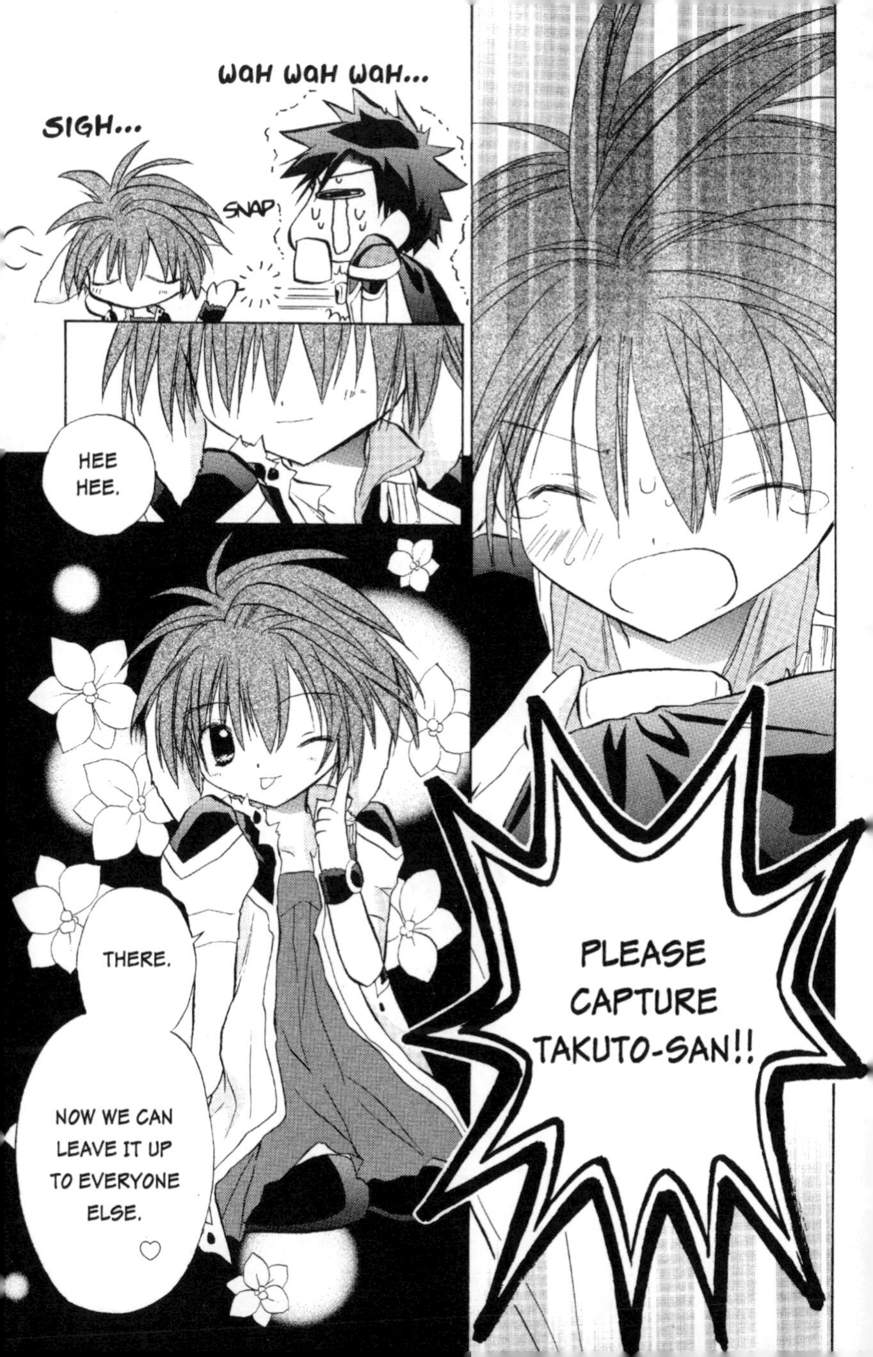
PLEASE CAPTURE TAKUTO-SAN!!
WAH WAH WAH...
SNAP
SIGH...
HEE HEE.
THERE.
NOW WE CAN LEAVE IT UP TO EVERYONE ELSE.

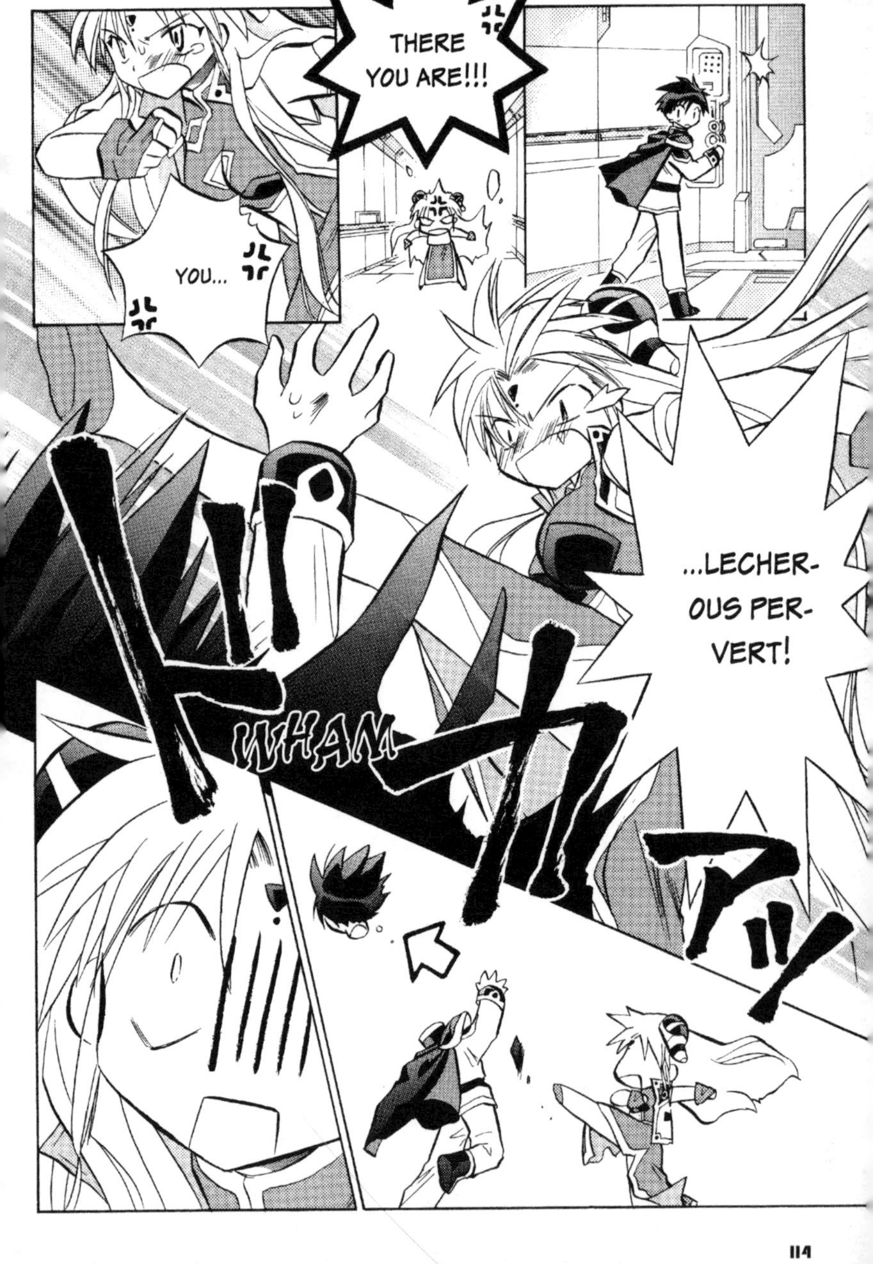
THERE YOU ARE!!!
YOU...
...LECHER-OUS PER-VERT!
WHAM

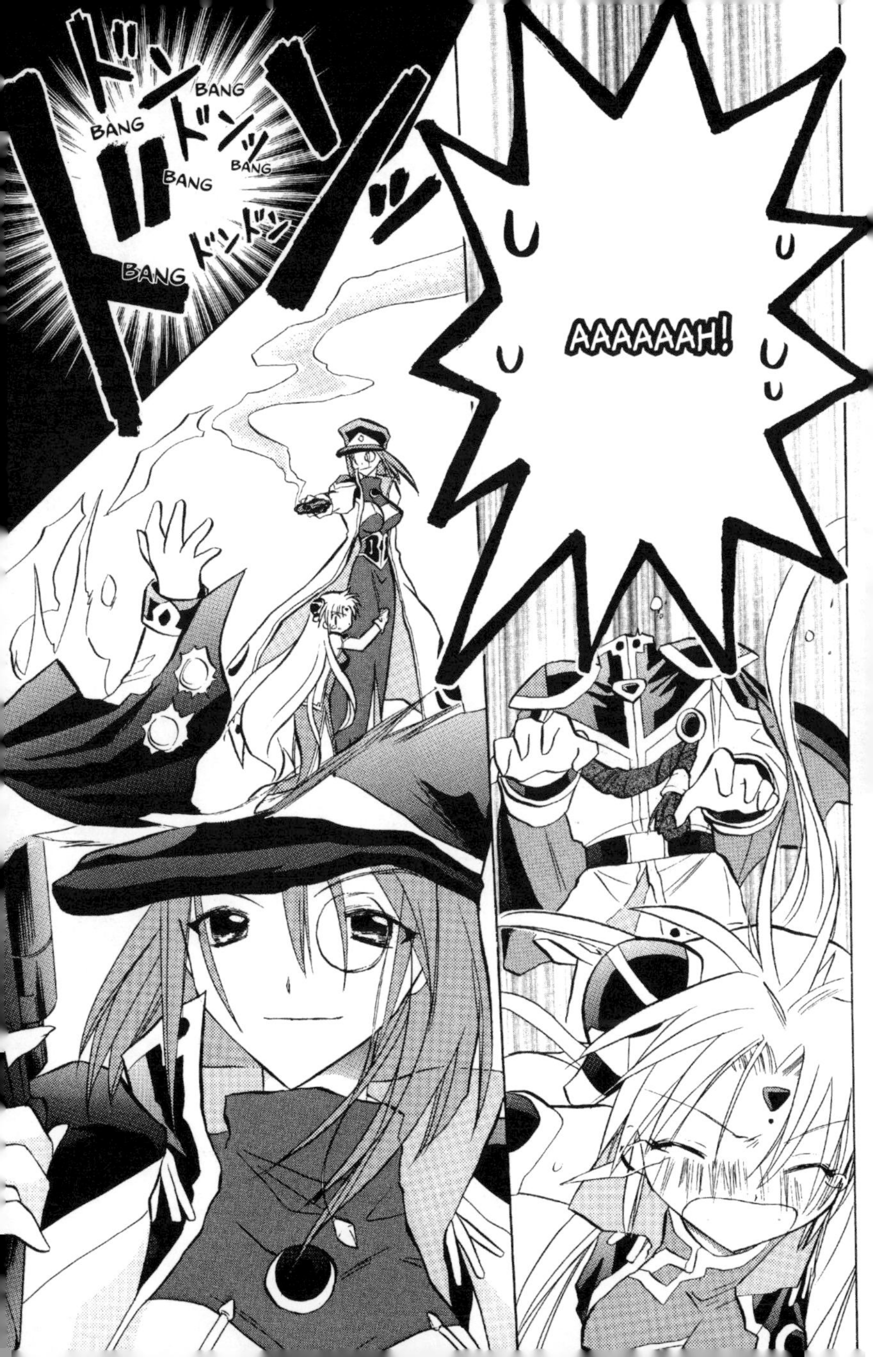
AAAAAAH!
BANG
BANG
BANG
BANG
BANG

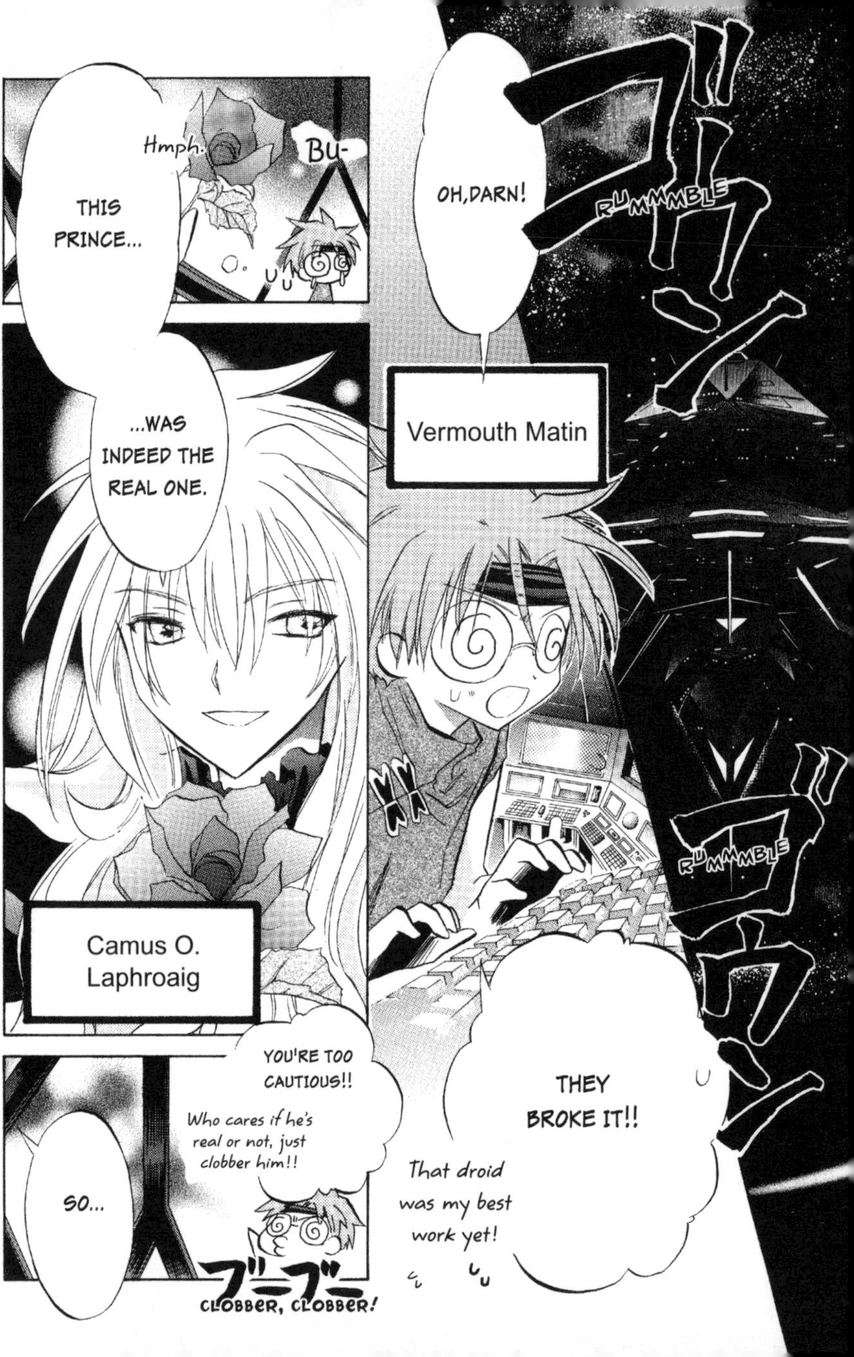
OH, DARN!
RUMMMBLE
Vermouth Matin
RUMMMBLE
THEY BROKE IT!!
That droid was my best work yet!
Hmph.
BU-
THIS PRINCE...
...WAS INDEED THE REAL ONE.
Camus O. Laphroaig
YOU'RE TOO CAUTIOUS!!
Who cares if he's real or not, just clobber him!!
SO...
CLOBBER, CLOBBER!

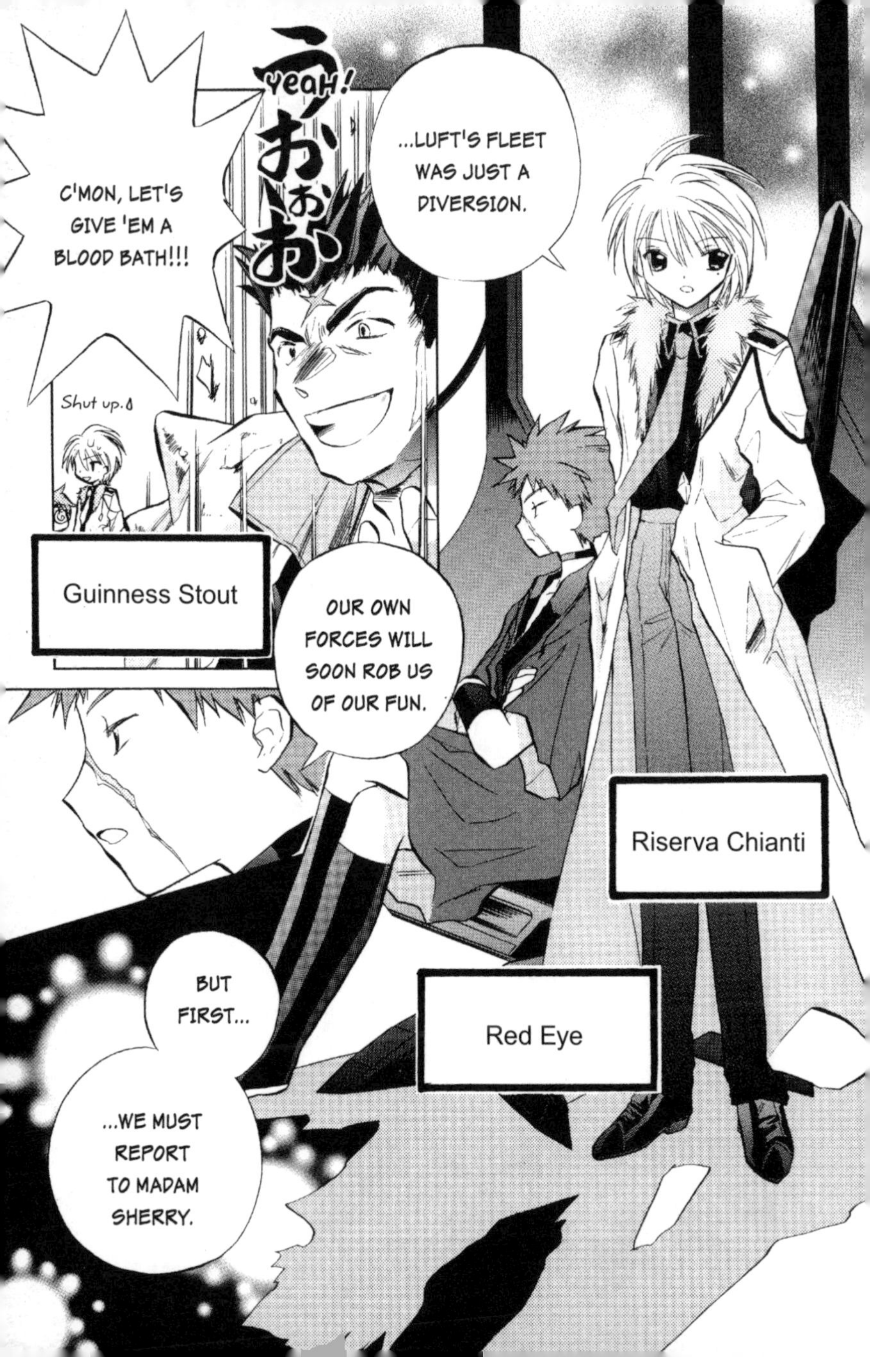
...LUFT'S FLEET WAS JUST A DIVERSION.
YEAH!
うおおお
C'MON, LET'S GIVE 'EM A BLOOD BATH!!!
Shut up.
Guinness Stout
OUR OWN FORCES WILL SOON ROB US OF OUR FUN.
Riserva Chianti
Red Eye
BUT FIRST...
...WE MUST REPORT TO MADAM SHERRY.

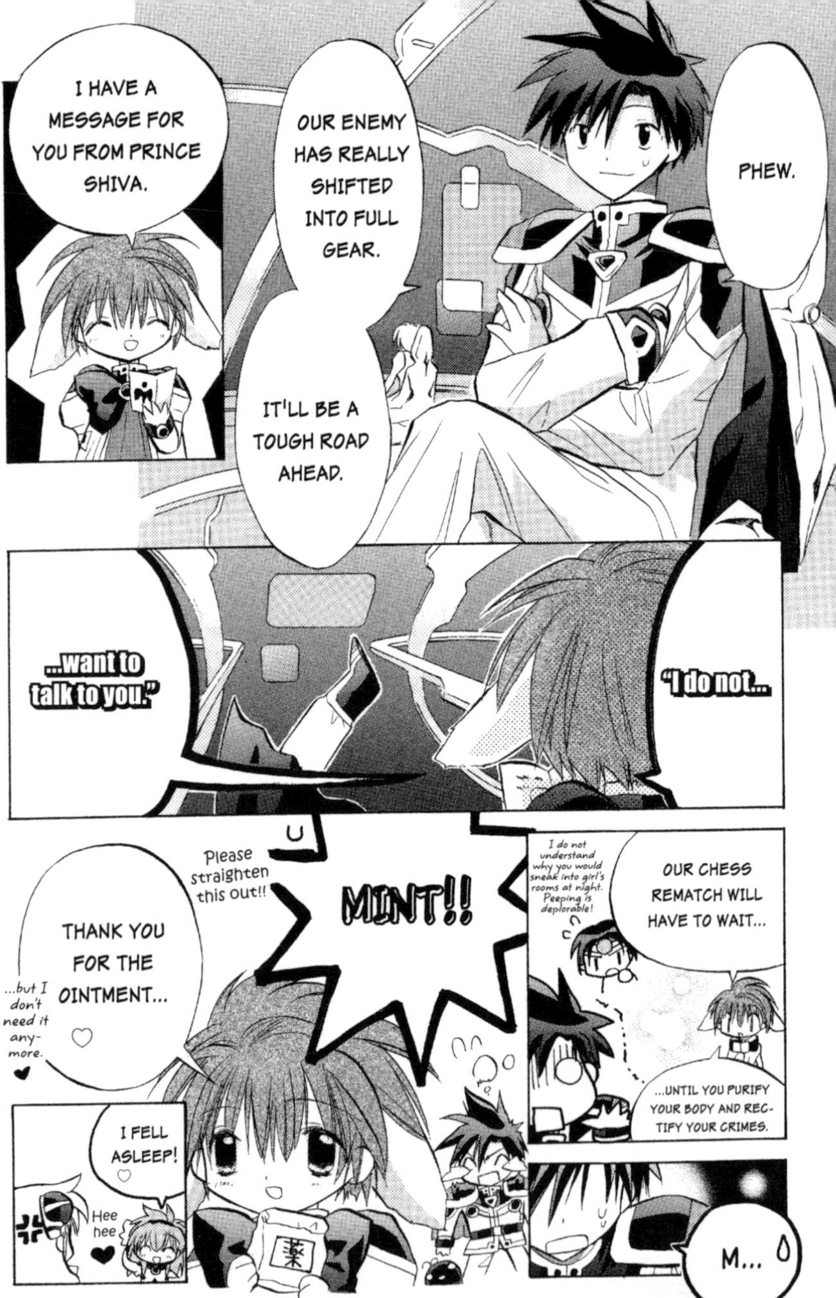
PHEW.
OUR ENEMY HAS REALLY SHIFTED INTO FULL GEAR.
IT'LL BE A TOUGH ROAD AHEAD.
I HAVE A MESSAGE FOR YOU FROM PRINCE SHIVA.
"I do not...
...want to talk to you."
OUR CHESS REMATCH WILL HAVE TO WAIT...
I do not understand why you would sneak into girl's rooms at night. Peeping is deplorable!
...UNTIL YOU PURIFY YOUR BODY AND RECTIFY YOUR CRIMES.
M...
MINT!!
Please straighten this out!!
THANK YOU FOR THE OINTMENT...
...but I don't need it anymore.
I FELL ASLEEP!
Hee hee

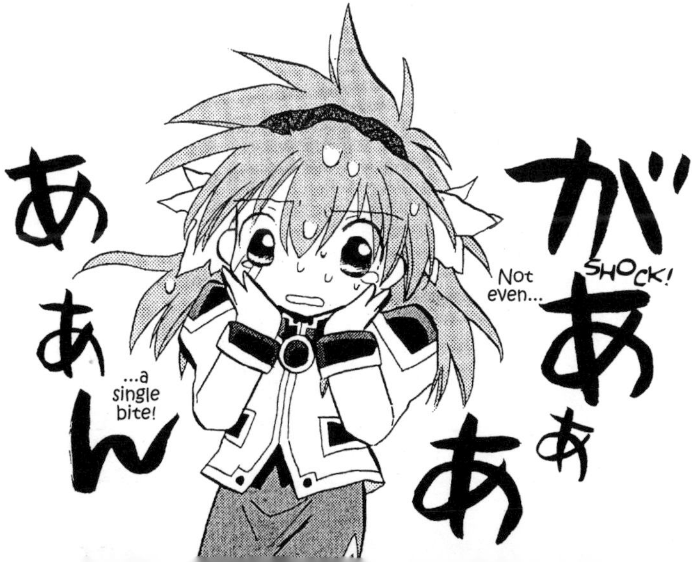

があぁあ
SHOCK!
Not even...
ああん
...a single bite!

ギャラクシーエンジェル
Galaxy Angel

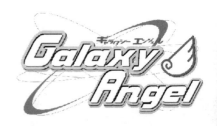

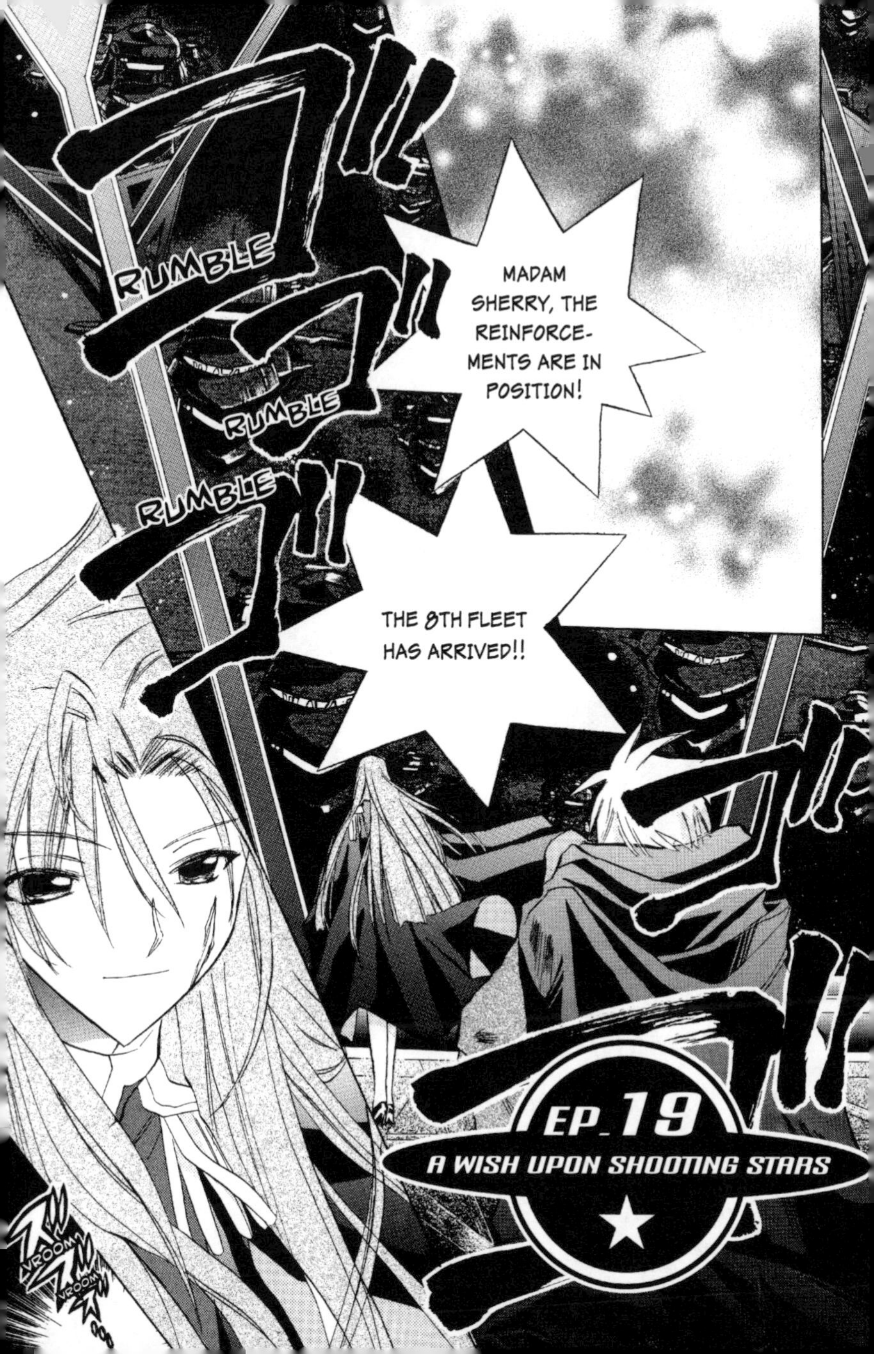
MADAM SHERRY, THE REINFORCE-MENTS ARE IN POSITION!
RUMBLE
RUMBLE
RUMBLE
THE 8TH FLEET HAS ARRIVED!!
EP_19
A WISH UPON SHOOTING STARS
VROOM
VROOM

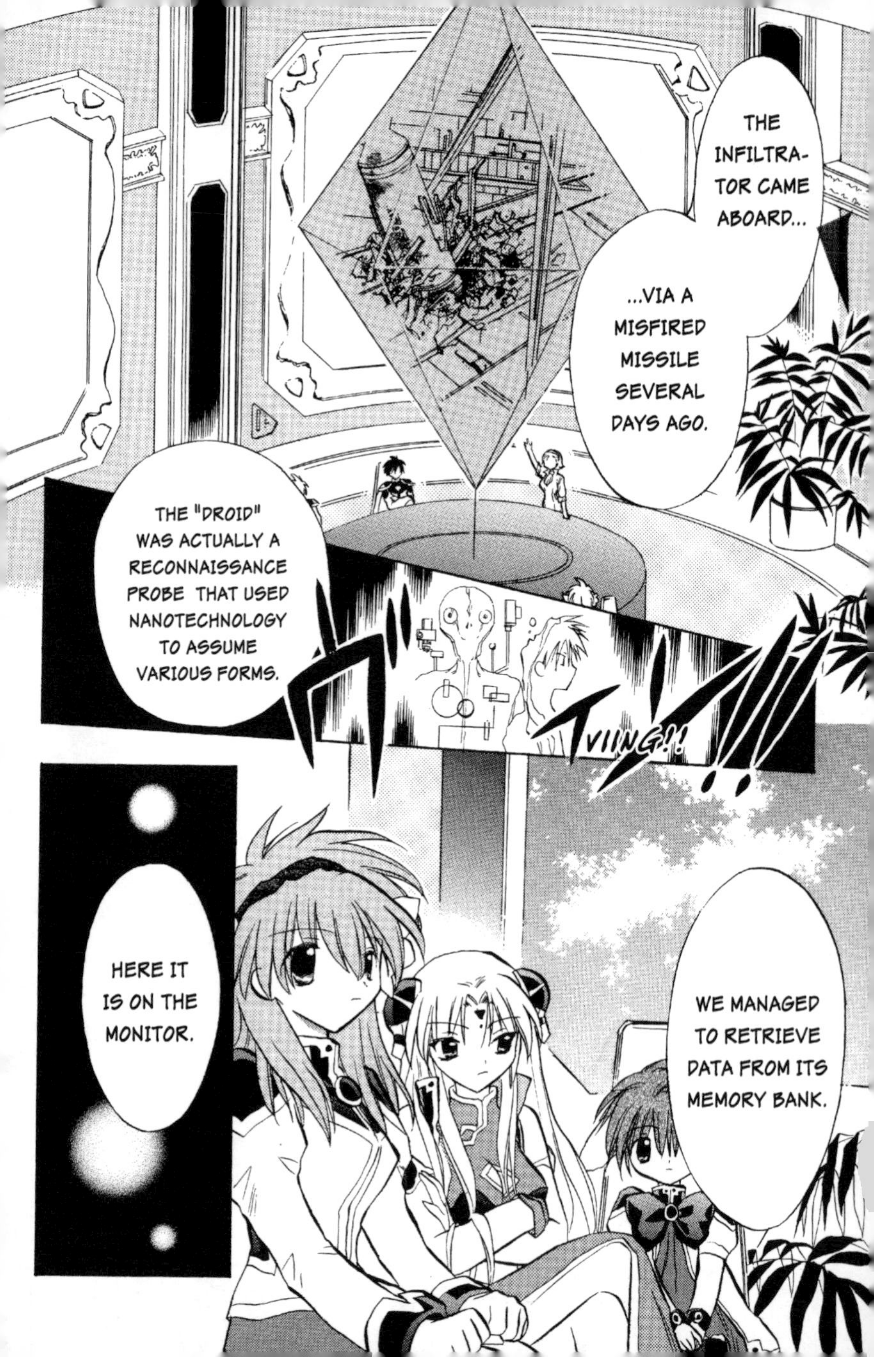
THE INFILTRATOR CAME ABOARD...
...VIA A MISFIRED MISSILE SEVERAL DAYS AGO.
THE "DROID" WAS ACTUALLY A RECONNAISSANCE PROBE THAT USED NANOTECHNOLOGY TO ASSUME VARIOUS FORMS.
VIING!!
WE MANAGED TO RETRIEVE DATA FROM ITS MEMORY BANK.
HERE IT IS ON THE MONITOR.

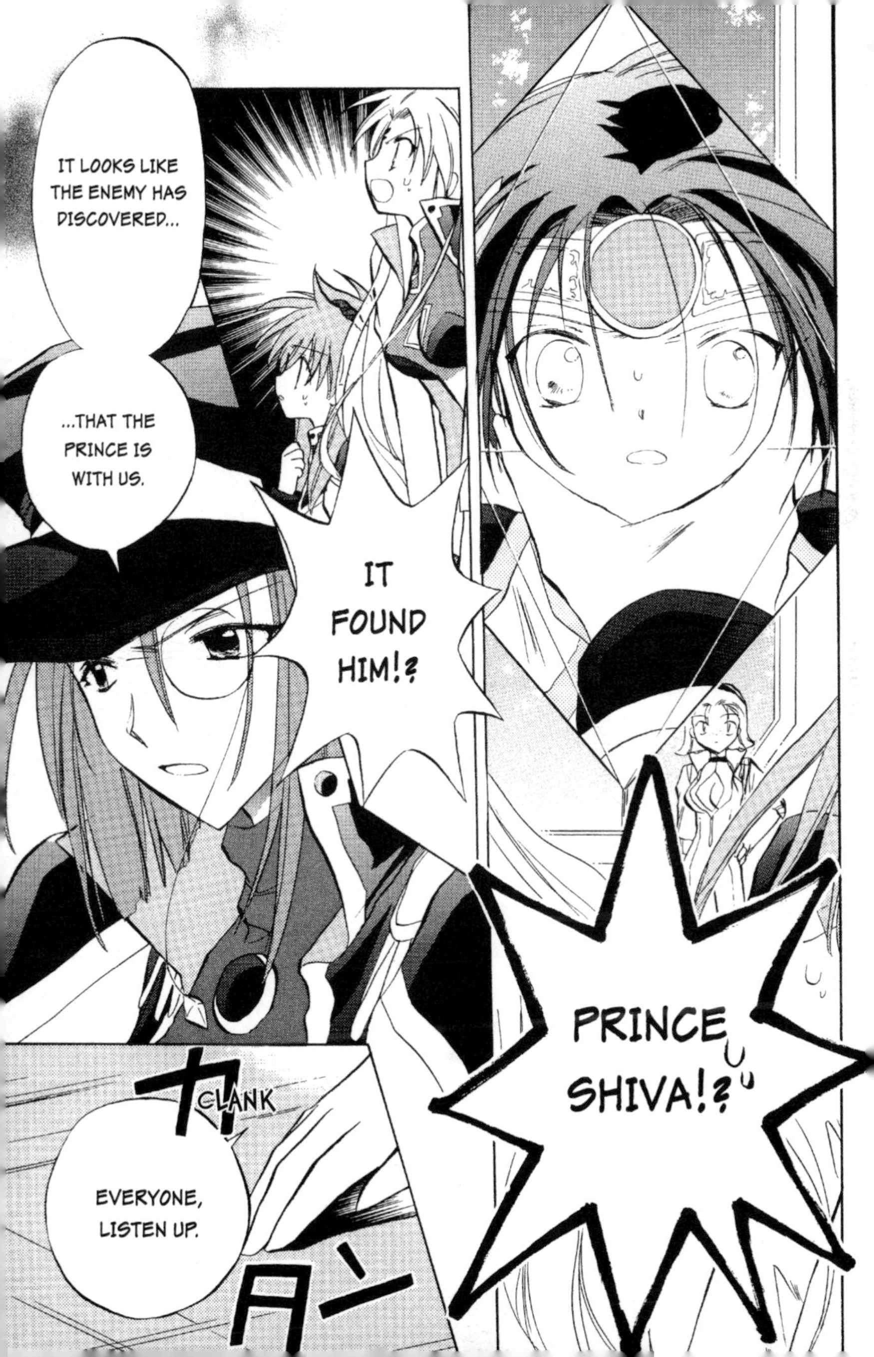
IT LOOKS LIKE THE ENEMY HAS DISCOVERED...
...THAT THE PRINCE IS WITH US.
IT FOUND HIM!?
PRINCE SHIVA!?
CLANK
EVERYONE, LISTEN UP.

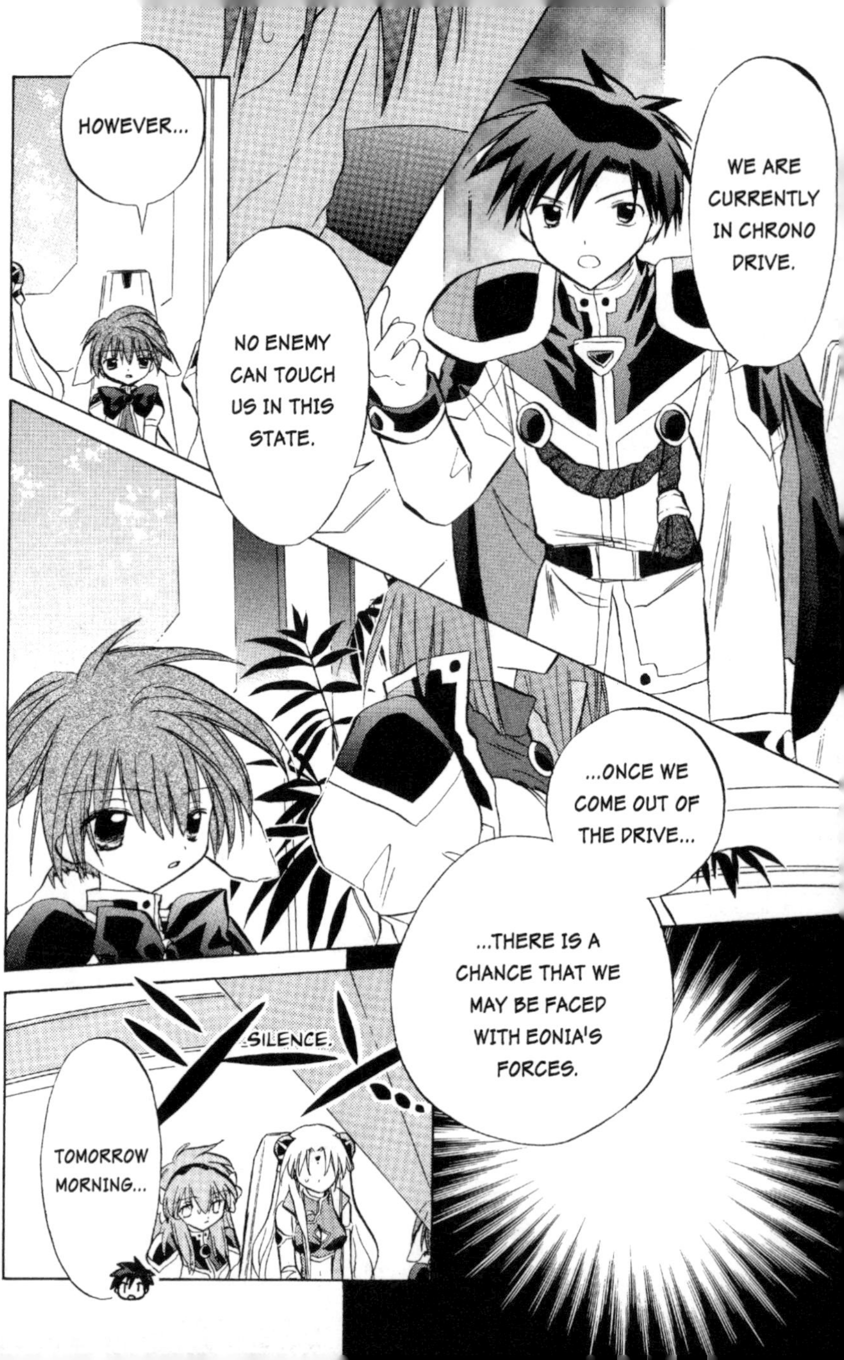
WE ARE CURRENTLY IN CHRONO DRIVE.
NO ENEMY CAN TOUCH US IN THIS STATE.
HOWEVER...
...ONCE WE COME OUT OF THE DRIVE...
...THERE IS A CHANCE THAT WE MAY BE FACED WITH EONIA'S FORCES.
SILENCE.
TOMORROW MORNING...

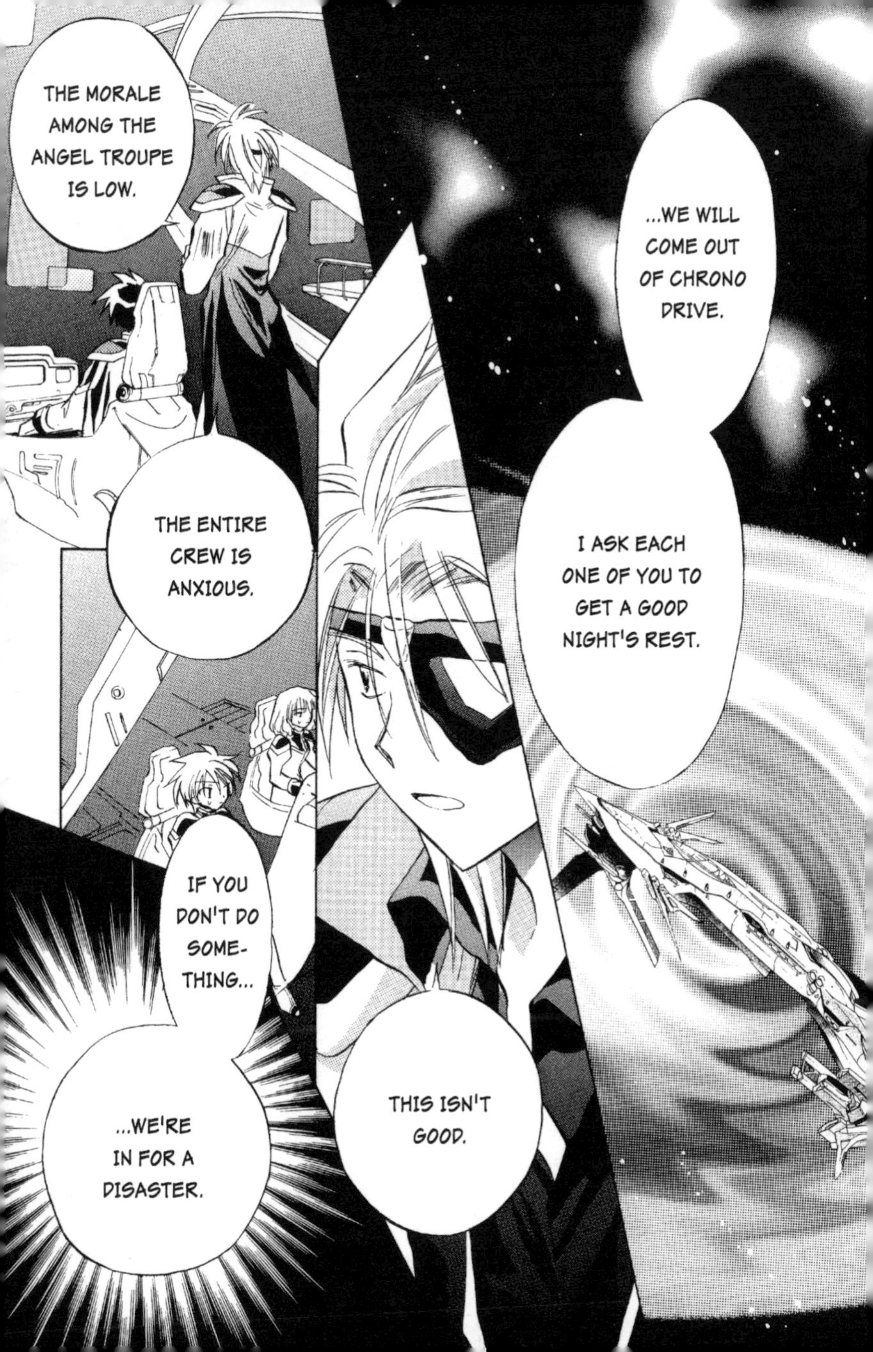
...WE WILL COME OUT OF CHRONO DRIVE.
I ASK EACH ONE OF YOU TO GET A GOOD NIGHT'S REST.
THIS ISN'T GOOD.
THE MORALE AMONG THE ANGEL TROUPE IS LOW.
THE ENTIRE CREW IS ANXIOUS.
IF YOU DON'T DO SOME-THING...
...WE'RE IN FOR A DISASTER.

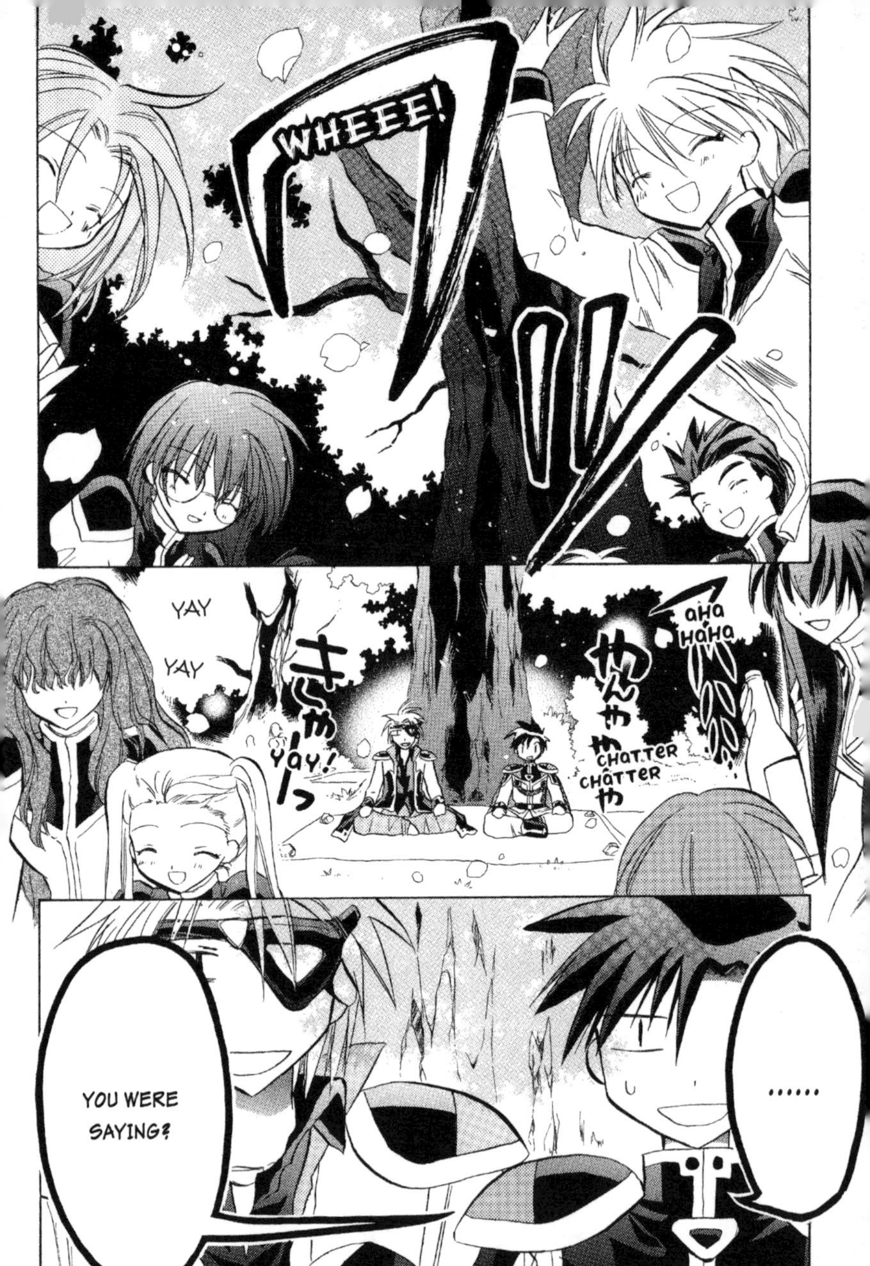
WHEEE!
AHA HAHA
CHATTER CHATTER
YAY!
YAY
YAY
......
YOU WERE SAYING?

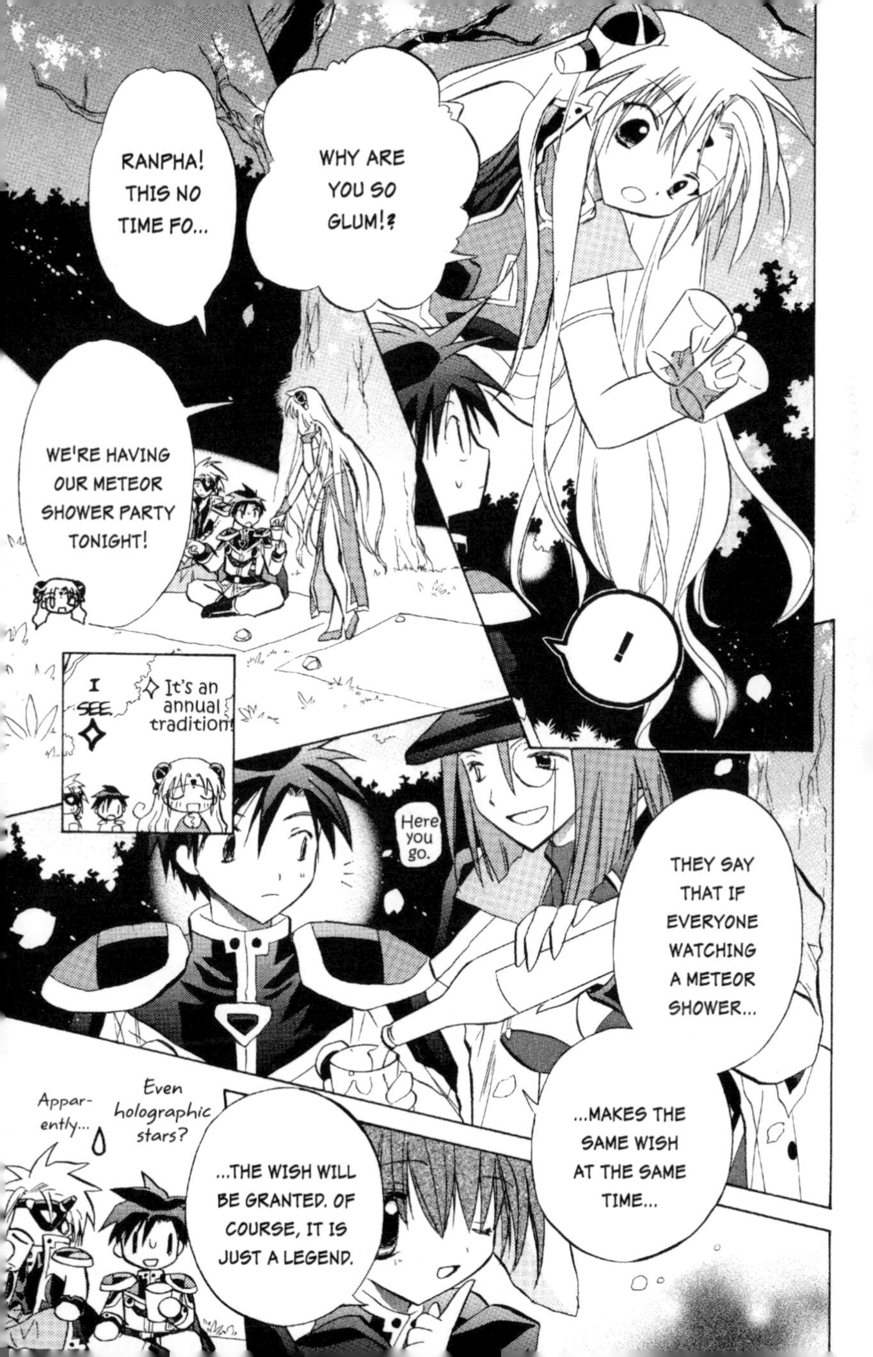
WHY ARE YOU SO GLUM!?
RANPHA! THIS NO TIME FO...
!
WE'RE HAVING OUR METEOR SHOWER PARTY TONIGHT!
It's an annual tradition!
I SEE.
Here you go.
THEY SAY THAT IF EVERYONE WATCHING A METEOR SHOWER...
...MAKES THE SAME WISH AT THE SAME TIME...
...THE WISH WILL BE GRANTED. OF COURSE, IT IS JUST A LEGEND.
Even holographic stars?
Apparently...

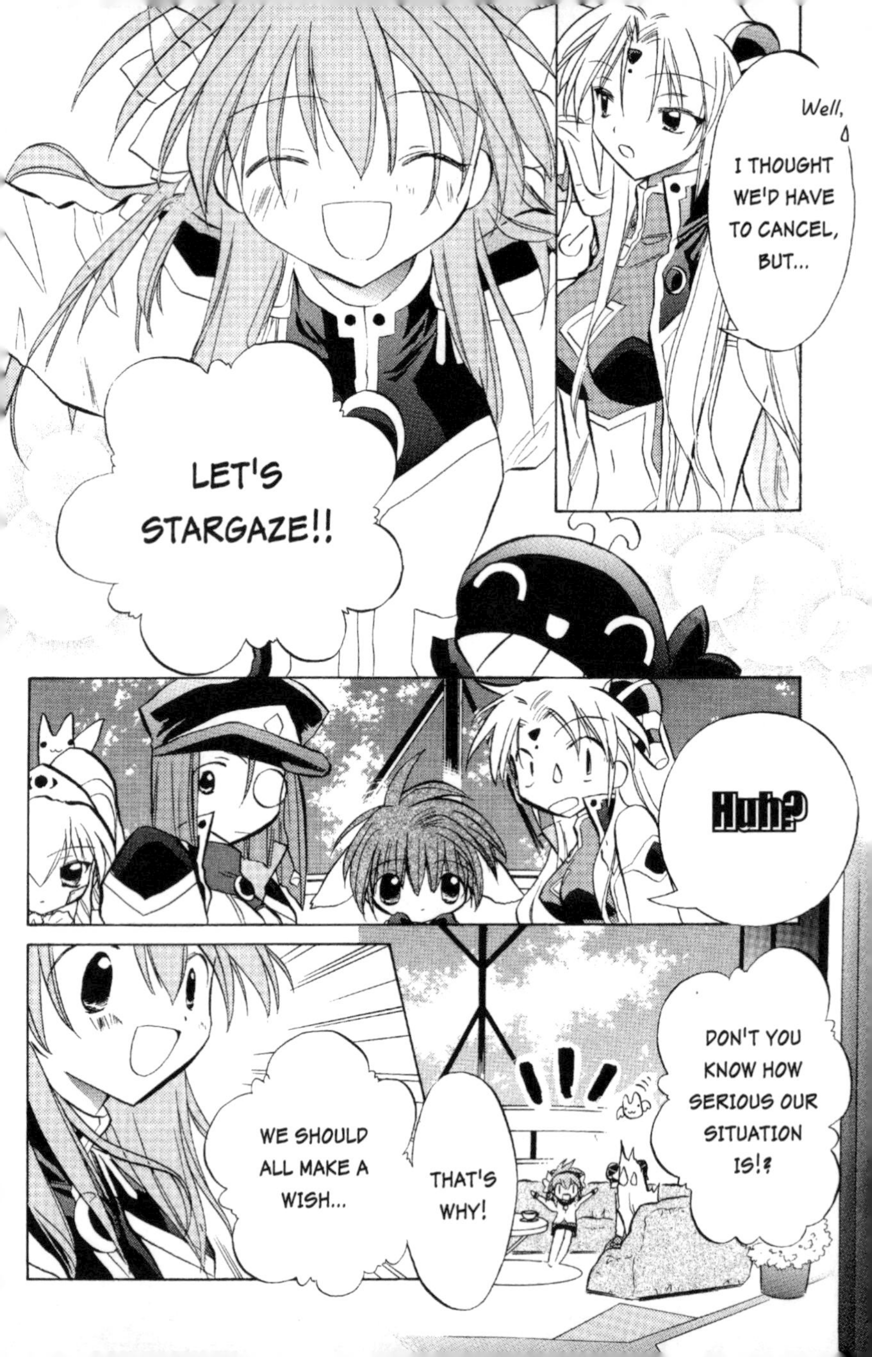
Well, I THOUGHT WE'D HAVE TO CANCEL, BUT...
LET'S STARGAZE!!
Huh?
DON'T YOU KNOW HOW SERIOUS OUR SITUATION IS!?
THAT'S WHY!
WE SHOULD ALL MAKE A WISH...

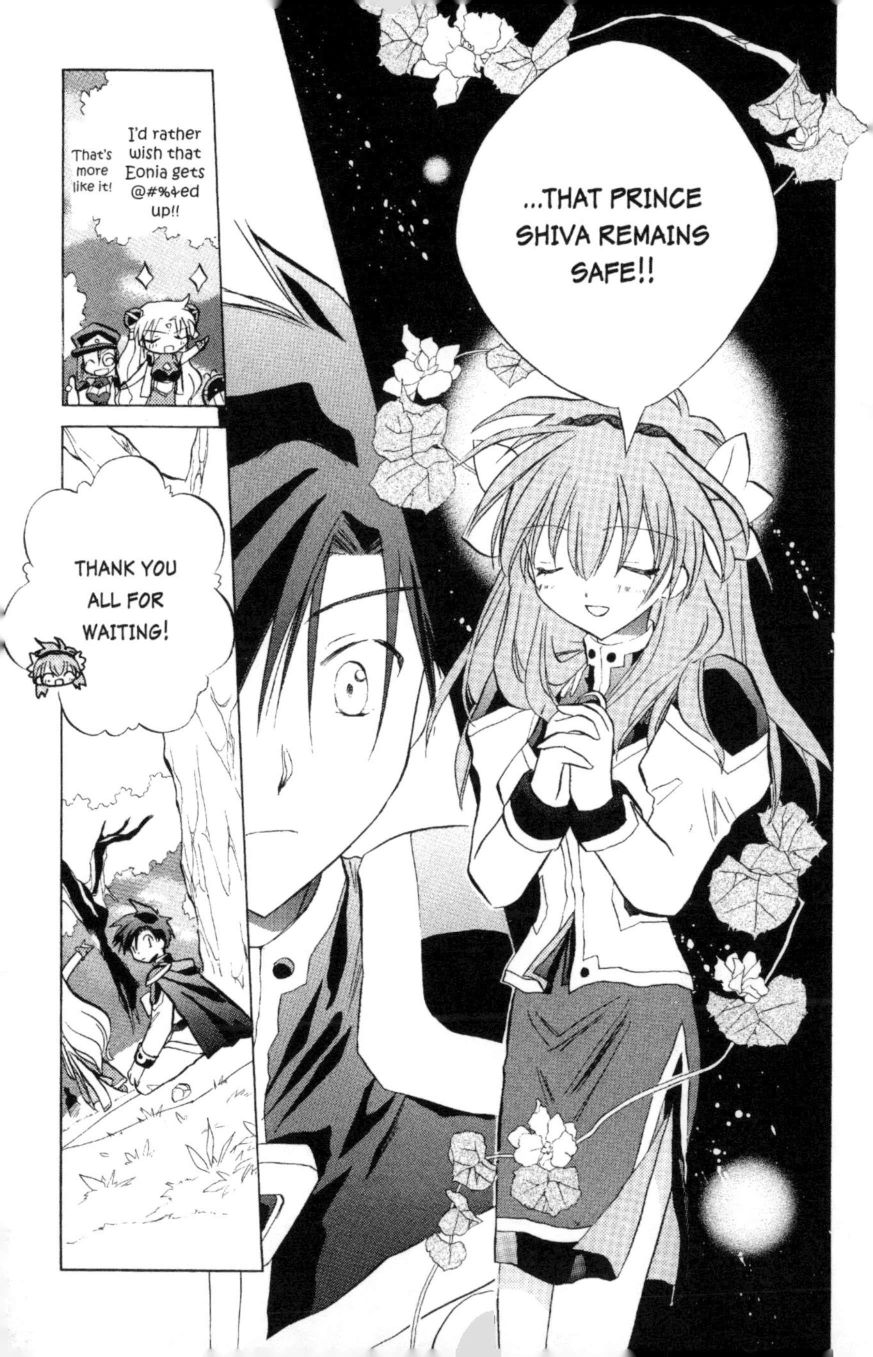
...THAT PRINCE SHIVA REMAINS SAFE!!
I'd rather wish that Eonia gets @#%&ed up!!
That's more like it!
THANK YOU ALL FOR WAITING!

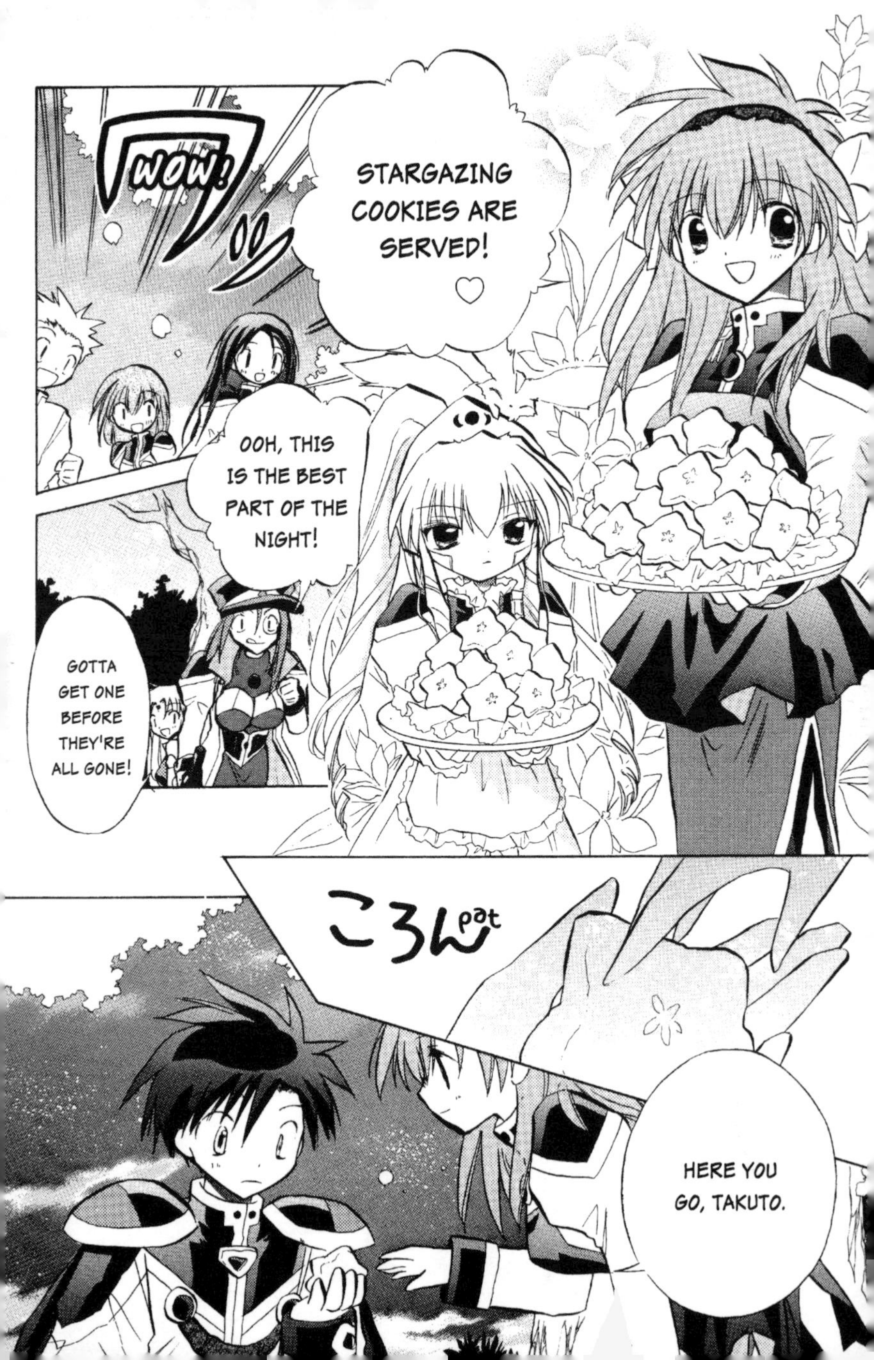
STARGAZING COOKIES ARE SERVED! ♡
WOW!
OOH, THIS IS THE BEST PART OF THE NIGHT!
GOTTA GET ONE BEFORE THEY'RE ALL GONE!
ころん pat
HERE YOU GO, TAKUTO.

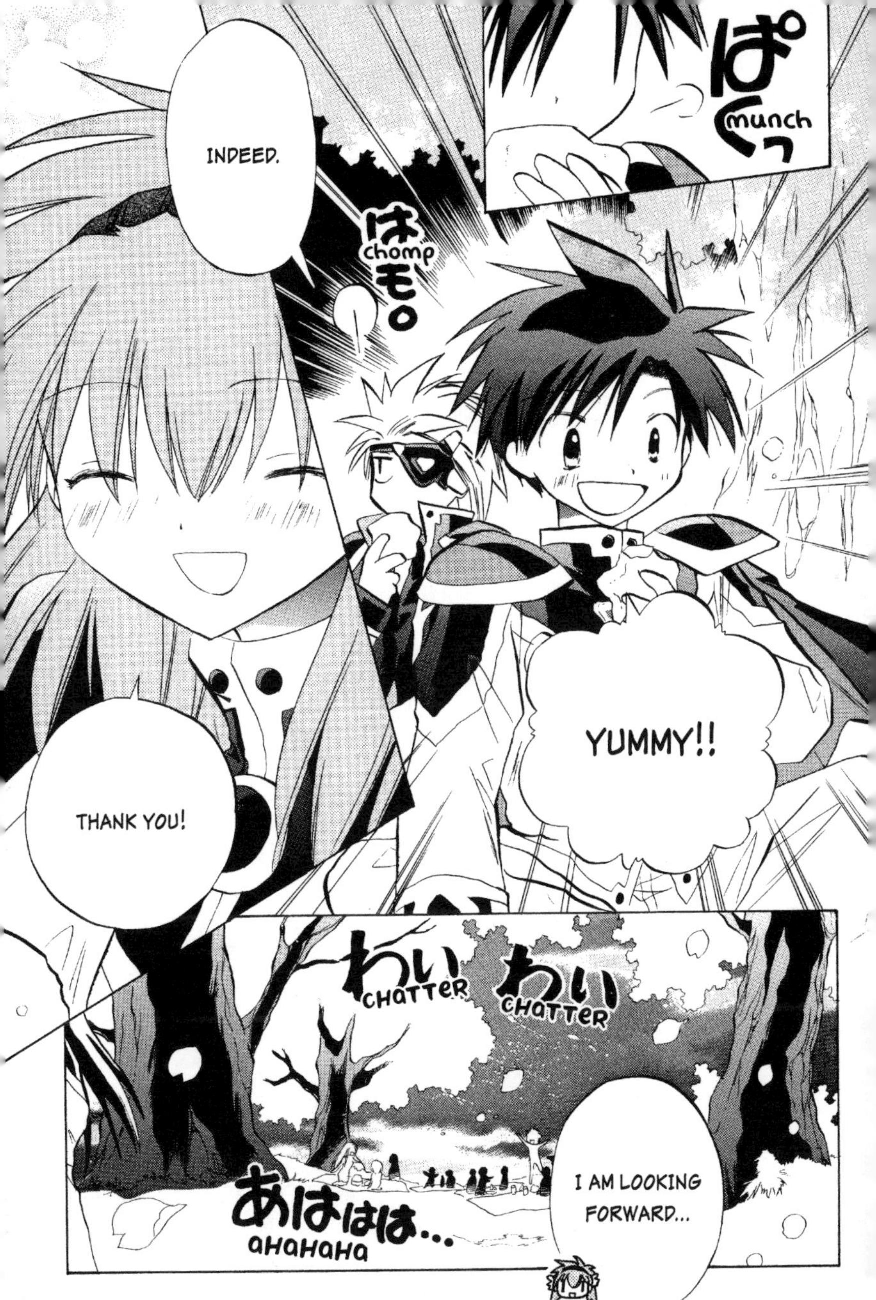

ぱくっ
munch
はもっ
chomp
YUMMY!!
INDEED.
THANK YOU!
わい
CHATTER
わい
CHATTER
あははは…
aHaHaHa
I AM LOOKING FORWARD...

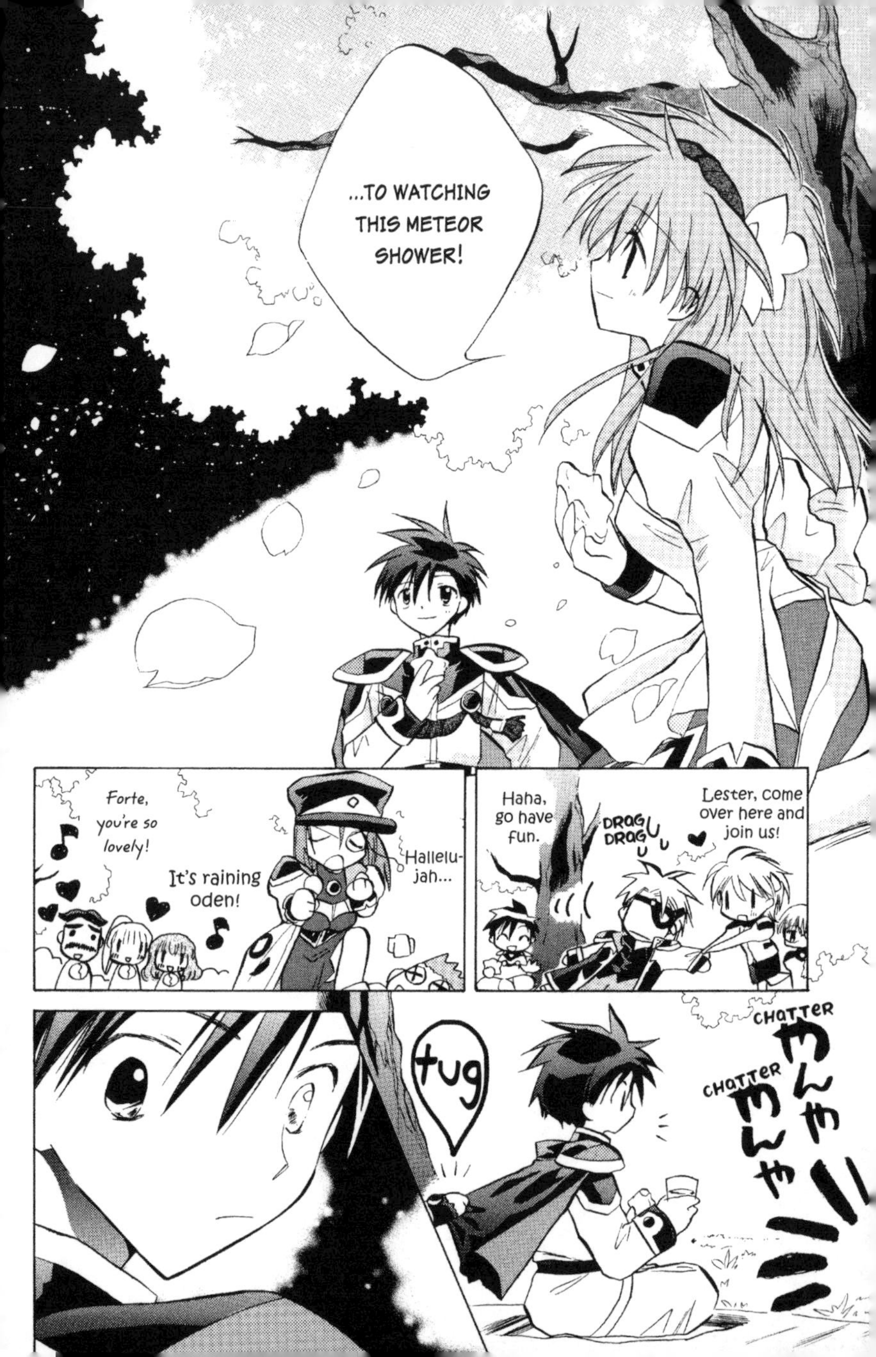
...TO WATCHING THIS METEOR SHOWER!
Lester, come over here and join us!
DRAG DRAG
Haha, go have fun.
Hallelu-jah...
Forte, you're so lovely!
It's raining oden!
CHATTER
CHATTER
tug

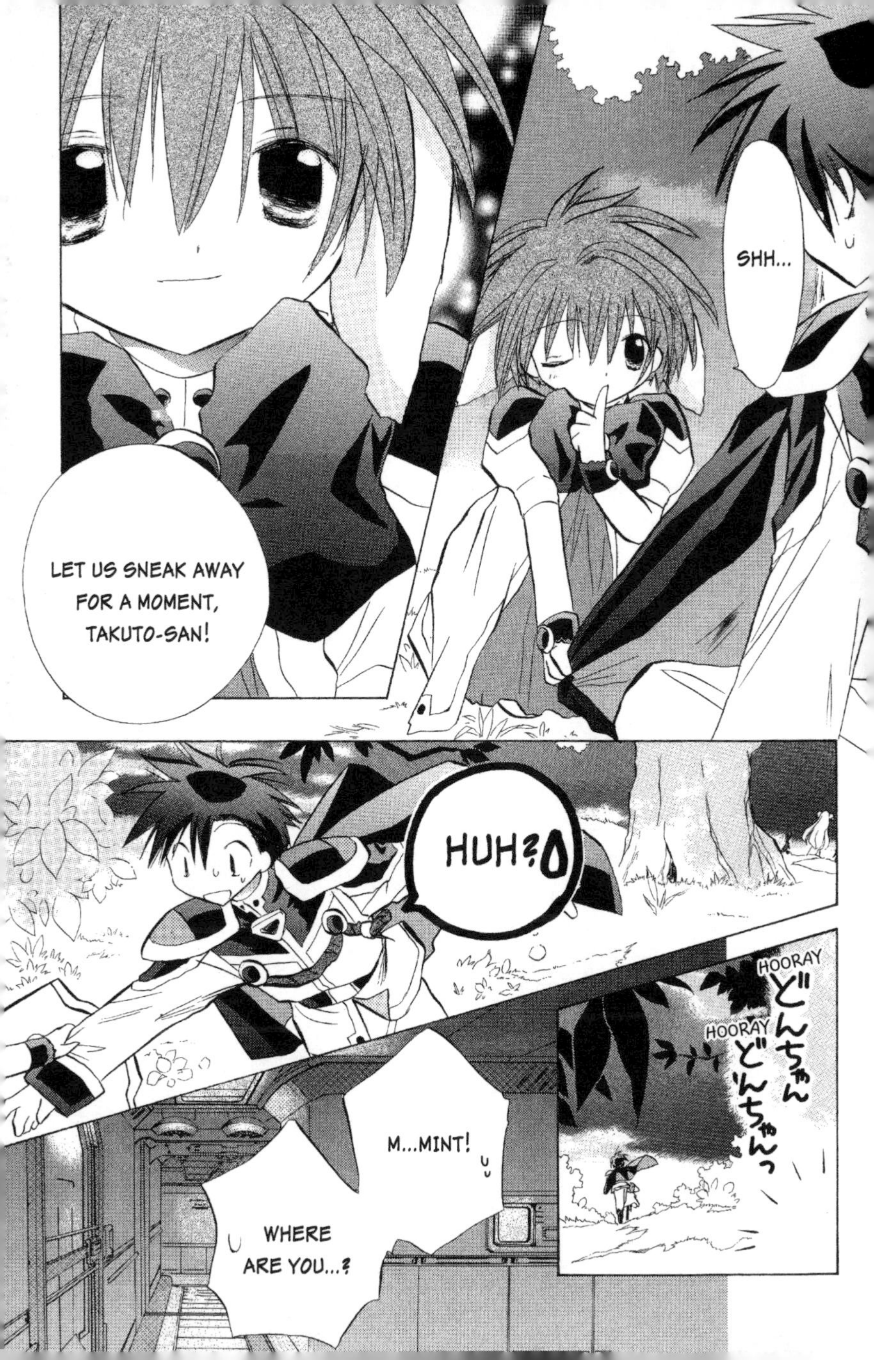
SHH...
LET US SNEAK AWAY FOR A MOMENT, TAKUTO-SAN!
HUH?
HOORAY どんちゃん
HOORAY どんちゃんっ
M...MINT!
WHERE ARE YOU...?

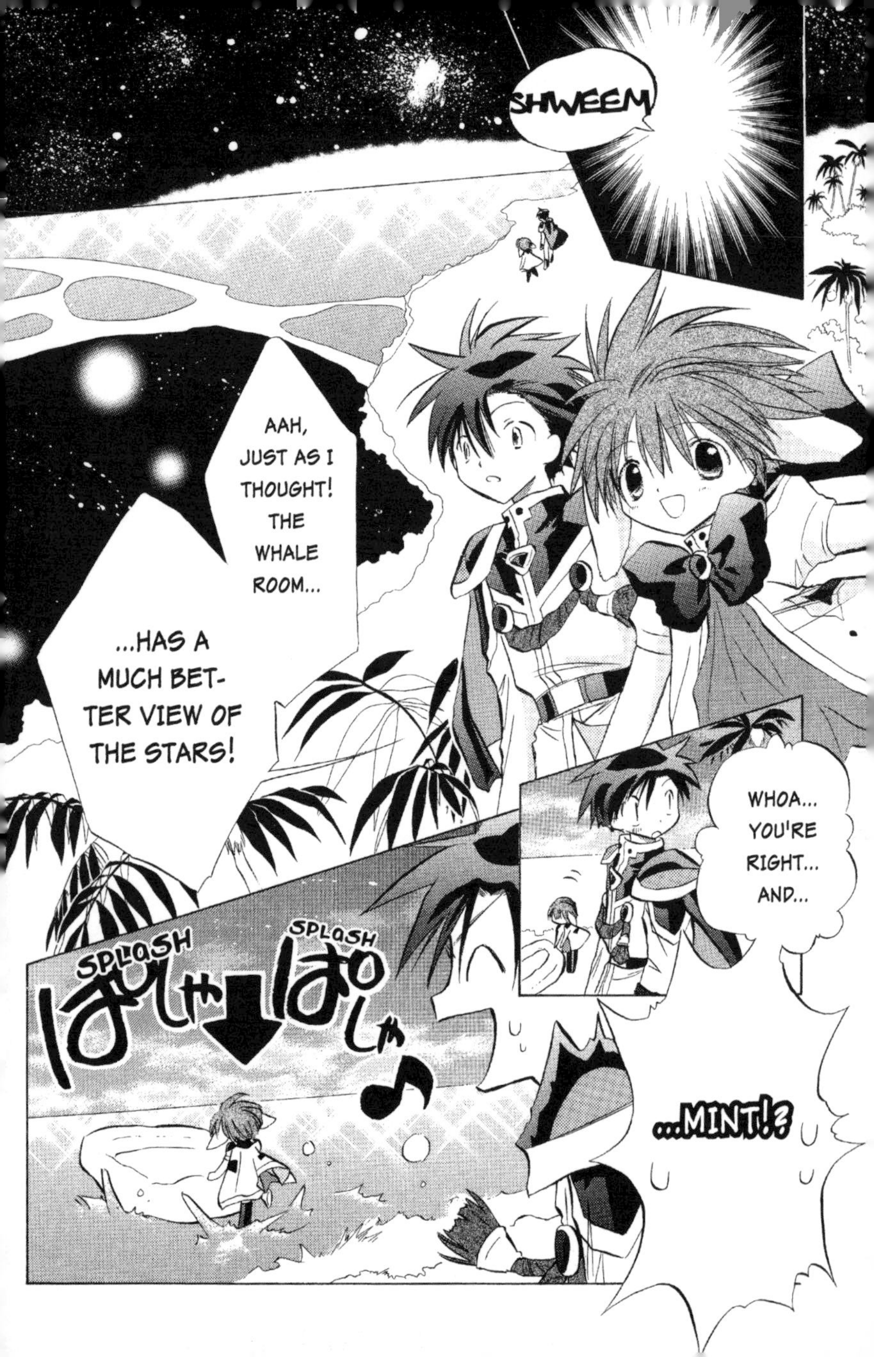
SHWEEM
AAH, JUST AS I THOUGHT! THE WHALE ROOM...
...HAS A MUCH BET-TER VIEW OF THE STARS!
WHOA... YOU'RE RIGHT... AND...
...MINT!?
SPLASH SPLASH
ぱしゃぱしゃ

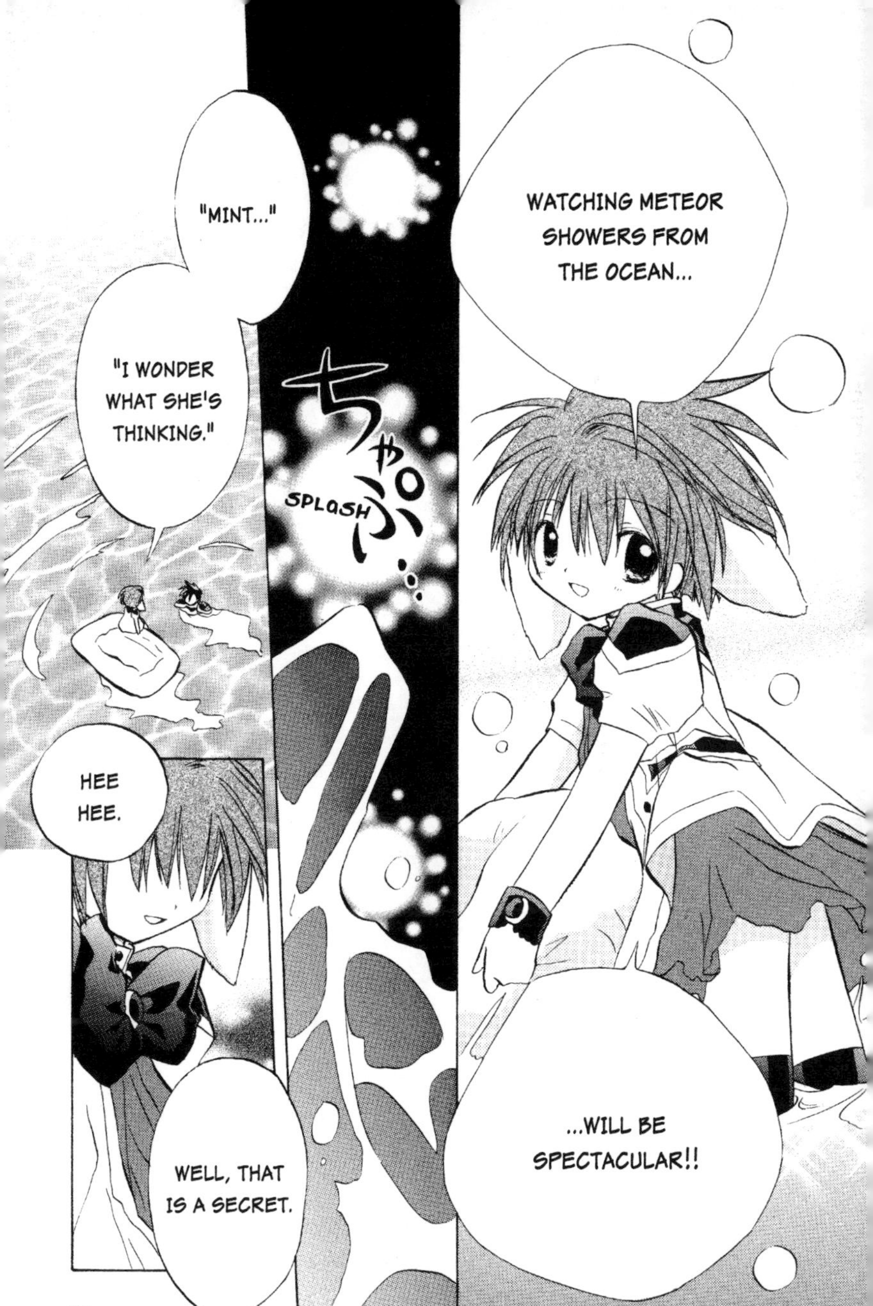
WATCHING METEOR SHOWERS FROM THE OCEAN...
...WILL BE SPECTACULAR!!
ちゃぷ...
SPLASH
"MINT..."
"I WONDER WHAT SHE'S THINKING."
HEE HEE.
WELL, THAT IS A SECRET.

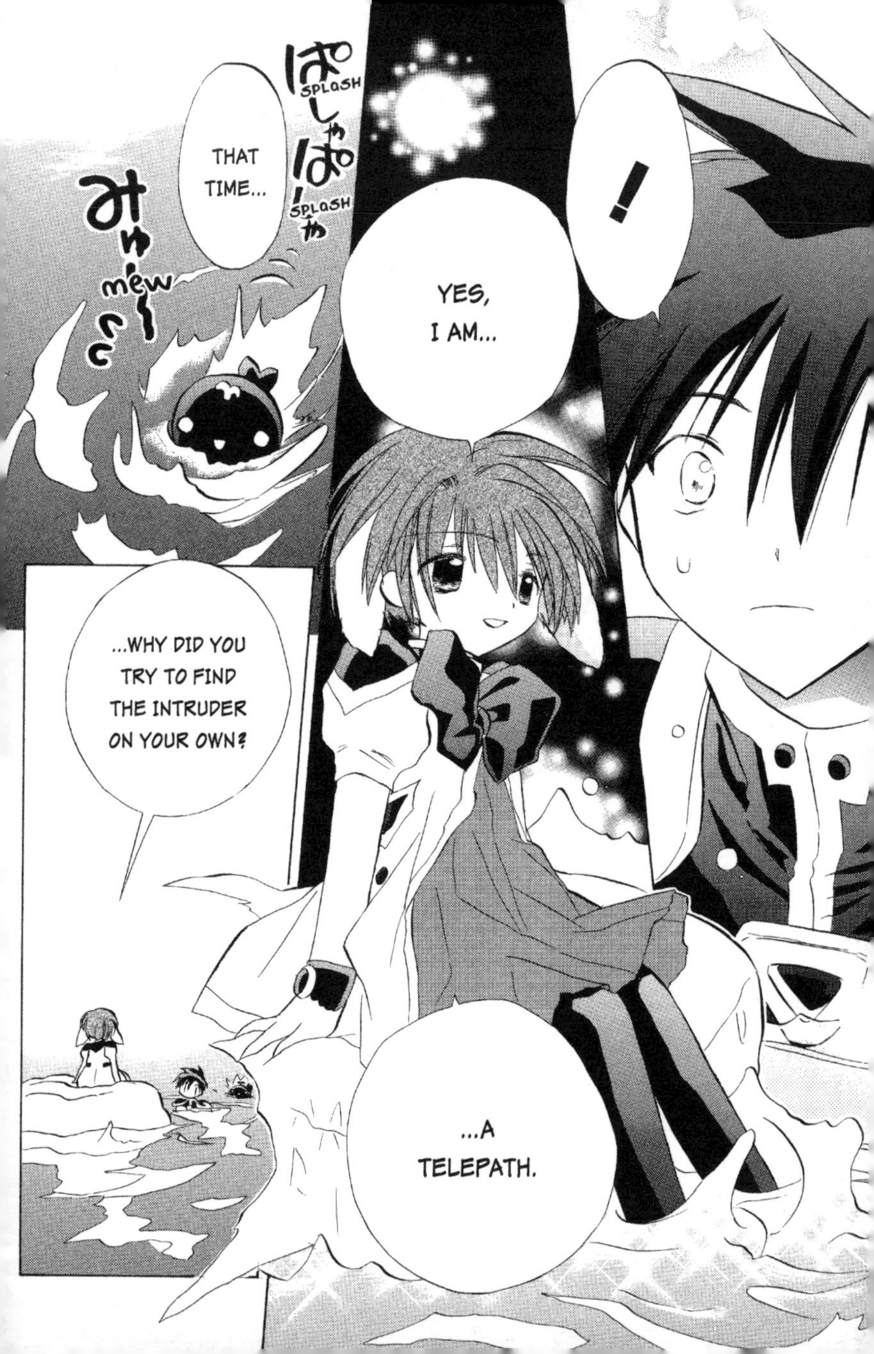

!
YES, I AM...
...A TELEPATH.
ぱしゃぱしゃ
SPLASH SPLASH
THAT TIME...
みゅ~~
mew
...WHY DID YOU TRY TO FIND THE INTRUDER ON YOUR OWN?

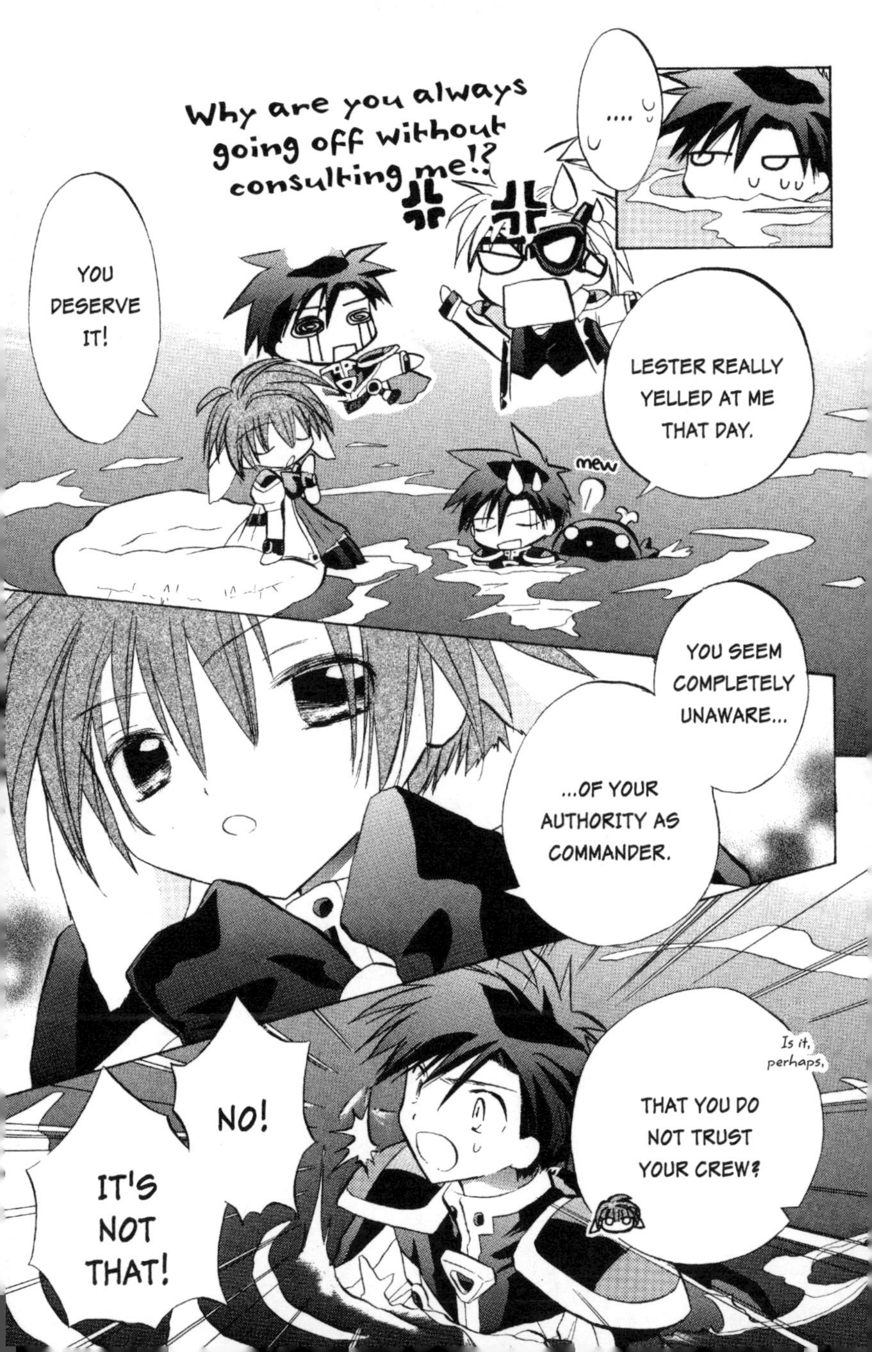
....
Why are you always going off without consulting me!?
LESTER REALLY YELLED AT ME THAT DAY.
mew
YOU DESERVE IT!
YOU SEEM COMPLETELY UNAWARE...
...OF YOUR AUTHORITY AS COMMANDER.
Is it, perhaps,
THAT YOU DO NOT TRUST YOUR CREW?
NO!
IT'S NOT THAT!

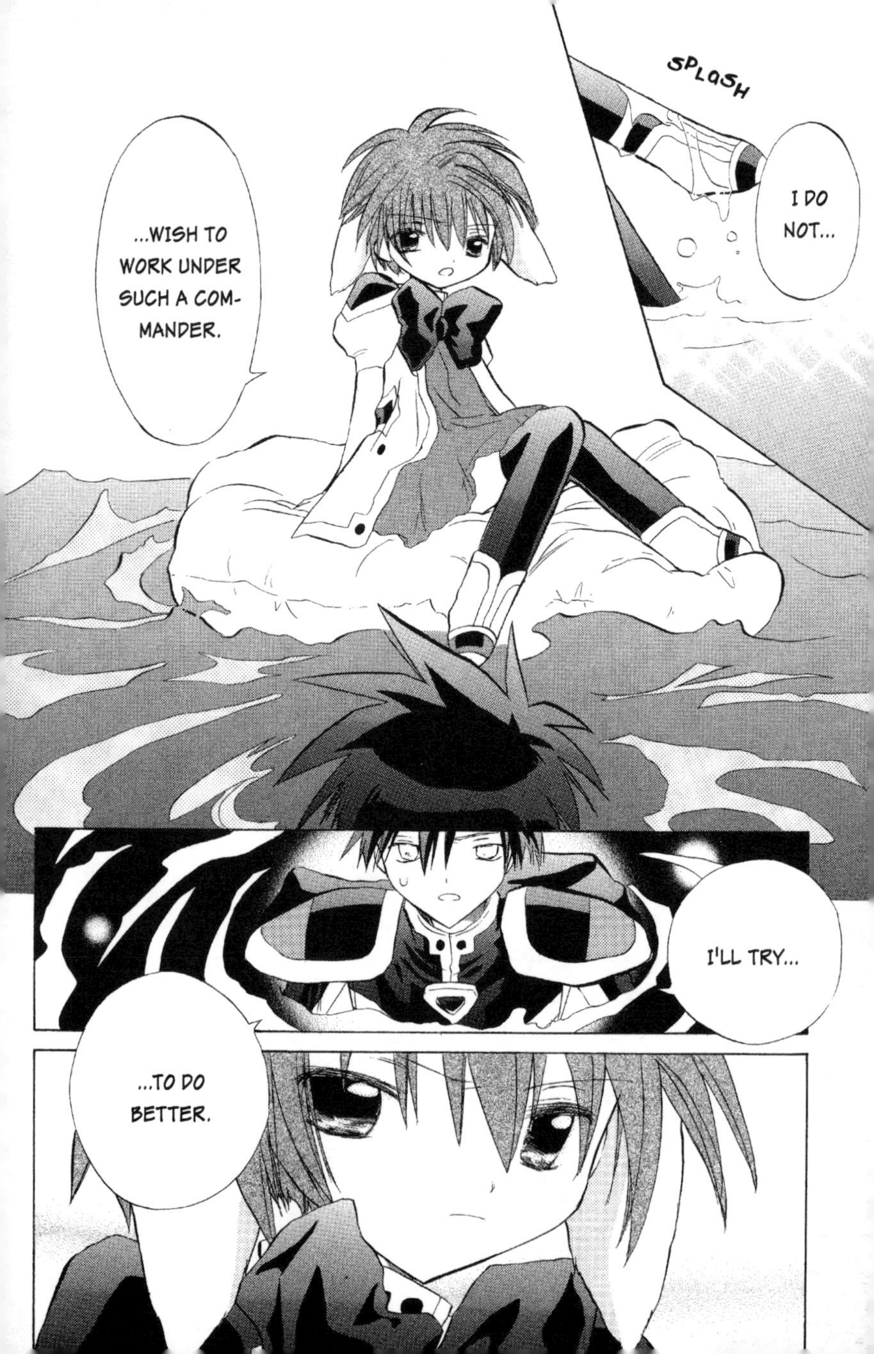
SPLASH
I DO NOT...
...WISH TO WORK UNDER SUCH A COM-MANDER.
I'LL TRY...
...TO DO BETTER.

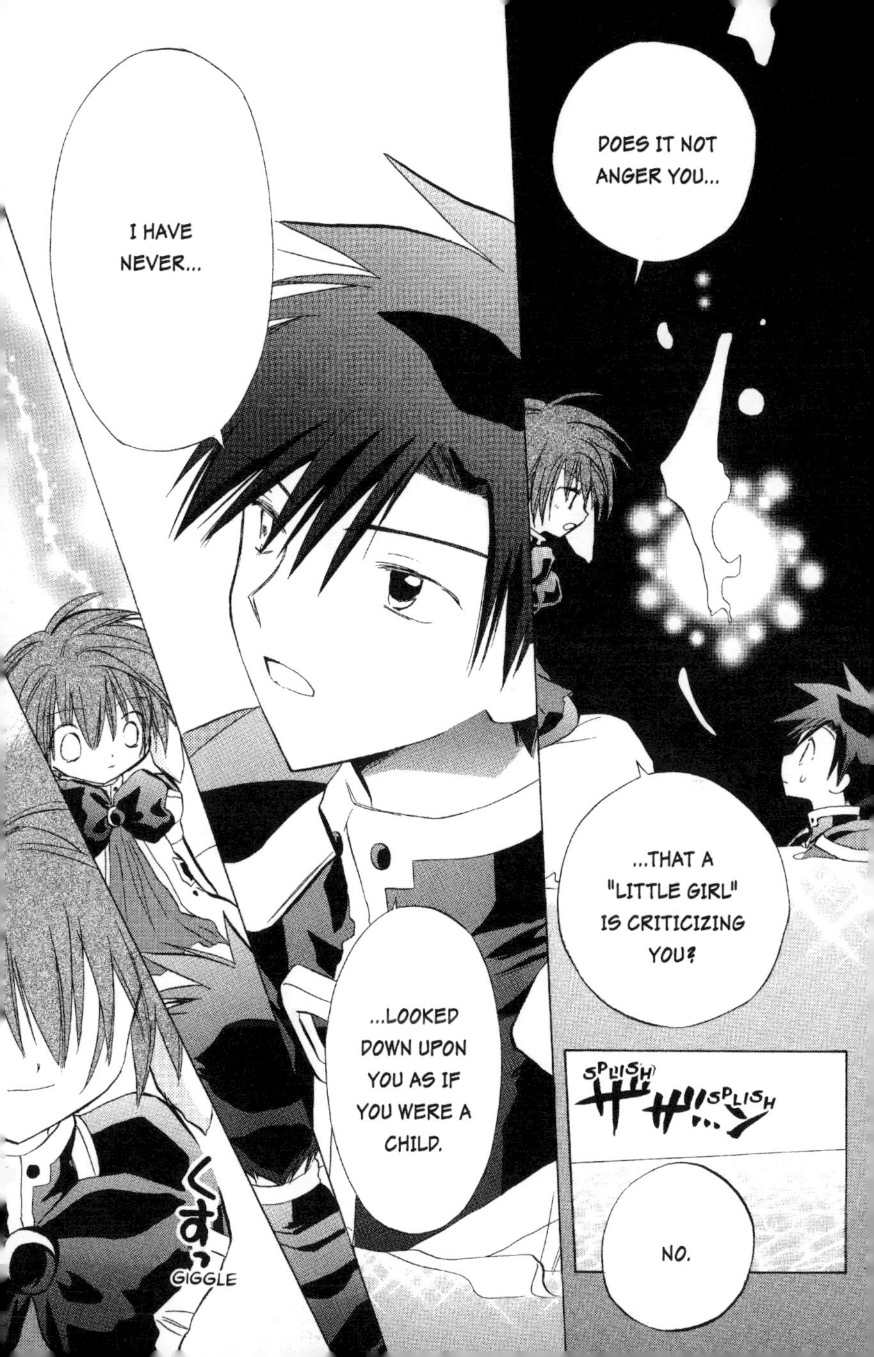
DOES IT NOT ANGER YOU...
...THAT A "LITTLE GIRL" IS CRITICIZING YOU?
SPLISH
ザザ!!ッ
SPLISH
NO.
I HAVE NEVER...
...LOOKED DOWN UPON YOU AS IF YOU WERE A CHILD.
くすっ
GIGGLE

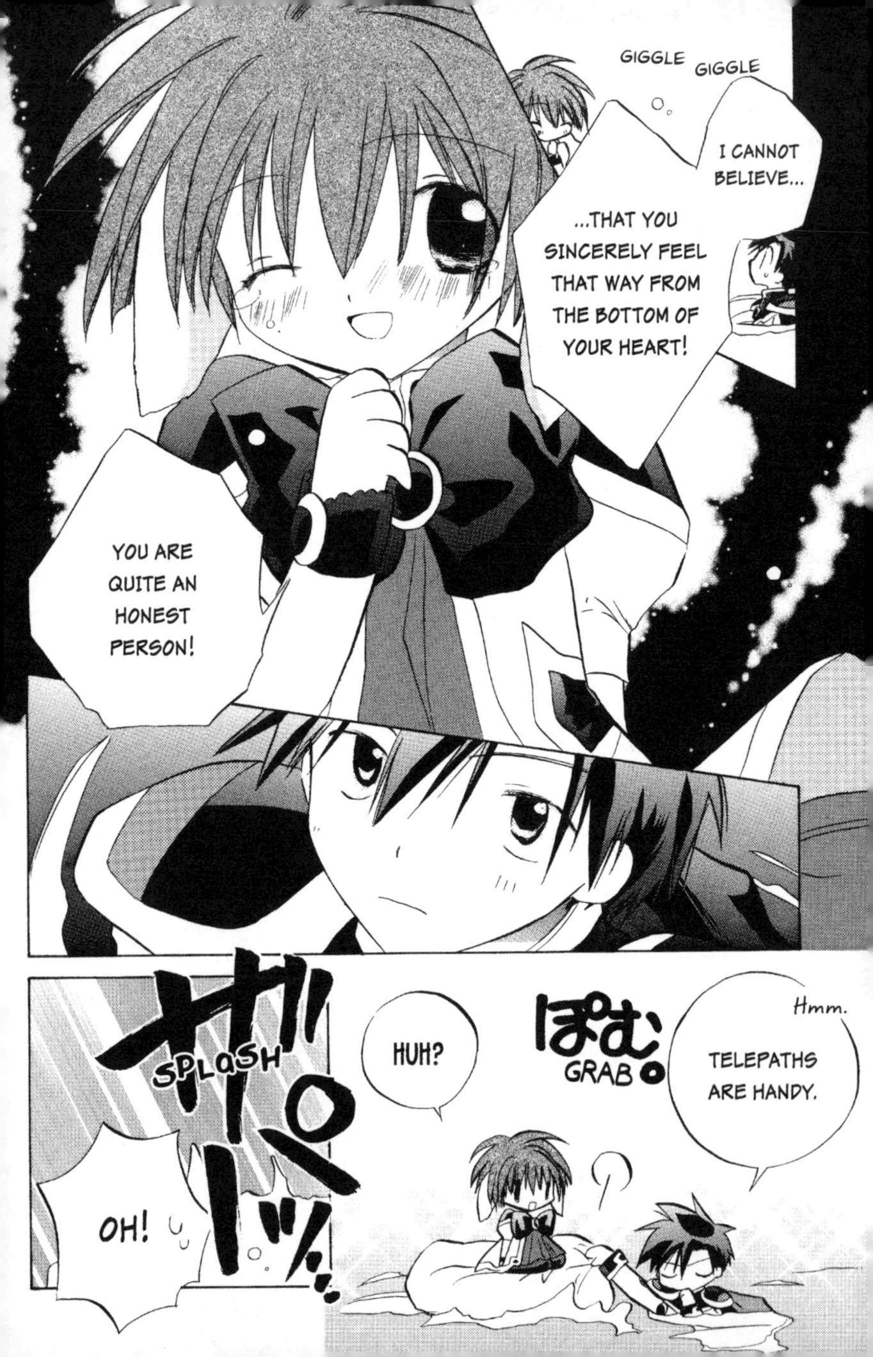
GIGGLE GIGGLE
I CANNOT BELIEVE...
...THAT YOU SINCERELY FEEL THAT WAY FROM THE BOTTOM OF YOUR HEART!
YOU ARE QUITE AN HONEST PERSON!
Hmm.
TELEPATHS ARE HANDY.
ぽむ
GRAB
HUH?
SPLASH
OH!

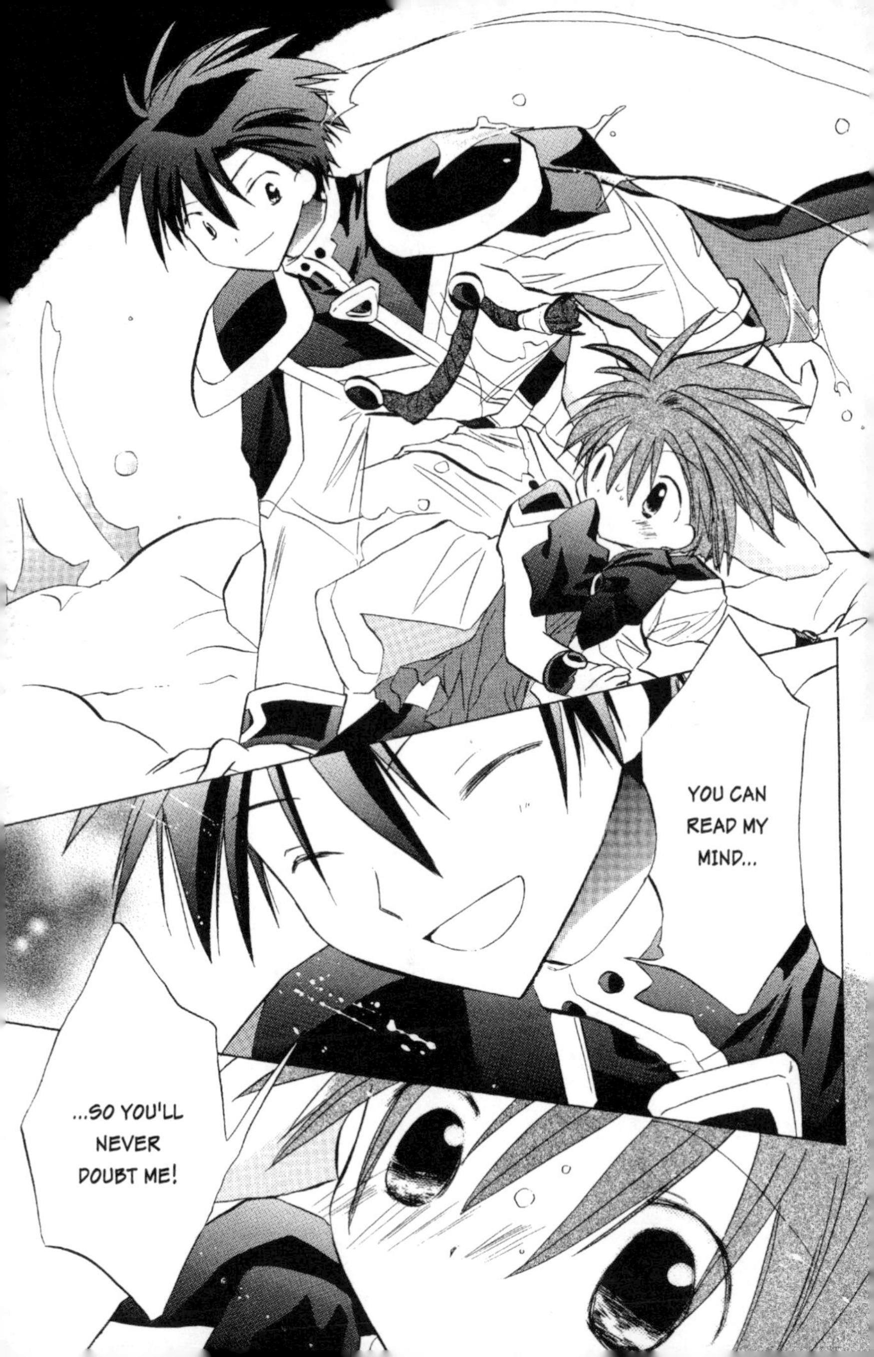
YOU CAN READ MY MIND...
...SO YOU'LL NEVER DOUBT ME!

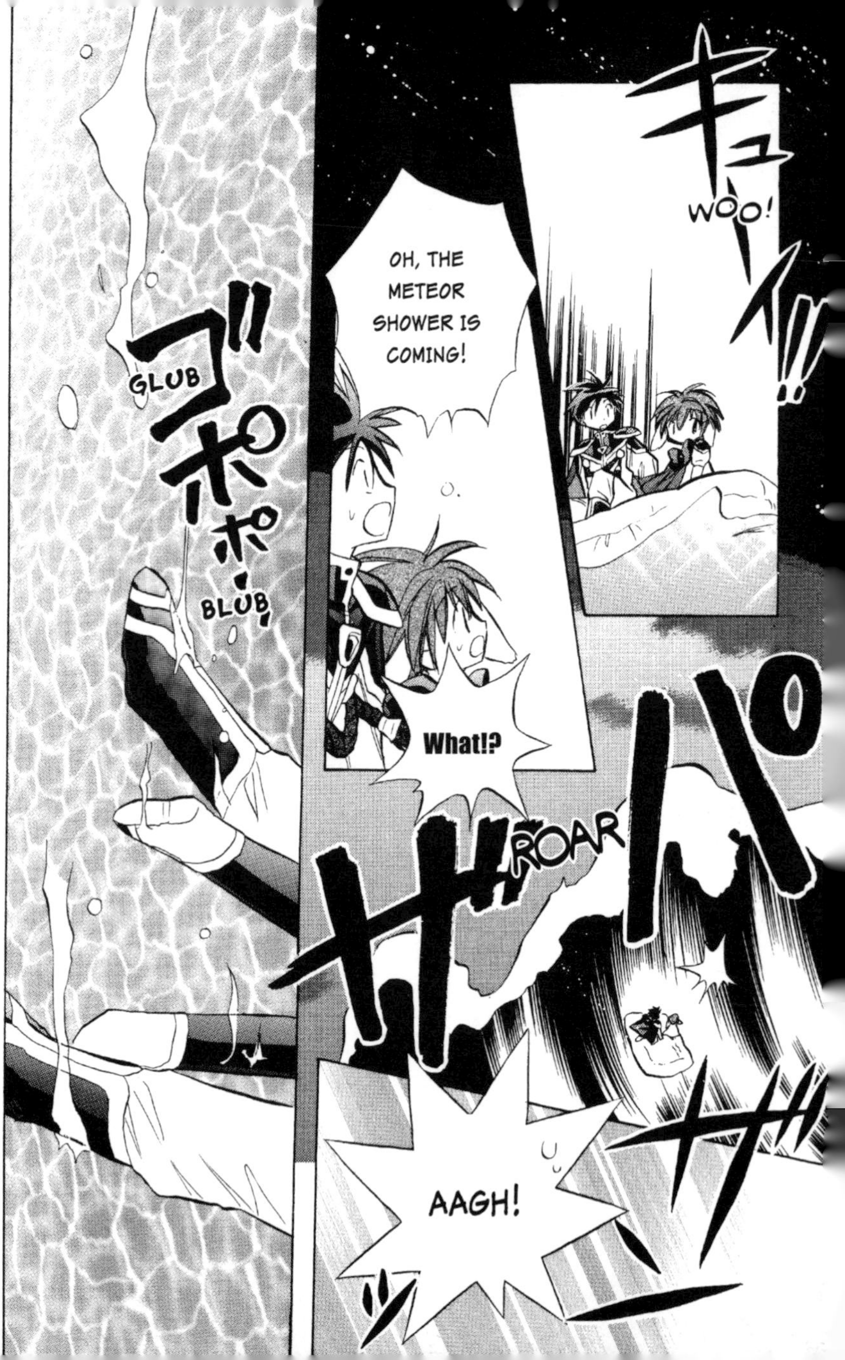
WOO!
OH, THE METEOR SHOWER IS COMING!
What!?
ROAR
AAGH!
GLUB
BLUB

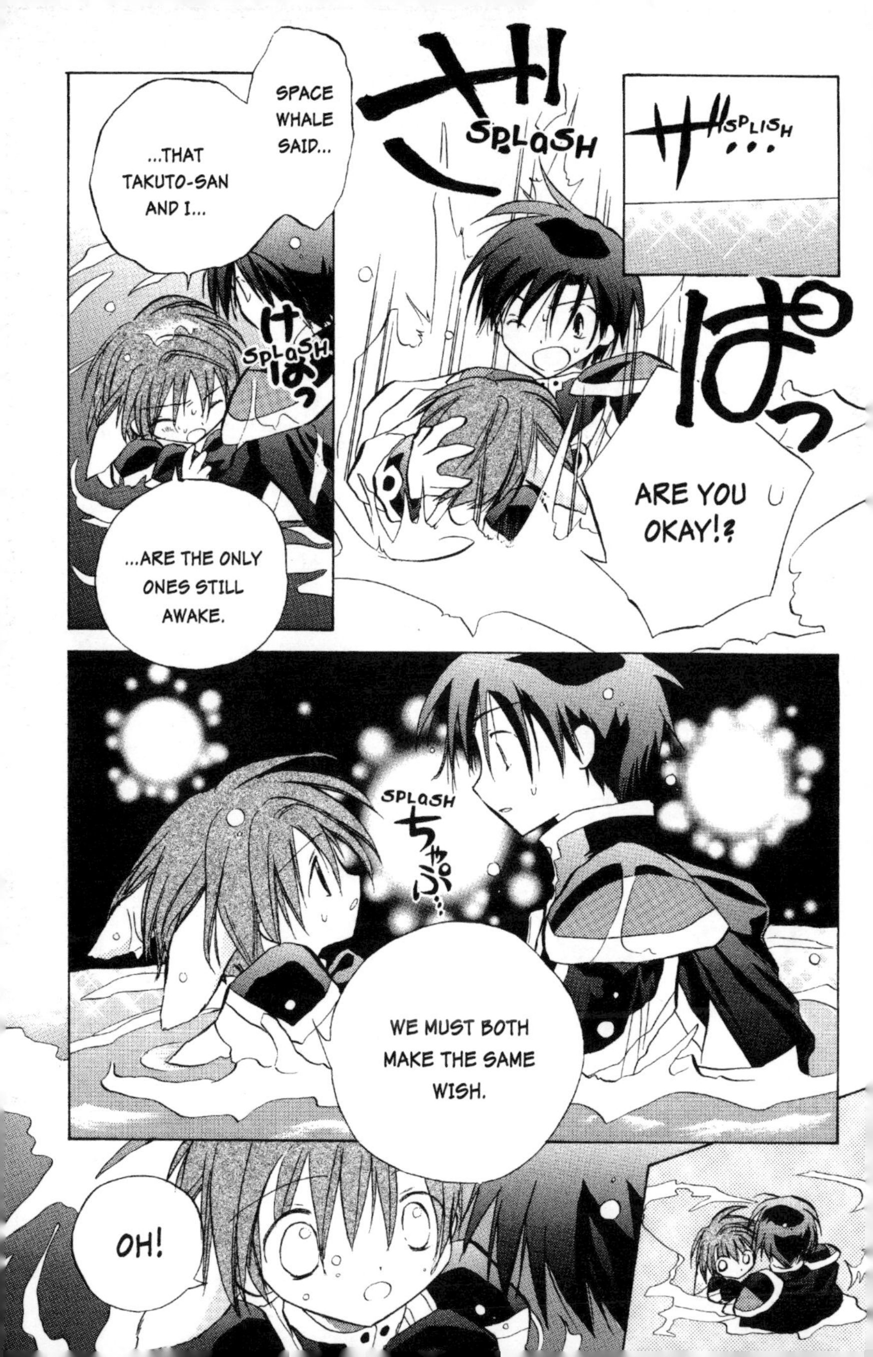
ザッ
SPLISH...
さっ
SPLASH
ぱっ
ARE YOU OKAY!?
SPACE WHALE SAID...
...THAT TAKUTO-SAN AND I...
けほっ
SPLASH
...ARE THE ONLY ONES STILL AWAKE.
SPLASH
ちゃぷ...
WE MUST BOTH MAKE THE SAME WISH.
OH!

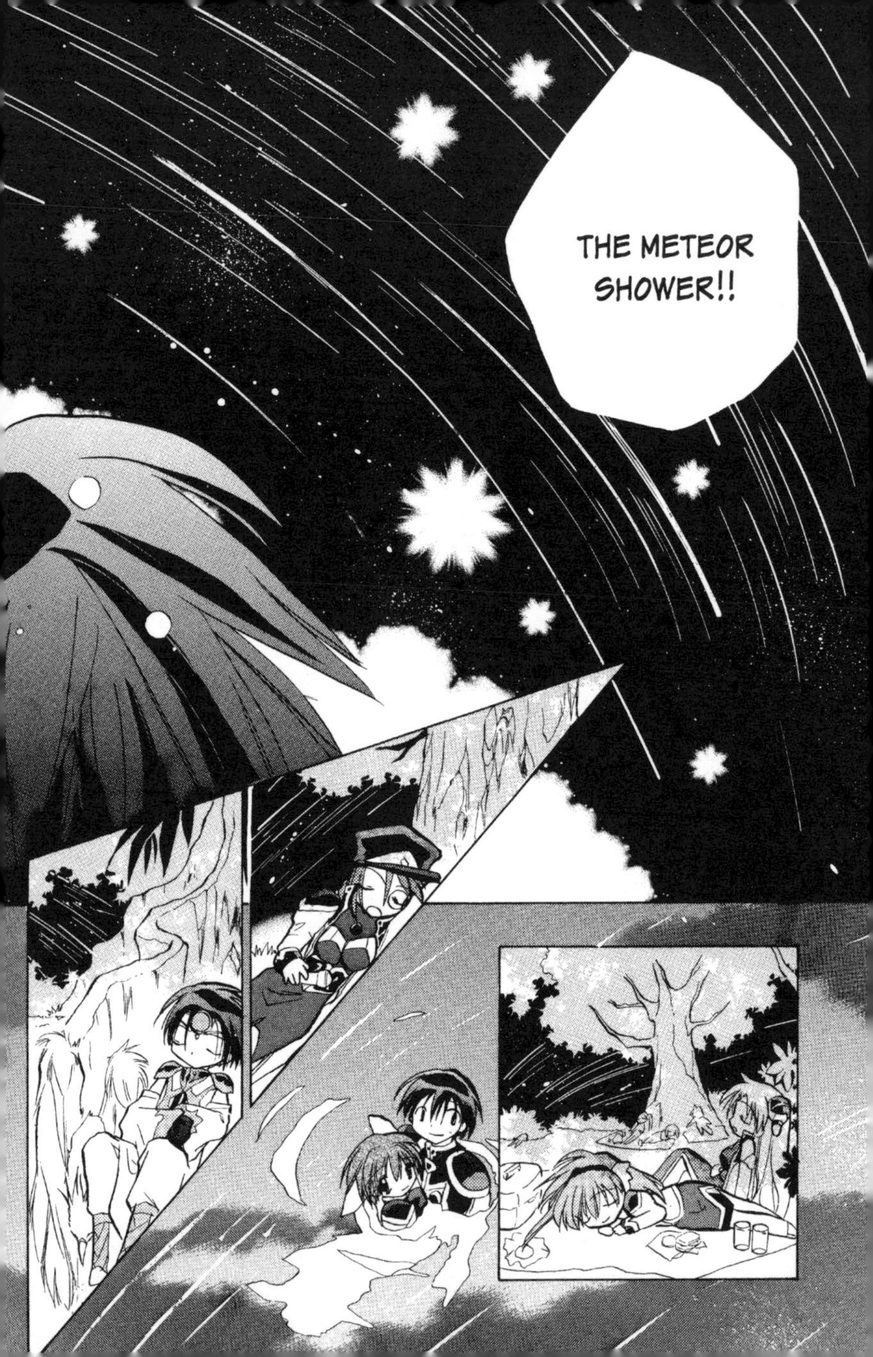
THE METEOR SHOWER!!

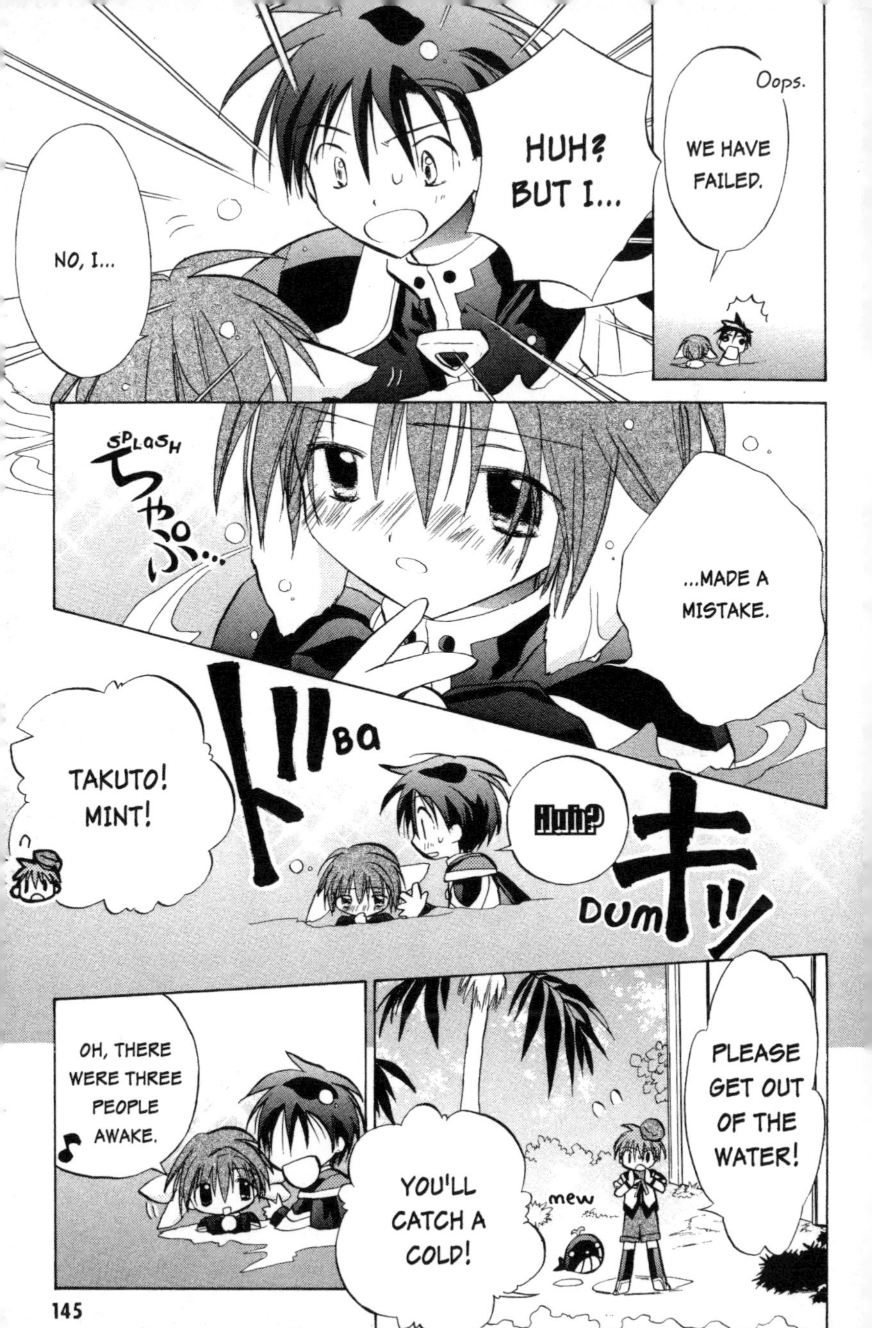
Oops.
WE HAVE FAILED.
HUH? BUT I...
NO, I...
...MADE A MISTAKE.
SPLASH ちゃぷ...
DUM ホッ
Huh?
BA ドバ
TAKUTO! MINT!
PLEASE GET OUT OF THE WATER!
YOU'LL CATCH A COLD!
mew
OH, THERE WERE THREE PEOPLE AWAKE.

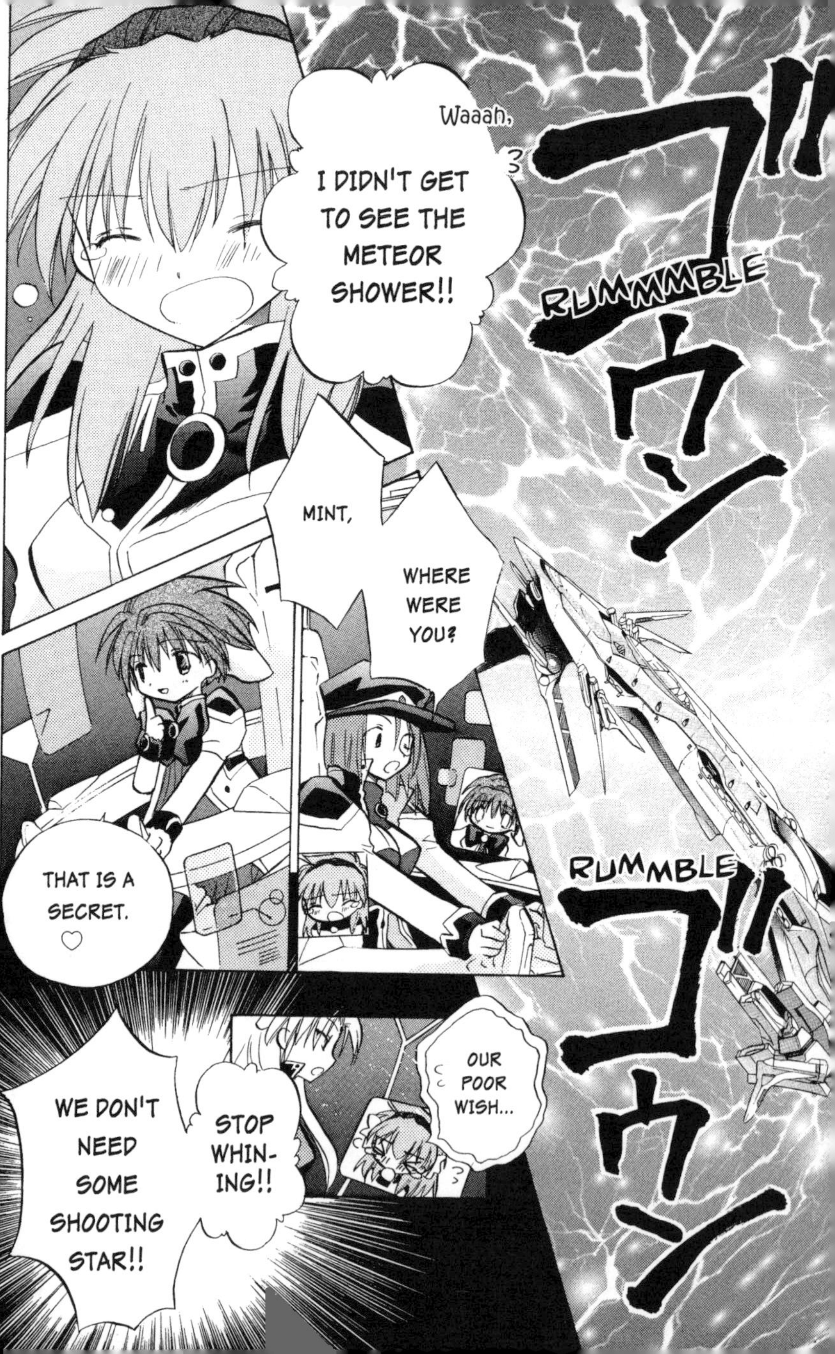
ゴウーン
RUMMMMBLE
Waaah,
I DIDN'T GET TO SEE THE METEOR SHOWER!!
MINT,
WHERE WERE YOU?
THAT IS A SECRET. ♡
ゴウン
RUMMBLE
OUR POOR WISH...
STOP WHINING!!
WE DON'T NEED SOME SHOOTING STAR!!

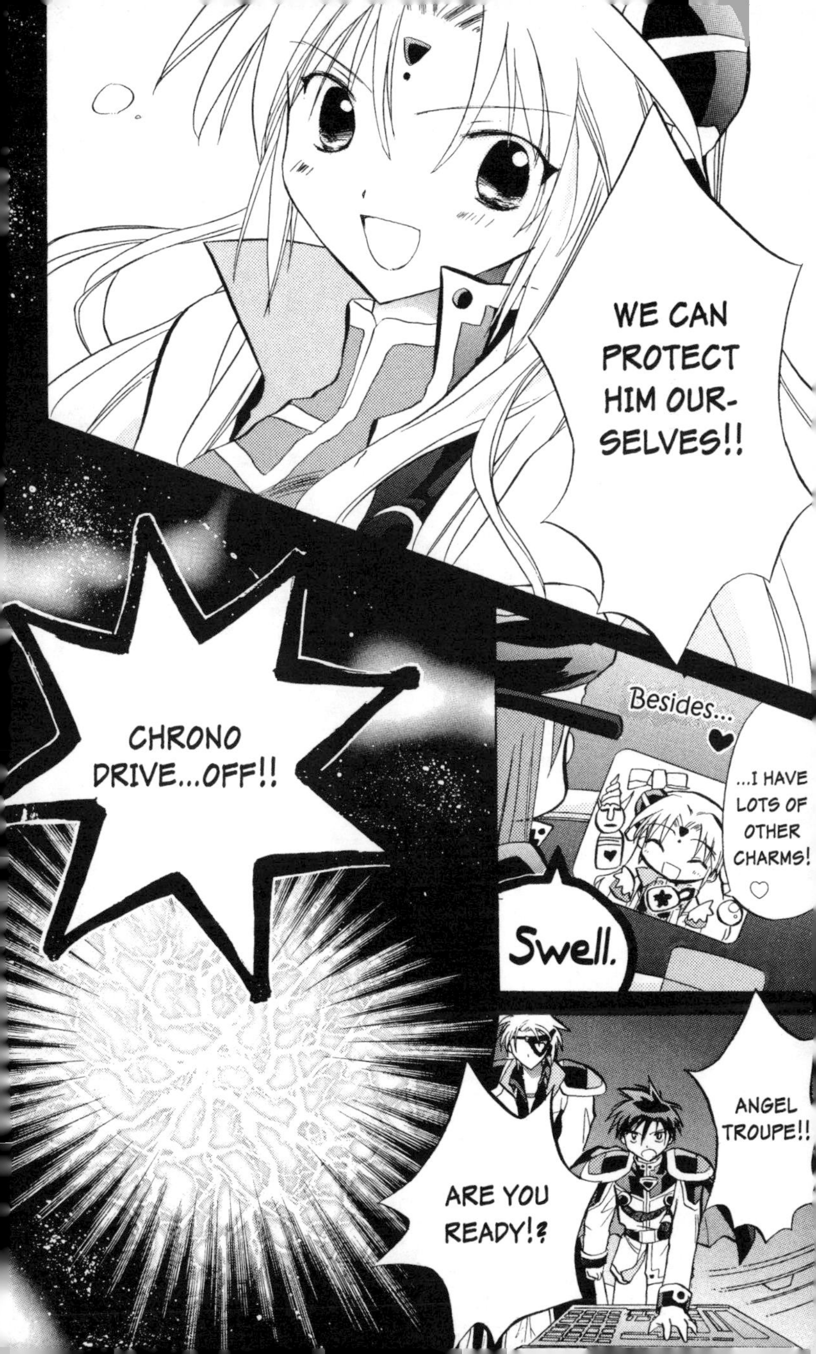
WE CAN PROTECT HIM OUR-SELVES!!
Besides...
...I HAVE LOTS OF OTHER CHARMS!
Swell.
ANGEL TROUPE!!
ARE YOU READY!?
CHRONO DRIVE...OFF!!

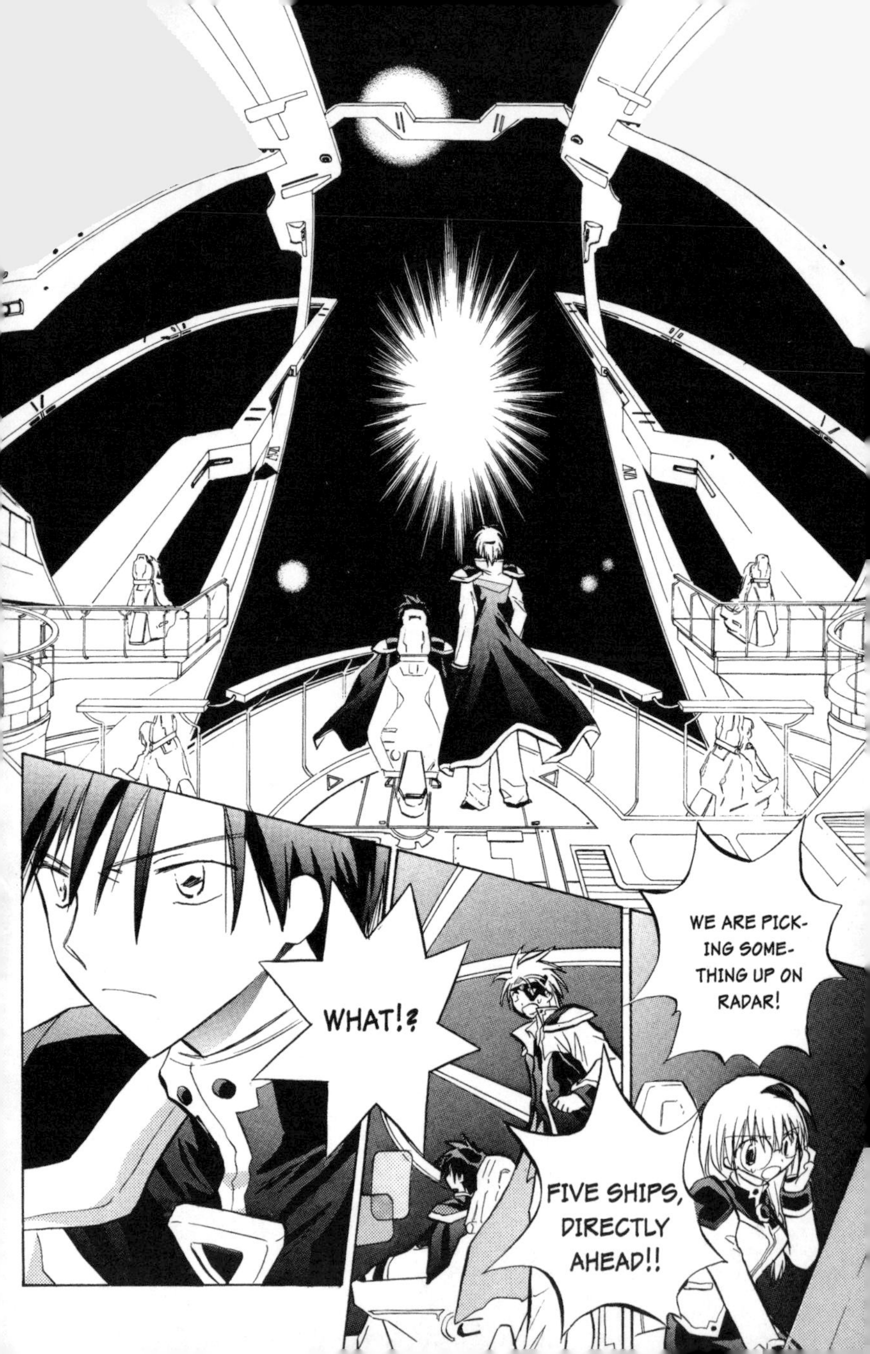
WE ARE PICK-ING SOME-THING UP ON RADAR!
WHAT!?
FIVE SHIPS, DIRECTLY AHEAD!!

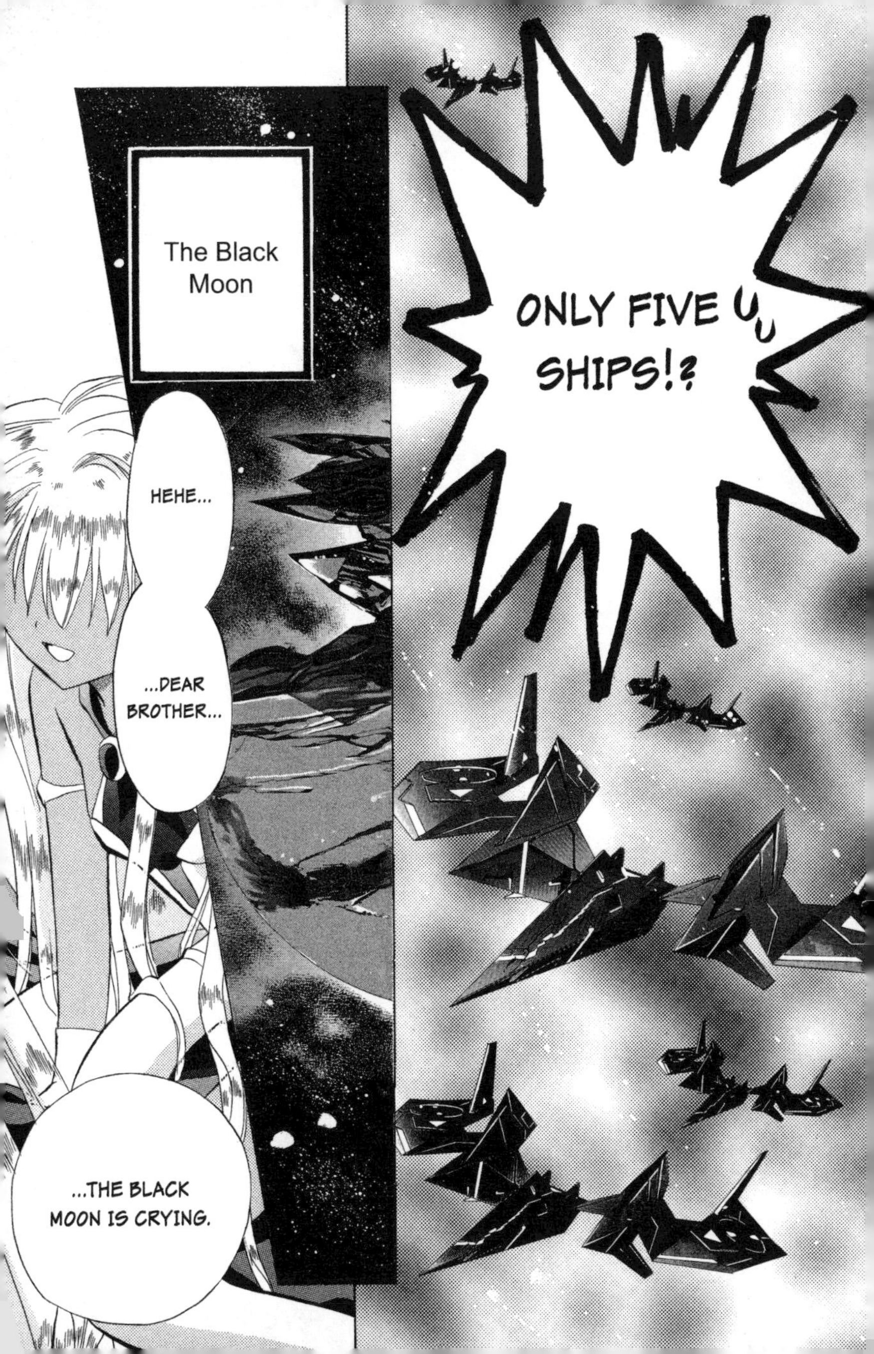
ONLY FIVE SHIPS!?
The Black Moon
HEHE...
...DEAR BROTHER...
...THE BLACK MOON IS CRYING.

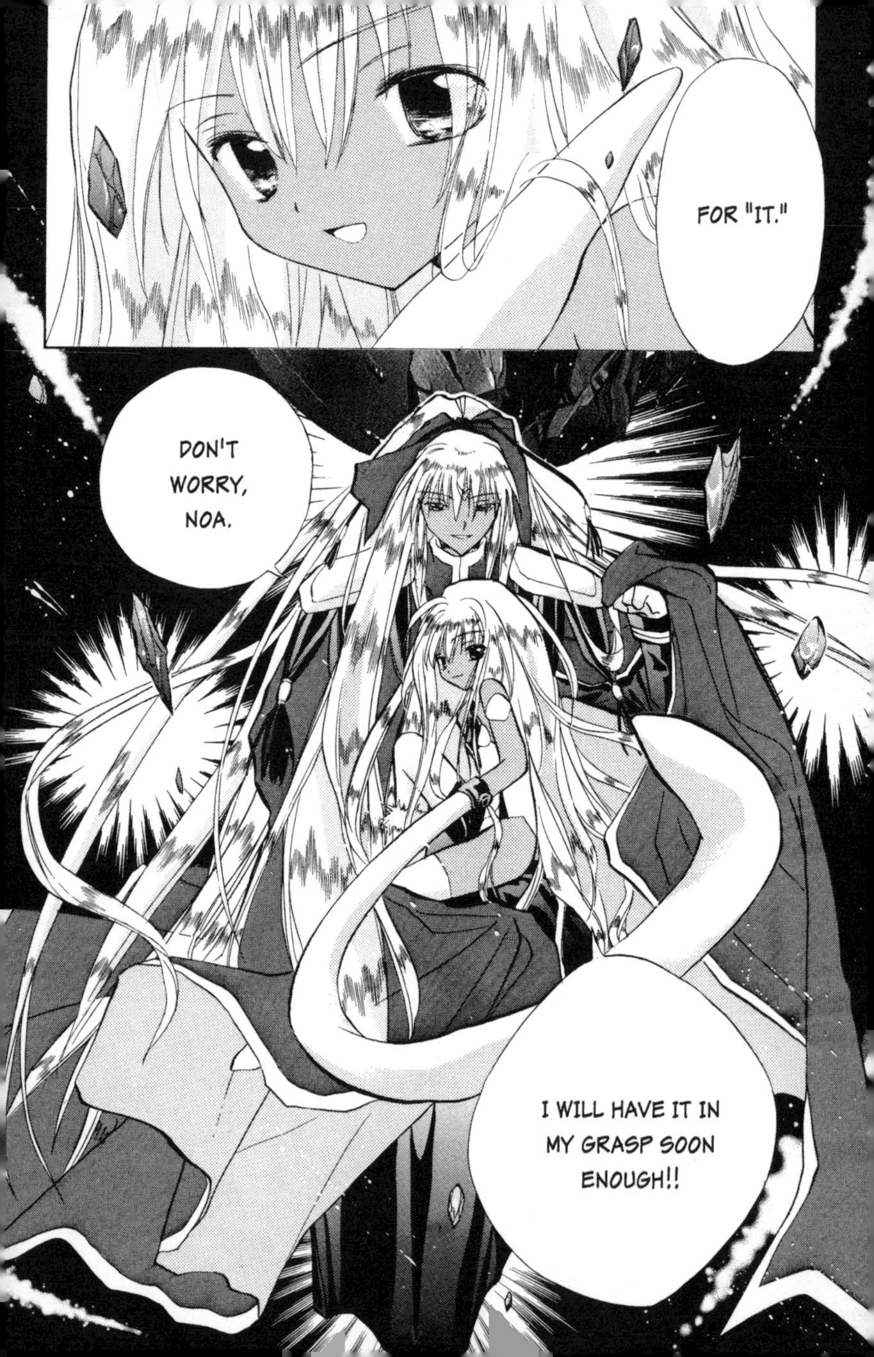
FOR "IT."
DON'T WORRY, NOA.
I WILL HAVE IT IN MY GRASP SOON ENOUGH!!

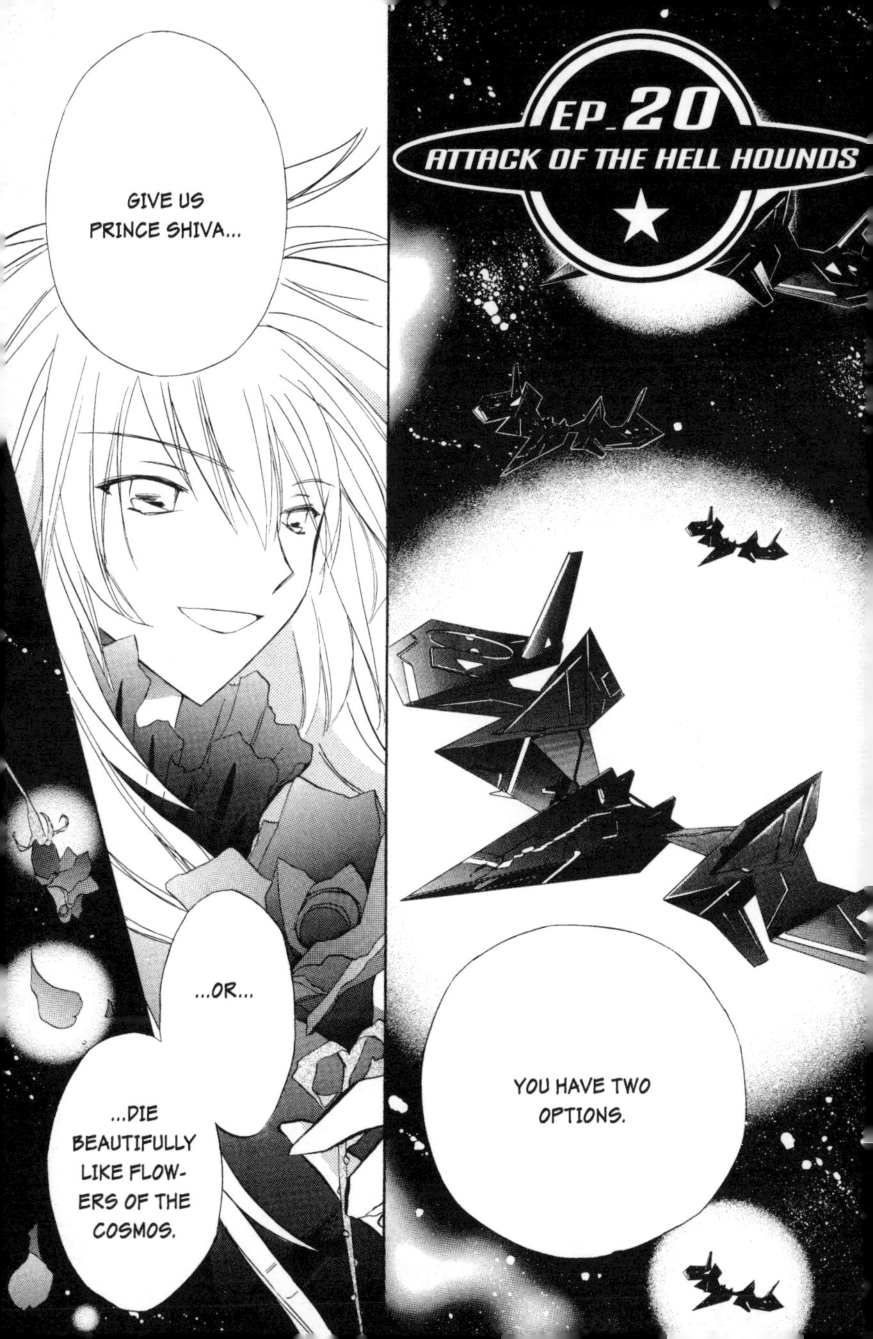
EP_20
ATTACK OF THE HELL HOUNDS
YOU HAVE TWO OPTIONS.
GIVE US PRINCE SHIVA...
...OR...
...DIE BEAUTIFULLY LIKE FLOWERS OF THE COSMOS.

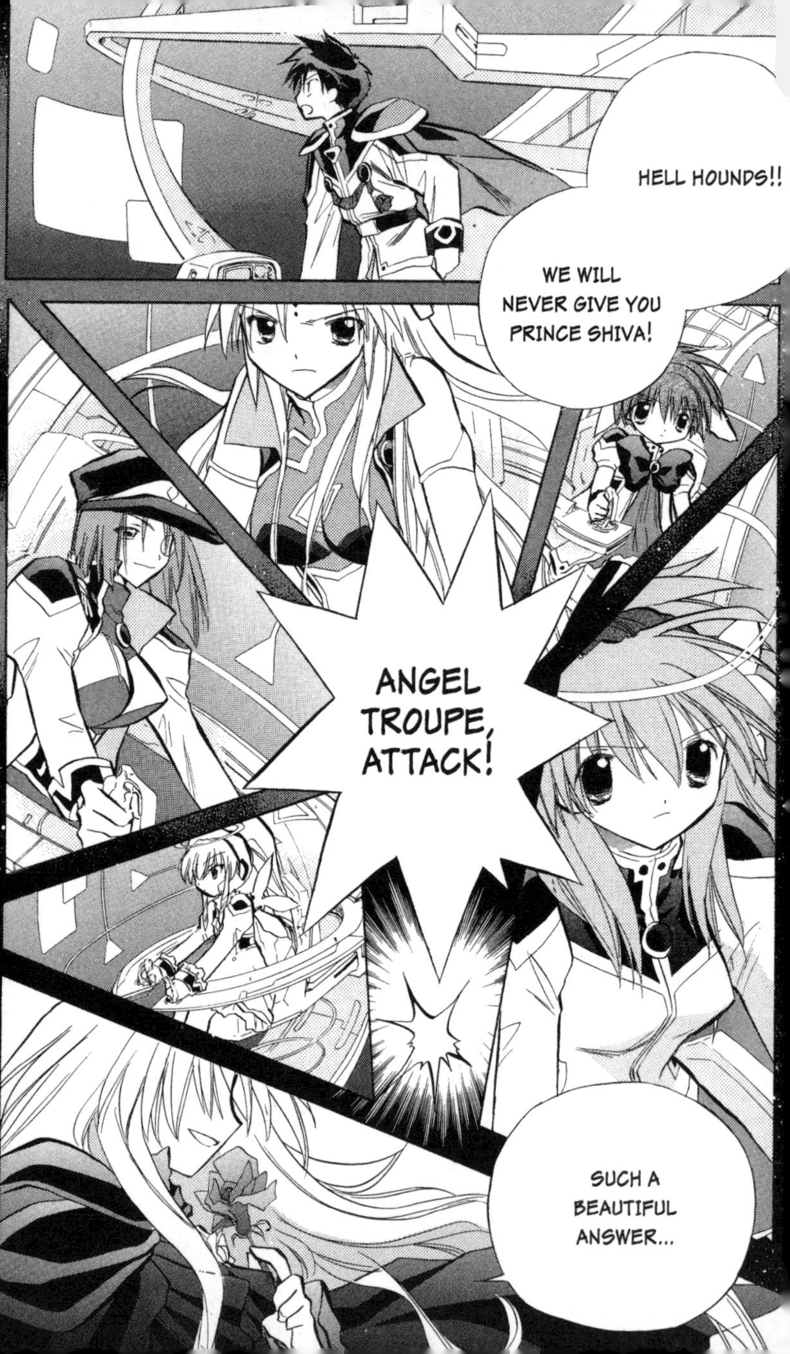
HELL HOUNDS!!
WE WILL NEVER GIVE YOU PRINCE SHIVA!
ANGEL TROUPE, ATTACK!
SUCH A BEAUTIFUL ANSWER...

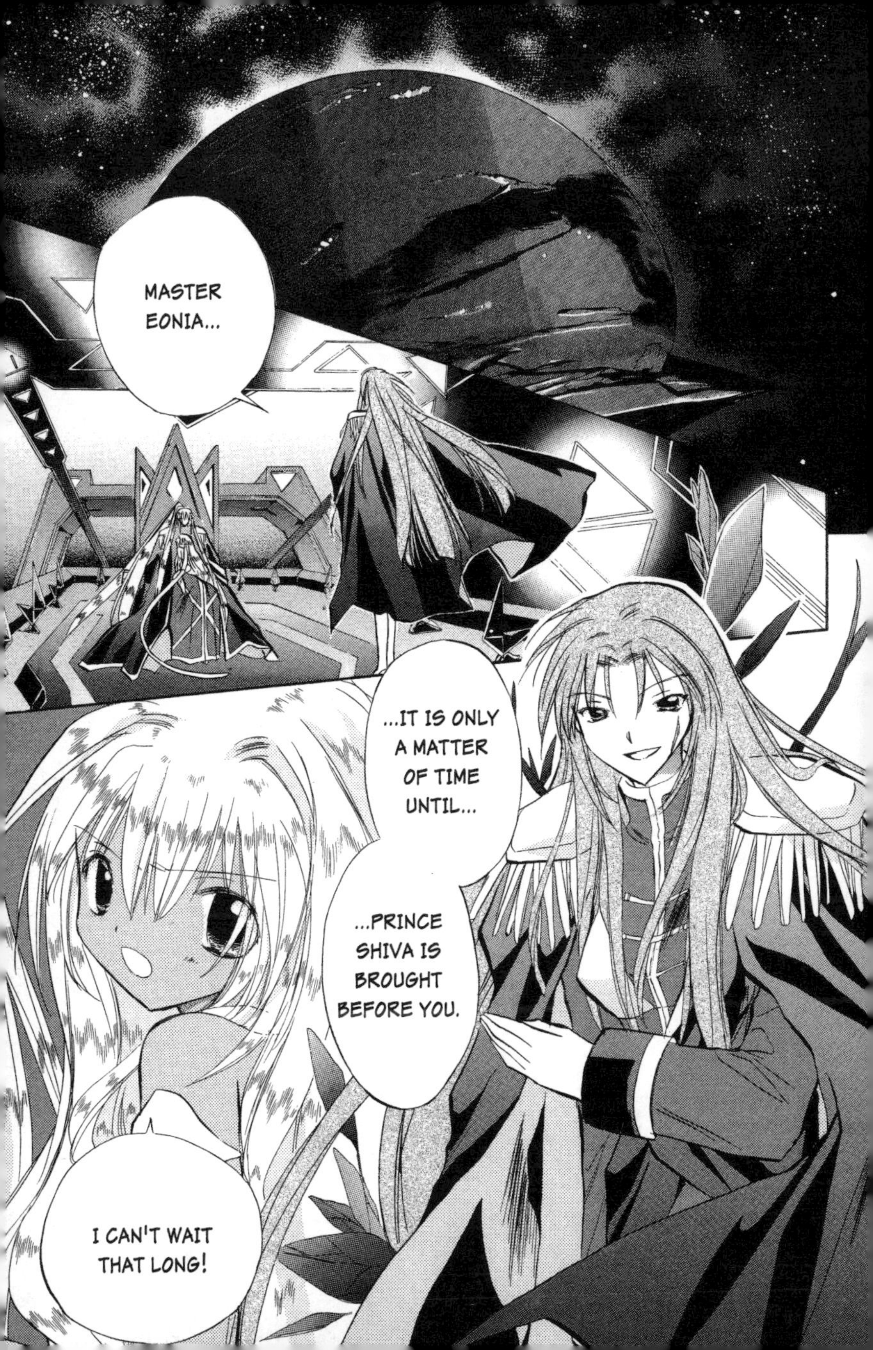
MASTER EONIA...
...IT IS ONLY A MATTER OF TIME UNTIL...
...PRINCE SHIVA IS BROUGHT BEFORE YOU.
I CAN'T WAIT THAT LONG!

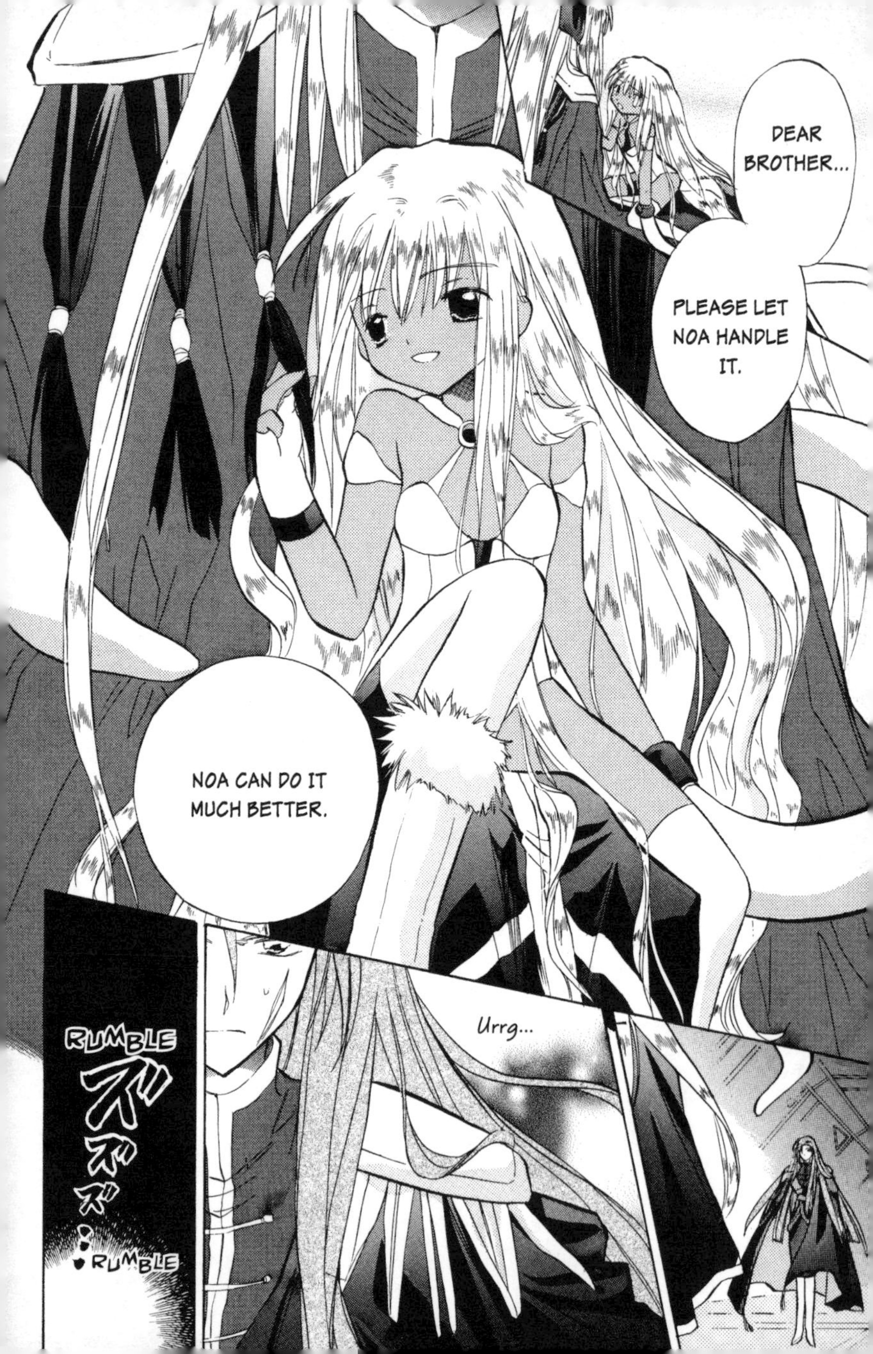
DEAR BROTHER...
PLEASE LET NOA HANDLE IT.
NOA CAN DO IT MUCH BETTER.
Urrg...
RUMBLE
ズズズ
RUMBLE

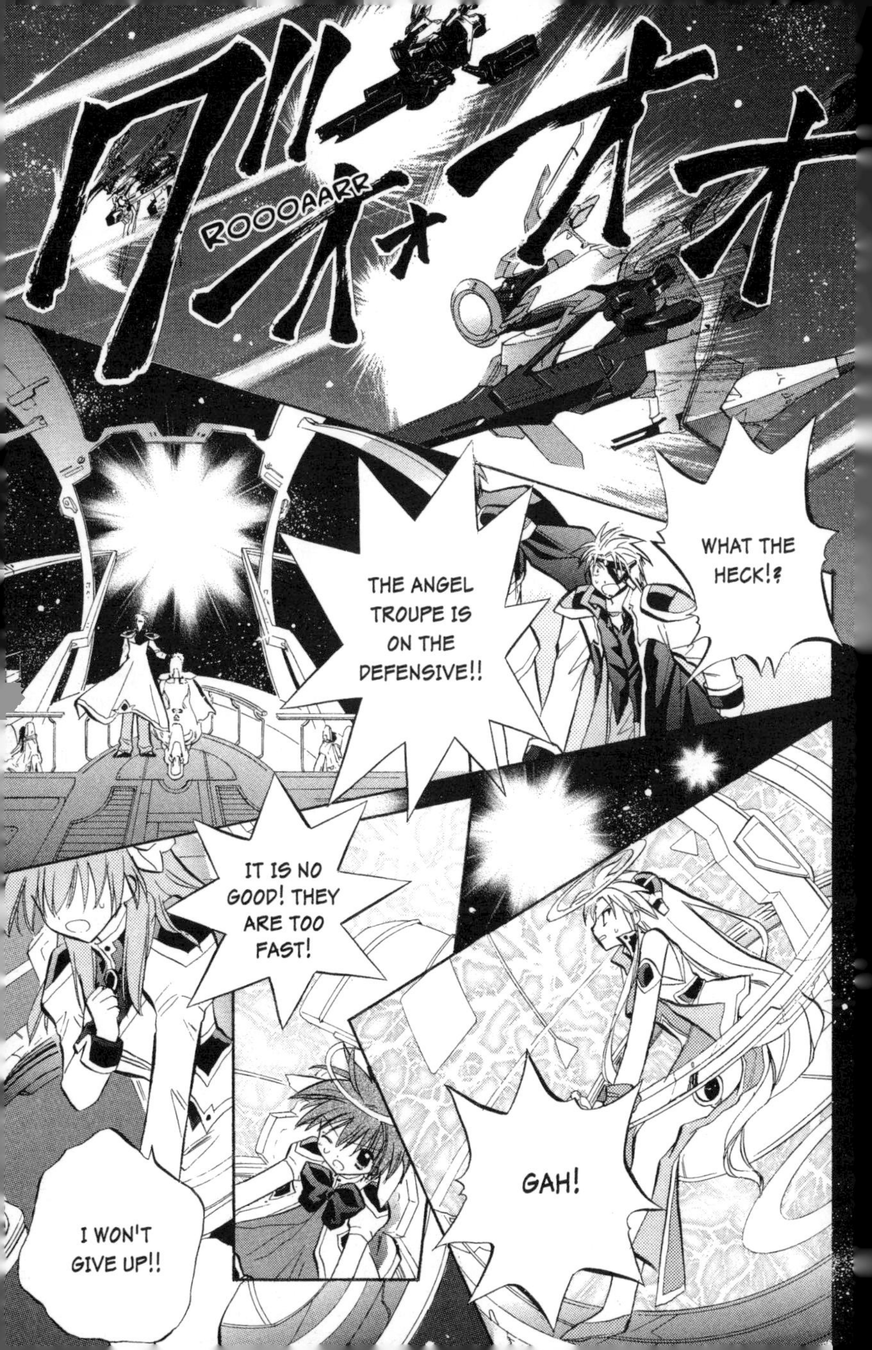
ROOOAARR
WHAT THE HECK!?
THE ANGEL TROUPE IS ON THE DEFENSIVE!!
GAH!
IT IS NO GOOD! THEY ARE TOO FAST!
I WON'T GIVE UP!!

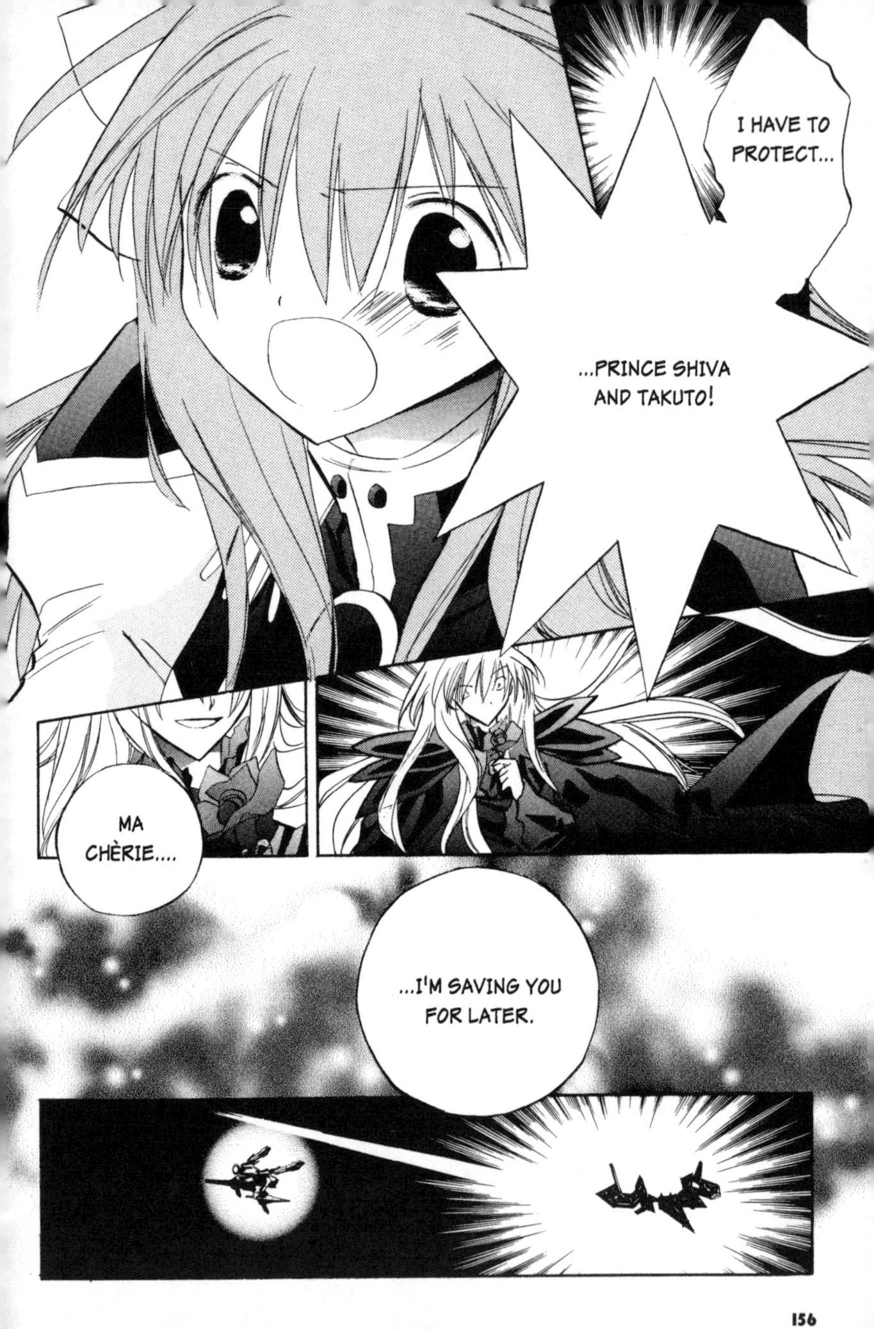
I HAVE TO PROTECT...
...PRINCE SHIVA AND TAKUTO!
MA CHÈRIE....
...I'M SAVING YOU FOR LATER.

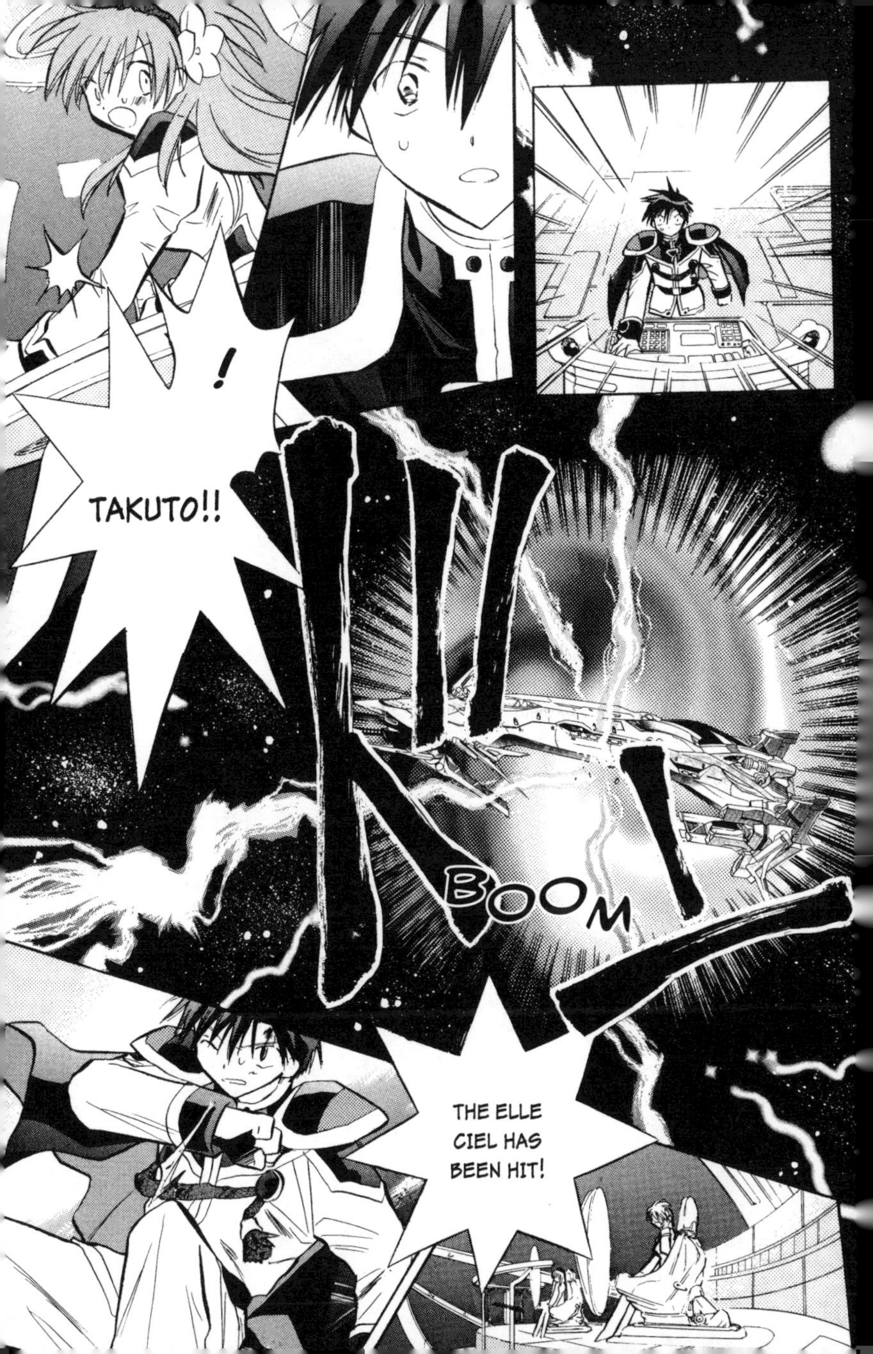
!
TAKUTO!!
BOOM
THE ELLE CIEL HAS BEEN HIT!

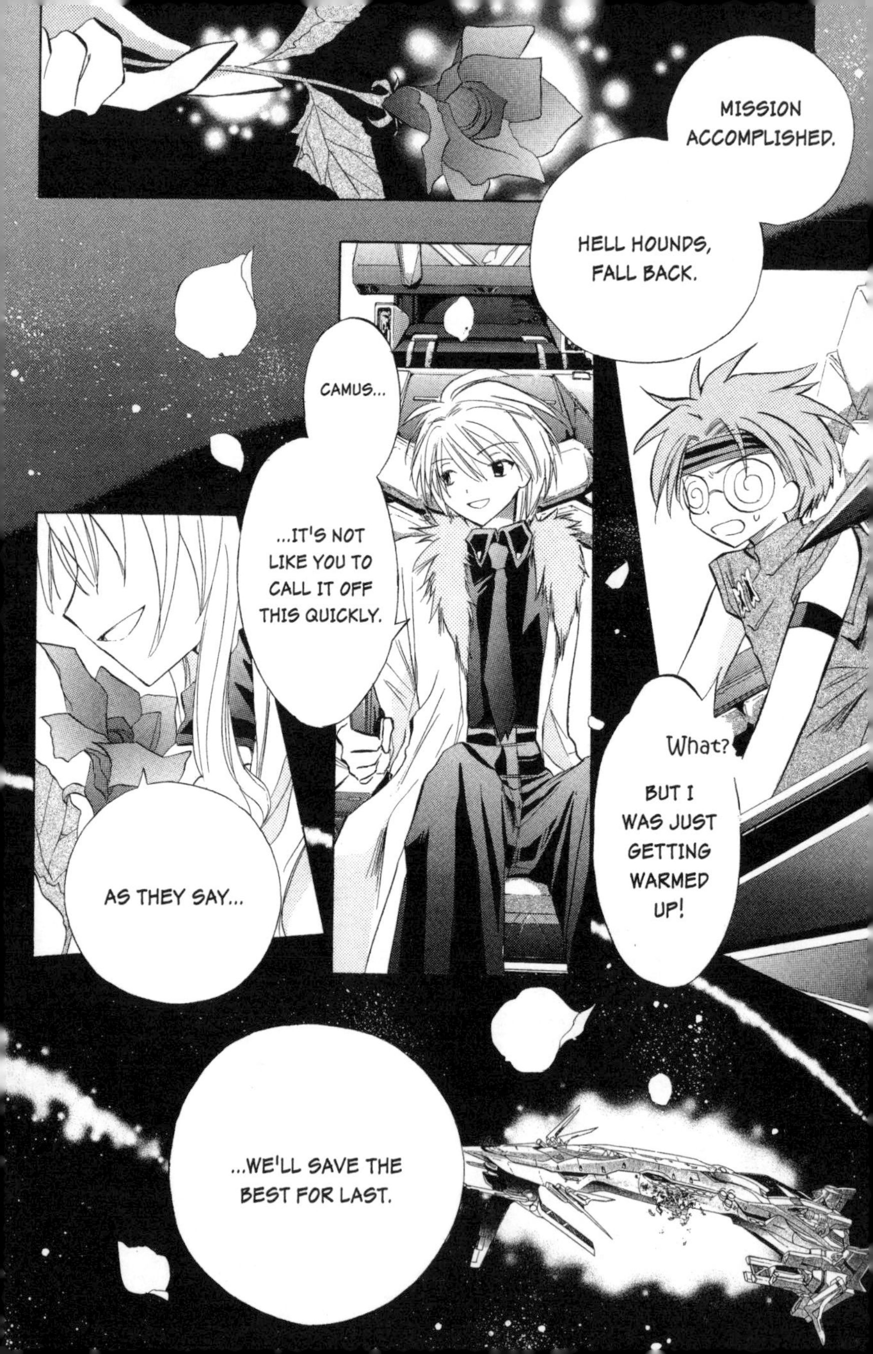
MISSION ACCOMPLISHED.
HELL HOUNDS, FALL BACK.
What?
BUT I WAS JUST GETTING WARMED UP!
CAMUS...
...IT'S NOT LIKE YOU TO CALL IT OFF THIS QUICKLY.
AS THEY SAY...
...WE'LL SAVE THE BEST FOR LAST.

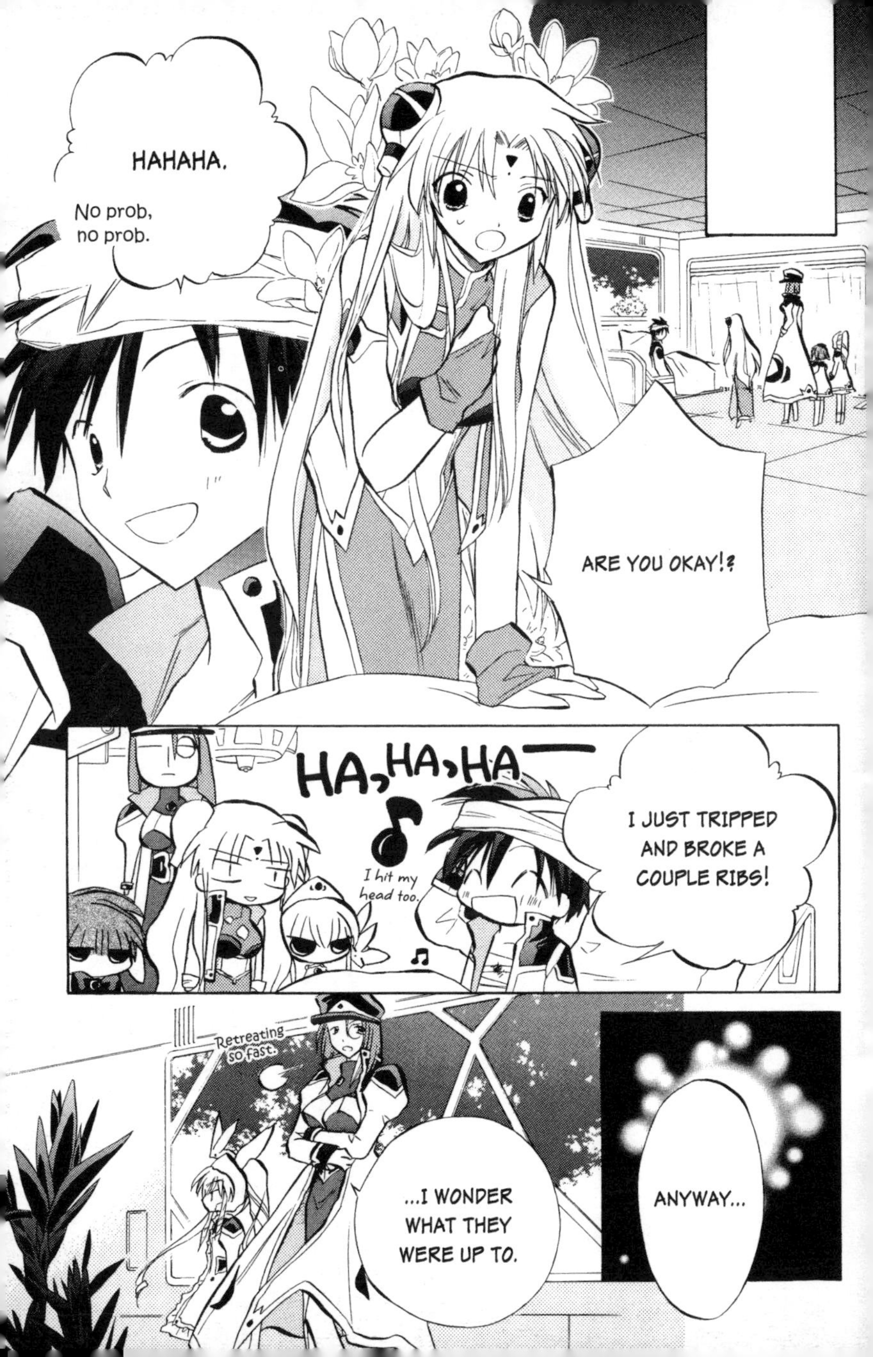
ARE YOU OKAY!?
HAHAHA.
No prob, no prob.
I JUST TRIPPED AND BROKE A COUPLE RIBS!
HA, HA, HA—
I hit my head too.
ANYWAY...
...I WONDER WHAT THEY WERE UP TO.
Retreating so fast.

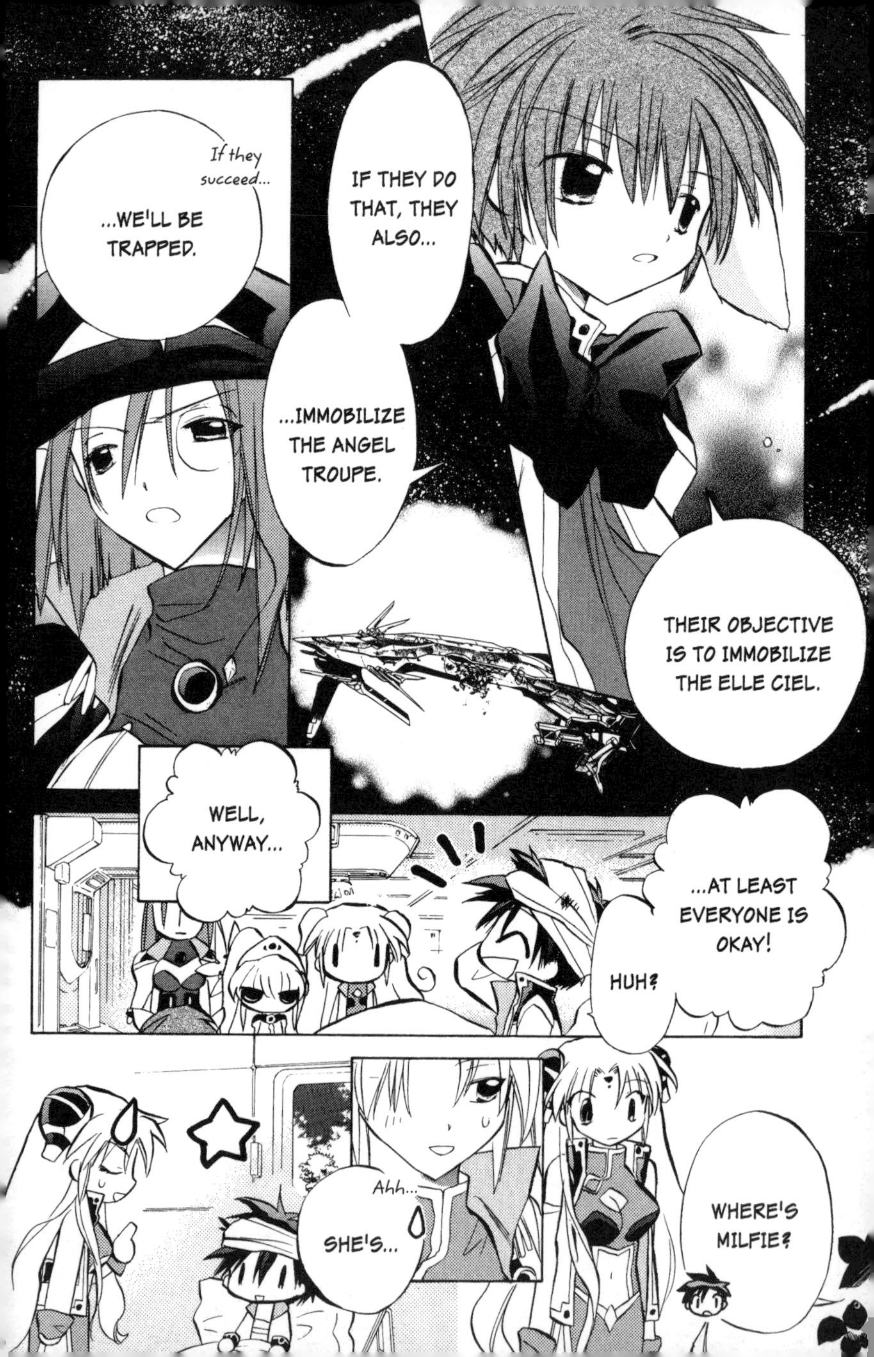
THEIR OBJECTIVE IS TO IMMOBILIZE THE ELLE CIEL.
IF THEY DO THAT, THEY ALSO...
...IMMOBILIZE THE ANGEL TROUPE.
If they succeed...
...WE'LL BE TRAPPED.
WELL, ANYWAY...
...AT LEAST EVERYONE IS OKAY!
HUH?
WHERE'S MILFIE?
Ahh...
SHE'S...

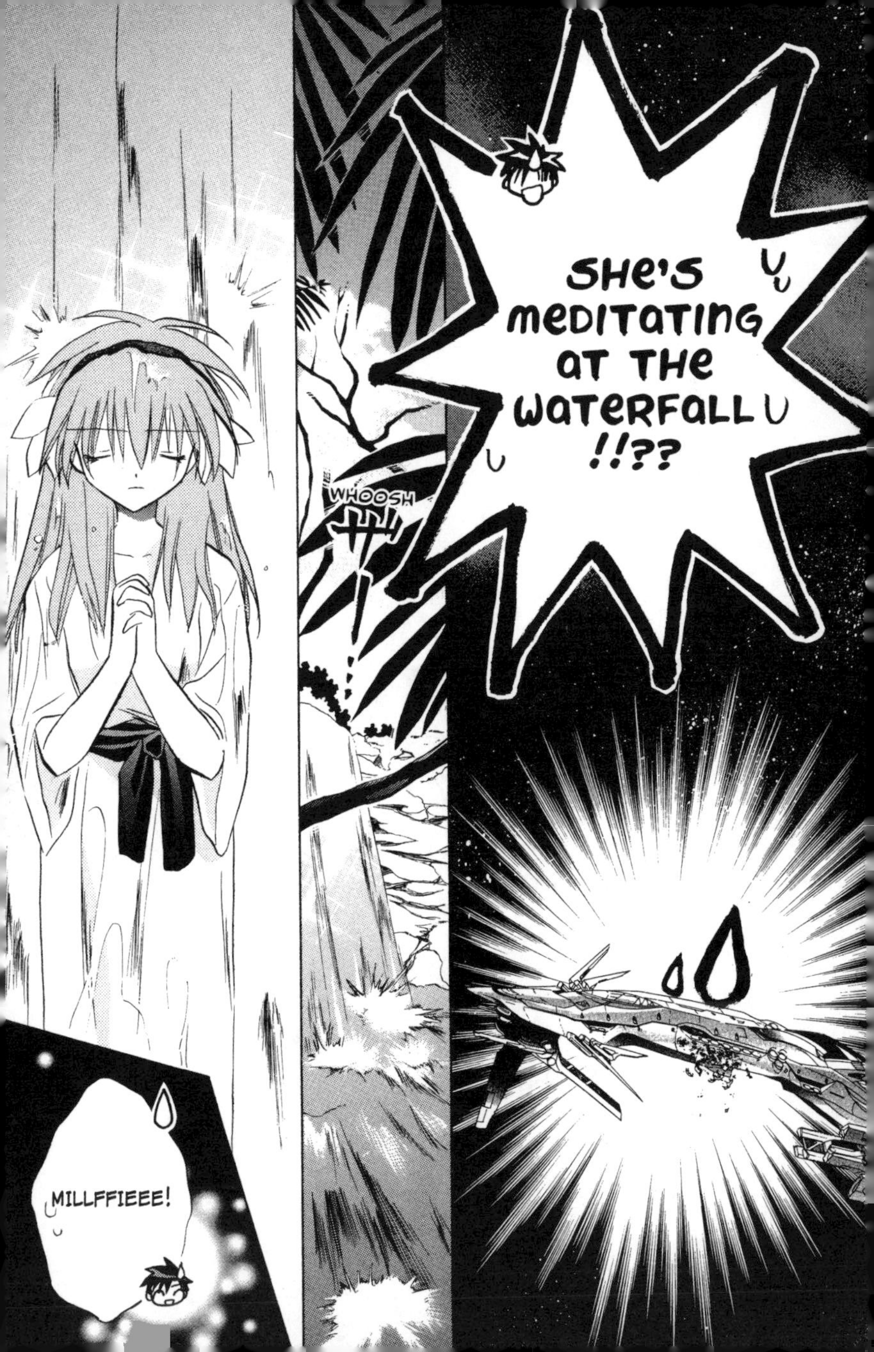
SHE'S MEDITATING AT THE WATERFALL !!??
WHOOSH
MILLFFIEEE!

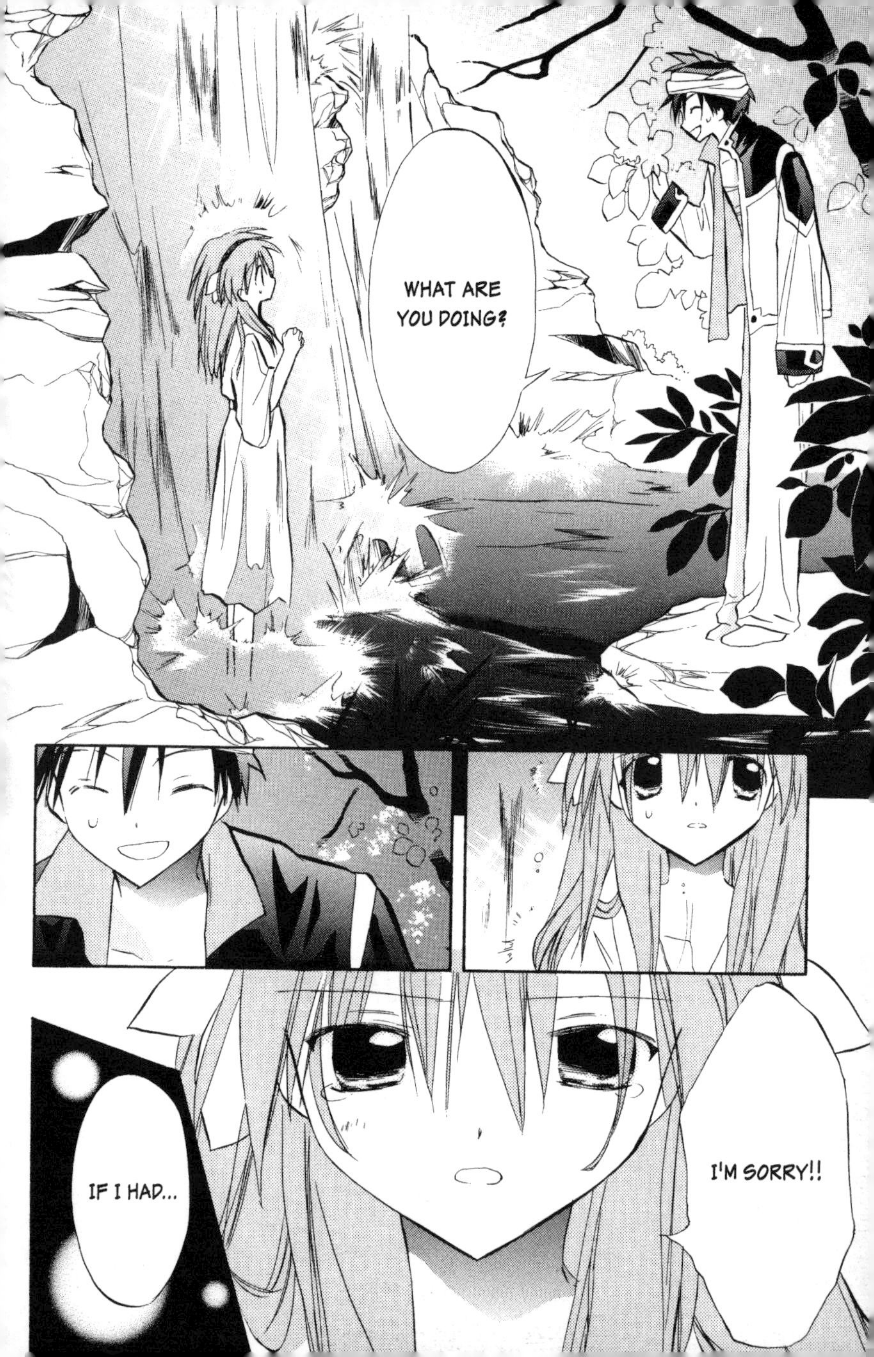
WHAT ARE YOU DOING?
I'M SORRY!!
IF I HAD...

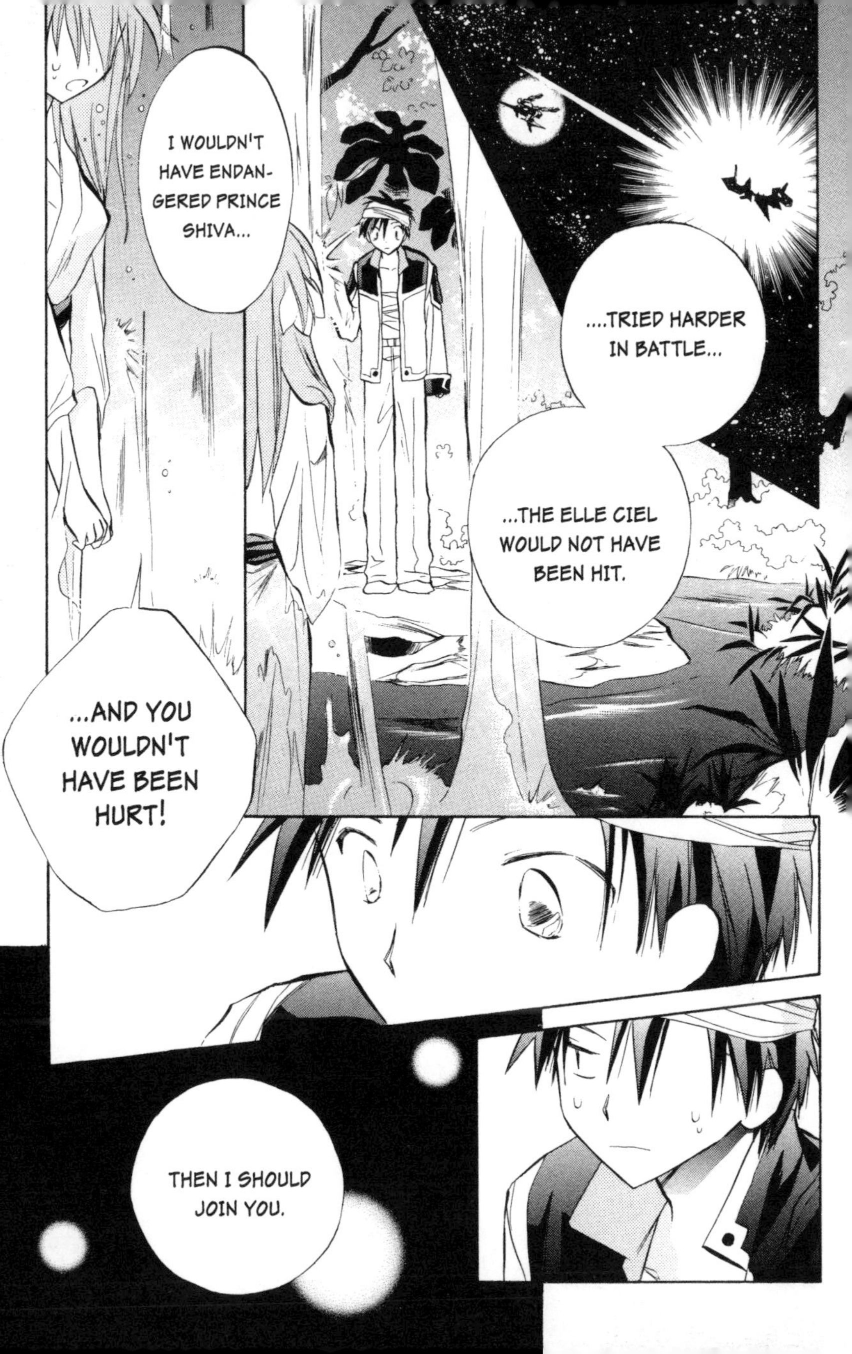
....TRIED HARDER IN BATTLE...
...THE ELLE CIEL WOULD NOT HAVE BEEN HIT.
I WOULDN'T HAVE ENDANGERED PRINCE SHIVA...
...AND YOU WOULDN'T HAVE BEEN HURT!
THEN I SHOULD JOIN YOU.

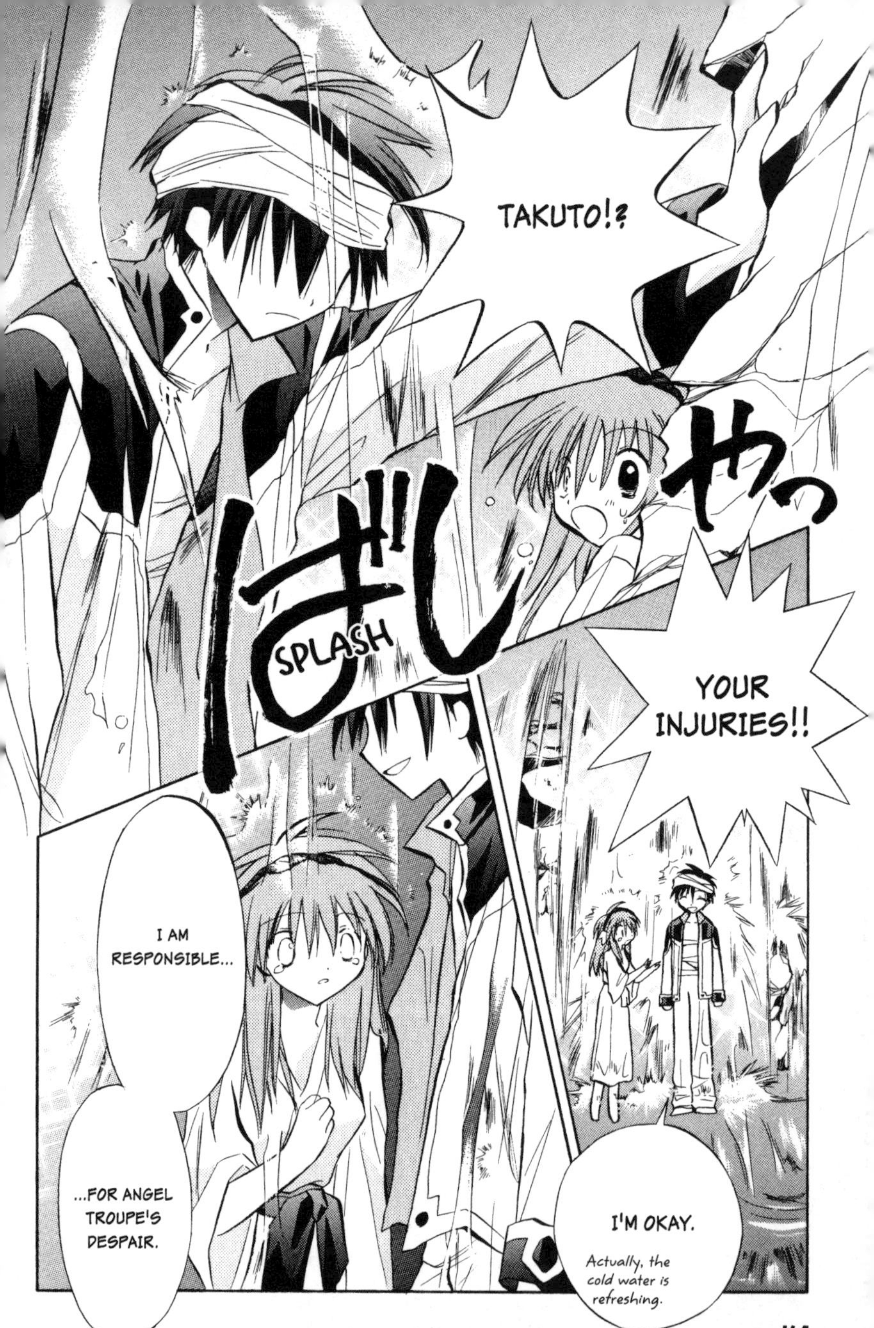
TAKUTO!?
ばしゃっ
SPLASH
YOUR INJURIES!!
I'M OKAY.
Actually, the cold water is refreshing.
I AM RESPONSIBLE...
...FOR ANGEL TROUPE'S DESPAIR.

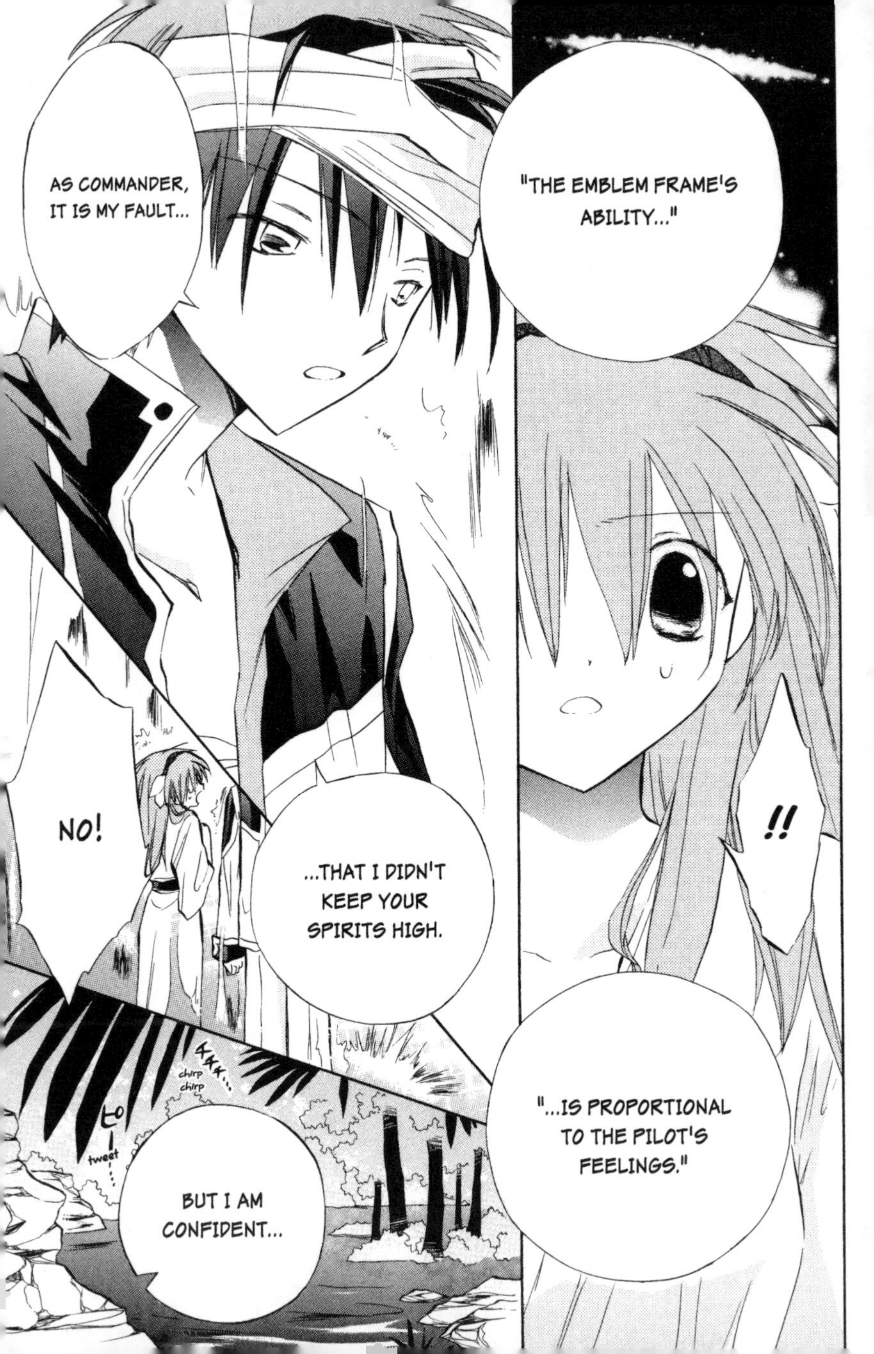
AS COMMANDER, IT IS MY FAULT...
...THAT I DIDN'T KEEP YOUR SPIRITS HIGH.
NO!
chirp chirp
tweet
BUT I AM CONFIDENT...
"THE EMBLEM FRAME'S ABILITY..."
!!
"...IS PROPORTIONAL TO THE PILOT'S FEELINGS."

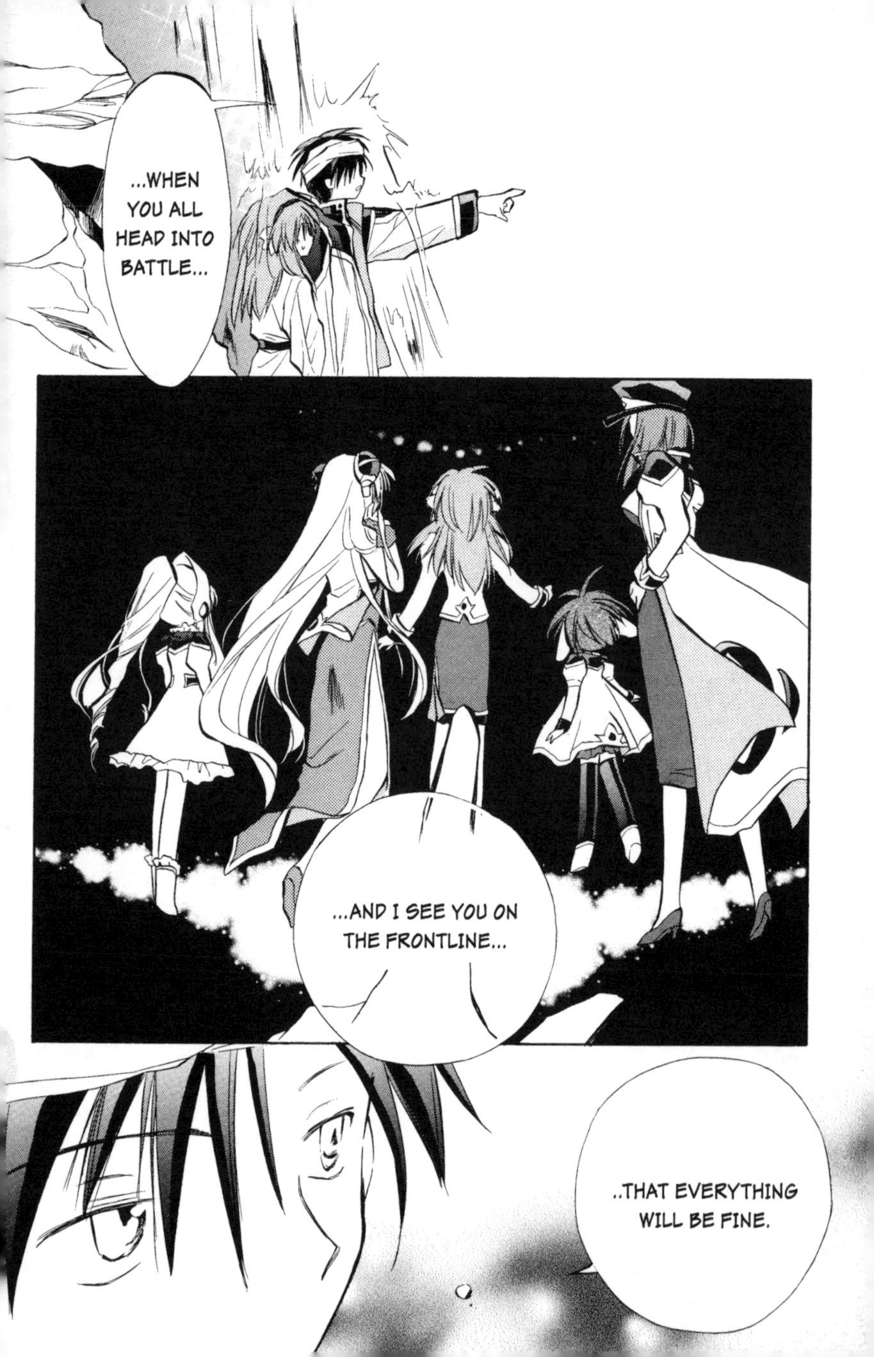
...WHEN YOU ALL HEAD INTO BATTLE...
...AND I SEE YOU ON THE FRONTLINE...
..THAT EVERYTHING WILL BE FINE.

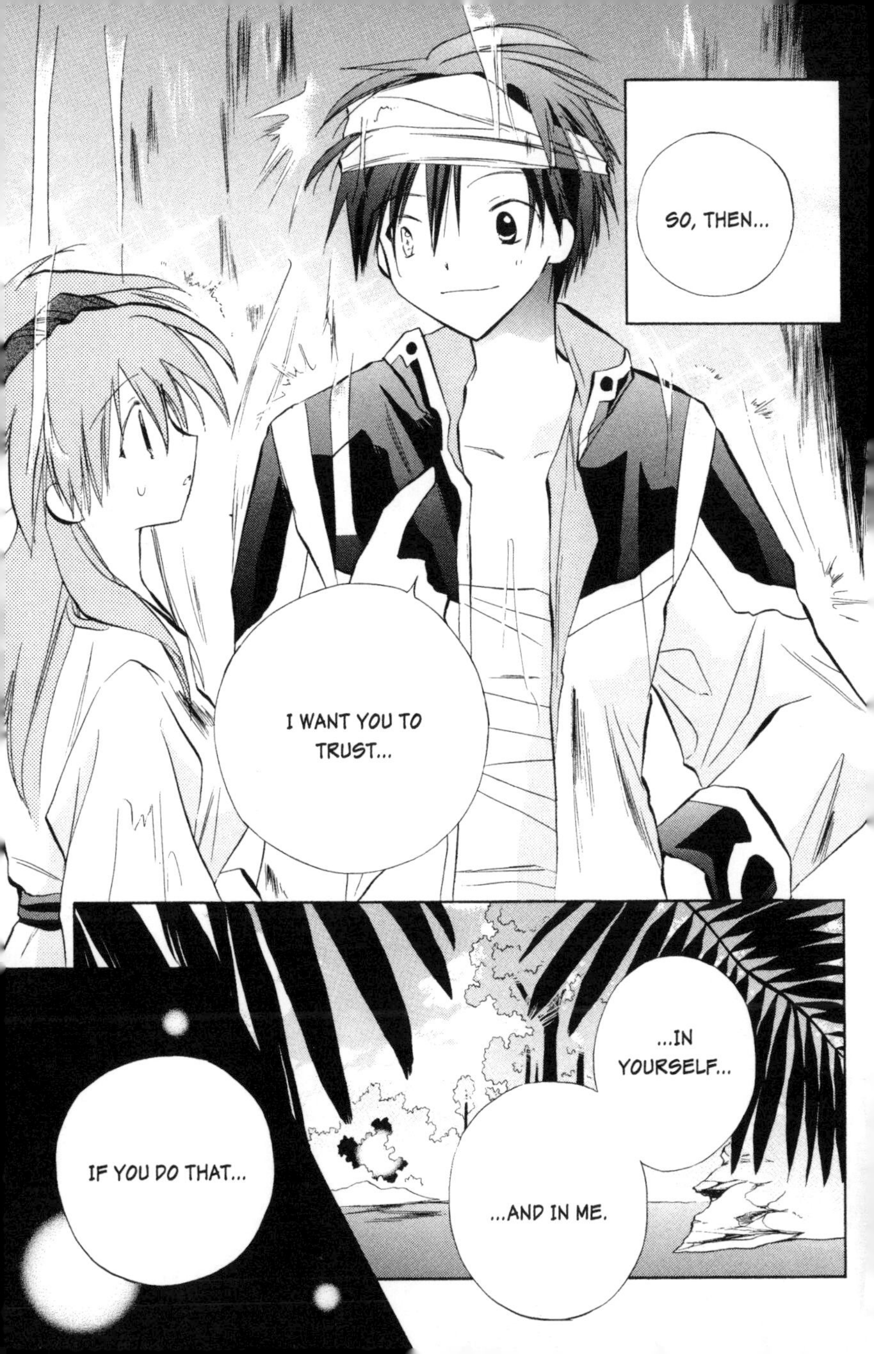
SO, THEN...
I WANT YOU TO TRUST...
...IN YOURSELF...
...AND IN ME.
IF YOU DO THAT...

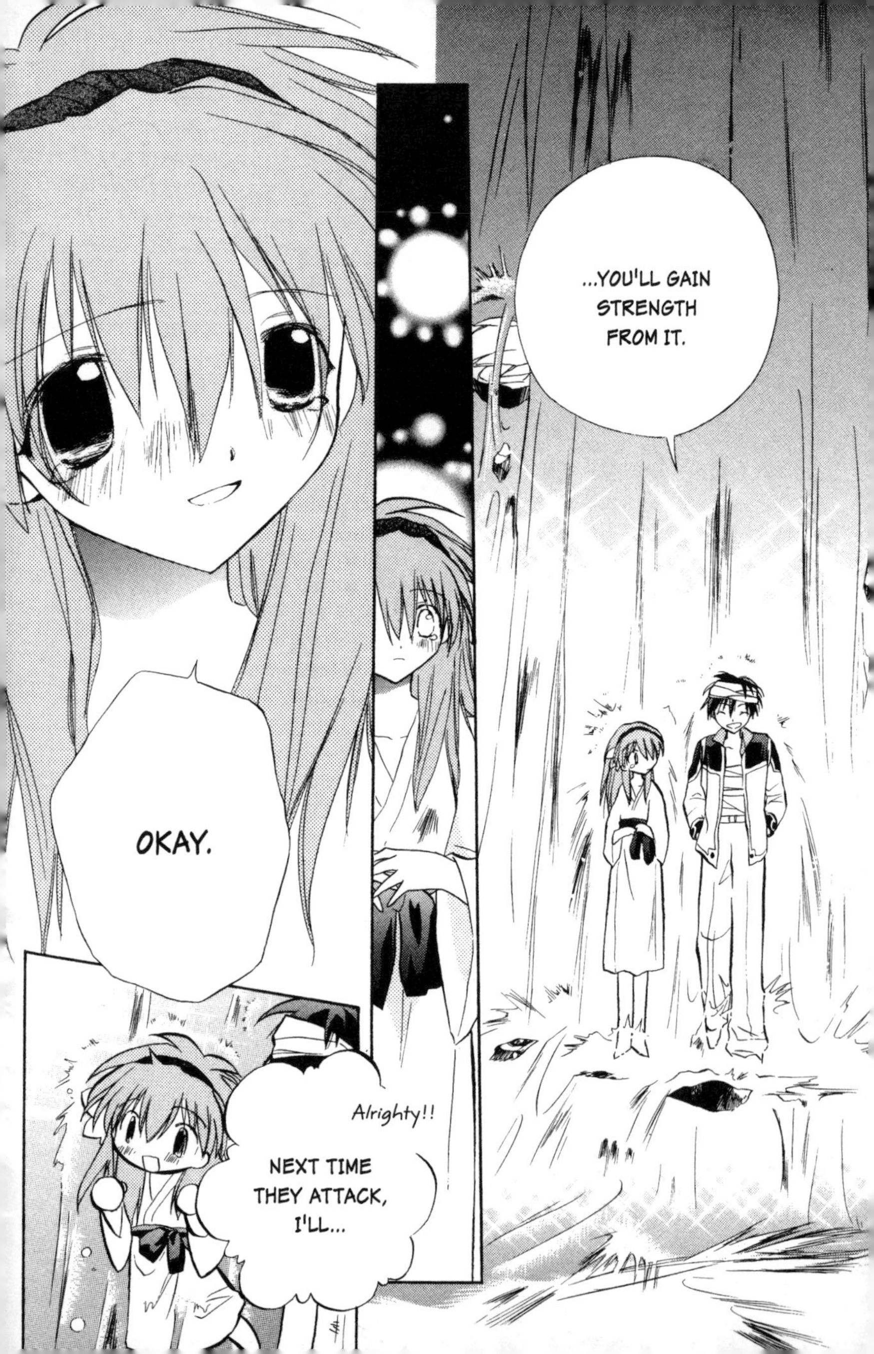
...YOU'LL GAIN STRENGTH FROM IT.
OKAY.
Alrighty!!
NEXT TIME THEY ATTACK, I'LL...

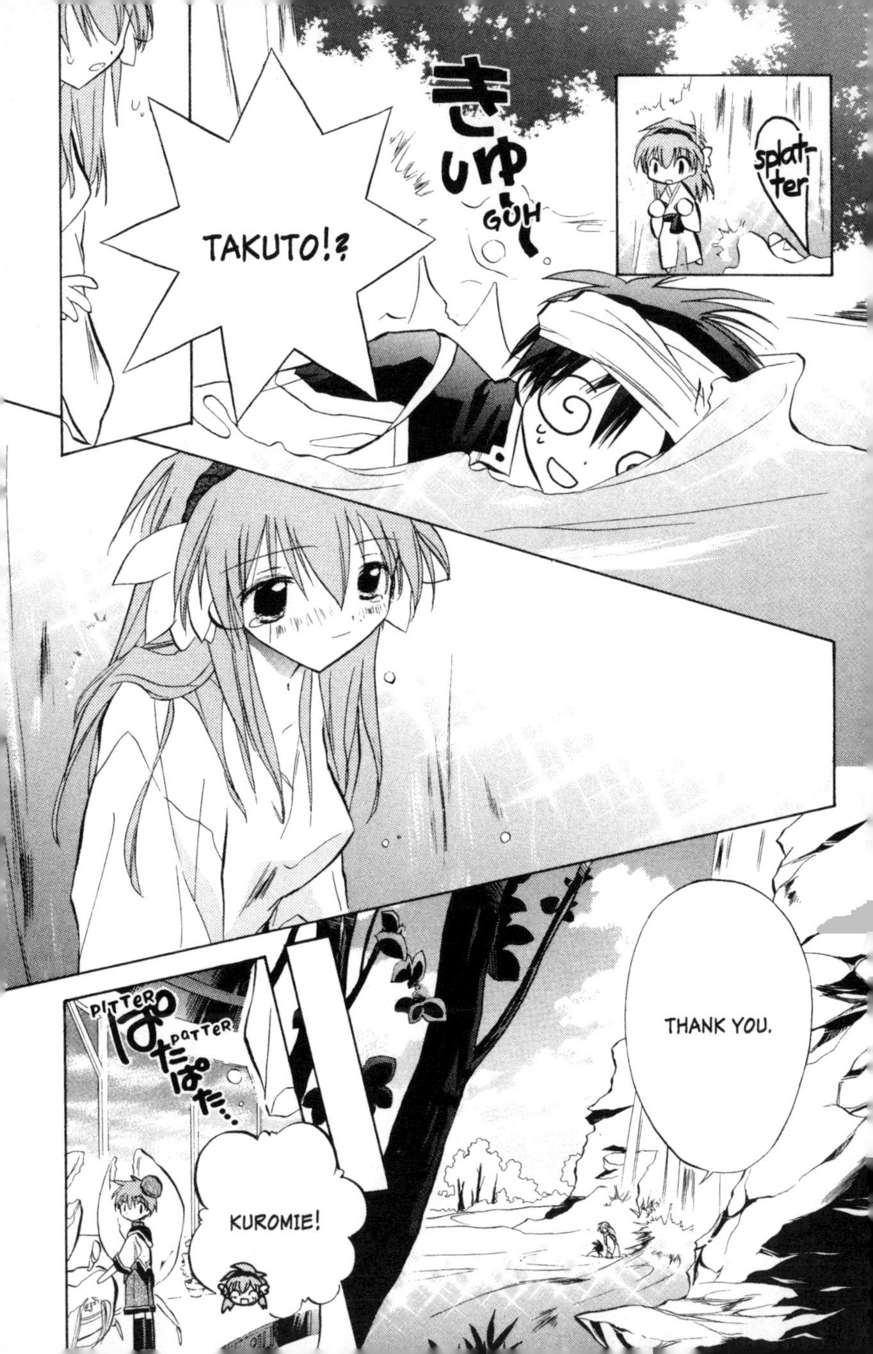
splat-ter
きゅ〜
GUH
TAKUTO!?
THANK YOU.
PITTER PATTER
ぱたぱた...
KUROMIE!

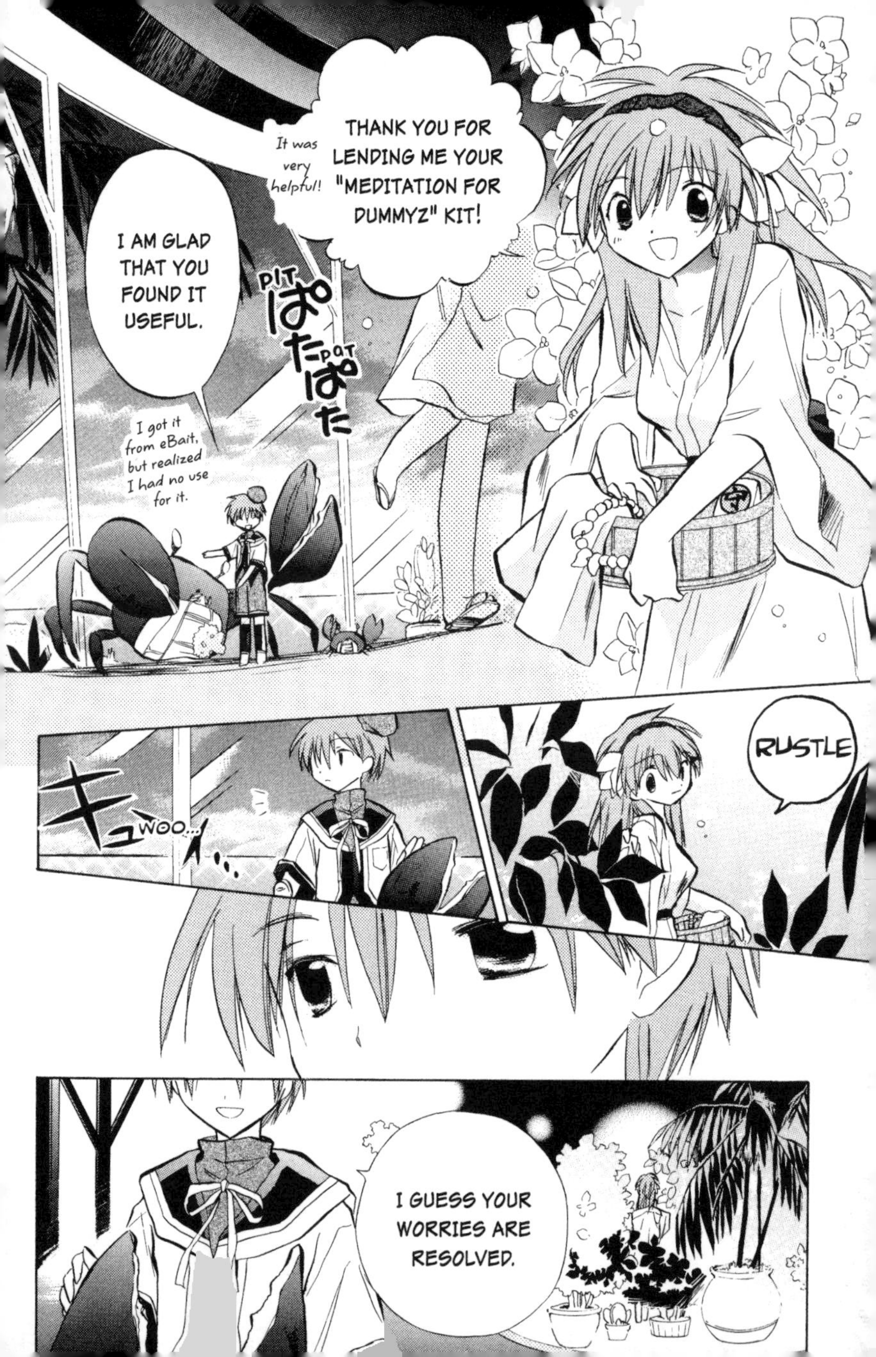
THANK YOU FOR LENDING ME YOUR "MEDITATION FOR DUMMYZ" KIT!
It was very helpful!
I AM GLAD THAT YOU FOUND IT USEFUL.
ぱたぱた
PIT PAT
I got it from eBait, but realized I had no use for it.
RUSTLE
キュ
WOO...
...
I GUESS YOUR WORRIES ARE RESOLVED.

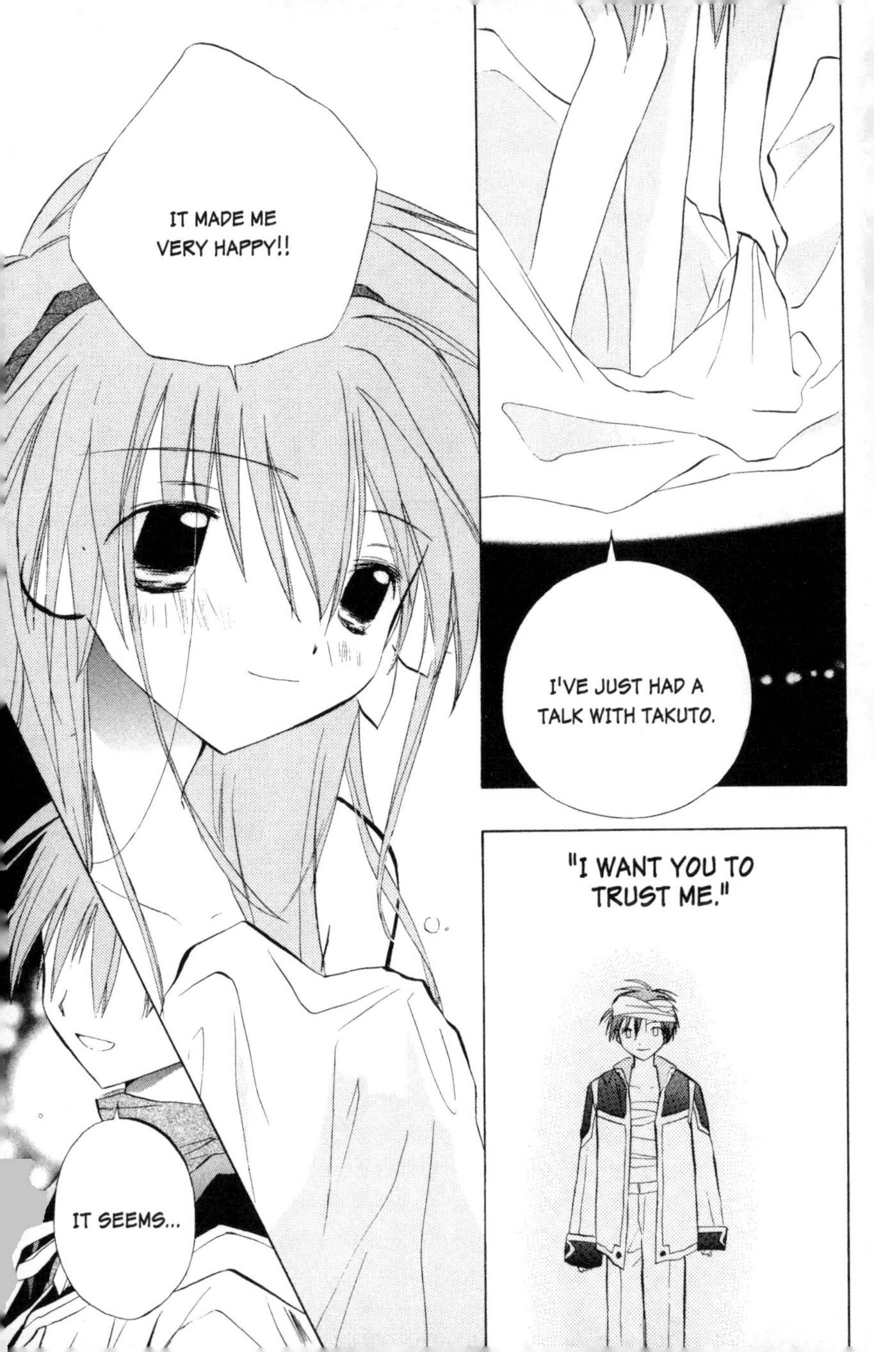
I'VE JUST HAD A TALK WITH TAKUTO.
"I WANT YOU TO TRUST ME."
IT MADE ME VERY HAPPY!!
IT SEEMS...

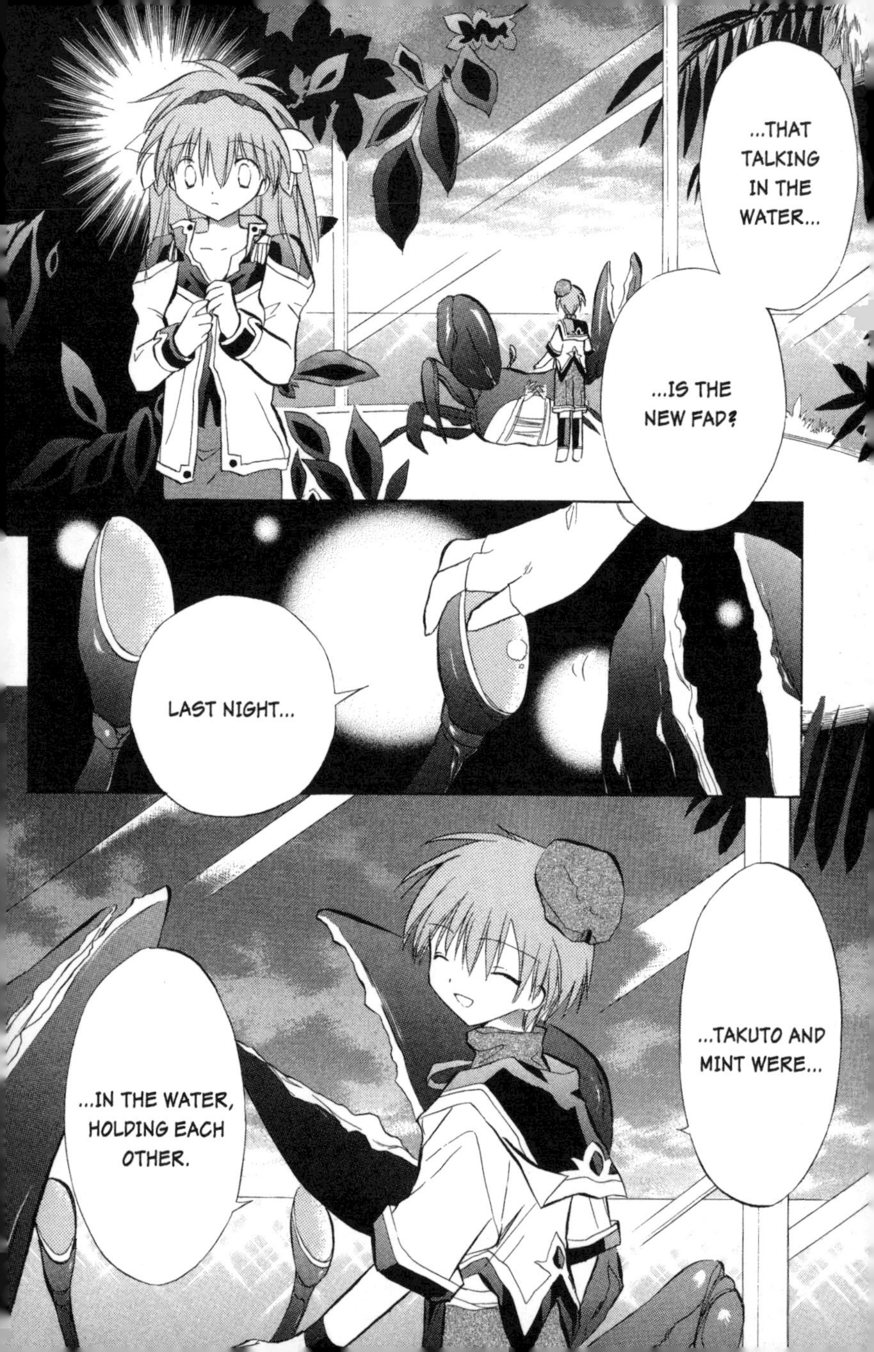
...THAT TALKING IN THE WATER...
...IS THE NEW FAD?
LAST NIGHT...
...TAKUTO AND MINT WERE...
...IN THE WATER, HOLDING EACH OTHER.

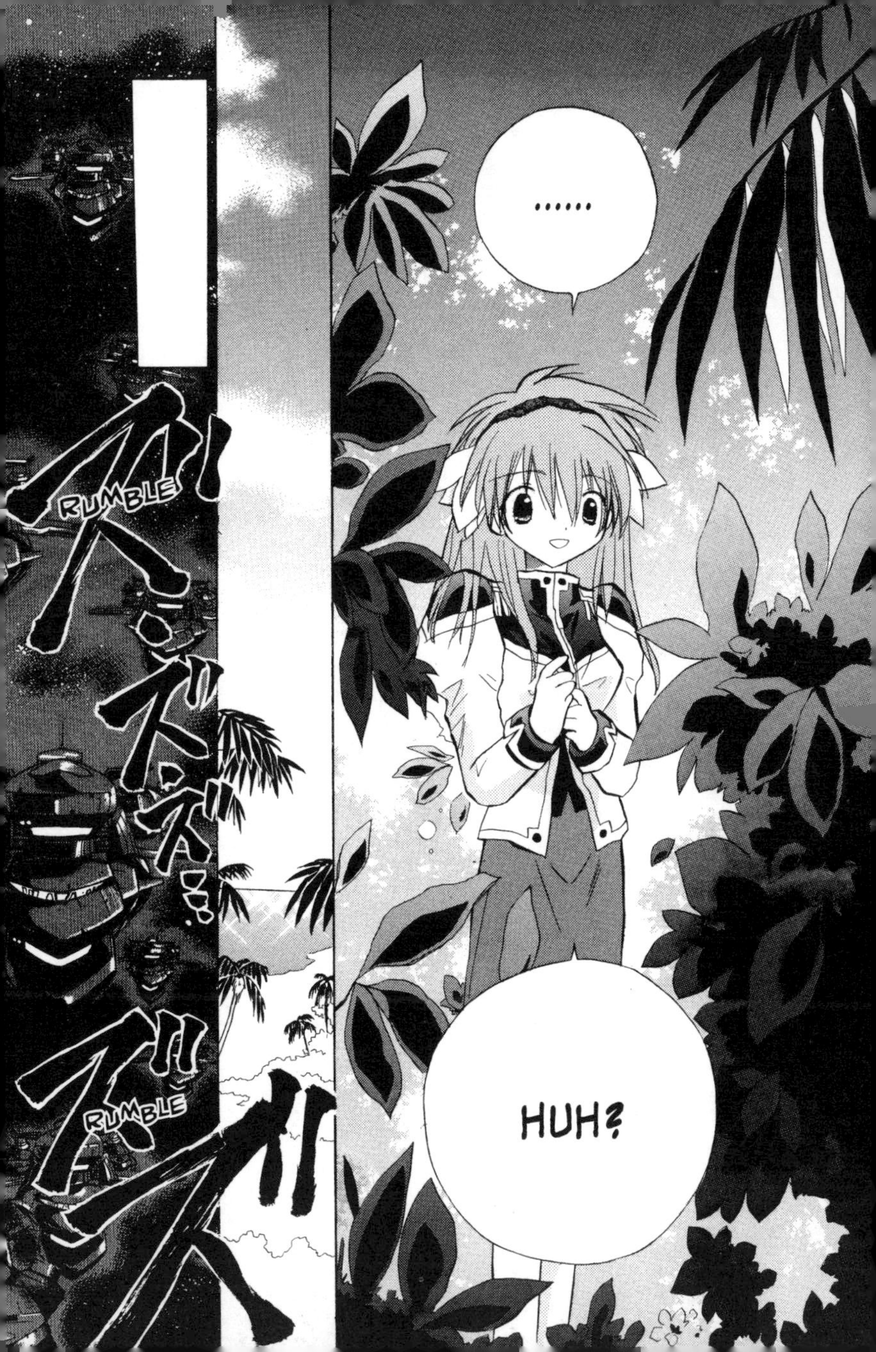
......
HUH?
RUMBLE
RUMBLE

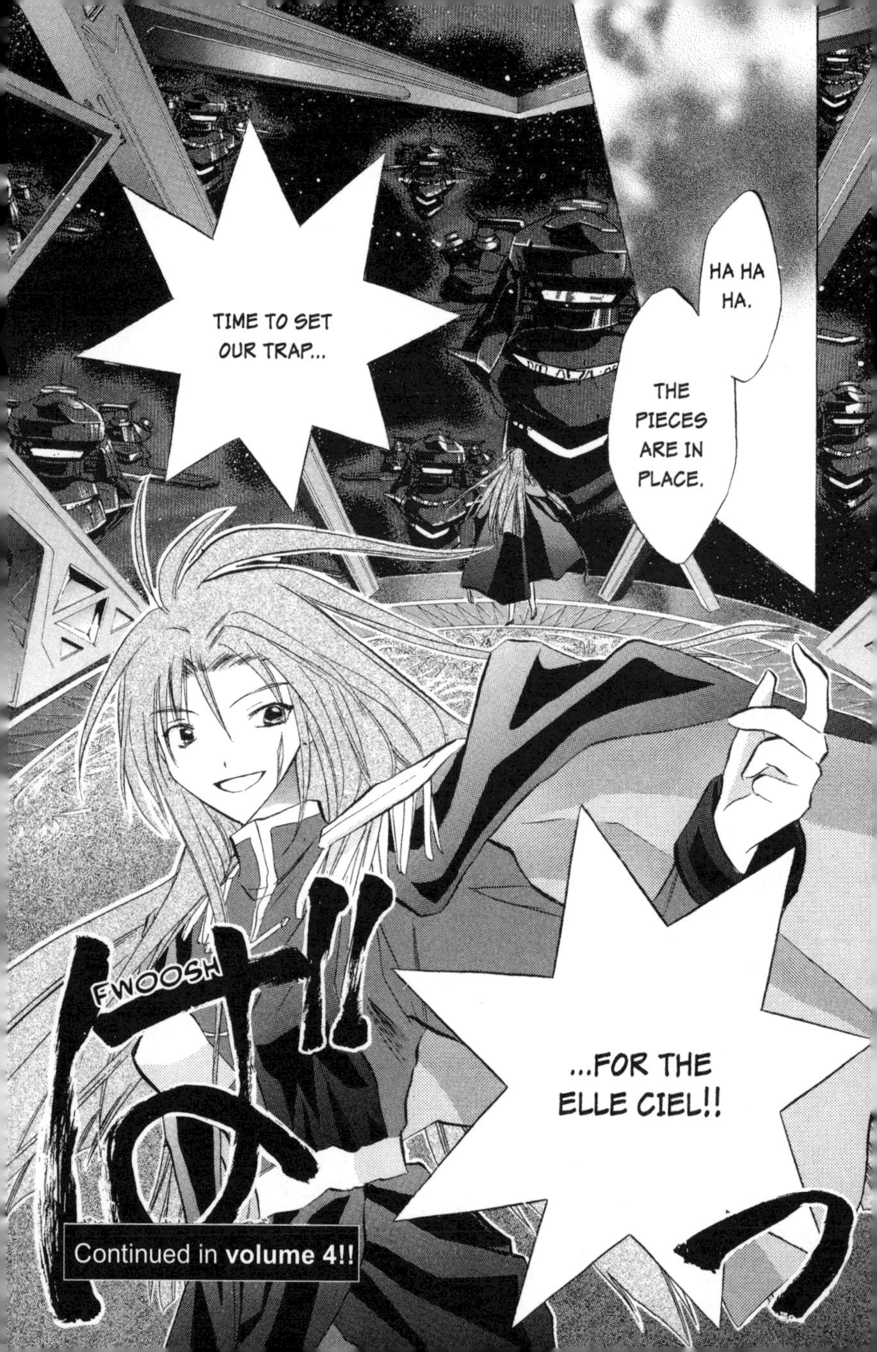
HA HA HA.
THE PIECES ARE IN PLACE.
TIME TO SET OUR TRAP...
...FOR THE ELLE CIEL!!
FWOOSH
Continued in **volume 4!!**

●SPECIAL THANKS●

<STORYBOARD CHECKING & IDEA>
Ryo Mizuno

<SPACESHIP ETC. MATERIALS>
IKUSABUNE

<SPACESHIPS>
Kokoro Takei

<COLORING>
Mitsuru Yamazaki

<SPECIAL THANKS>
Arikui Fujimaru

●MAIN STAFF●

Meiko Araki   **Kaori Sato**
Kyoko Tarasawa   **Chori Harumaki**

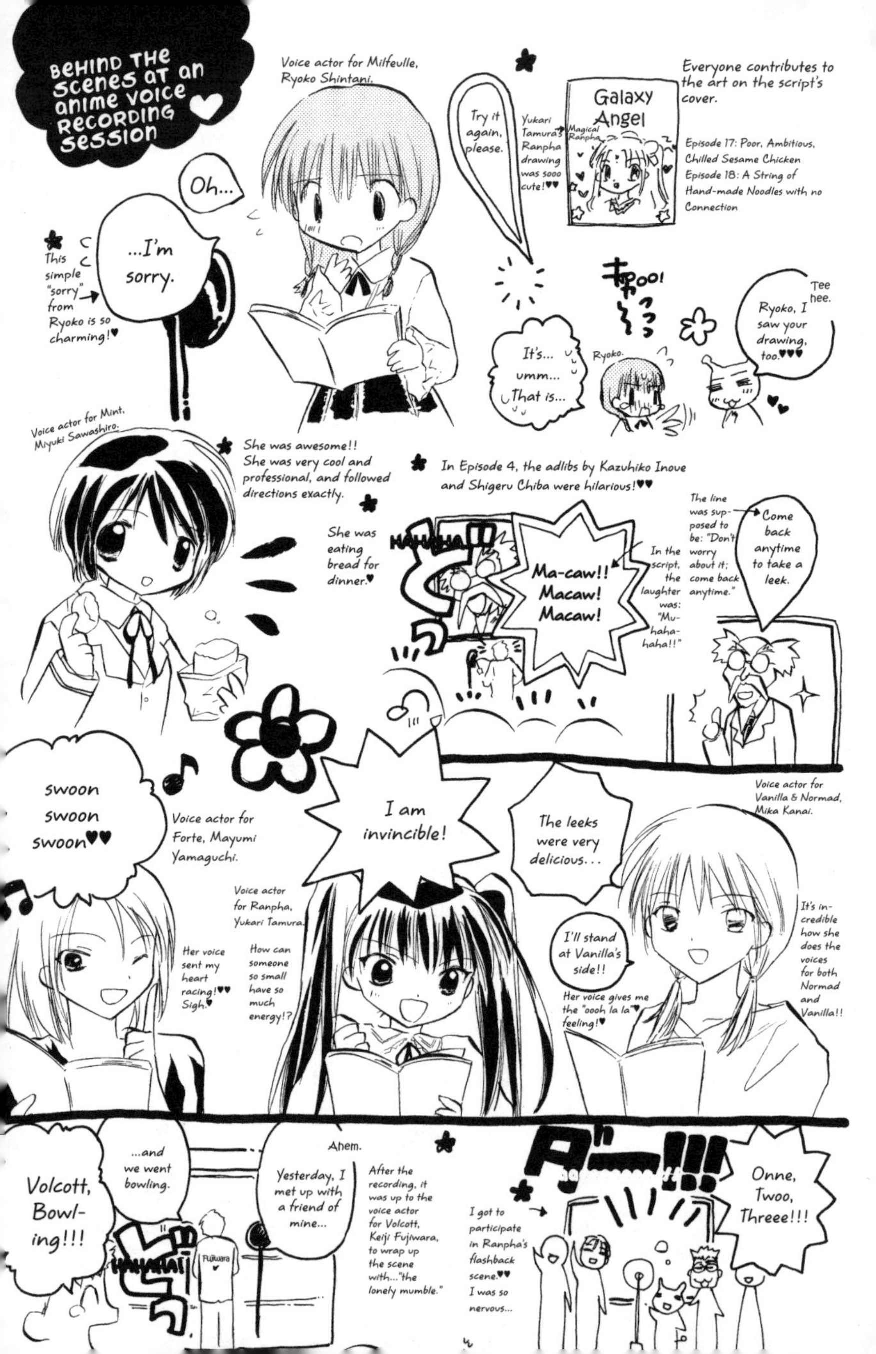
Behind the scenes at an anime voice recording session
Everyone contributes to the art on the script's cover.
Galaxy Angel
Magical Ranpha
Episode 17: Poor, Ambitious, Chilled Sesame Chicken
Episode 18: A String of Hand-made Noodles with no Connection
Yukari Tamura's Ranpha drawing was sooo cute!♥♥
Try it again, please.
Tee hee.
Ryoko, I saw your drawing, too.♥♥♥
Ryoko.
It's... umm... That is...
Voice actor for Milfeulle, Ryoko Shintani.
Oh...
...I'm sorry.
This simple "sorry" from Ryoko is so charming!♥
In Episode 4, the adlibs by Kazuhiko Inoue and Shigeru Chiba were hilarious!♥♥
The line was supposed to be: "Don't worry about it; come back anytime."
Come back anytime to take a leek.
In the script, the laughter was: "Mu-haha-haha!!"
Ma-caw!! Macaw! Macaw!
HAHAHA!!
She was eating bread for dinner.♥
Voice actor for Mint, Miyuki Sawashiro.
She was awesome!! She was very cool and professional, and followed directions exactly.
Voice actor for Vanilla & Normad, Mika Kanai.
It's incredible how she does the voices for both Normad and Vanilla!!
The leeks were very delicious...
I'll stand at Vanilla's side!!
Her voice gives me the "oooh la la"♥ feeling!♥
I am invincible!
Voice actor for Ranpha, Yukari Tamura.
How can someone so small have so much energy!?
Her voice sent my heart racing!♥♥ Sigh.♥
Voice actor for Forte, Mayumi Yamaguchi.
swoon swoon swoon♥♥
Onne, Twoo, Threee!!!
I got to participate in Ranpha's flashback scene.♥♥ I was so nervous...
After the recording, it was up to the voice actor for Volcott, Keiji Fujiwara, to wrap up the scene with..."the lonely mumble."
Ahem.
Yesterday, I met up with a friend of mine...
...and we went bowling.
Volcott, Bowl-ing!!!
HAHAHA!!
Fujiwara

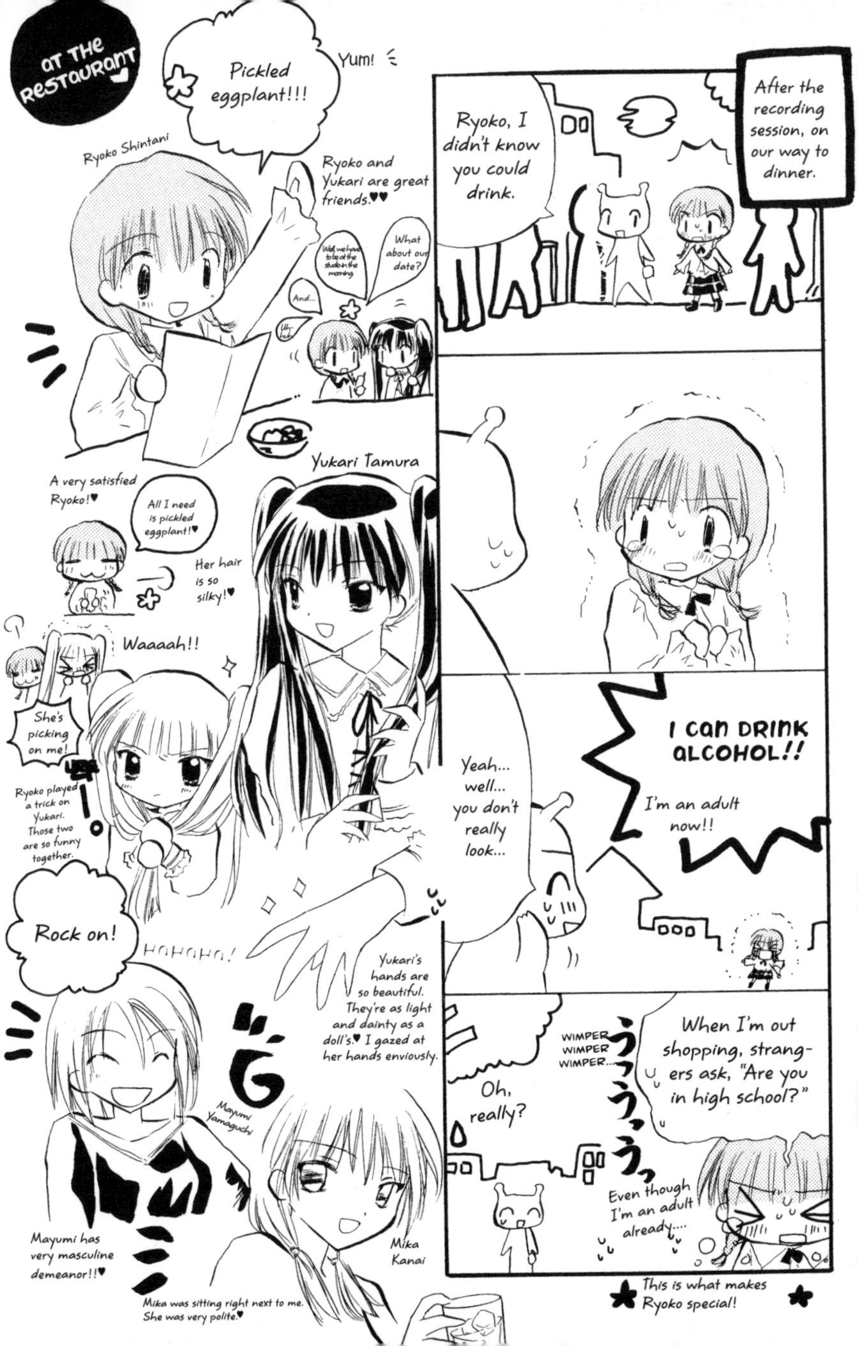
After the recording session, on our way to dinner.
Ryoko, I didn't know you could drink.
I can DRINK ALCOHOL!!
I'm an adult now!!
Yeah... well... you don't really look...
When I'm out shopping, strangers ask, "Are you in high school?"
WIMPER WIMPER WIMPER...
Even though I'm an adult already....
Oh, really?
This is what makes Ryoko special!
AT THE RESTAURANT
Pickled eggplant!!!
Yum!
Ryoko Shintani
Ryoko and Yukari are great friends.♥♥
What about our date?
Well, we have to be at the studio in the morning.
And...
Uh-huh
A very satisfied Ryoko!♥
All I need is pickled eggplant!♥
Her hair is so silky!♥
Yukari Tamura
Waaaah!!
She's picking on me!
Ryoko played a trick on Yukari. Those two are so funny together.
Rock on!
HAHAHA!
Yukari's hands are so beautiful. They're as light and dainty as a doll's.♥ I gazed at her hands enviously.
Mayumi Yamaguchi
Mayumi has very masculine demeanor!!♥
Mika Kanai
Mika was sitting right next to me. She was very polite.♥

★ That's it for GA Volume 3. Thank you for reading this far!! There are many people who have supported me. Truly, they have been a tremendous help. Thank you all very much!! I'll keep going one step at a time... at my own pace... hopefully in the right direction. And I won't give up.

Galaxy
G A Angel

I will do my best!

Best wishes,♥

Kanan

✿A little advertisement:✿ Broccoli gave me the opportunity to publish my first illustration book. It consists mostly of my GA illustrations. (Also included are Aquarian Age drawings and rough sketches of GA.) I even did some original color illustrations for the book!♥ If you are interested, please check them out.♥ For information about the illustration book's availability, please check out www.animegamers. com.♥ The book is called KANAN. Thank you very much!♥

ギャラクシーエンジェル

Galaxy Angel™

4

BROCCOLI BOOKS DELUXE
Galaxy Angel
4
BY Kanan

IT'S THE CALM BEFORE THE STORM FOR THE ANGEL TROUPE. AS THEY HEAD TOWARD PLANET LOME, HOME OF THE ANTI-EONIA HEADQUARTERS, THE DANGER IS GROWING. WITH PRINCE SHIVA THREATENED, THE ANGEL TROUPE MUST FOCUS ON THE MISSION AT HAND. NOW, IF ONLY MILFEULLE CAN MANAGE TO THINK STRAIGHT!

SO WHAT IF RANPHA AND TAKUTO KISS? WHY SHOULD IT MATTER TO HER? FOR SOME REASON, IT KEEPS EATING AT HER, BUT THE ENEMY WAITS FOR NO WOMAN. EONIA AND THE HELL HOUNDS ARE ON THE MOVE AND THE ELLE CIEL IS IN FOR THE FIGHT OF ITS LIFE!

VOLUME 4 WILL BE AVAILABLE THIS COMING JANUARY AT YOUR LOCAL BOOKSTORES!

HERE ARE SOME PREVIEW PAGES TO GIVE YOU A SNEAK PEEK!

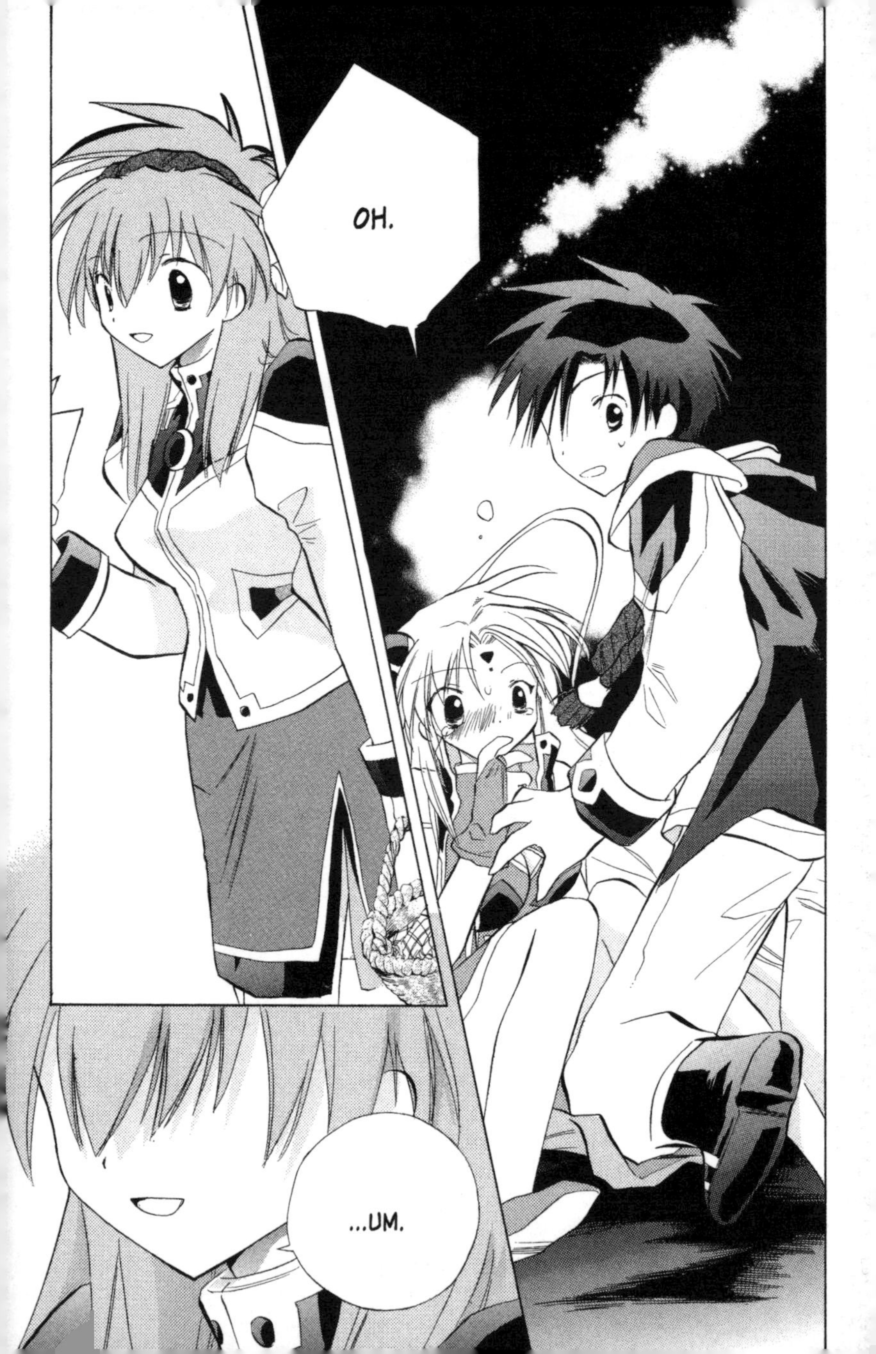
OH.
...UM.

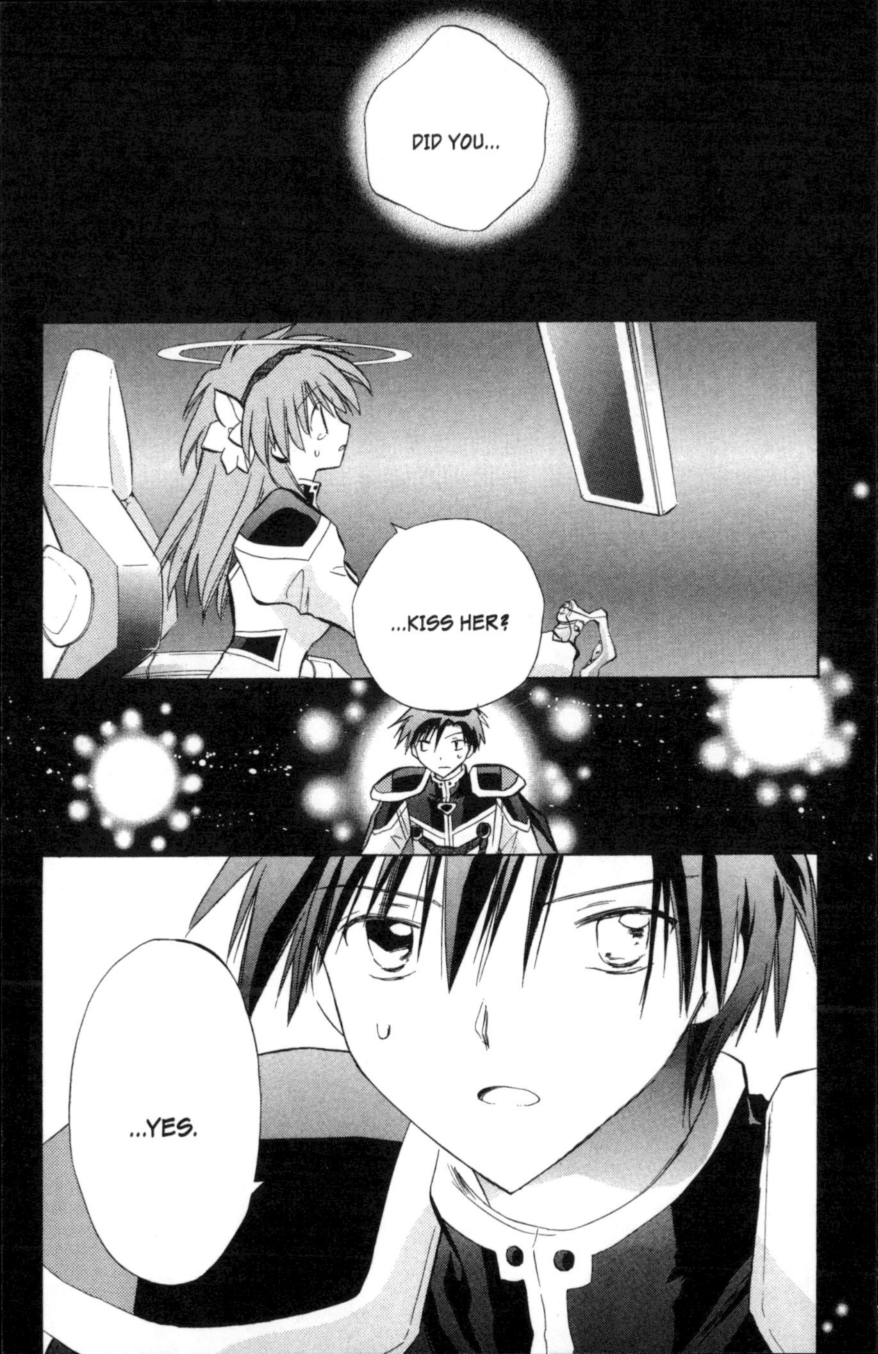
DID YOU...
...KISS HER?
...YES.

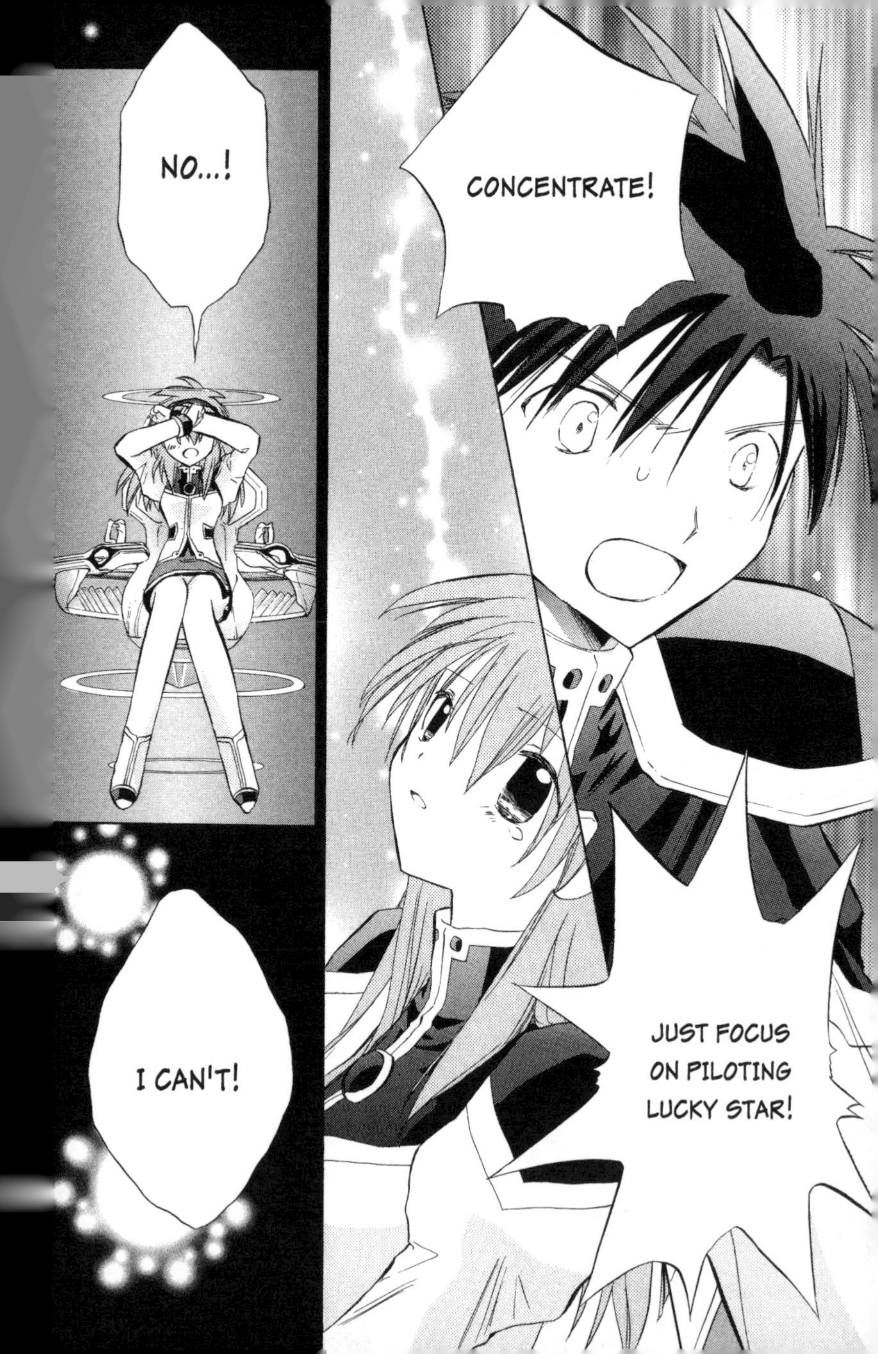
CONCENTRATE!
JUST FOCUS ON PILOTING LUCKY STAR!
NO...!
I CAN'T!

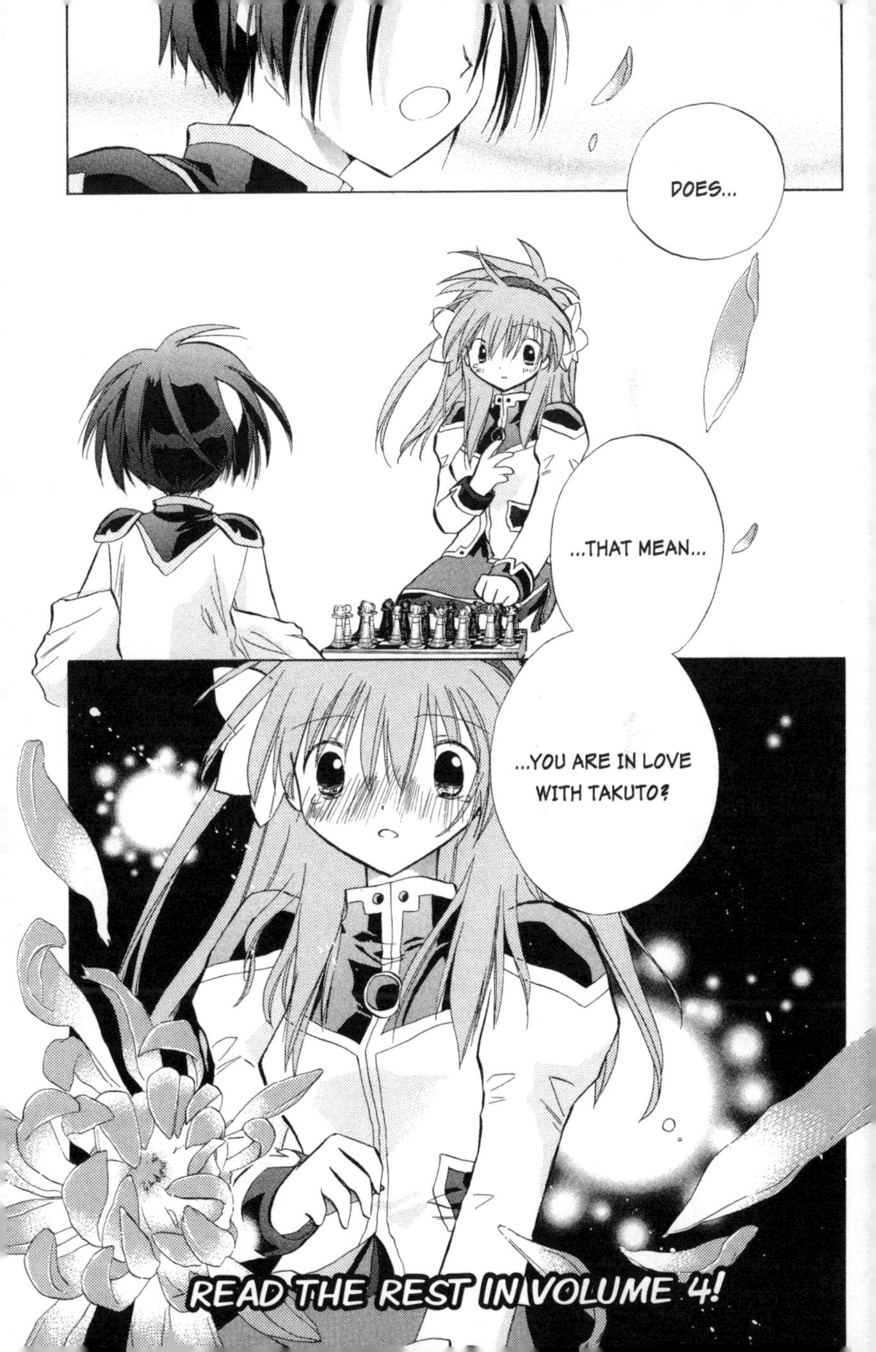
DOES...
...THAT MEAN...
...YOU ARE IN LOVE WITH TAKUTO?
READ THE REST IN VOLUME 4!

Vanilla H

Vanilla is a taciturn girl who does not express her feelings. Although she will answer questions, she rarely speaks on her own. She has a special ability to control nanotechnology and can frequently be seen with a squirrel-like nanotech pet, which is made of a group of microscopic machines. This device enables her to fix any machine and heal any living organism.

Vanilla does everything she is told. She has no personal desires or will, but has a strong sense of duty, which is supported by an almighty faith in her religion.

Age: 13
Rank: Second Lieutenant
Height: 4'4"

Favorite food:
None in particular
(She is a religious-based vegetarian.)

Hobbies:
Worshipping,
scripture recitation

Special abilities:
Healing with her
nanotech pet

GA-005 Harvester

Harvester can transport a high number of nanomachines for the repair of damaged fighters. It plays a supporting role among the Emblem Frames. Its artillery is weak, but it possesses the strongest defensive system out of the Emblem Frames.

Length: 133'2"
Width: 165'4"
Height: 63'

Favorite food:
N/A

Hobbies:
N/A

Special abilities:
N/A

Eonia Transbaal

As nephew of King Gerald, Eonia had a legitimate claim to the lineage of the royal throne. He was stripped of his rights, however, and banished into the outskirts of space for an unnamed offense.

Highly intelligent, he will do anything to achieve his goals.

Age: 26

Noa

Noa is a little girl who is always with Eonia. She refers to Eonia as her big brother and acts as if she is his little sister.

Much of Noa remains a mystery, and is yet to be revealed.

Sherry Bristol

Cool and calm, Sherry is a brilliant tactician who is Eonia's right-hand person. She served alongside Eonia before he was banished and remained with him during his exile. She is highly trusted by Eonia, and she has extreme loyalty towards him (although her true motivation has more to do with love). Although she is well aware of the Imperial Forces' true capability, her attitudes are distorted by her feeling that anyone who is a threat to Master Eonia should be destroyed immediately. If the situation calls for it, she will charge headlong into the battlefield.

Rezon Mayzom

Rezon is a former Imperial Force lieutenant who betrayed his platoon during the coup. He makes numerous attempts to destroy the Elle Ciel and kill the Angel Troupe.

Age: unknown

Kuromie Quark

Kuromie is the caretaker of the space whales onboard the Elle Ciel. The space whales can read people's minds, and Kuromie has the ability to communicate with them to gather information.

Age: 15
Height: 4'7"

Kela

She tends to the health and well being of the Elle Ciel crewmembers. She also looks after Vanilla, who occasionally helps out in the medical ward. Her specialty is psychological counseling. Her interests include knitting and reading. Kela is very fond of coffee.

Age: 29

Galaxy Angel Files: Almo, Coco & Creta

Almo

Almo is one of the Elle Ciel's bridge staff, mainly in charge of correspondence and communication. She is a friendly and outgoing girl. She is secretly in love with Lester.

Age: 19

Coco

Coco handles and analyzes the radar control of the Elle Ciel. Quiet and mild mannered, she is Almo's good friend.

Age: 19

Creta

A specialist in the Lost Technology, Creta is responsible for the maintenance of the Emblem Frames. It is rumored that Creta is a huge fan of boy bands.

Age: 24

The Emblem Frames

The **Angel Troupe** pilots the **Emblem Frames**. These huge ships use a variety of **Lost Technology** equipment, ranging from a **Gravitational Control System** to a **Chronostring Engine**, which allows hyperspace travel. The ships incorporate the **Human-Brain and Artificial-Brain Linking Organization (H.A.L.O.)** system, which allows the pilot to control the Emblem Frame via a direct mental link. As a result of this unique system, the usefulness and strength of the Emblem Frame varies in proportion to the psychological state of the pilot. Put simply: if the pilot is feeling well, the Emblem Frame works well. If, on the other hand, the pilot is depressed, the Emblem Frame will not function. Pilots must additionally possess the innate ability to synch with the system in order for the link to work. Without this ability, a pilot will be unable to move an Emblem Frame so much as an inch, regardless of her skill as a pilot. For this reason, a vast search was conducted across the galaxy for pilots with this special gift. The resulting group consists of the five girls who make up the Angel Troupe today. Not all of the pilots could be found in existing military reserves, which is why there are civilians such as Vanilla and Mint in the troupe.

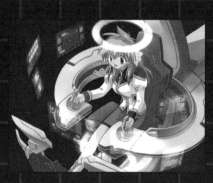

When an **Angel Troupe** member sits in the cockpit, the **H.A.L.O.** system's **Angel Ring** appears above the pilot's head.

THE UNIVERSE OF GALAXY ANGEL

About G.A. in a Nutshell

The following comics and notes are part of a serialization in the monthly informational magazine *From Gamers*. Originally titled "Kanan's Secret Notes," Kanan used the comics to introduce and give more personality to the different characters from Galaxy Angel.

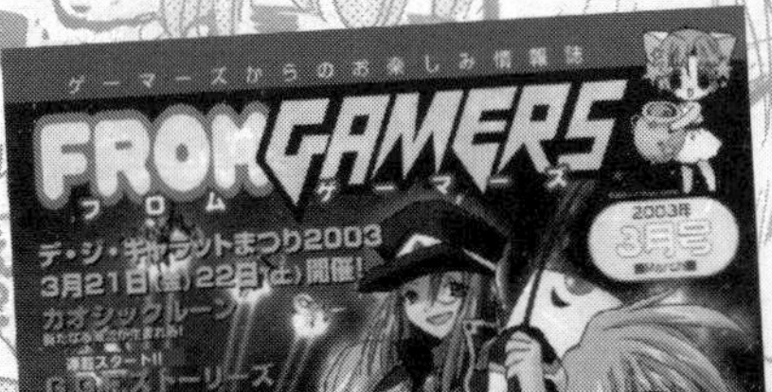
ゲーマーズからのお楽しみ情報誌
FROMGAMERS
フロムゲーマーズ
2003年 3月号
デ・ジ・キャラットまつり2003
3月21日(金)22日(土)開催!
カオシックルーン
G.G.F.ストーリーズ
デ・ジ・キャラット
新作アニメ情報
4月17日(木)
PS2でエンジェル隊に会える

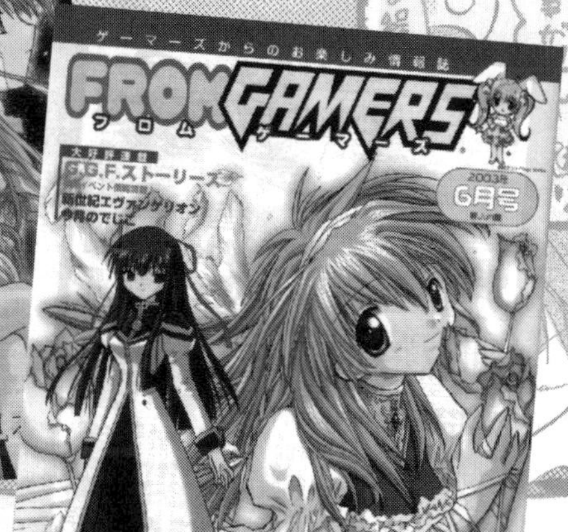
ゲーマーズからのお楽しみ情報誌
FROMGAMERS
フロムゲーマーズ
G.G.F.ストーリーズ
新世紀エヴァンゲリオン
今月のでじこ
2003年 6月号
新展開!?

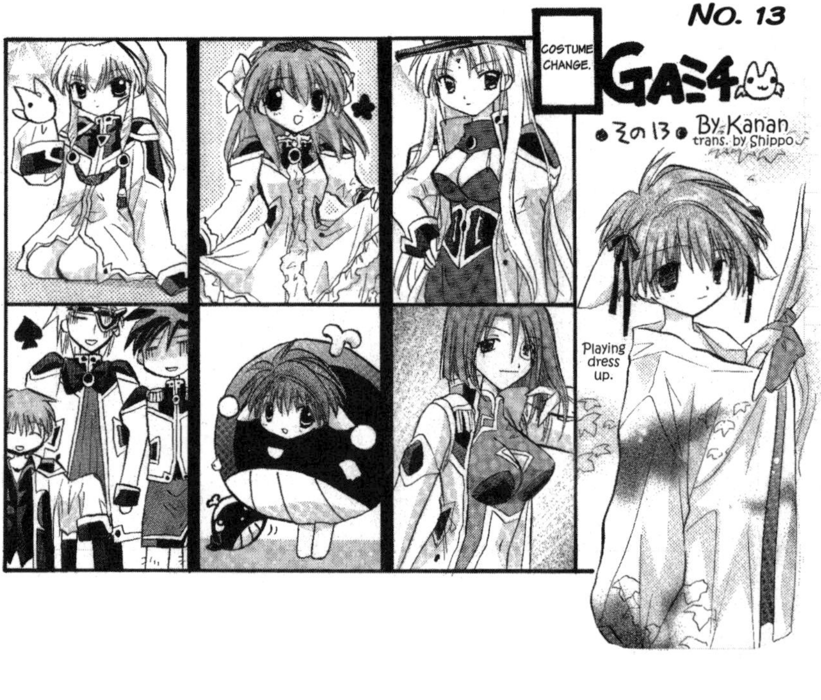
NO. 13
GAミ4
●その13●
By Kanan
trans. by Shippo
COSTUME CHANGE.
Playing dress up.

First appeared in *From Gamers* November 2001 issue.

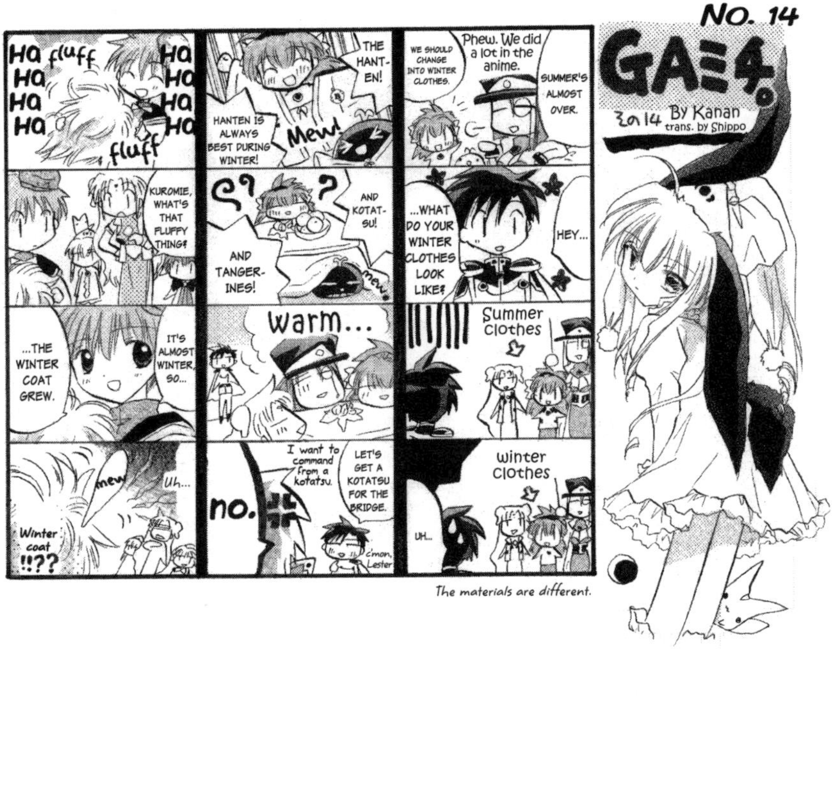
NO. 14
その14
By Kanan
trans. by Shippo
Phew. We did a lot in the anime.
SUMMER'S ALMOST OVER.
WE SHOULD CHANGE INTO WINTER CLOTHES.
HEY...
...WHAT DO YOUR WINTER CLOTHES LOOK LIKE?
Summer clothes
winter clothes
UH...
The materials are different.
THE HANTEN!
HANTEN IS ALWAYS BEST DURING WINTER!
Mew!
?
AND KOTATSU!
AND TANGERINES!
mew.
warm...
LET'S GET A KOTATSU FOR THE BRIDGE.
I want to command from a kotatsu.
no.
c'mon, Lester
Ha Ha Ha Ha
fluff
Ha Ha Ha Ha
fluff
KUROMIE, WHAT'S THAT FLUFFY THING?
IT'S ALMOST WINTER, SO...
...THE WINTER COAT GREW.
mew
Uh...
Winter coat !!??

First appeared in *From Gamers* December 2001 issue.

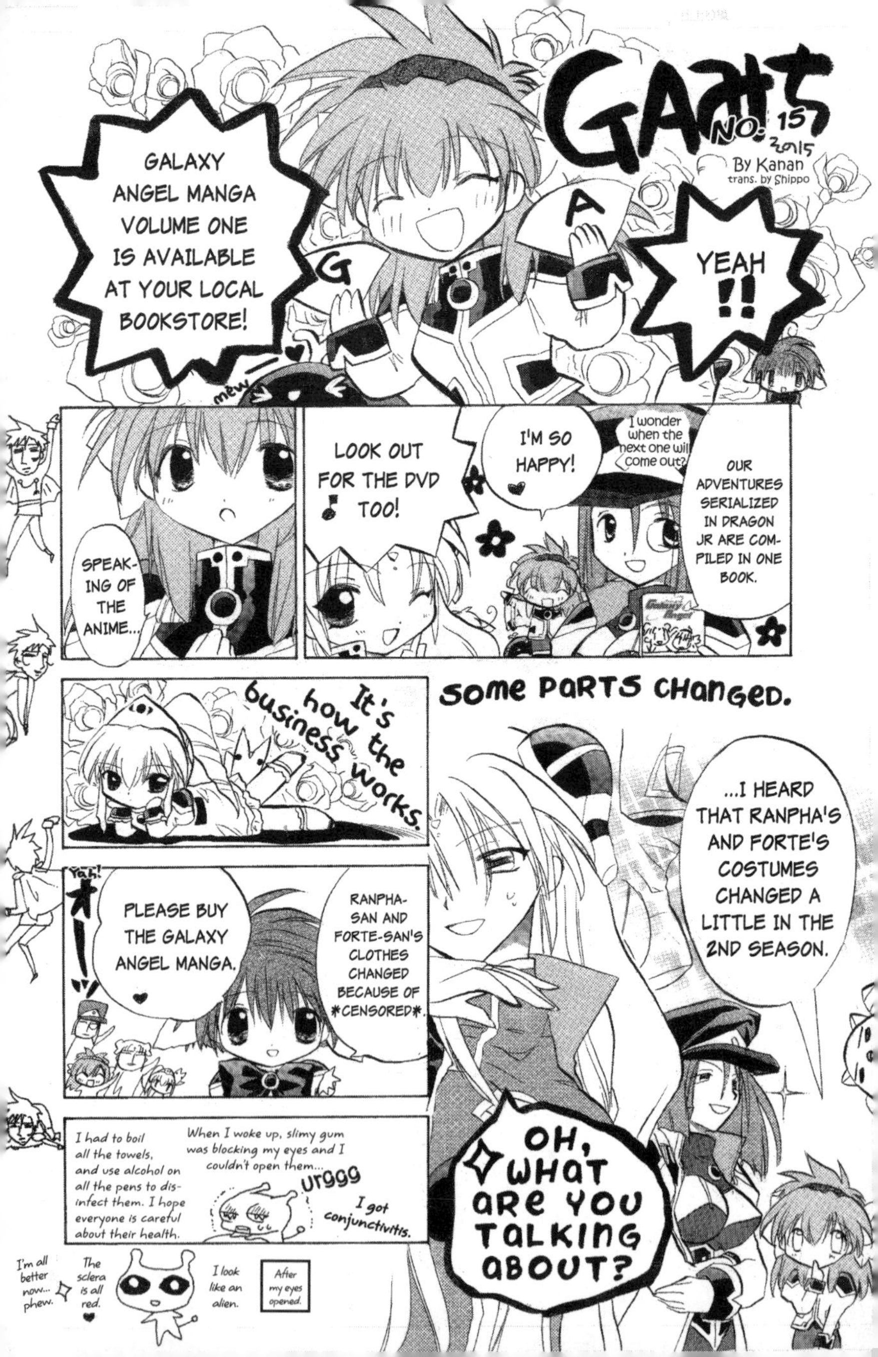
GAみち
NO. 157
By Kanan
trans. by Shippo
YEAH!!
GALAXY ANGEL MANGA VOLUME ONE IS AVAILABLE AT YOUR LOCAL BOOKSTORE!
mew
OUR ADVENTURES SERIALIZED IN DRAGON JR ARE COMPILED IN ONE BOOK.
I wonder when the next one will come out?
I'M SO HAPPY!
LOOK OUT FOR THE DVD TOO!
SPEAKING OF THE ANIME...
Some parts changed.
...I HEARD THAT RANPHA'S AND FORTE'S COSTUMES CHANGED A LITTLE IN THE 2ND SEASON.
OH, WHAT ARE YOU TALKING ABOUT?
It's how the business works.
Yah!
RANPHA-SAN AND FORTE-SAN'S CLOTHES CHANGED BECAUSE OF *CENSORED*.
PLEASE BUY THE GALAXY ANGEL MANGA.
When I woke up, slimy gum was blocking my eyes and I couldn't open them...
Urggg
I got conjunctivitis.
I had to boil all the towels, and use alcohol on all the pens to disinfect them. I hope everyone is careful about their health.
After my eyes opened.
I look like an alien.
The sclera is all red.
I'm all better now... phew.

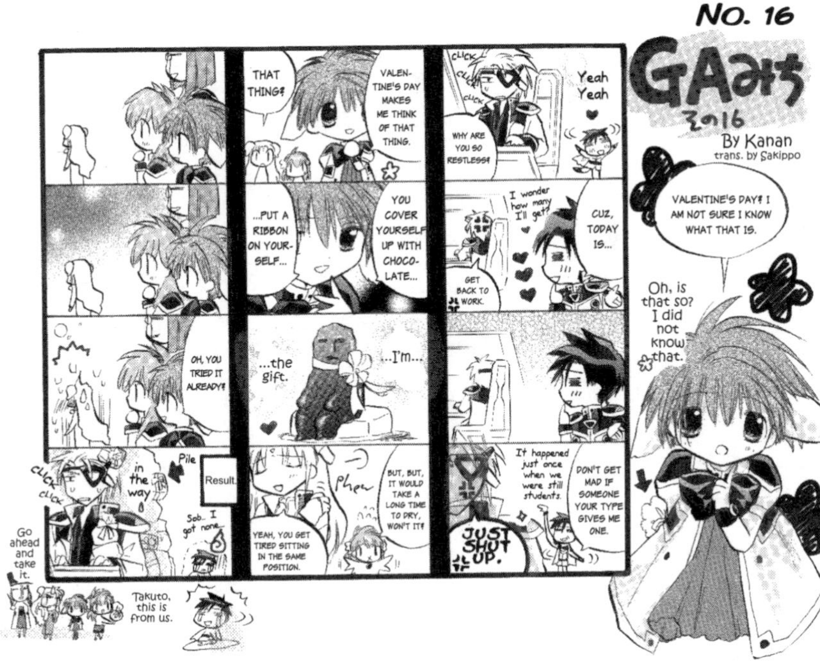
NO. 16
GAみち
その16
By Kanan
trans. by Sakippo
VALENTINE'S DAY? I AM NOT SURE I KNOW WHAT THAT IS.
Oh, is that so? I did not know that.
CLICK CLICK CLICK
Yeah Yeah
WHY ARE YOU SO RESTLESS?
CUZ, TODAY IS...
I wonder how many I'll get?
GET BACK TO WORK.
DON'T GET MAD IF SOMEONE YOUR TYPE GIVES ME ONE.
It happened just once when we were still students.
JUST SHUT UP.
VALEN-TINE'S DAY MAKES ME THINK OF THAT THING.
THAT THING?
YOU COVER YOURSELF UP WITH CHOCO-LATE...
...PUT A RIBBON ON YOUR-SELF...
...I'm...
...the gift.
BUT, BUT, IT WOULD TAKE A LONG TIME TO DRY, WON'T IT?
Phew
YEAH, YOU GET TIRED SITTING IN THE SAME POSITION.
OH, YOU TRIED IT ALREADY?
Result.
Pile
in the way
CLICK CLICK
Sob.. I got none.
Go ahead and take it.
Takuto, this is from us.

First appeared in *From Gamers* March 2002 issue.

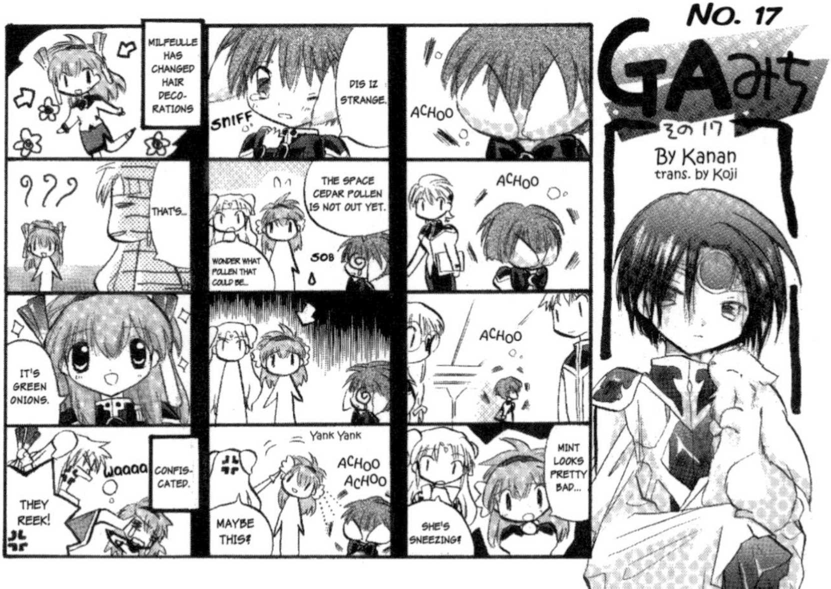
NO. 17
GAみち
その17
By Kanan
trans. by Koji
ACHOO
ACHOO
ACHOO
MINT LOOKS PRETTY BAD...
SHE'S SNEEZING?
DIS IZ STRANGE.
SNIFF
THE SPACE CEDAR POLLEN IS NOT OUT YET.
SOB
WONDER WHAT POLLEN THAT COULD BE...
Yank Yank
ACHOO ACHOO
MAYBE THIS?
MILFEULLE HAS CHANGED HAIR DECO-RATIONS
THAT'S...
???
IT'S GREEN ONIONS.
CONFIS-CATED.
Waaaa
THEY REEK!

First appeared in *From Gamers* April 2002 issue.

NO. 18

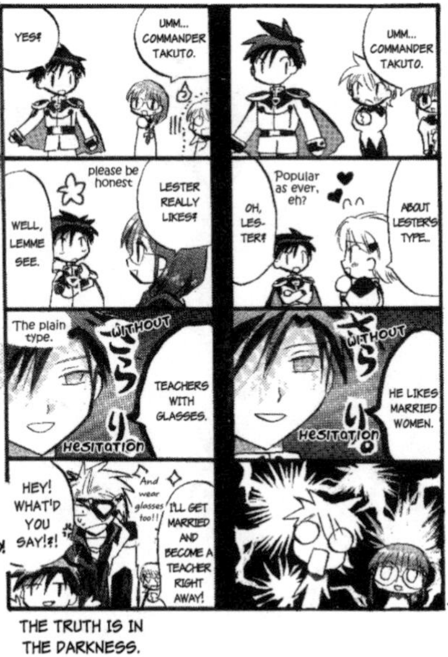
UMM... COMMANDER TAKUTO.
Popular as ever, eh?
ABOUT LESTER'S TYPE..
OH, LES-TER?
WITHOUT HESITATION
HE LIKES MARRIED WOMEN.
UMM... COMMANDER TAKUTO.
YES?
please be honest
LESTER REALLY LIKES?
WELL, LEMME SEE.
The plain type.
WITHOUT HESITATION
TEACHERS WITH GLASSES.
I'LL GET MARRIED AND BECOME A TEACHER RIGHT AWAY!
And wear glasses too!!
HEY! WHAT'D YOU SAY!?!
TAKUTO!
THE TRUTH IS IN THE DARKNESS.

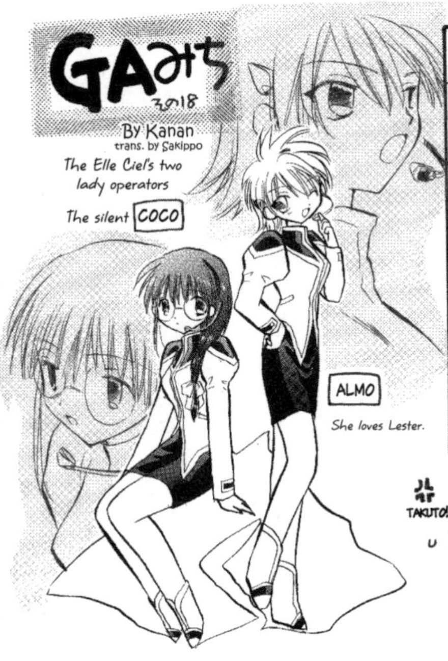
GAみち
その18
By Kanan
trans. by Sakippo
The Elle Ciel's two lady operators
The silent COCO
ALMO
She loves Lester.

First appeared in *From Gamers* May 2002 issue.

Translation Notes

pg. 9 Forte and Mint are wearing yukatas. Yukatas are a type of kimono worn usually in the summer at festivals. Historically, they have been worn after one takes a bath, but by the Meiji Period people began to wear them outside.

pg. 55 Kid's Meal - In Japanese restaurants, the kids' meal usually has a little flag on it.

pg. 68 San - A suffix; can be put after any name to indicate respect.

pg. 132 Oden - A type of Japanese food served during the winter. It is a hot pot dish which includes daikon radish, fish cakes, boiled eggs, seaweed, mochi, and other items.

pg. 161 Meditation - In Japan, there is a type of mental training in which one stands under a waterfall to meditate. One would wear a certain type of clothing and join hands to reach a state of selflessness in the waterfall. This exercise can also be used to pray for a wish to be fulfilled.

pg. 176 Ryoko Shintani - The Japanese voice actor for Milfeulle in the anime. She was the winner of the Prism Palette Broccoli audition and was chosen to play the main part, Yayoi Sakuragi.

pg. 176 Yukari Tamura - The Japanese voice actor for Ranpha in the anime. Her other work includes Misha from Pita-Ten.

pg. 176 Miyuki Sawashiro - The Japanese voice actor for Mint in the anime. Her other work includes Puchiko from Di Gi Charat.

pg. 176 Kazuhiko Inoue - The Japanese voice actor for Professor Asagaya Minami. He is a guest character for this episode. Dejiko and Puchiko also have a part in this episode.

pg. 176 Shigeru Chiba - The Japanese voice actor for Mr. God. He is a guest character for this episode.

pg. 176 Vanilla and Normad - Both Japanese voices for Vanilla and Normad are done by the same voice actor, Mika Kanai. She also sings for both characters.

pg. 176 Mayumi Yamaguchi - The Japanese voice actor for Forte in the anime. Her other work includes Envy from Full Metal Alchemist.

pg. 176 One, Two, Three, Daaaaa! - This is a famous line coined by the professional Japanese wrestler Antonio Inoki.

pg. 176 Volcott - A character from the anime.

pg. 176 Keiji Fujiwara - The Japanese voice actor for Volcott. His other work includes the dad in Crayon Shinchan.

pg. 176 "The Lonely Mumble" - The original title is "Hitori Gottsu," a TV show featuring comedian Hitoshi Matsumoto.

pg. 178 GA - Short for Galaxy Angel.

pg. 178 Broccoli - The company that created Galaxy Angel, along with other titles such as Di Gi Charat, Aquarian Age, and Bushi Lord.

pg. 178 Aquarian Age - An original trading card game created by Broccoli, with popular illustrations by various artists and a unique game system rivaled by no other card game. Some artists include CLAMP, Haruhiko Mikimoto, Aoi Nanase, and Koge-Donbo. Aquarian Age is a multi-platformed media, featured in anime, manga, and novels. Juvenile Orion is also set in the Aquarian Age universe.

pg. 193 Hanten - A puffy, cotton coat-like outerwear the Japanese wear during the winter to keep warm. Mainly used inside the home. Very comfortable.

pg. 193 Kotatsu - A blanket-table the Japanese use during the winter to keep warm. It is a table with a quilt over it, and there is a heat generator attached to keep one's feet warm.

pg. 193 Tangerines - Japanese people tend to eat tangerines when they sit at a kotatsu. Tangerines are the most widely consumed fruit in Japan.

pg. 194 Dragon Jr. - The monthly anthology magazine that featured the Galaxy Angel manga. It is now called Dragon Age.

pg. 195 Valentine's Day - In Japan, Valentine's Day is celebrated differently from the United States. The females are the only ones who send gifts , which are usually chocolates to their love interests. Most girls use Valentine's Day as a day to confess their love to someone. Aside from that, girls give obligation chocolates to friends, family, and colleagues to

DVDs by ■ Synch-Point

AquarianAge
the movie

The danger caused by the ERASER fleet has been eliminated thanks to the combined powers of the ARAYASHIKI, DARK-LORE, E.G.O., and WIZ-DOM factions. But a new threat looms in the horizon. Calling themselves the POLESTAR EMPIRE, they seek to take over the world by any means. Now it is up to five young women to come to terms with themselves and accept their true calling...

I'm Gonna Be An Angel!

On his way to school, Yuusuke stumbles upon a naked Noelle sleeping in the forest. Now, everyone's calling him her husband! But Yuusuke already has a crush on his classmate Natsumi. To make matters worse, Noelle's family of monsters has moved into his house. On top of that, the evil Dispel, who is trying to kidnap Noelle, sends all sorts of creatures after her. Wrestlers, catgirls, and aliens... Oh my!

DI GI CHARAT ™

Di Gi Charat (Dejiko for short) is an alien hybrid-cat-eared girl with the ambition of becoming a superstar on planet Earth. However, the cost of living is quite high in Tokyo. Luckily she gets both work and housing at an anime chain store called Gamers, and quickly becomes popular with the fans who shop there. But this is only the beginning of her misadventures!

For more information visit:
www.bro-usa.com

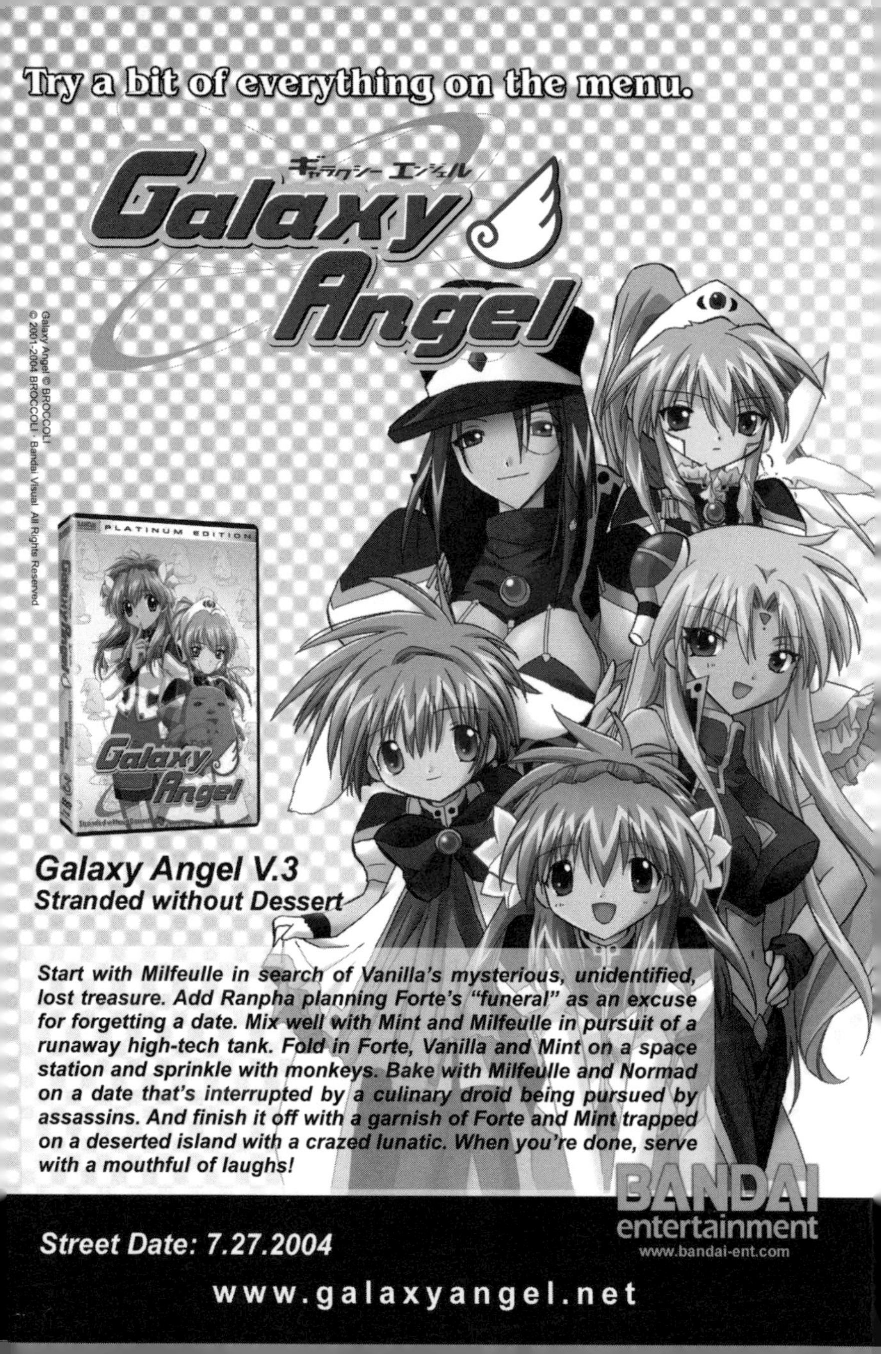
Try a bit of everything on the menu.
ギャラクシーエンジェル
Galaxy Angel
Galaxy Angel © BROCCOLI
© 2001-2004 BROCCOLI · Bandai Visual. All Rights Reserved
PLATINUM EDITION
Galaxy Angel
Galaxy Angel V.3
Stranded without Dessert
Start with Milfeulle in search of Vanilla's mysterious, unidentified, lost treasure. Add Ranpha planning Forte's "funeral" as an excuse for forgetting a date. Mix well with Mint and Milfeulle in pursuit of a runaway high-tech tank. Fold in Forte, Vanilla and Mint on a space station and sprinkle with monkeys. Bake with Milfeulle and Normad on a date that's interrupted by a culinary droid being pursued by assassins. And finish it off with a garnish of Forte and Mint trapped on a deserted island with a crazed lunatic. When you're done, serve with a mouthful of laughs!
BANDAI
entertainment
www.bandai-ent.com
Street Date: 7.27.2004
www.galaxyangel.net

YOU'RE READING THE WRONG WAY!

This is the end of the book! In Japan, manga is generally read from right to left. All reading starts on the upper right corner, and ends on the lower left. American comics are generally read from left to right, starting on the upper left of each page. In order to preserve the true nature of the work, we printed this book in a right to left fashion. Those who are unfamiliar with manga may find this confusing at first, but once you start getting into the story, you will wonder how you ever read manga any other way!

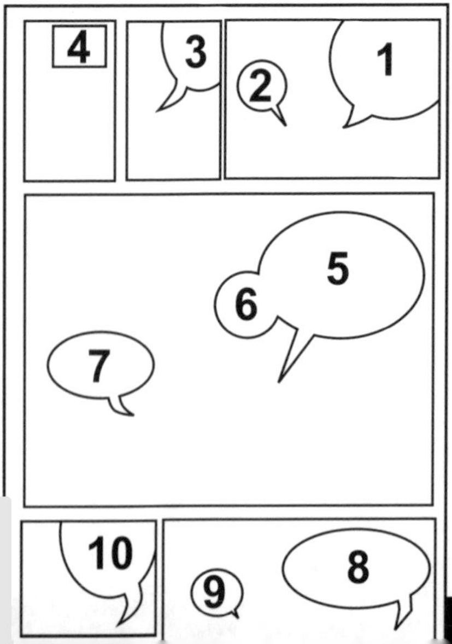
1
2
3
4
5
6
7
8
9
10

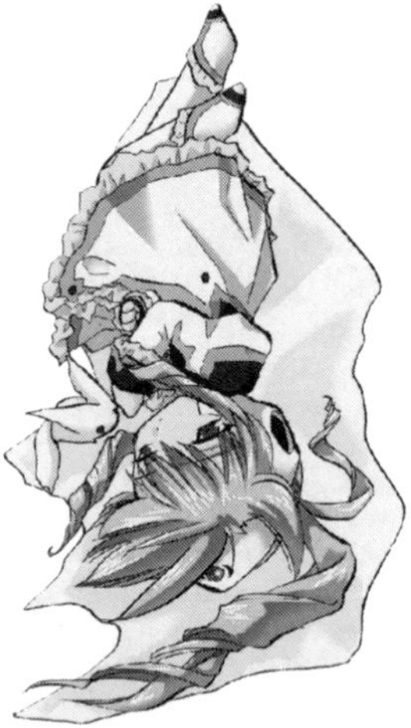

THIS QUESTIONNAIRE IS REDEEMABLE FOR:

Galaxy Angel Volume 3 Dust Jacket

Broccoli Books Questionnaire

Fill out and return to Broccoli Books to receive your corresponding dust jacket!*

PLEASE MAIL THE COMPLETE FORM, ALONG WITH UNITED STATES POSTAGE STAMPS
WORTH $1.50 ENCLOSED IN THE ENVELOPE TO:**

Broccoli International
Attn: Broccoli Books Dust Jacket Committee
12211 W Washington Blvd #110
Los Angeles, CA 90066

(Please write legibly)

Name: _____

Address: _____

City, State, Zip: _____

E-mail: _____

Gender: ☐ Male ☐ Female **Age:** _____

(If you are under 13 years old, parental consent is required)

Parent/Guardian signature: _____

Occupation: _____

Where did you hear about this title?

☐ Magazine (Please specify): _____

☐ Flyer from: a store   convention   club   other: _____

☐ Website (Please specify): _____

☐ At a store (Please specify): _____

☐ Word of Mouth

☐ Other (Please specify): _____

Where was this title purchased? (If known)

_____

Why did you buy this title?

_____
_____
_____

CUT ALONG HERE

CUT ALONG HERE

How would you rate the following features of this manga?

	Excellent	Good	Satisfactory	Poor
Translation	☐	☐	☐	☐
Art quality	☐	☐	☐	☐
Cover	☐	☐	☐	☐
Extra/Bonus Material	☐	☐	☐	☐

What would you like to see improved in Broccoli Books manga?

____

Would you recommend this manga to someone else? ☐ Yes ☐ No

What related products would you be interested in?

☐ Posters ☐ Apparel Other: _______________

Which magazines do you read on a regular basis?

____

What manga titles would you like to see in English?

____

Favorite manga titles: _______________

Favorite manga artists: _______________

What race/ethnicity do you consider yourself? (Please check one)

☐ Asian/Pacific Islander ☐ Native American/Alaskan Native

☐ Black/African American ☐ White/Caucasian

☐ Hispanic/Latino ☐ Other: _______________

Final comments about this manga:

____

____

____

Thank you!

* While supplies last.

** For residents of Canada, please send an International Reply Coupon (IRC) of $3.00 US made out to "Broccoli International."

All information provided will be used for internal purposes only. We will not sell or otherwise divulge any of the information.

Requests not in compliance with all terms of this form will not be acknowledged or returned. All submissions are subject to verification and become the property of Broccoli International USA. Fraudulent submission, including use of multiple addresses or P.O. boxes to obtain additional Broccoli International USA information or offers may result in prosecution. Broccoli International USA reserves the right to withdraw or modify any terms of this form. Void where prohibited, taxed, or restricted by law. Broccoli International USA will not be liable for lost, misdirected, mutilated, illegible, incomplete, or postage-due mail. Dust jacket offer is only available to residents of the United States and Canada. For updates to the rules and regulations, please see www.bro-usa.com.